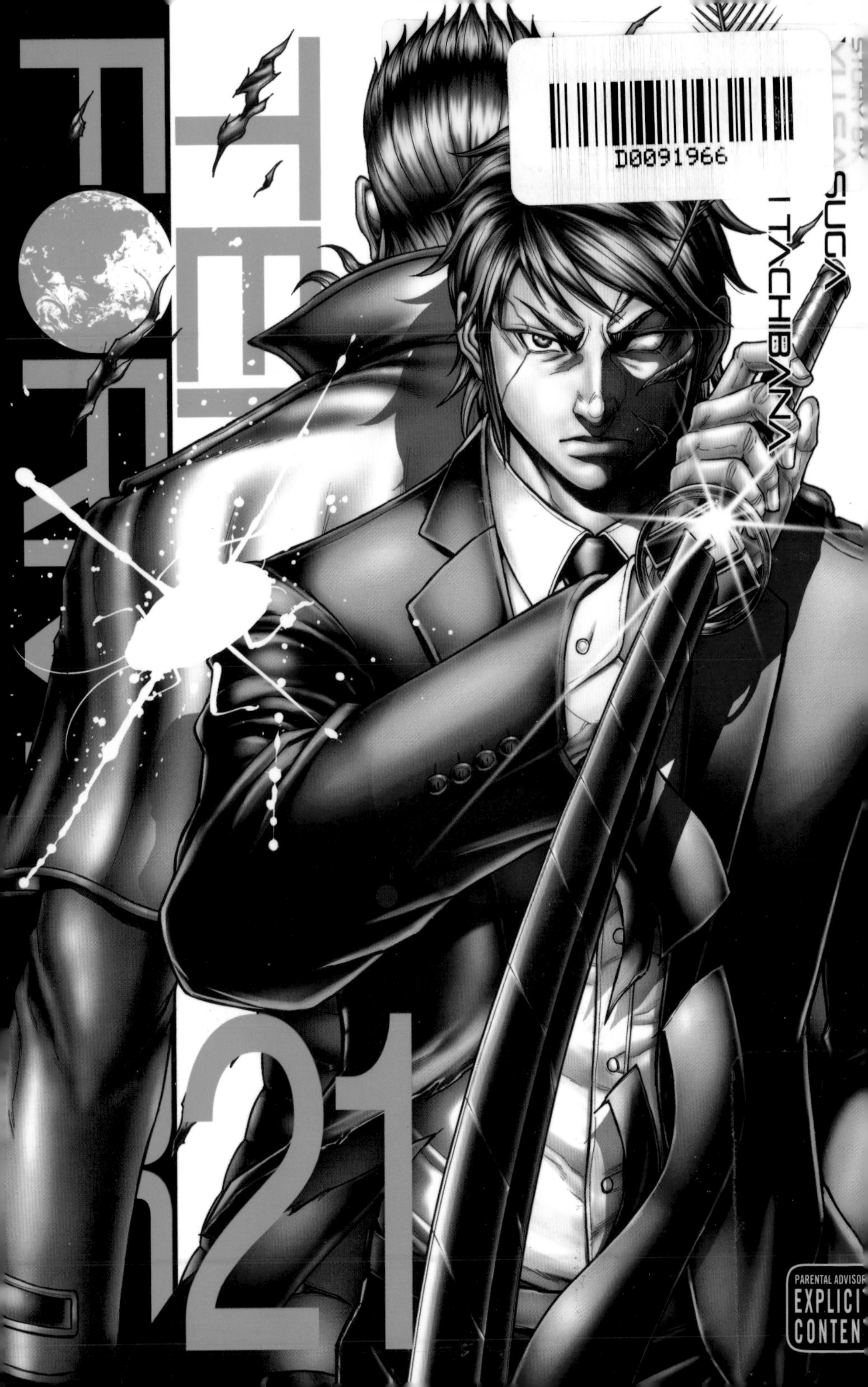
D0091966
SUGA
TACHIBANA
21
PARENTAL ADVISOR
EXPLICI
CONTEN

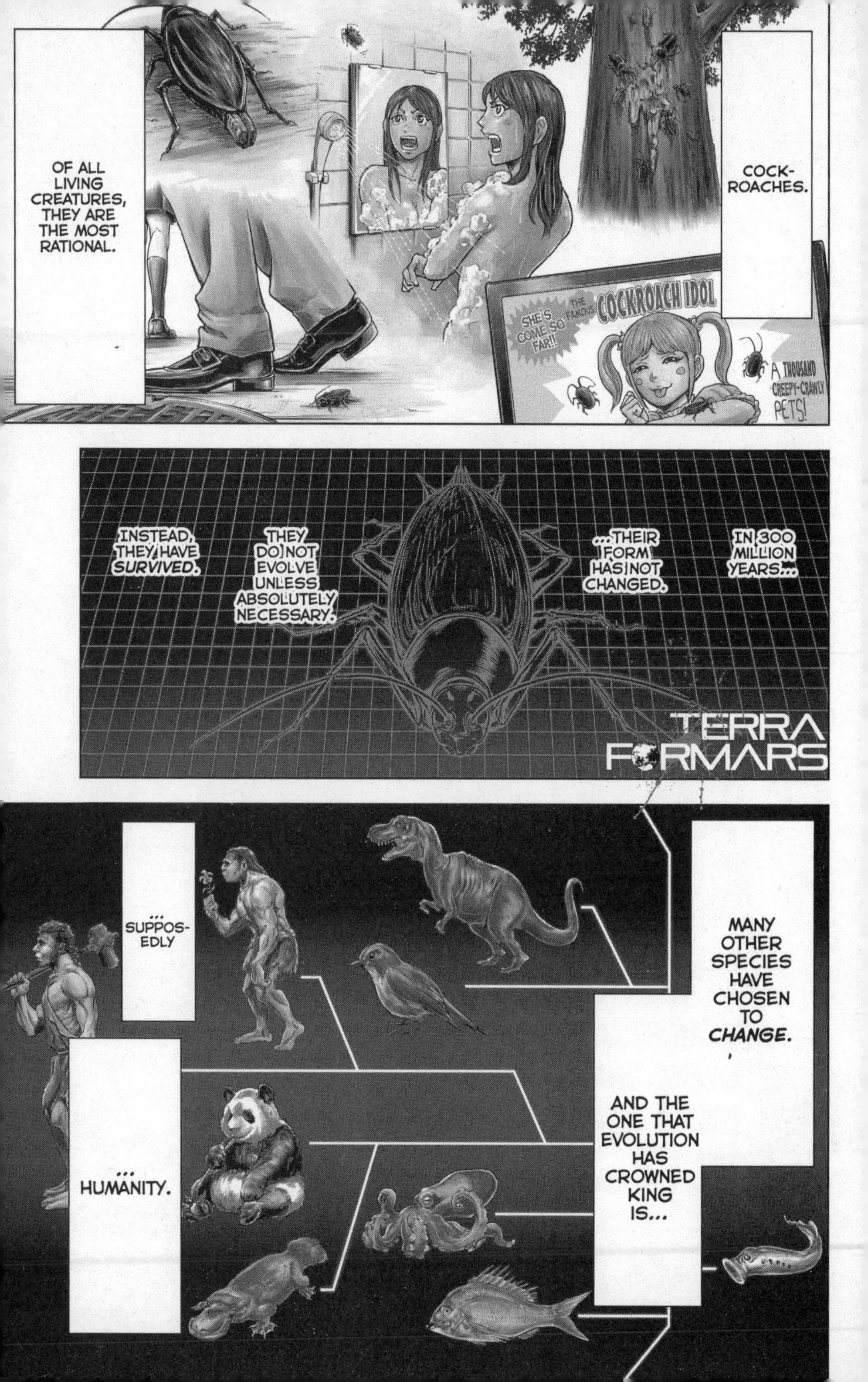
COCK-ROACHES.
THE FAMOUS COCKROACH IDOL
SHE'S COME SO FAR!!
A THOUSAND CREEPY-CRAWLY PETS!
OF ALL LIVING CREATURES, THEY ARE THE MOST RATIONAL.
IN 300 MILLION YEARS...
...THEIR FORM HAS NOT CHANGED.
THEY DO NOT EVOLVE UNLESS ABSOLUTELY NECESSARY.
INSTEAD, THEY HAVE *SURVIVED*.
TERRA FORMARS
MANY OTHER SPECIES HAVE CHOSEN TO *CHANGE*.
AND THE ONE THAT EVOLUTION HAS CROWNED KING IS...
...SUPPOS-EDLY
...HUMANITY.

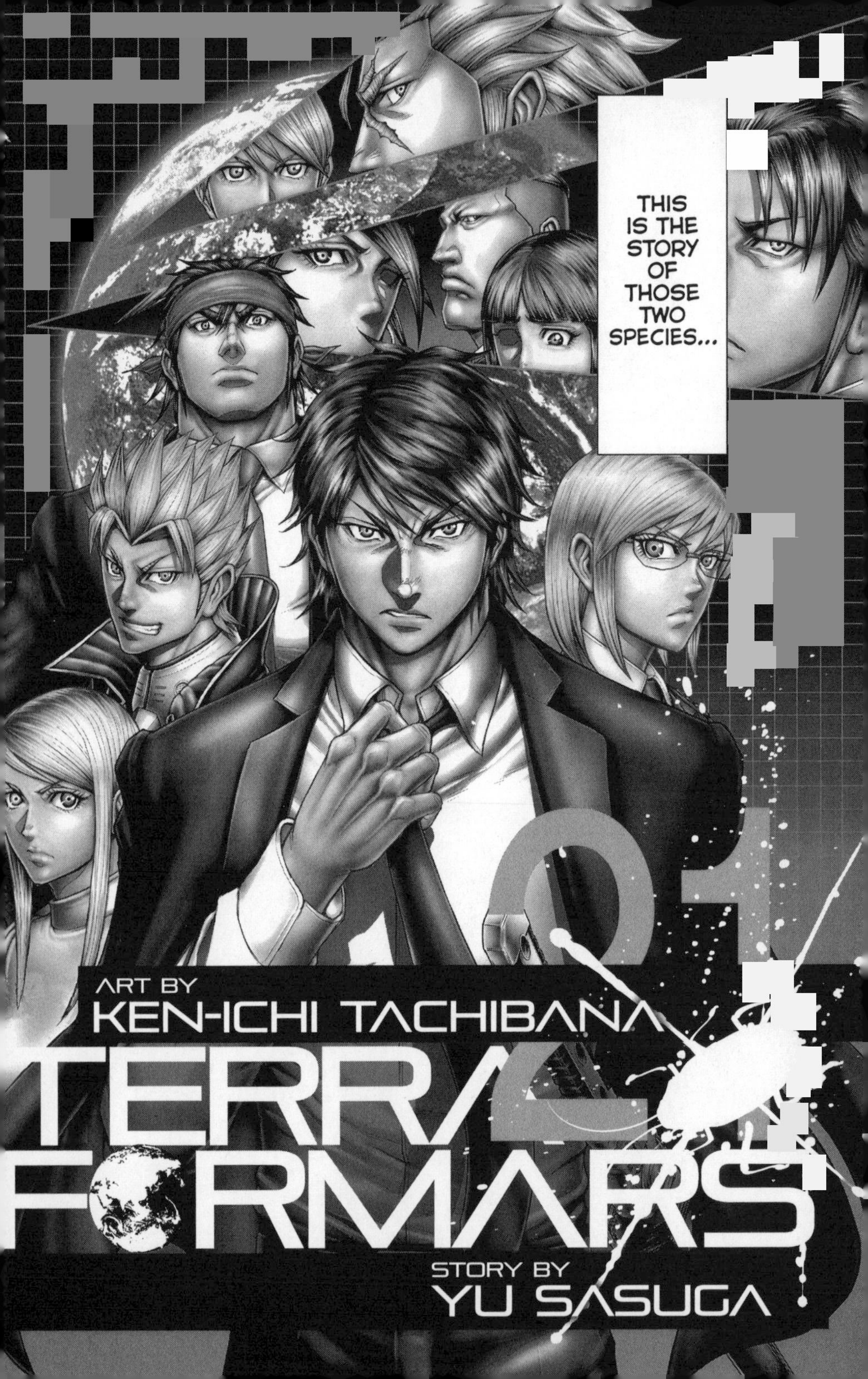
THIS IS THE STORY OF THOSE TWO SPECIES...
21
ART BY
KEN-ICHI TACHIBANA
TERRA FORMARS
STORY BY
YU SASUGA

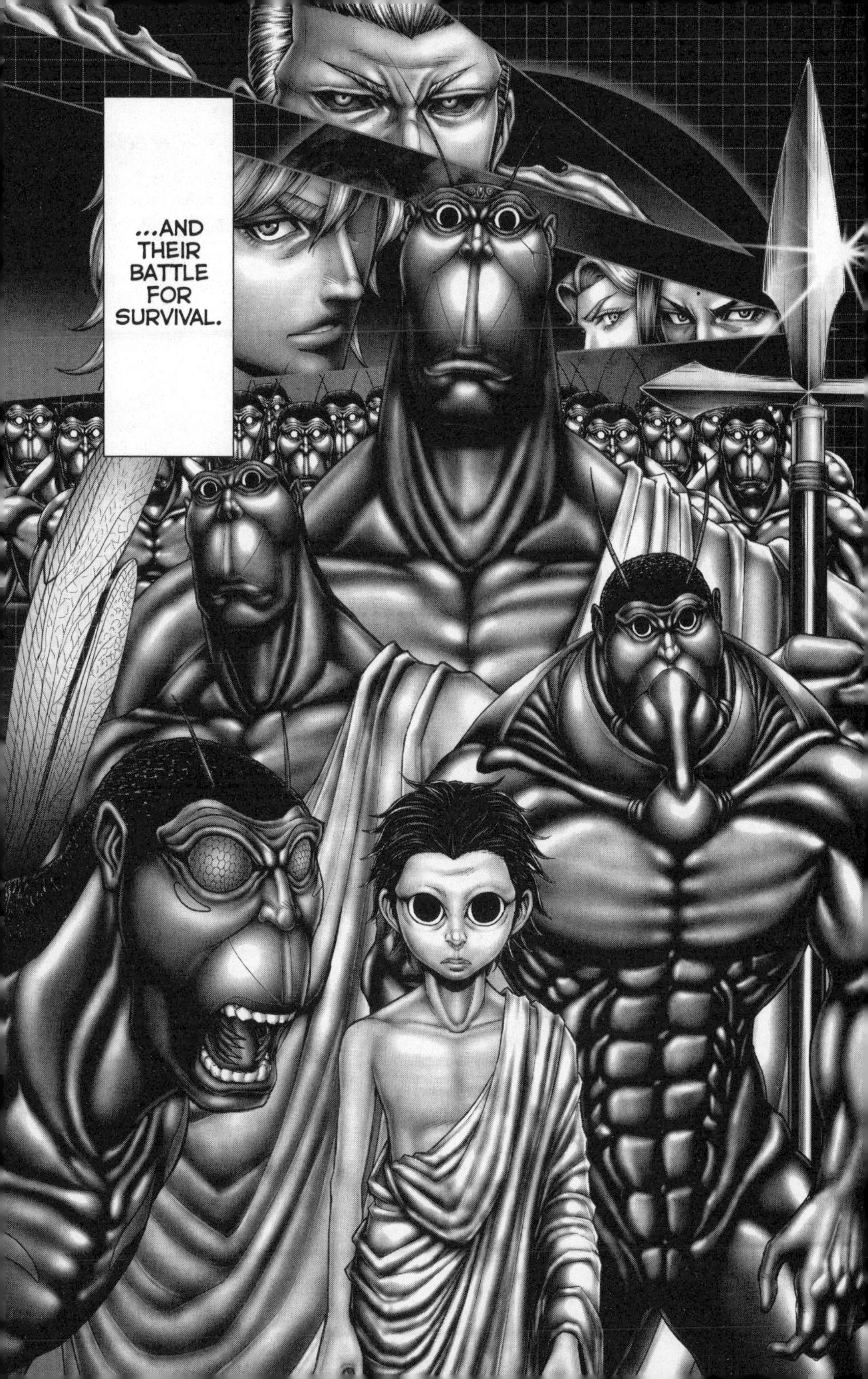
...AND THEIR BATTLE FOR SURVIVAL.

MARS

= ANTI-TERRAFORMAR PERSONNEL
= SNEAKERS

【ICHI KEIGO】 PRIVATE MILITARY COMPANY, MERCENARY GROUP

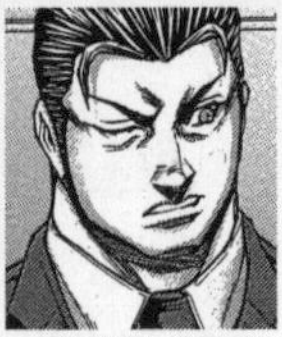

SHICHISEI HIRUMA

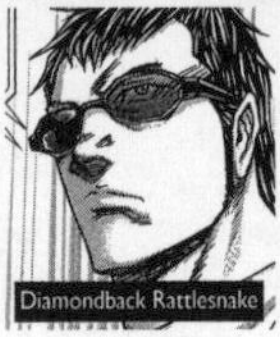
Diamondback Rattlesnake

KYO HYUGA

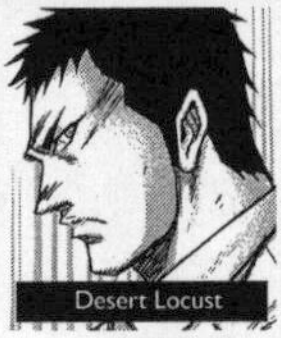
Desert Locust

JOICHI HONGO

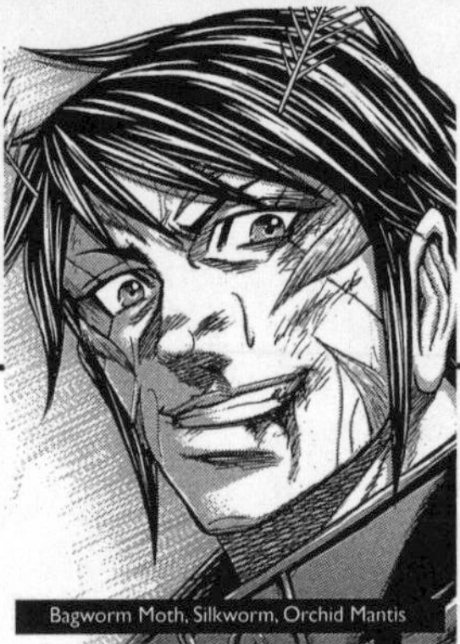
Bagworm Moth, Silkworm, Orchid Mantis

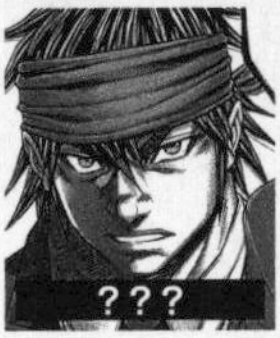
???

TATSUHIRO SOMEYA

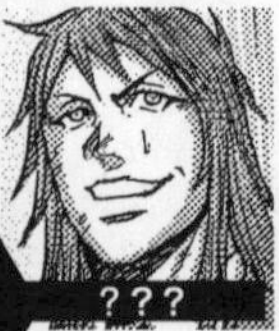
???

AKARI HIZAMARU

The main protagonist. Section Chief, Patrol Section, Capital Headquarters, Tokyo. Artificially created with an immune tolerance organ called the Mosaic Organ, he is known as the Second. Numerous countries want to experiment on him.

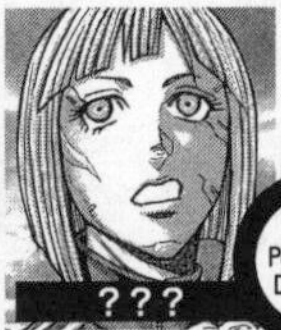
???

Boso Peninsula Defense

SAMURAI SWORD (code name)

Old friends.

【JAPANESE GOVERNMENT】

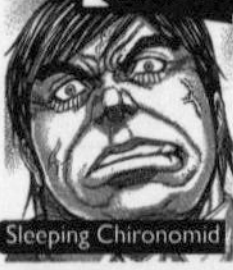
Sleeping Chironomid

ICHIRO HIRUMA

Former *Bugs 2* crew

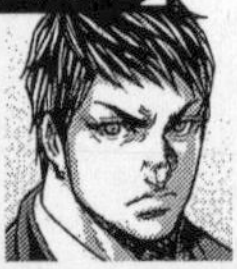

ROKKA HIRUMA

Tokaido Defense

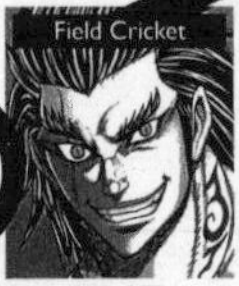
Field Cricket

SHO SAITO

Leader of a subterranean gang in Kanto. Defending the Tokaido region!

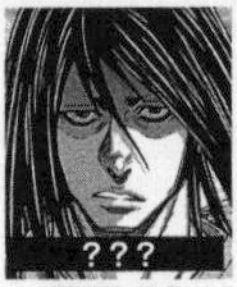
???

ITSUKI KAZEMURA

Imperial Palace Guard. Defending the Kii Peninsula!

Kii Peninsula Defense

【SPACIALS】 SPECIAL OPERATIONS UNIT OF THE AMERICAN SPACE FORCE

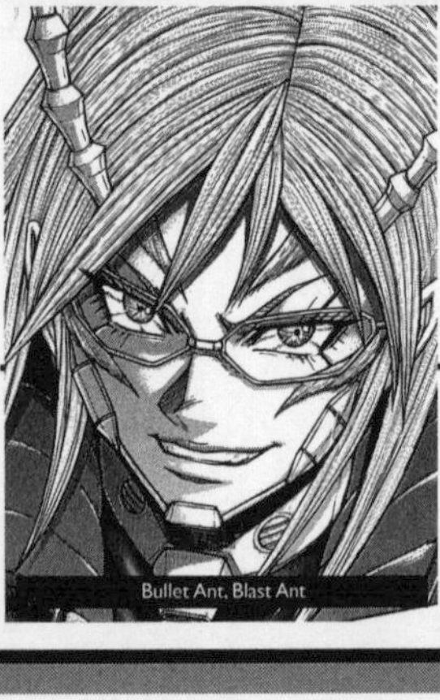
Bullet Ant, Blast Ant

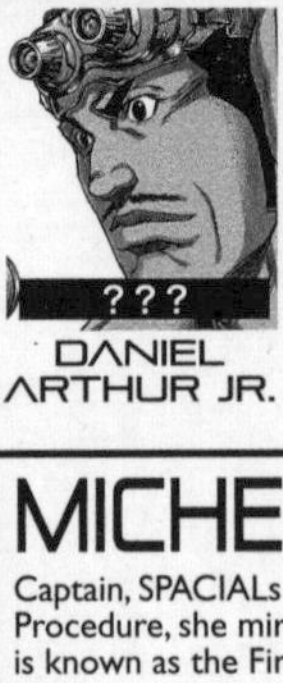
???

DANIEL ARTHUR JR.

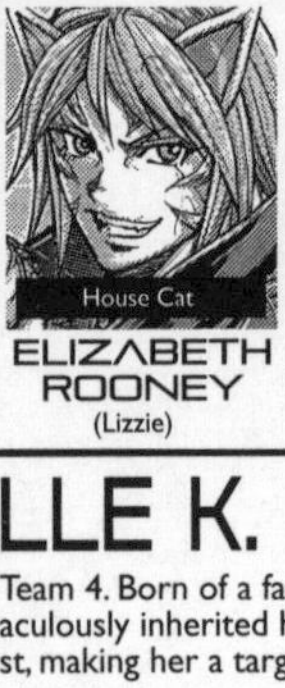
House Cat

ELIZABETH ROONEY (Lizzie)

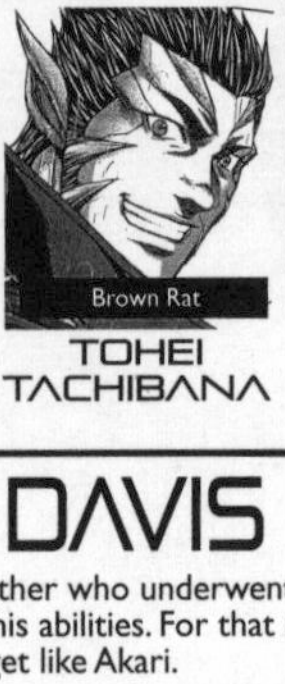
Brown Rat

TOHEI TACHIBANA

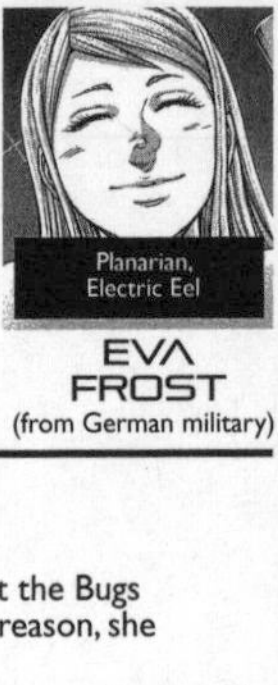
Planarian, Electric Eel

EVA FROST (from German military)

MICHELLE K. DAVIS

Captain, SPACIALs Team 4. Born of a father who underwent the Bugs Procedure, she miraculously inherited his abilities. For that reason, she is known as the First, making her a target like Akari.

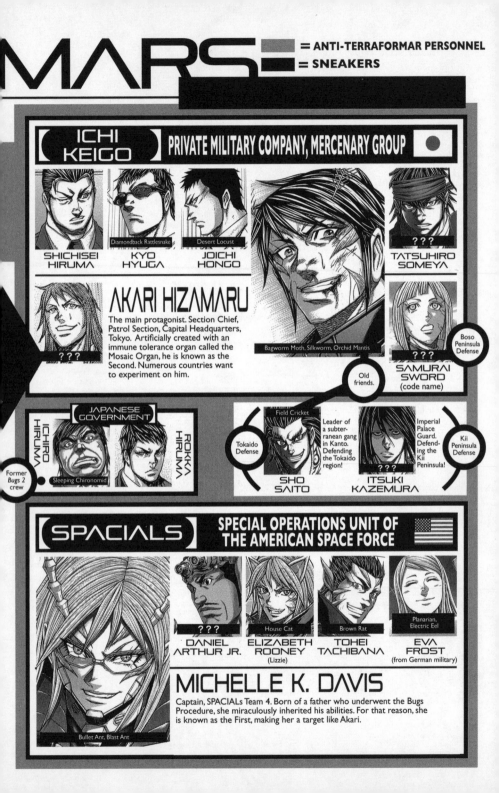

TERRAFORMARS

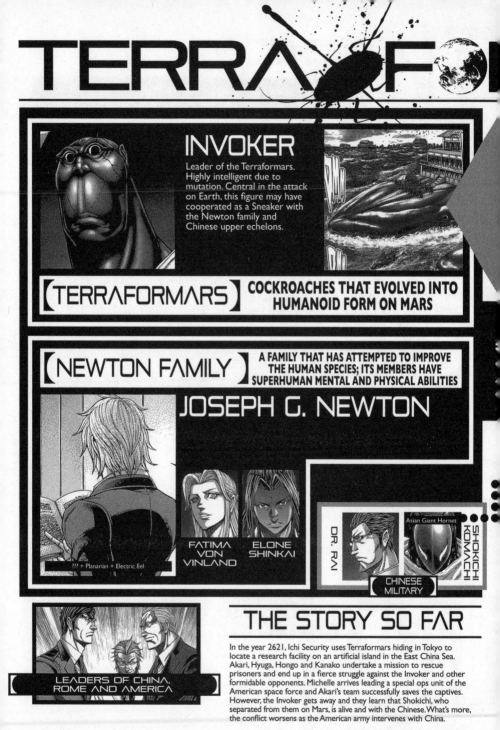

INVOKER

Leader of the Terraformars. Highly intelligent due to mutation. Central in the attack on Earth, this figure may have cooperated as a Sneaker with the Newton family and Chinese upper echelons.

[TERRAFORMARS] COCKROACHES THAT EVOLVED INTO HUMANOID FORM ON MARS

[NEWTON FAMILY] A FAMILY THAT HAS ATTEMPTED TO IMPROVE THE HUMAN SPECIES; ITS MEMBERS HAVE SUPERHUMAN MENTAL AND PHYSICAL ABILITIES

??? + Planarian + Electric Eel

JOSEPH G. NEWTON

FATIMA VON VINLAND

ELONE SHINKAI

DR. RAI

Asian Giant Hornet

SHOKICHI KOMACHI

[CHINESE MILITARY]

[LEADERS OF CHINA, ROME AND AMERICA]

THE STORY SO FAR

In the year 2621, Ichi Security uses Terraformars hiding in Tokyo to locate a research facility on an artificial island in the East China Sea. Akari, Hyuga, Hongo and Kanako undertake a mission to rescue prisoners and end up in a fierce struggle against the Invoker and other formidable opponents. Michelle arrives leading a special ops unit of the American space force and Akari's team successfully saves the captives. However, the Invoker gets away and they learn that Shokichi, who separated from them on Mars, is alive and with the Chinese. What's more, the conflict worsens as the American army intervenes with China.

One week after the battle on the artificial island, the Terraformars launch an all-out attack on Japan at the moment the entire Cabinet resigns. Former Prime Minister Ichiro Hiruma returns, however, and the government temporarily resumes functioning. As the intentions of the various nations and their camps grow increasingly tangled, warriors around Japan await the Terraformars. Just then, Michelle receives unexpected news from China!

CONTENTS

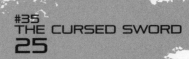

#34
THE ANCIENT FRONTIER SPIRIT
7

#35
THE CURSED SWORD
25

#36
ILLNESS
43

#37
DESCENDANT OF
THE GODS
61

#38
SOFT AND HARD
80

#39
OUTSIDE ASTROLOGY
99

#40
THE END OF THE CENTURY
118

#41
THE PROLOGUE TO THE EPILOGUE
137

#42
LE GRAND ROY D'ANGOLMOIS
187

TERRA FORMARS 21

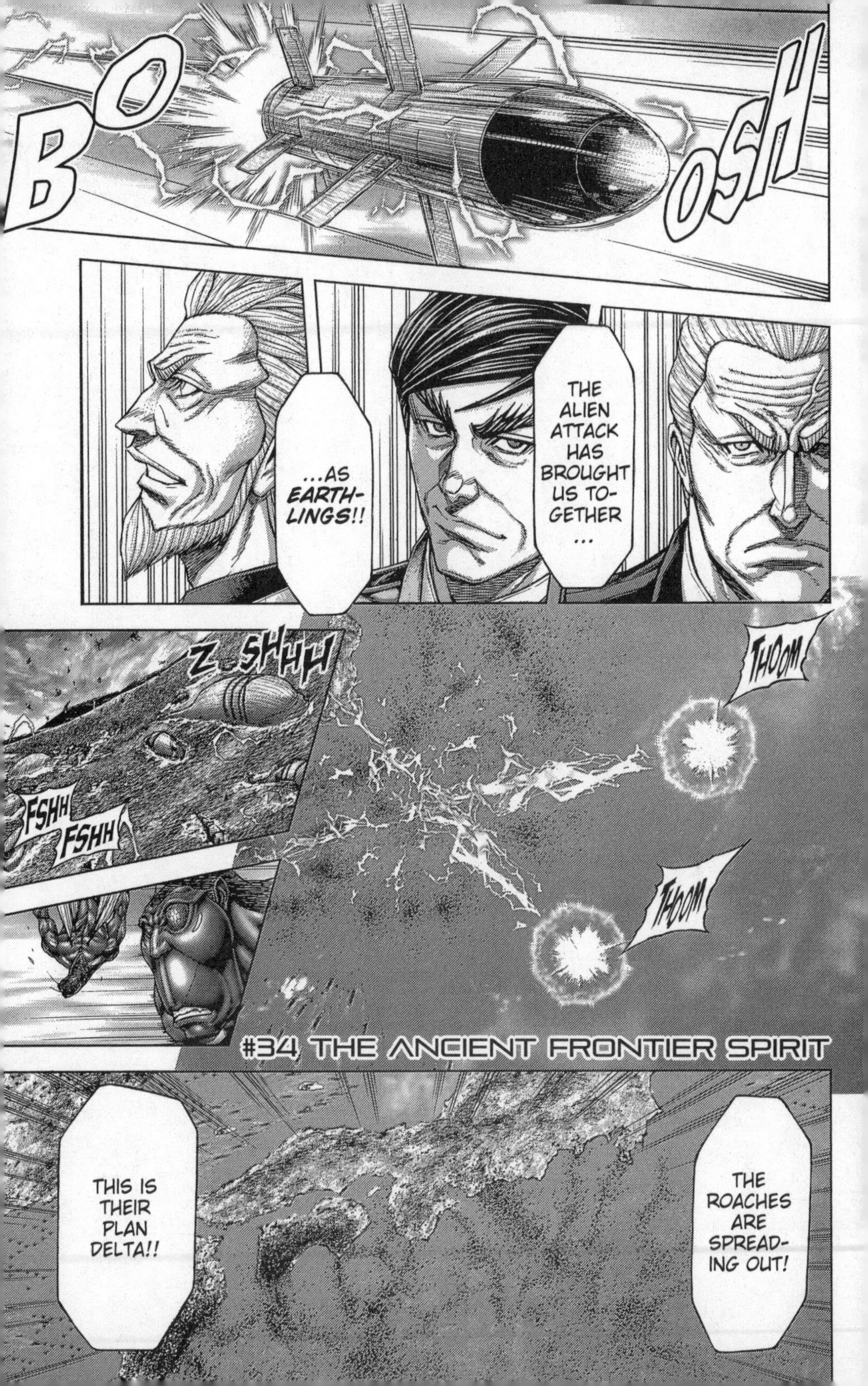
BOOSH
THE ALIEN ATTACK HAS BROUGHT US TO-GETHER ...
...AS EARTH-LINGS!!
THOOM!
THOOM
#34 THE ANCIENT FRONTIER SPIRIT
Z SHHH
FSHH FSHH
THE ROACHES ARE SPREAD-ING OUT!
THIS IS THEIR PLAN DELTA!!

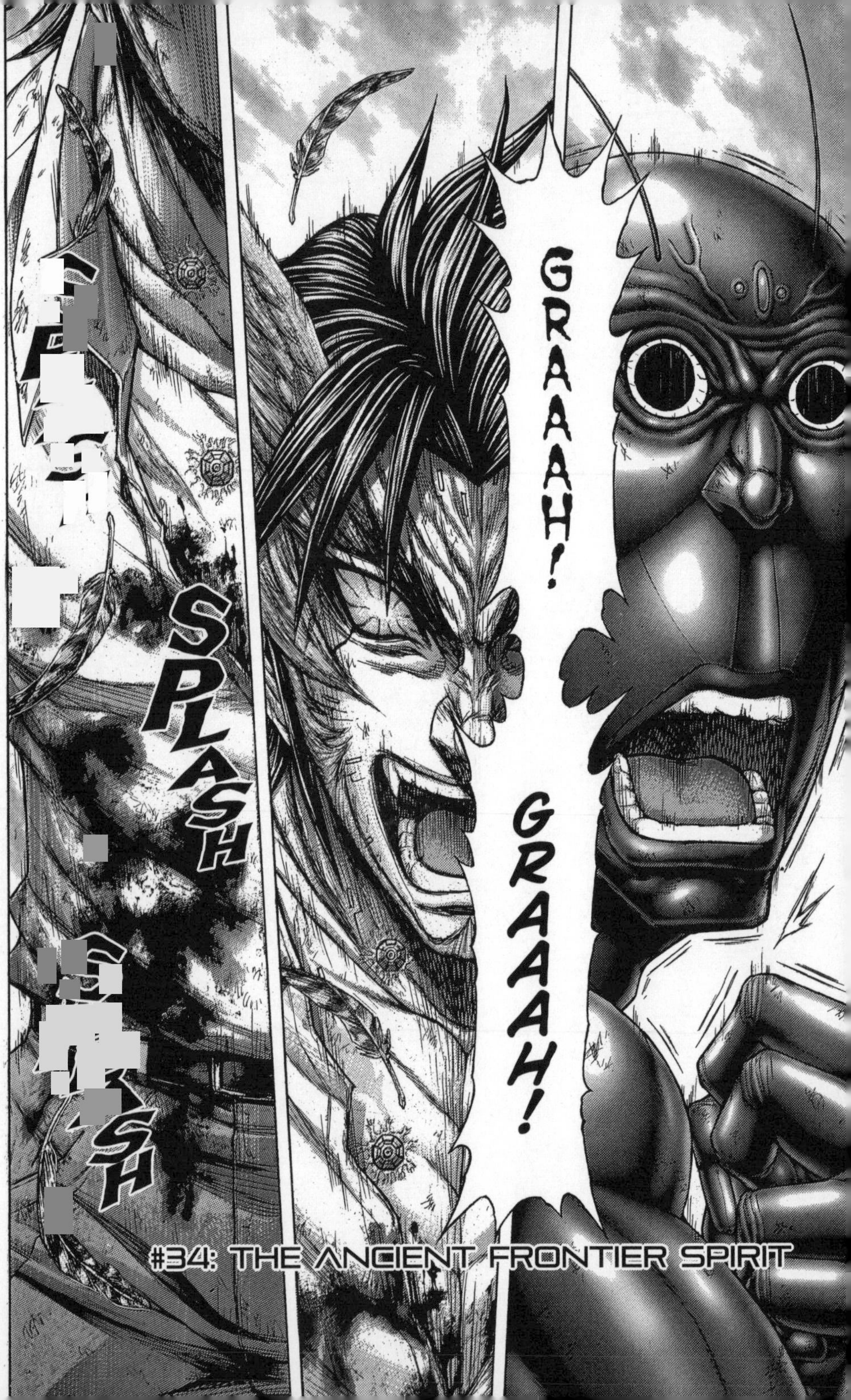
GRAAAAH! GRAAAAH!
SPLASH
#34: THE ANCIENT FRONTIER SPIRIT

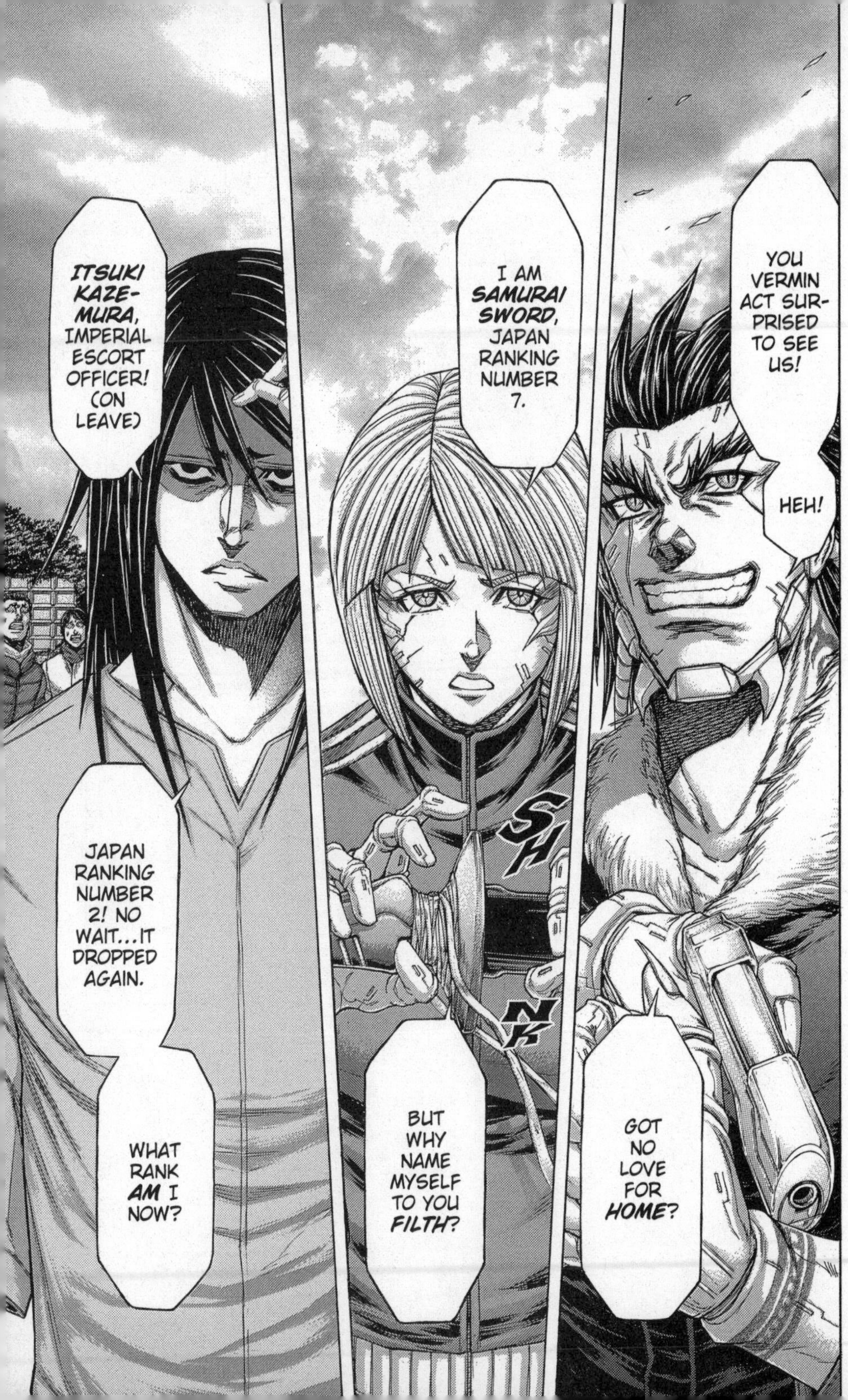
YOU VERMIN ACT SUR-PRISED TO SEE US!
HEH!
GOT NO LOVE FOR *HOME*?
I AM *SAMURAI SWORD*, JAPAN RANKING NUMBER 7.
BUT WHY NAME MYSELF TO YOU *FILTH*?
ITSUKI KAZE-MURA, IMPERIAL ESCORT OFFICER! (ON LEAVE)
JAPAN RANKING NUMBER 2! NO WAIT...IT DROPPED AGAIN.
WHAT RANK *AM* I NOW?

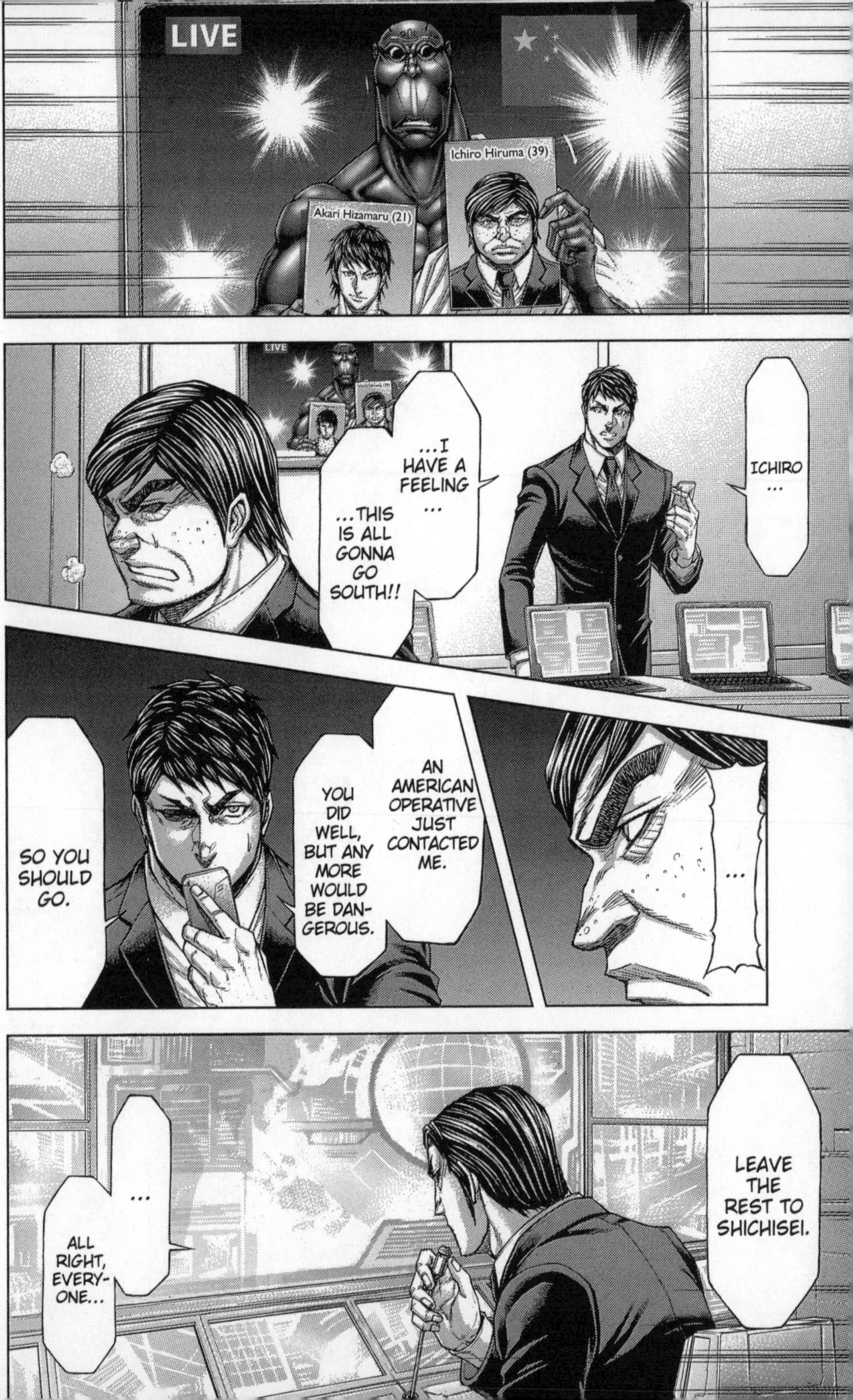
LIVE
Ichiro Hiruma (39)
Akari Hizamaru (21)
ICHIRO ...
...I HAVE A FEELING ...
...THIS IS ALL GONNA GO SOUTH!!
LIVE
...
AN AMERICAN OPERATIVE JUST CONTACTED ME.
YOU DID WELL, BUT ANY MORE WOULD BE DANGEROUS.
SO YOU SHOULD GO.
LEAVE THE REST TO SHICHISEI.
...
ALL RIGHT, EVERYONE...

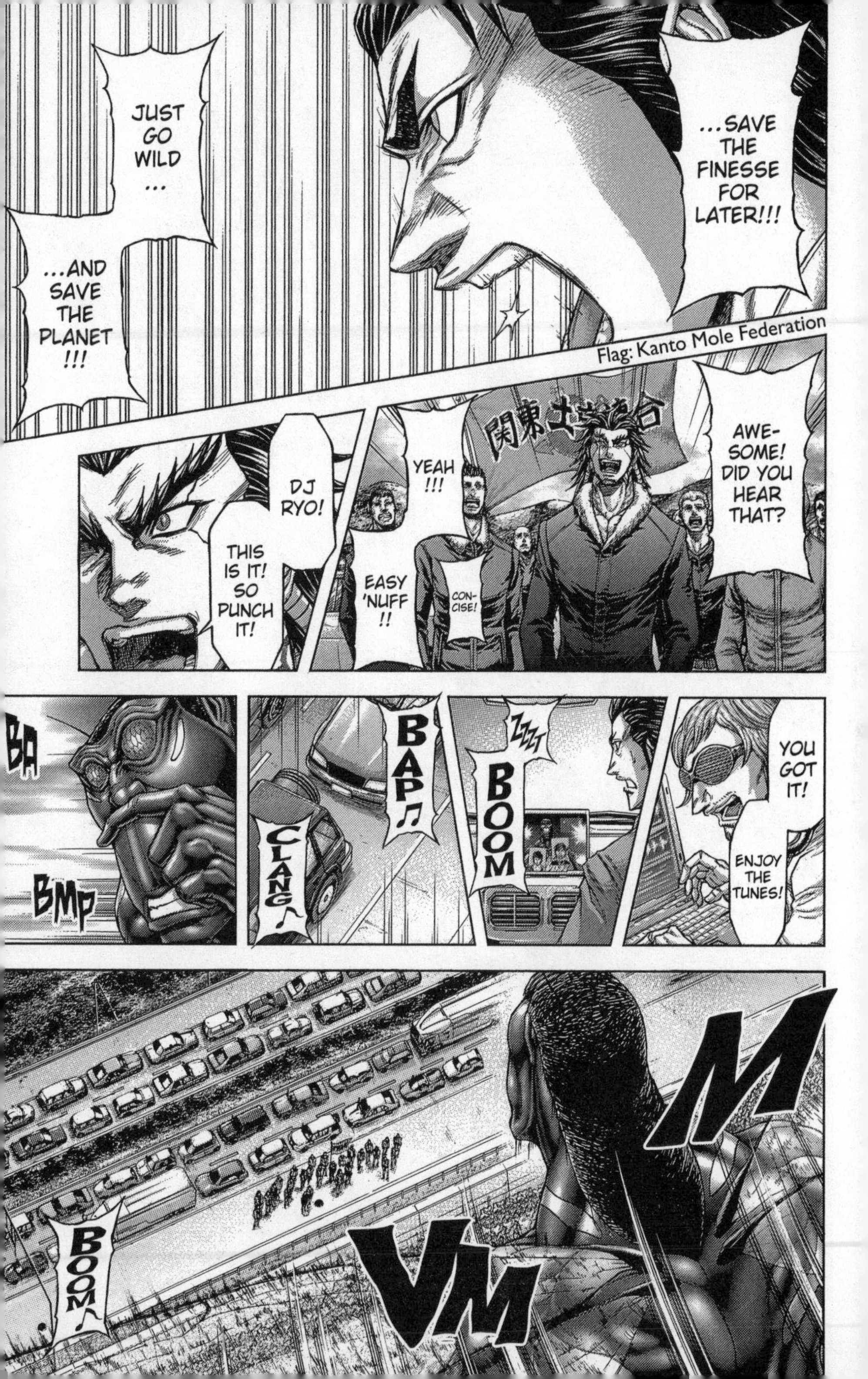
...SAVE THE FINESSE FOR LATER!!!
JUST GO WILD...
...AND SAVE THE PLANET!!!
Flag: Kanto Mole Federation
AWE-SOME! DID YOU HEAR THAT?
YEAH!!!
CON-CISE!
EASY 'NUFF!!
DJ RYO!
THIS IS IT! SO PUNCH IT!
YOU GOT IT!
ENJOY THE TUNES!
ZZZT
BOOM
BAP♫
CLANG♪
BA
BMP
M
VM
BOOM♪

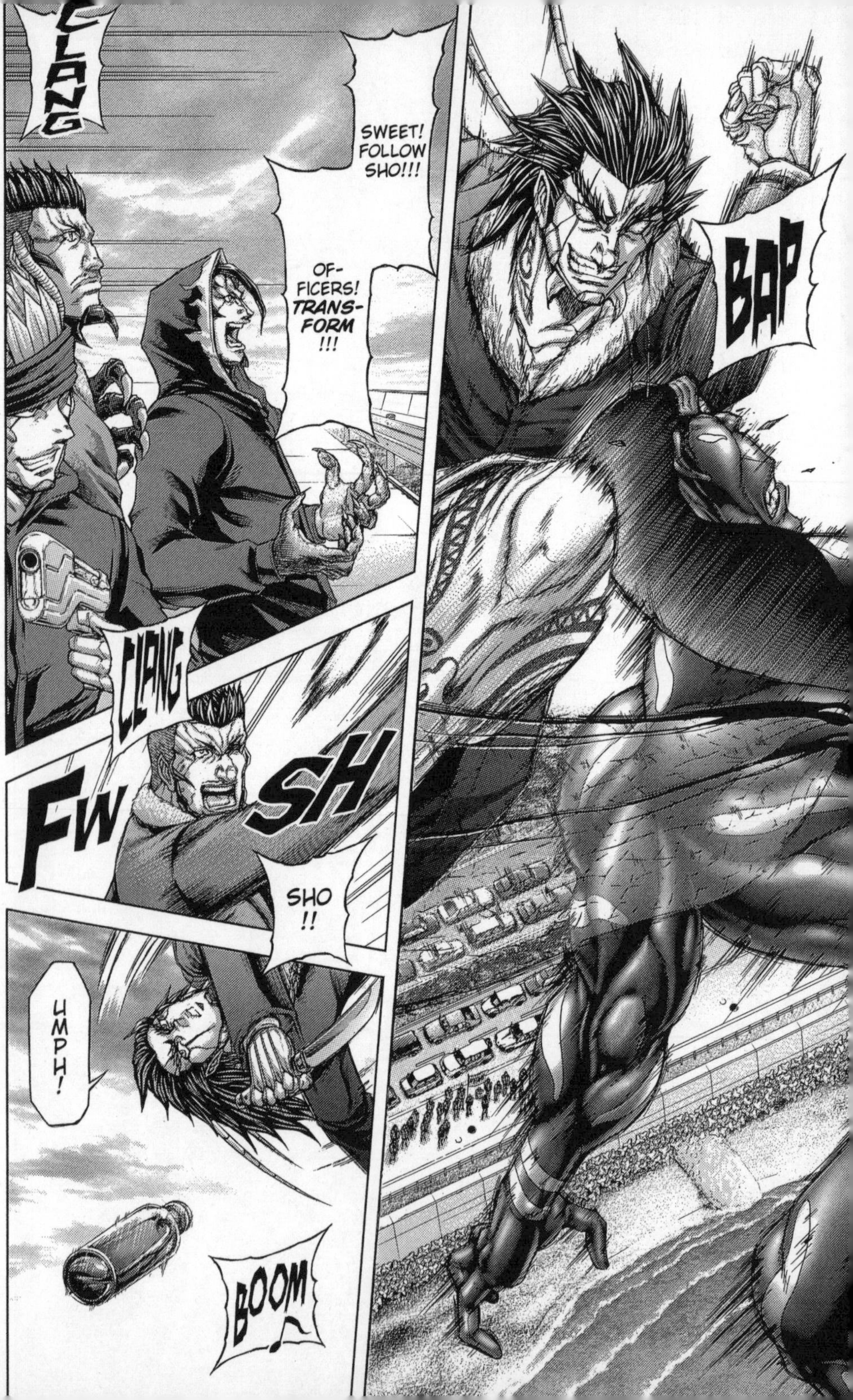

BAP
SWEET! FOLLOW SHO!!!
CLANG
OF-FICERS! TRANSFORM!!!
CLANG
FWSH
SHO!!
UMPH!
BOOM

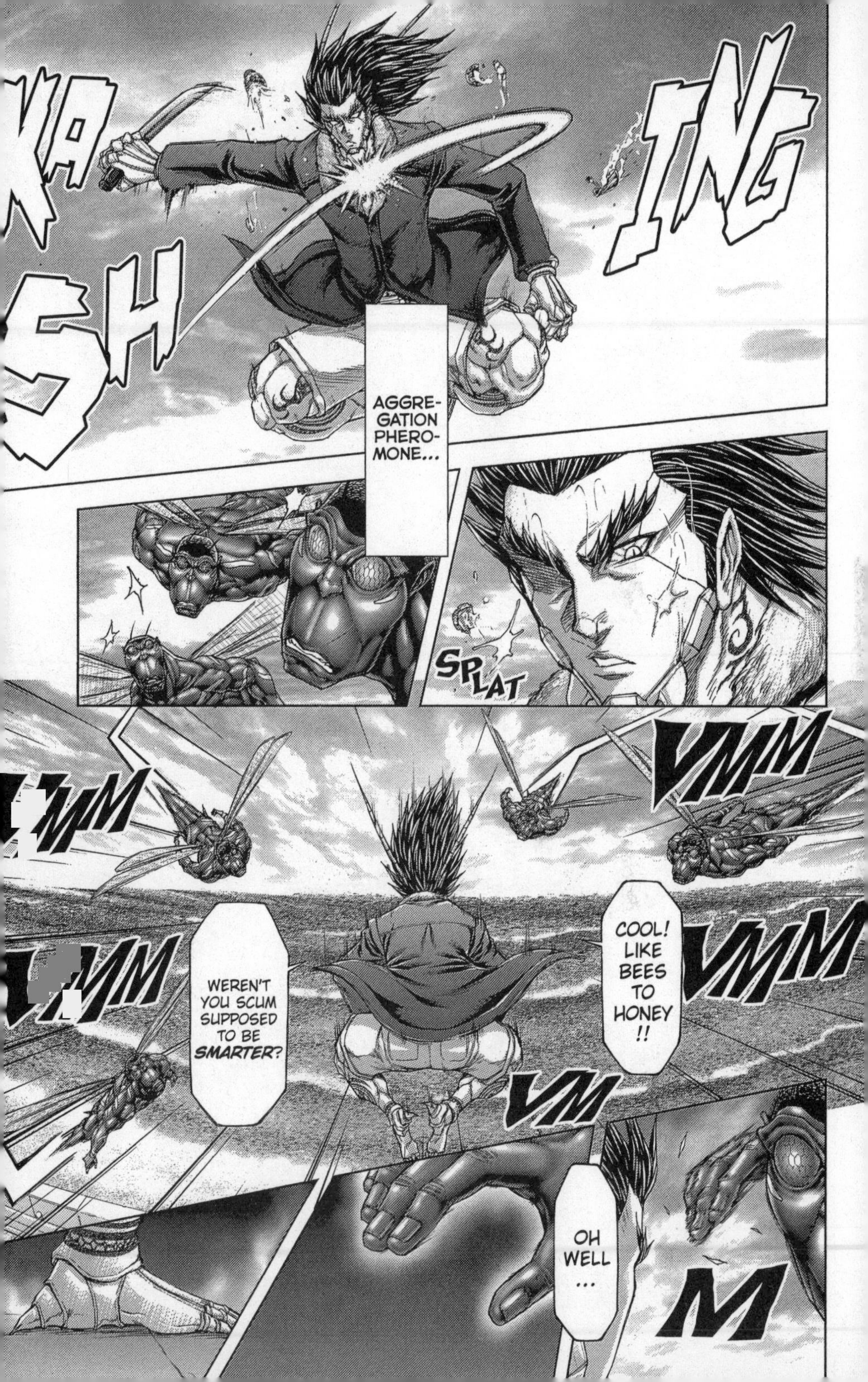
KA SH ING
AGGRE-GATION PHERO-MONE...
SPLAT
VMM
COOL! LIKE BEES TO HONEY!!
VMM
VM
WEREN'T YOU SCUM SUPPOSED TO BE SMARTER?
M
OH WELL...

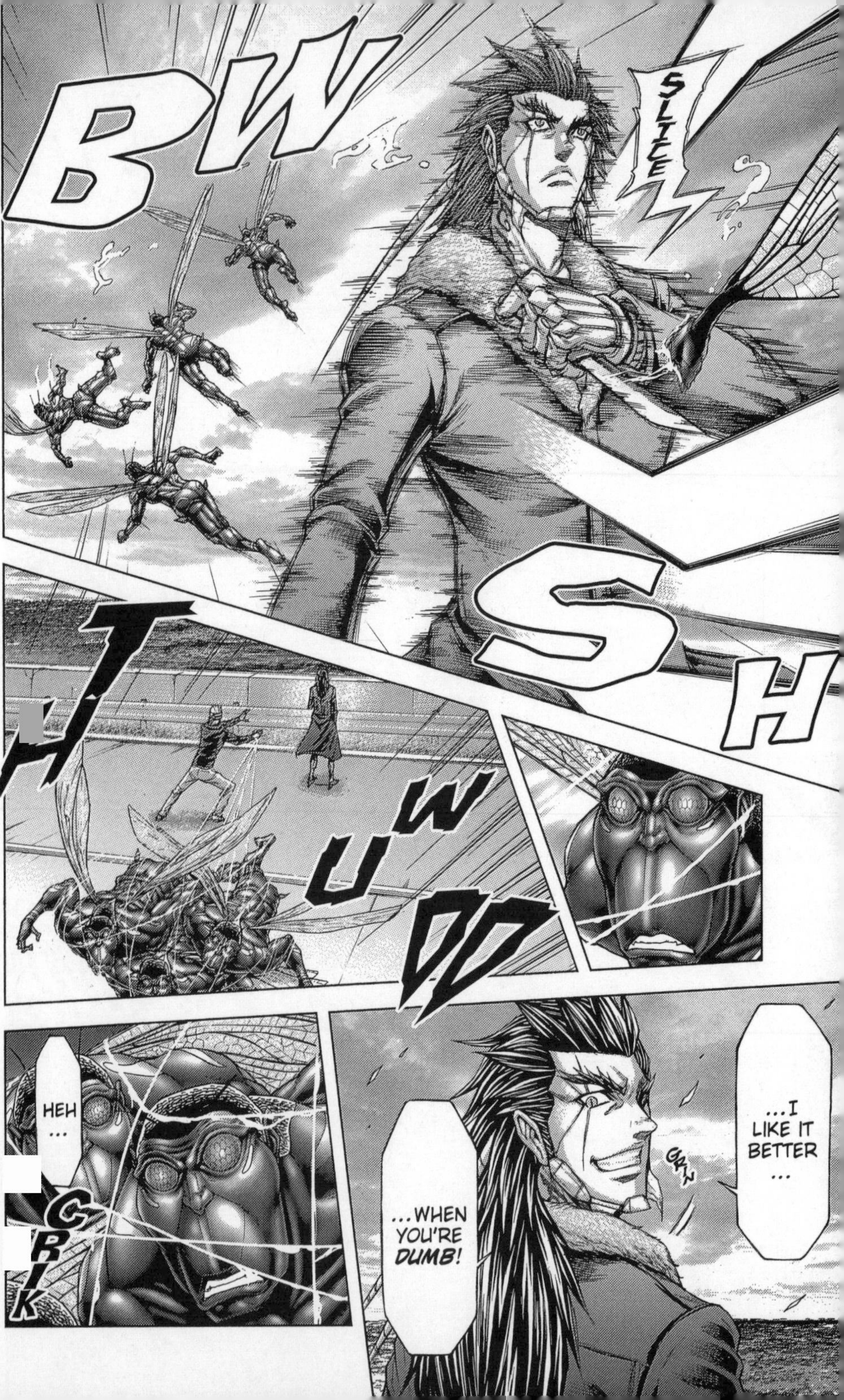
BW
SLICE
SH
H
WUDD
...I LIKE IT BETTER ...
GRIN
...WHEN YOU'RE DUMB!
HEH ...
CRIK

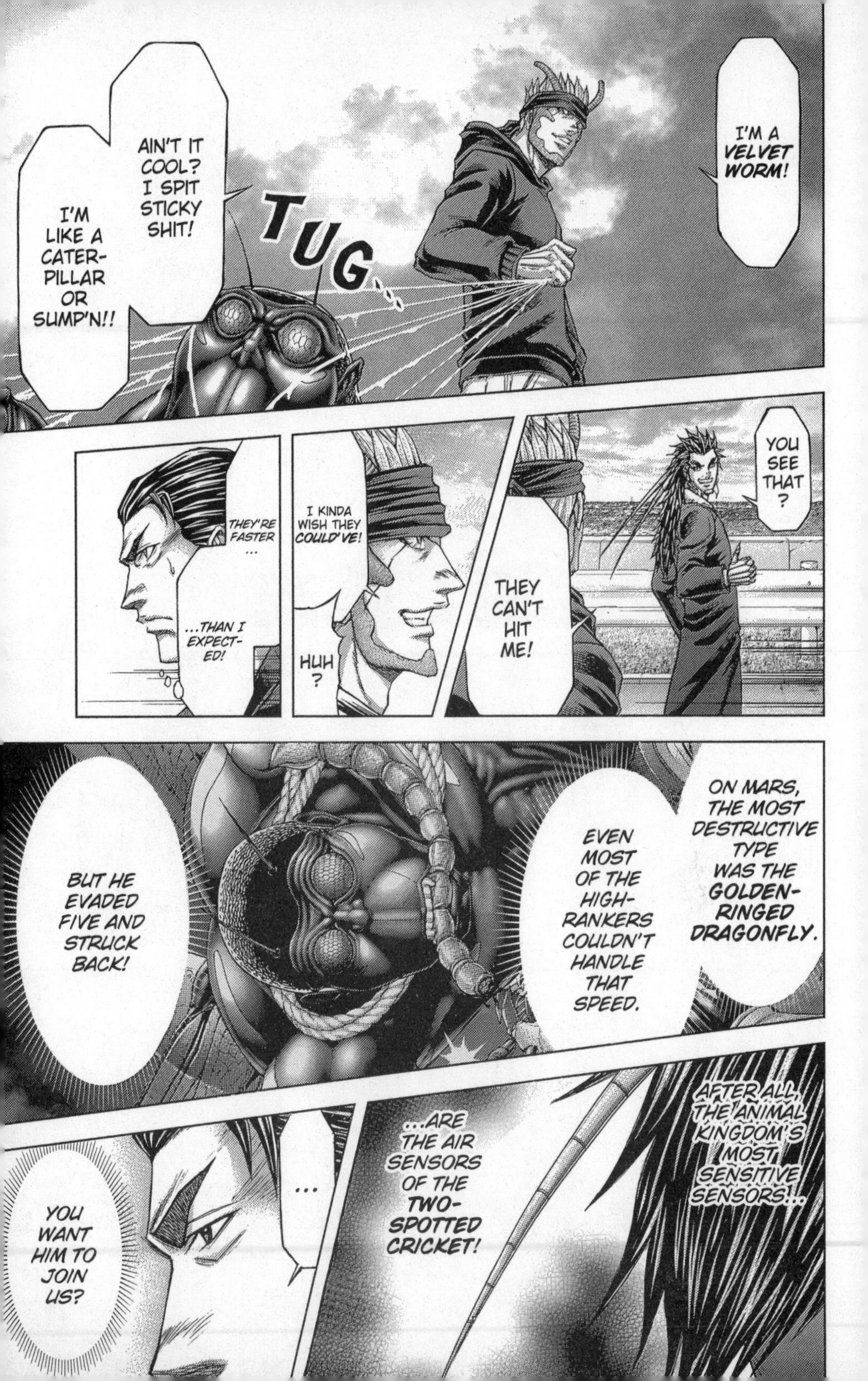

I'M A VELVET WORM!
TUG...
AIN'T IT COOL? I SPIT STICKY SHIT!
I'M LIKE A CATER-PILLAR OR SUMP'N!!
YOU SEE THAT?
THEY CAN'T HIT ME!
I KINDA WISH THEY COULD'VE!
HUH?
THEY'RE FASTER...
...THAN I EXPECT-ED!
ON MARS, THE MOST DESTRUCTIVE TYPE WAS THE GOLDEN-RINGED DRAGONFLY.
EVEN MOST OF THE HIGH-RANKERS COULDN'T HANDLE THAT SPEED.
BUT HE EVADED FIVE AND STRUCK BACK!
AFTER ALL, THE ANIMAL KINGDOM'S MOST SENSITIVE SENSORS...
...ARE THE AIR SENSORS OF THE TWO-SPOTTED CRICKET!
...
YOU WANT HIM TO JOIN US?

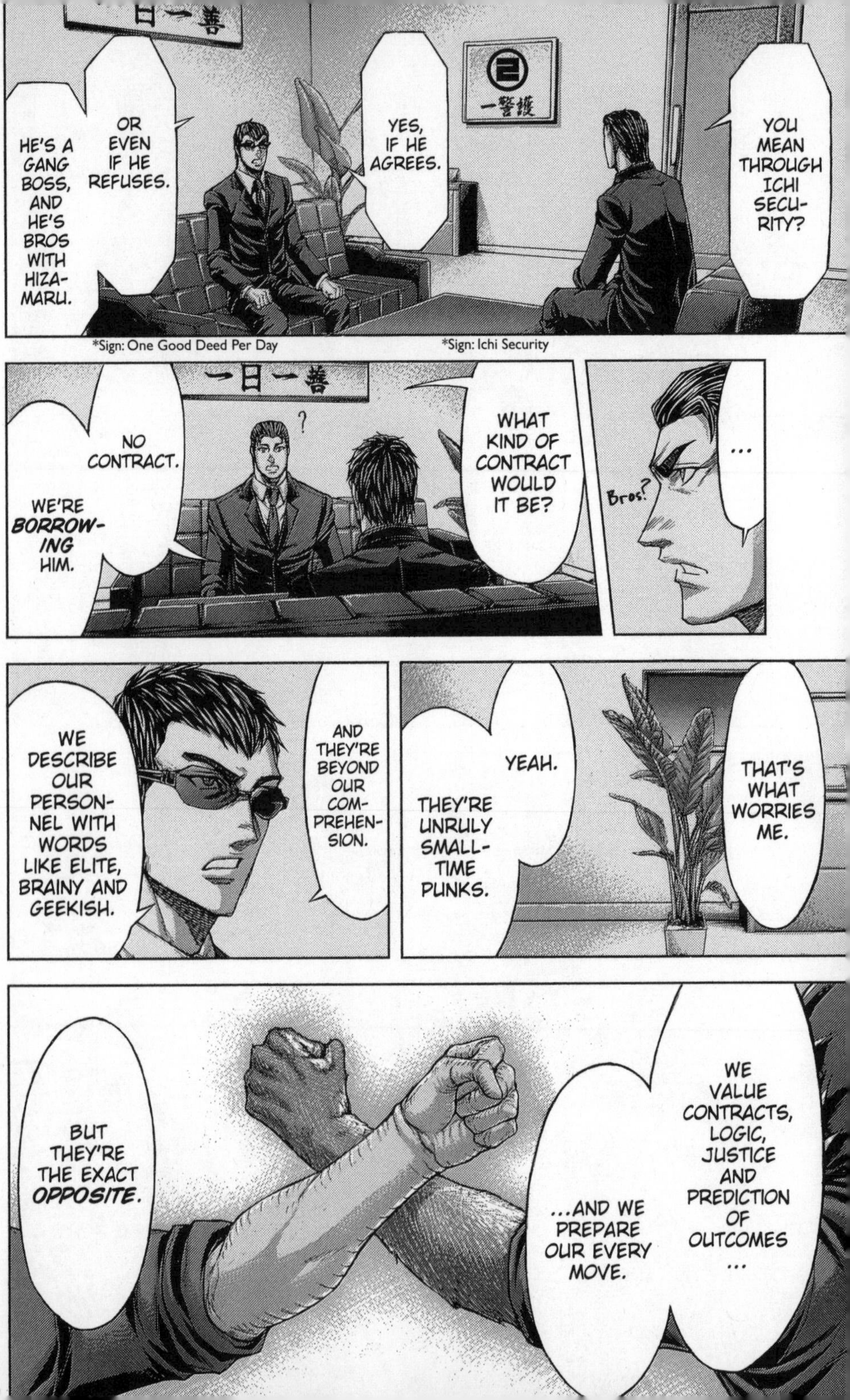
YOU MEAN THROUGH ICHI SECURITY?
YES, IF HE AGREES.
OR EVEN IF HE REFUSES.
HE'S A GANG BOSS, AND HE'S BROS WITH HIZAMARU.
*Sign: One Good Deed Per Day
*Sign: Ichi Security
...
Bros?
WHAT KIND OF CONTRACT WOULD IT BE?
NO CONTRACT.
WE'RE ***BORROWING*** HIM.
THAT'S WHAT WORRIES ME.
YEAH.
THEY'RE UNRULY SMALL-TIME PUNKS.
AND THEY'RE BEYOND OUR COMPREHENSION.
WE DESCRIBE OUR PERSONNEL WITH WORDS LIKE ELITE, BRAINY AND GEEKISH.
WE VALUE CONTRACTS, LOGIC, JUSTICE AND PREDICTION OF OUTCOMES...
...AND WE PREPARE OUR EVERY MOVE.
BUT THEY'RE THE EXACT ***OPPOSITE***.

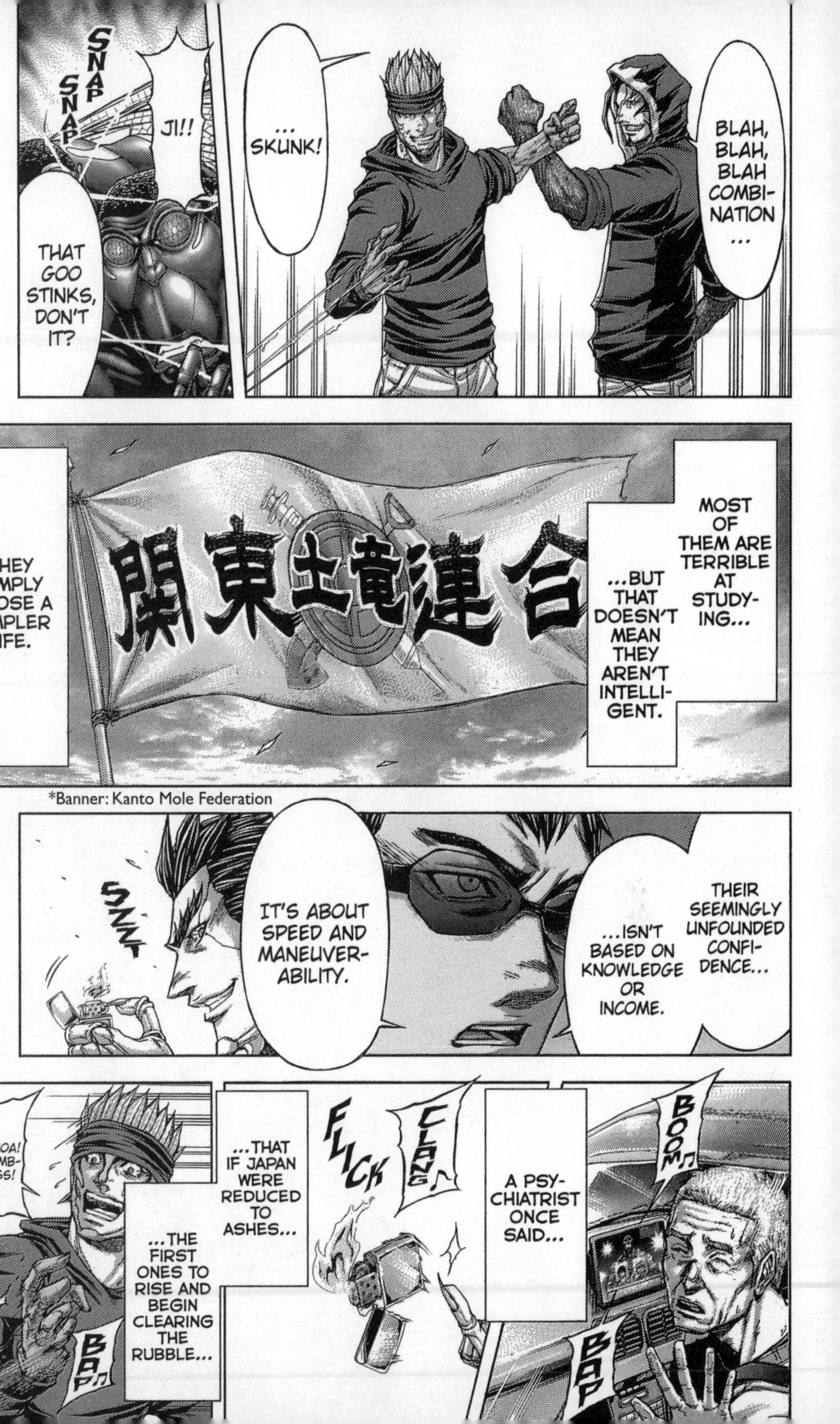
BLAH, BLAH, BLAH COMBINATION...
...SKUNK!
SNAP SNAP
JI!!
THAT GOO STINKS, DON'T IT?
MOST OF THEM ARE TERRIBLE AT STUDYING...
...BUT THAT DOESN'T MEAN THEY AREN'T INTELLIGENT.
関東土竜連合
THEY SIMPLY CHOSE A SIMPLER LIFE.
THEIR SEEMINGLY UNFOUNDED CONFIDENCE...
...ISN'T BASED ON KNOWLEDGE OR INCOME.
IT'S ABOUT SPEED AND MANEUVERABILITY.
SZZT
BOOM♫
A PSYCHIATRIST ONCE SAID...
BAP
CLANG♪
FLICK
...THAT IF JAPAN WERE REDUCED TO ASHES...
WHOA! DUMBASS!
...THE FIRST ONES TO RISE AND BEGIN CLEARING THE RUBBLE...
BAP♫
*Banner: Kanto Mole Federation

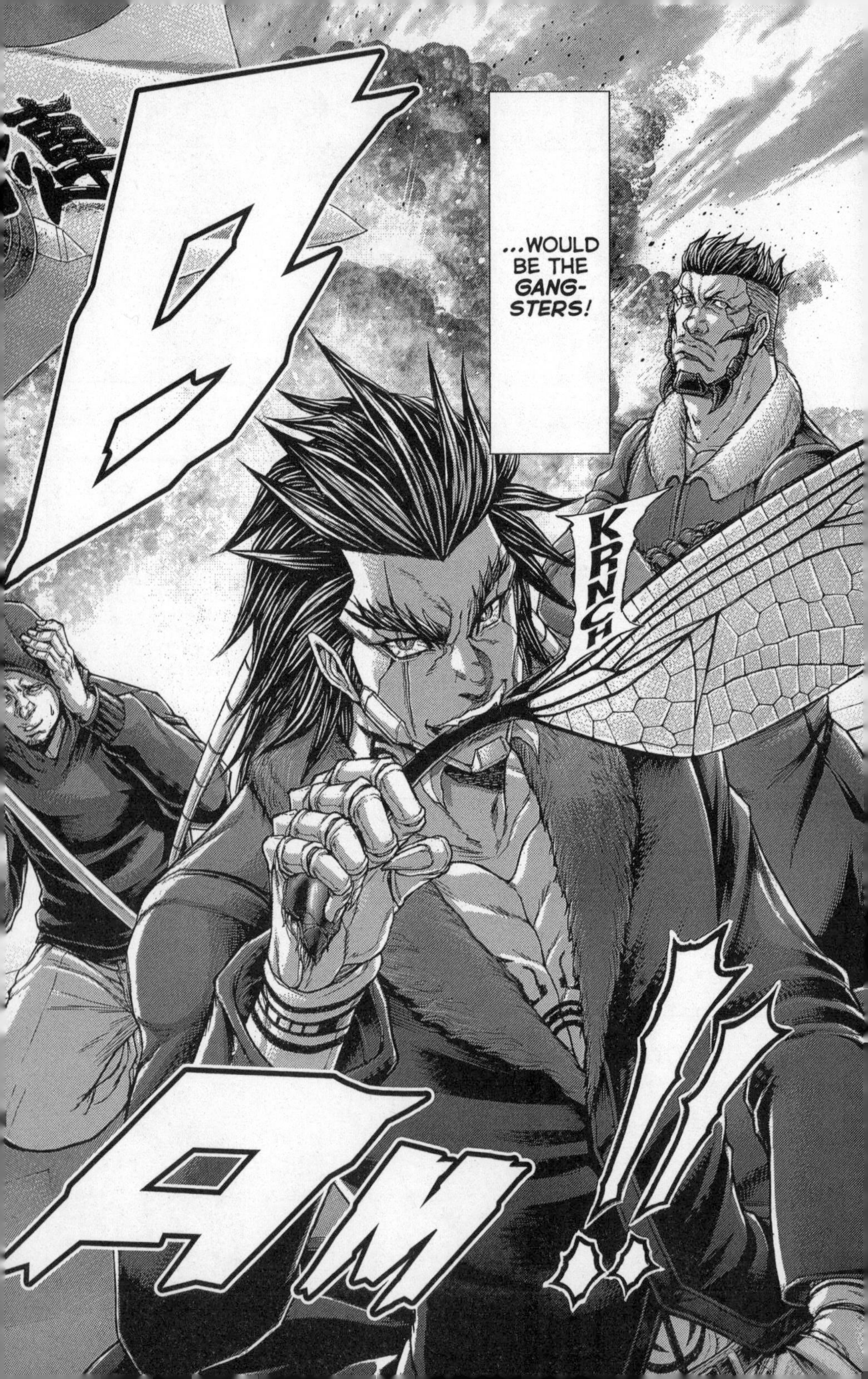
...WOULD BE THE GANGSTERS!
KRNCH
BAM!!

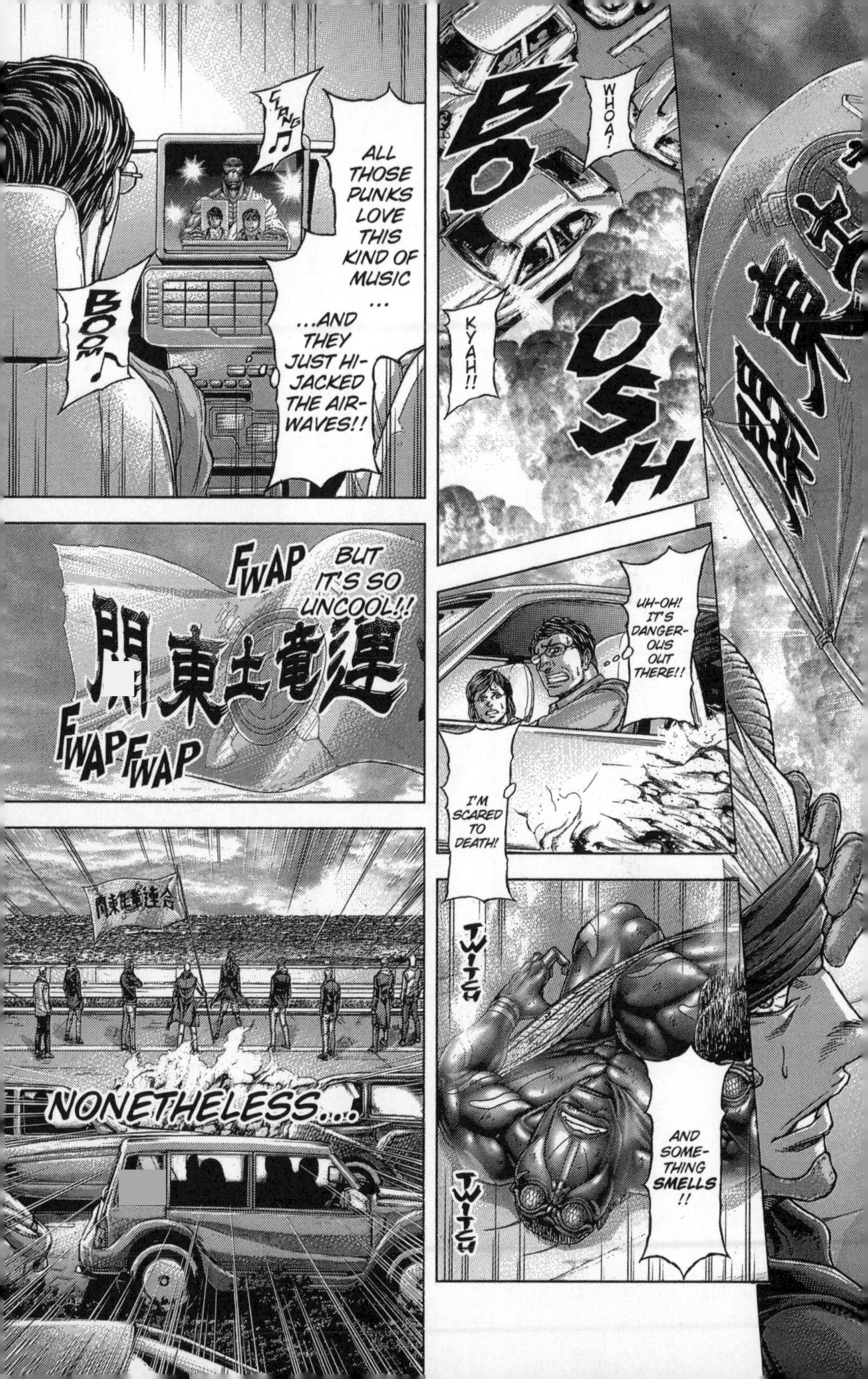
BOOSH
WHOA!
KYAH!!
UH-OH! IT'S DANGER-OUS OUT THERE!!
I'M SCARED TO DEATH!
TWITCH
TWITCH
AND SOME-THING SMELLS!!
CLANG ♫
ALL THOSE PUNKS LOVE THIS KIND OF MUSIC...
...AND THEY JUST HI-JACKED THE AIR-WAVES!!
BOOM ♪
FWAP
BUT IT'S SO UNCOOL!!
FWAP FWAP
NONETHELESS...

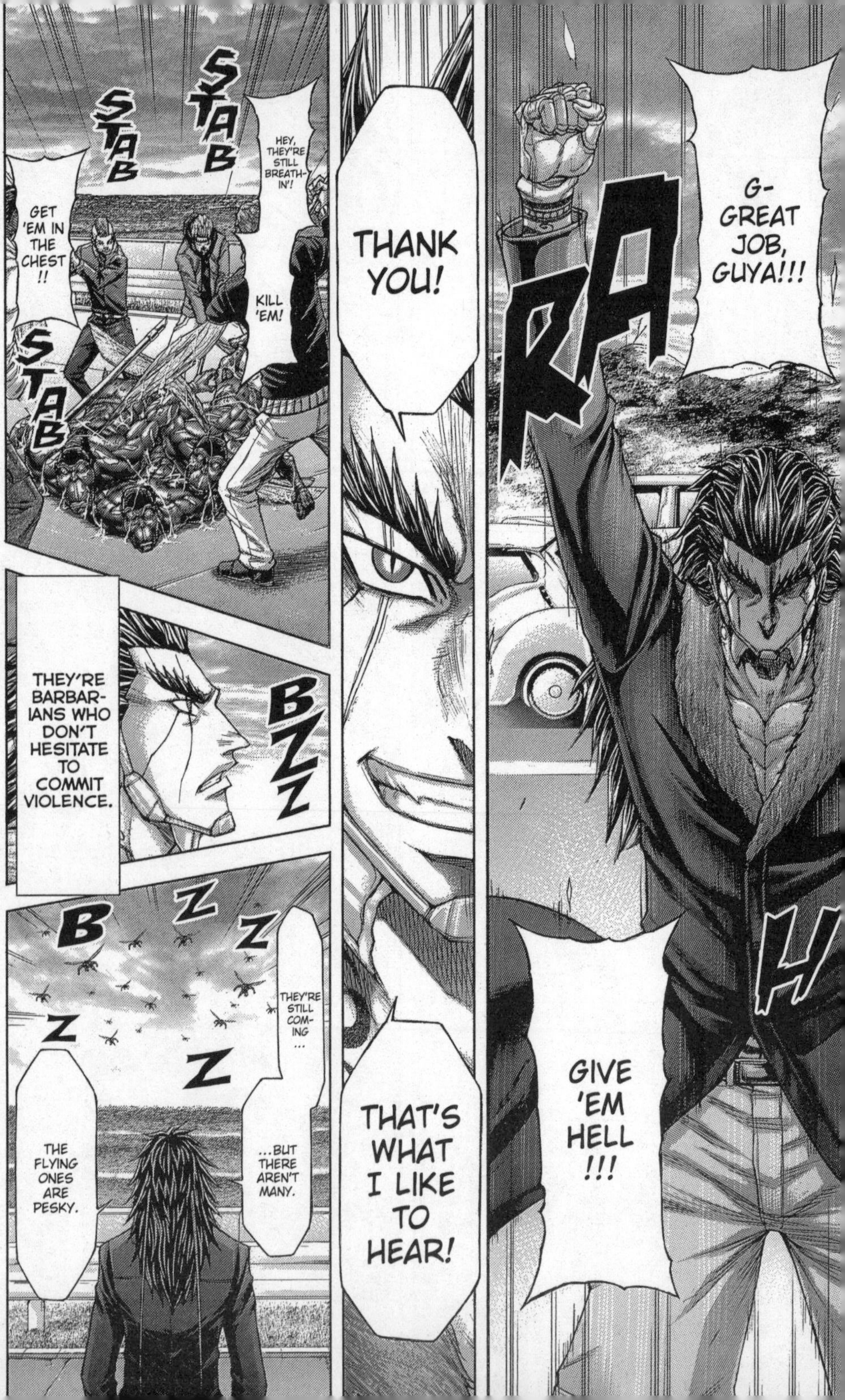
G-GREAT JOB, GUYA!!!
RA
H
GIVE 'EM HELL!!!
THANK YOU!
THAT'S WHAT I LIKE TO HEAR!
STAB
HEY, THEY'RE STILL BREATHIN'!
STAB
GET 'EM IN THE CHEST!!
KILL 'EM!
STAB
BZZ
THEY'RE BARBARIANS WHO DON'T HESITATE TO COMMIT VIOLENCE.
BZZZZ
THEY'RE STILL COMING...
...BUT THERE AREN'T MANY.
THE FLYING ONES ARE PESKY.

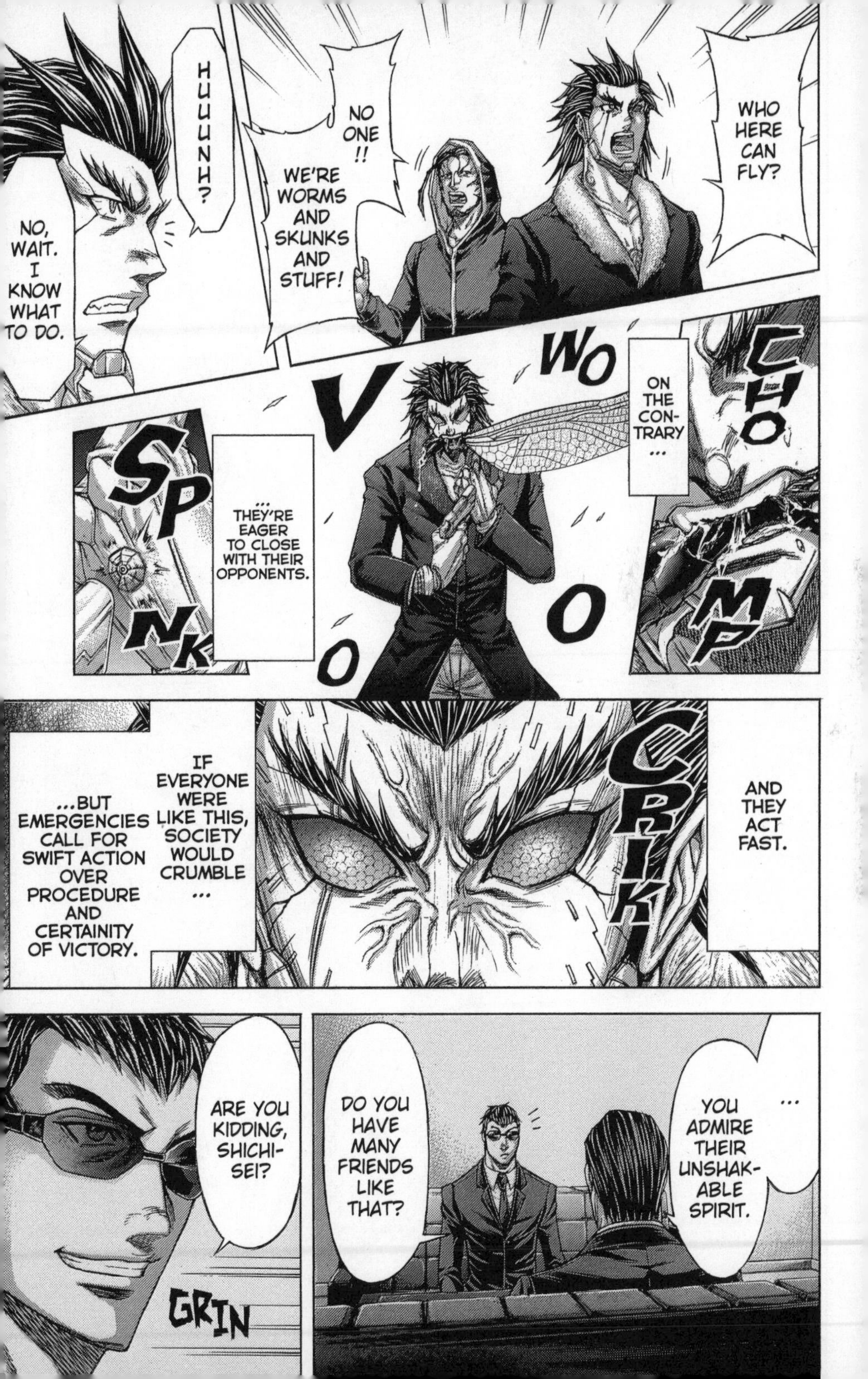
WHO HERE CAN FLY?
NO ONE!!
WE'RE WORMS AND SKUNKS AND STUFF!
HUUUNH?
NO, WAIT. I KNOW WHAT TO DO.
CHOMP
ON THE CONTRARY...
VWOOO
...THEY'RE EAGER TO CLOSE WITH THEIR OPPONENTS.
SPNK
AND THEY ACT FAST.
CRIK
IF EVERYONE WERE LIKE THIS, SOCIETY WOULD CRUMBLE...
...BUT EMERGENCIES CALL FOR SWIFT ACTION OVER PROCEDURE AND CERTAINITY OF VICTORY.
...
YOU ADMIRE THEIR UNSHAKABLE SPIRIT.
DO YOU HAVE MANY FRIENDS LIKE THAT?
ARE YOU KIDDING, SHICHISEI?
GRIN

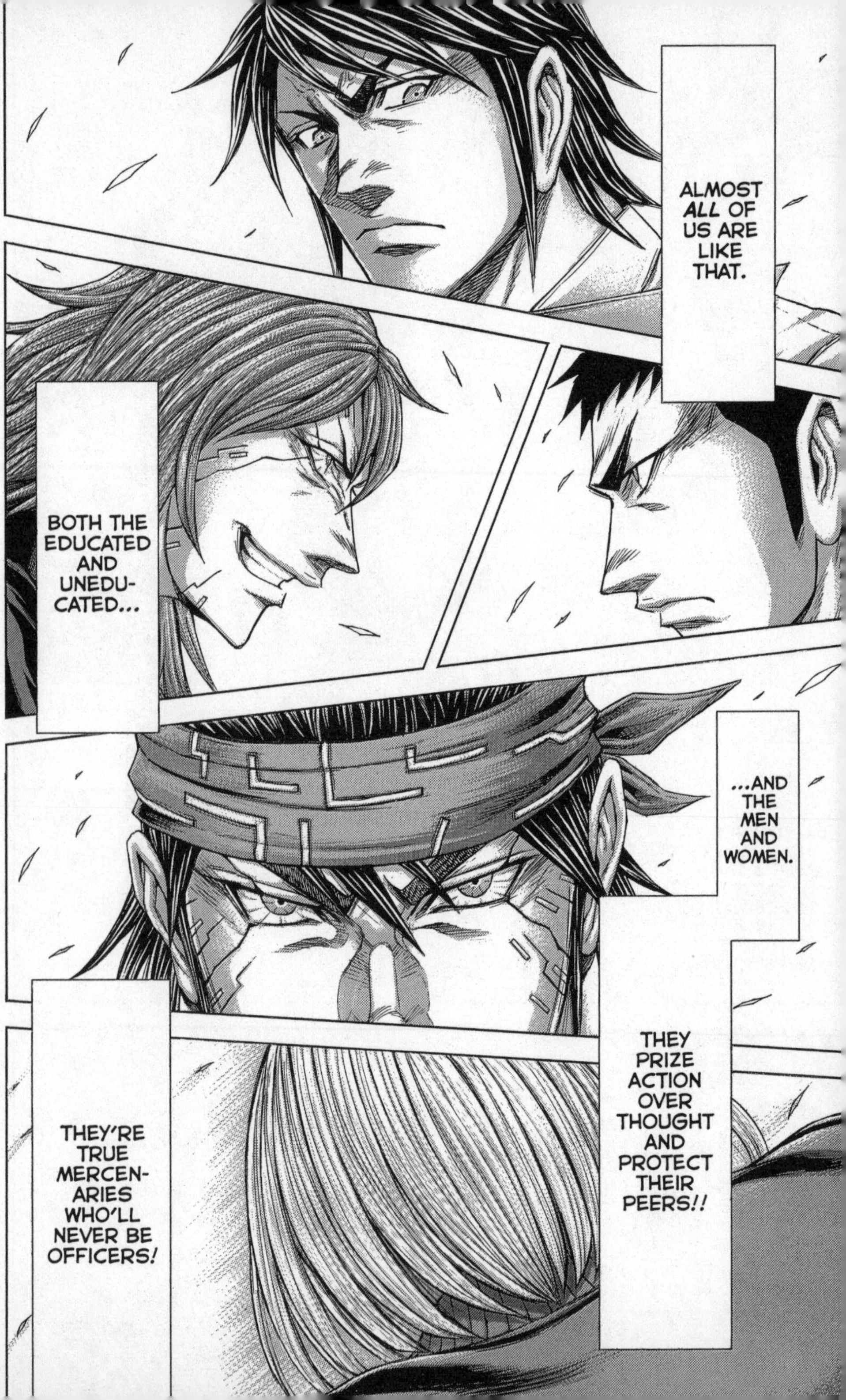
ALMOST *ALL* OF US ARE LIKE THAT.
BOTH THE EDUCATED AND UNEDU-CATED...
...AND THE MEN AND WOMEN.
THEY PRIZE ACTION OVER THOUGHT AND PROTECT THEIR PEERS!!
THEY'RE TRUE MERCEN-ARIES WHO'LL NEVER BE OFFICERS!

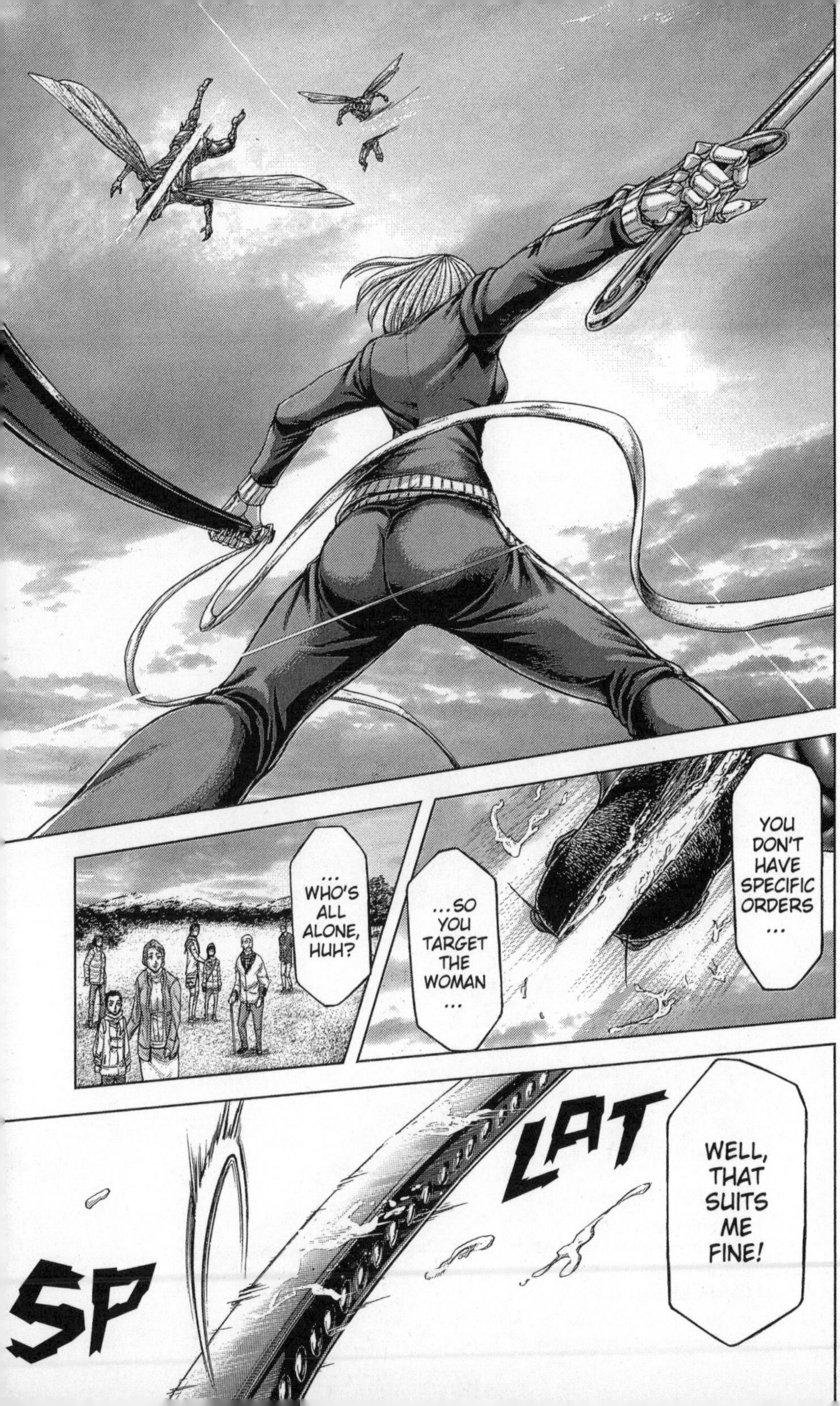
YOU DON'T HAVE SPECIFIC ORDERS ...
...SO YOU TARGET THE WOMAN ...
... WHO'S ALL ALONE, HUH?
WELL, THAT SUITS ME FINE!
LAT
SP

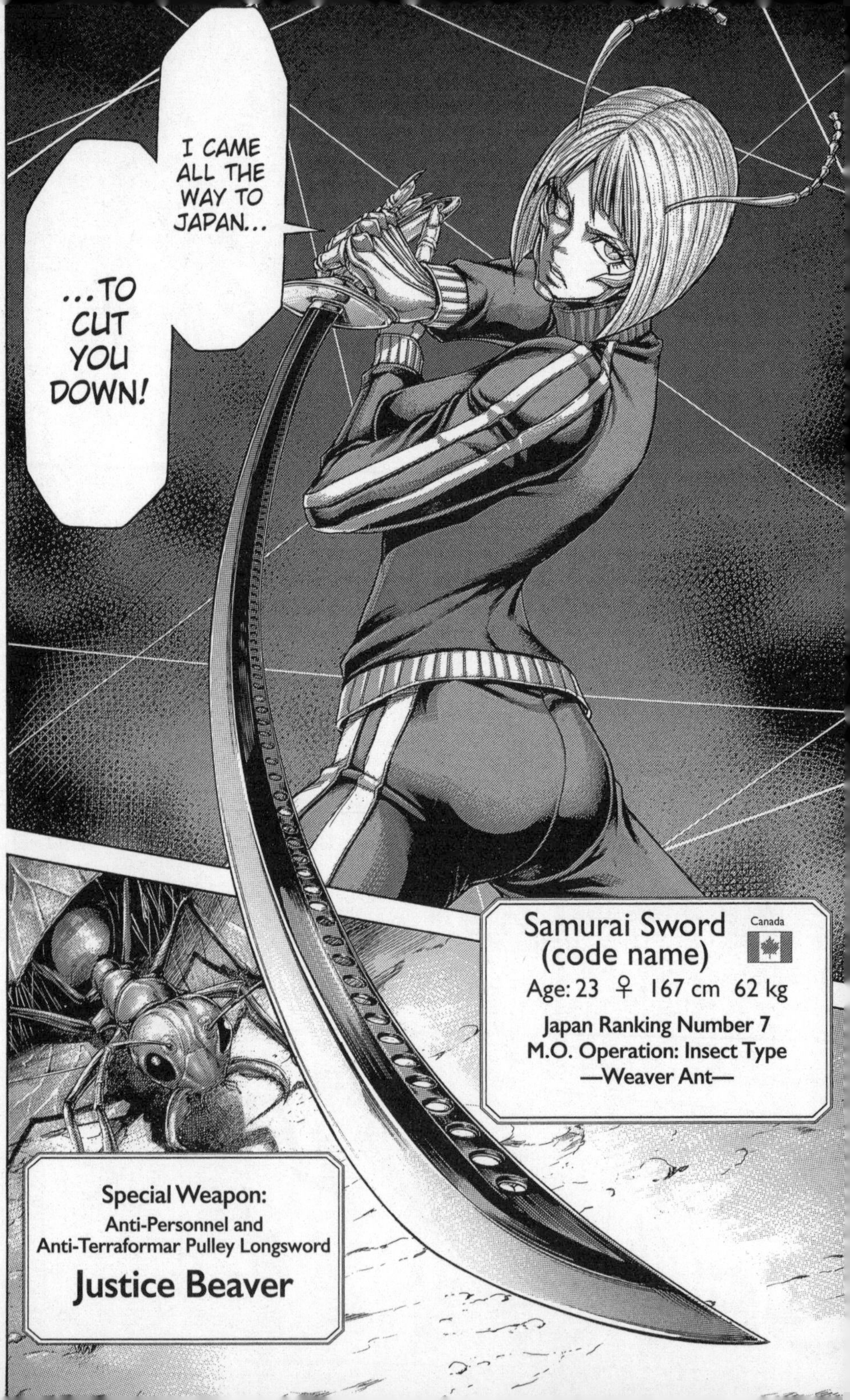
I CAME ALL THE WAY TO JAPAN...
...TO CUT YOU DOWN!
Samurai Sword (code name)
Canada
Age: 23 ♀ 167 cm 62 kg
Japan Ranking Number 7
M.O. Operation: Insect Type
—Weaver Ant—
Special Weapon:
Anti-Personnel and Anti-Terraformar Pulley Longsword
Justice Beaver

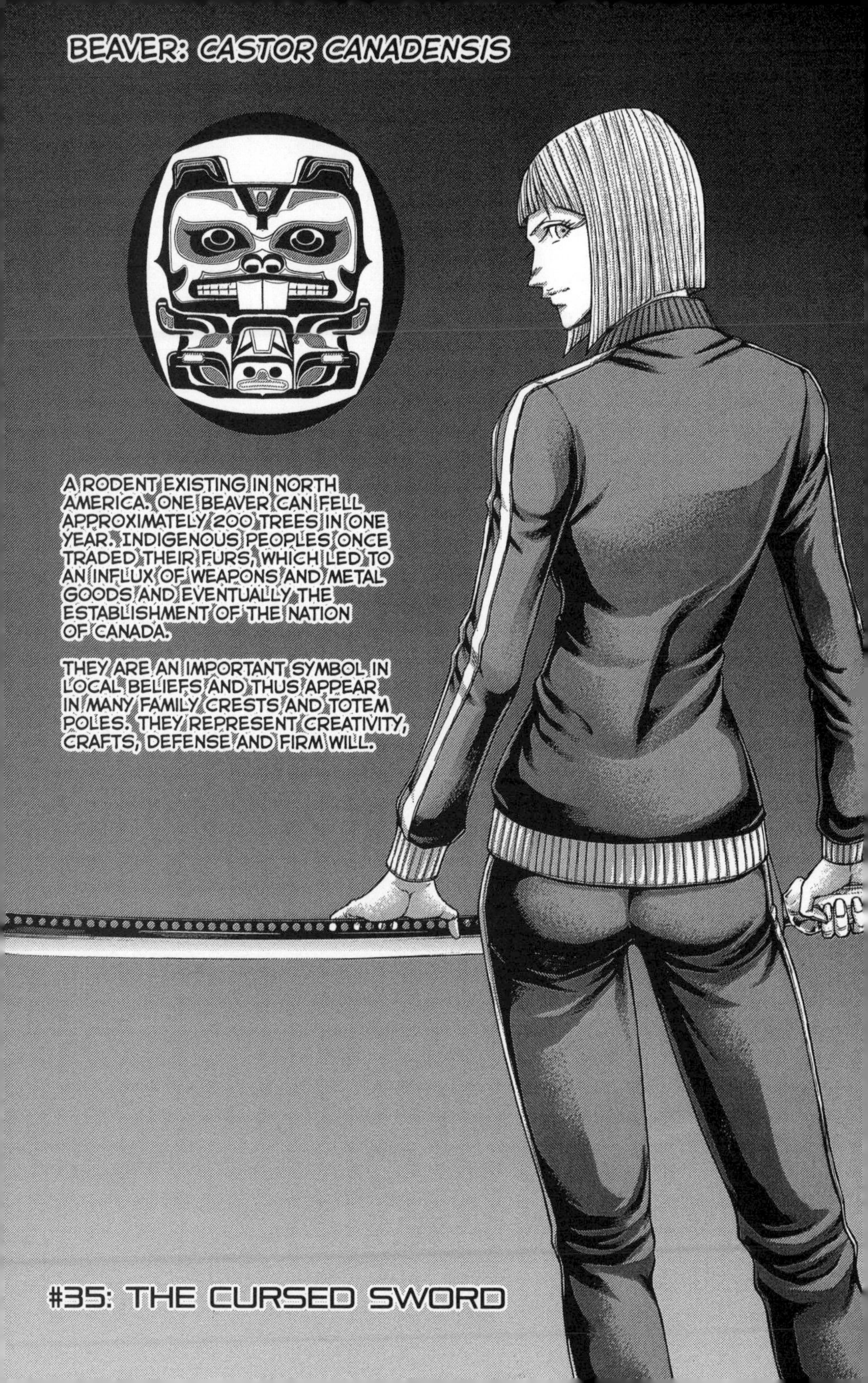
BEAVER: CASTOR CANADENSIS
A RODENT EXISTING IN NORTH AMERICA. ONE BEAVER CAN FELL APPROXIMATELY 200 TREES IN ONE YEAR. INDIGENOUS PEOPLES ONCE TRADED THEIR FURS, WHICH LED TO AN INFLUX OF WEAPONS AND METAL GOODS AND EVENTUALLY THE ESTABLISHMENT OF THE NATION OF CANADA.
THEY ARE AN IMPORTANT SYMBOL IN LOCAL BELIEFS AND THUS APPEAR IN MANY FAMILY CRESTS AND TOTEM POLES. THEY REPRESENT CREATIVITY, CRAFTS, DEFENSE AND FIRM WILL.
#35: THE CURSED SWORD

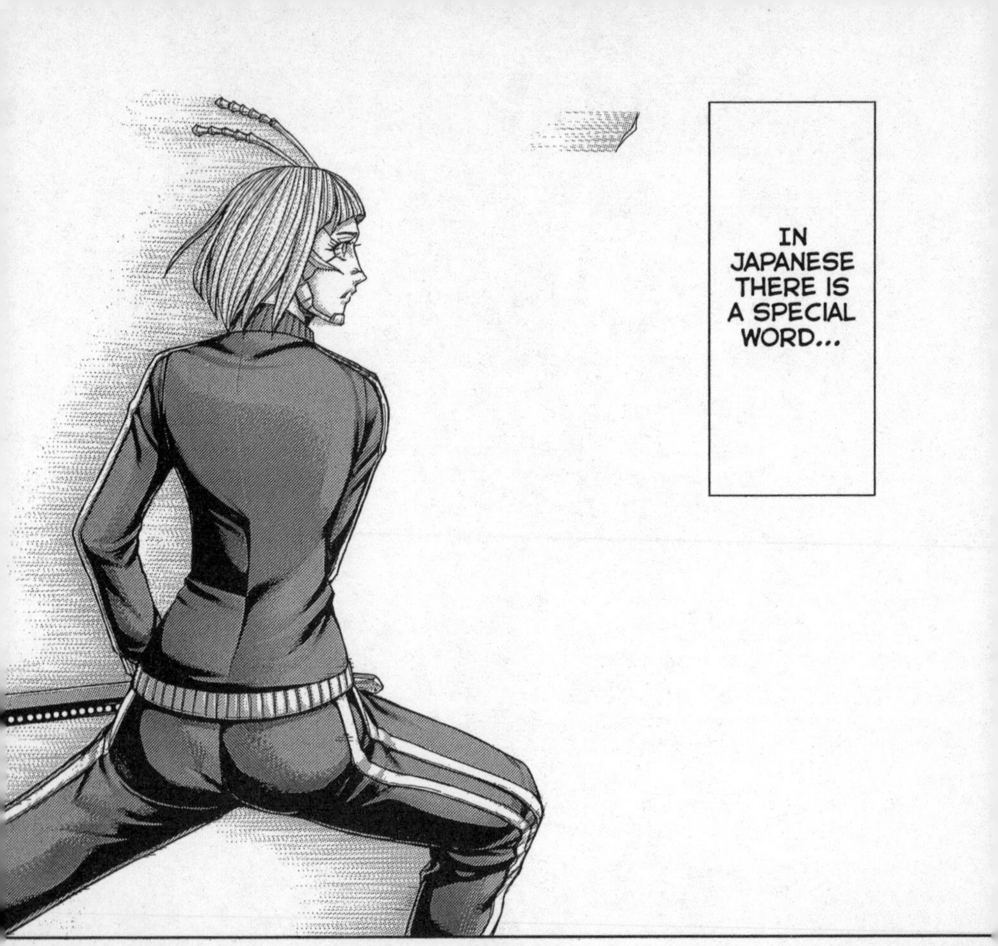
IN JAPANESE THERE IS A SPECIAL WORD...
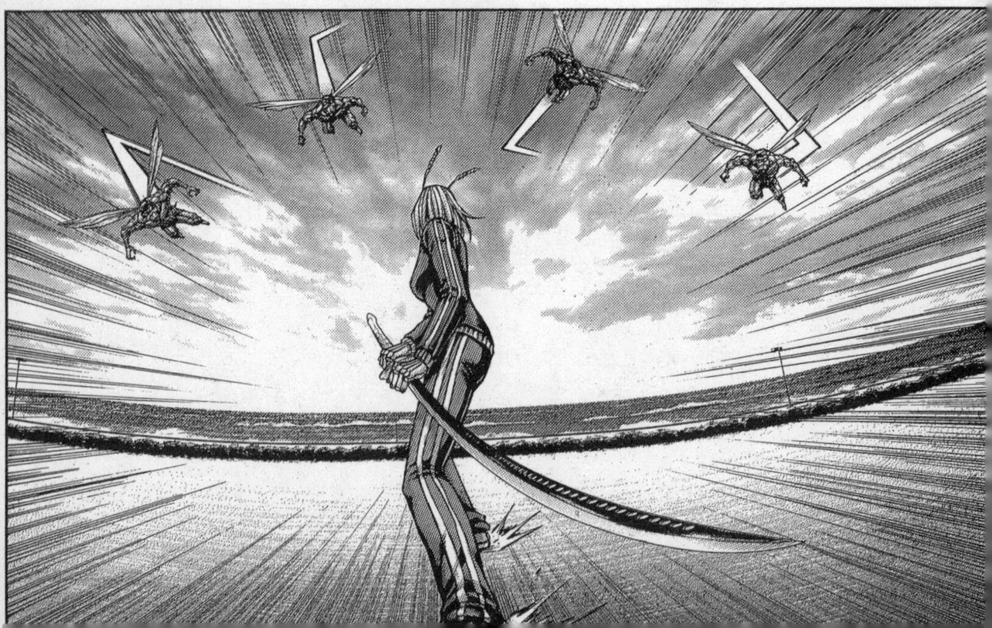

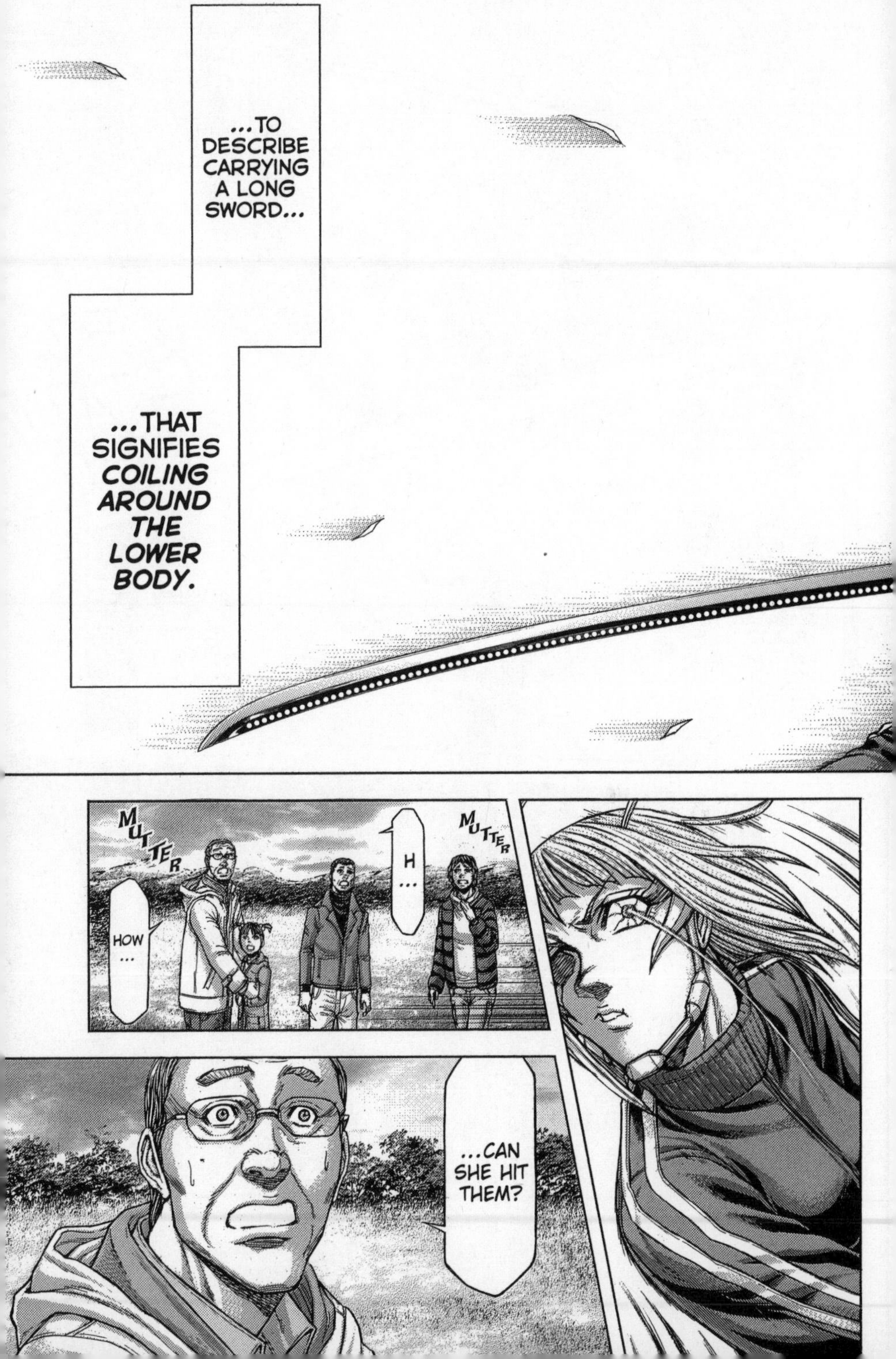
...TO DESCRIBE CARRYING A LONG SWORD...
...THAT SIGNIFIES COILING AROUND THE LOWER BODY.
MUTTER
H...
MUTTER
HOW...
...CAN SHE HIT THEM?

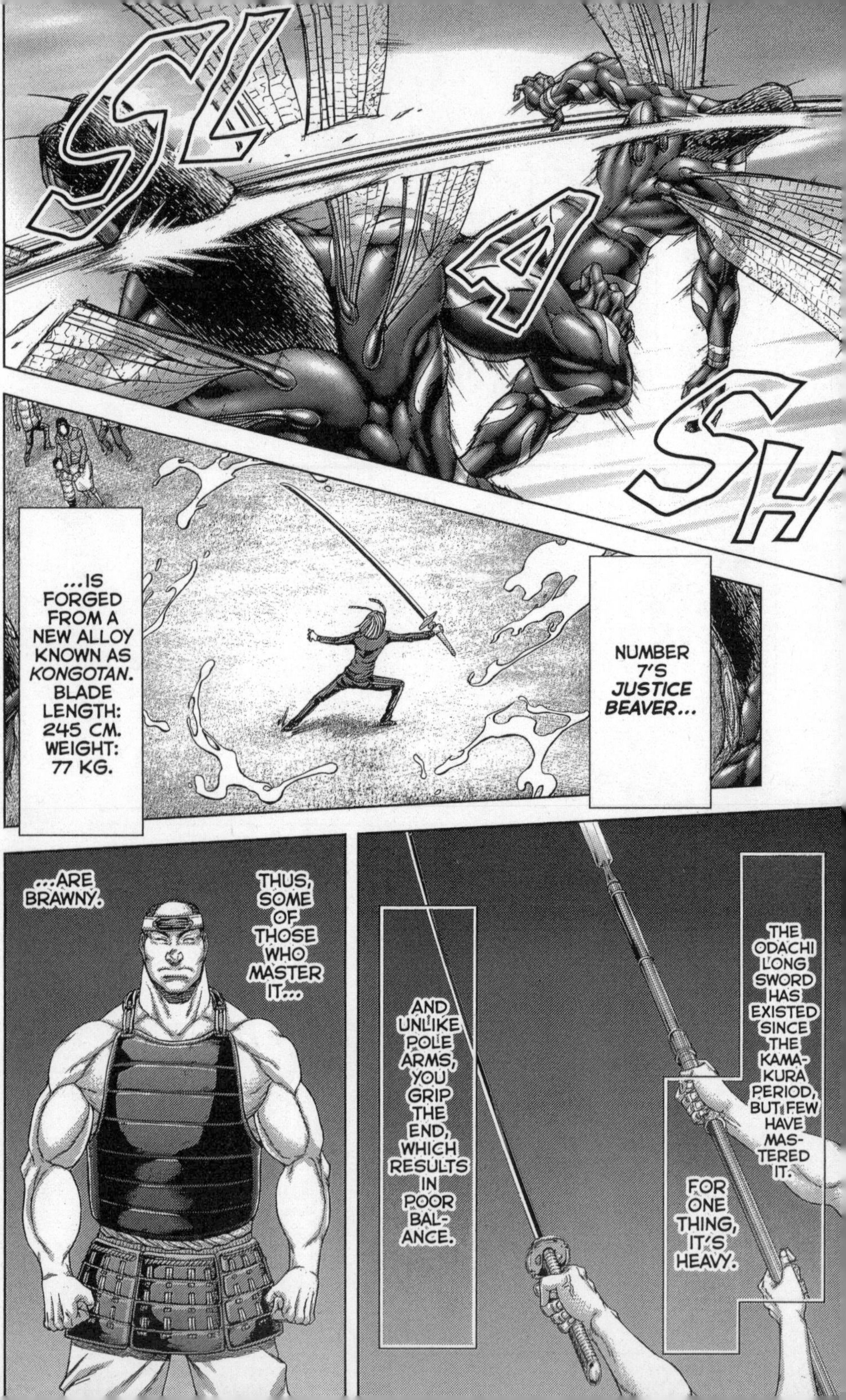
SL
A
SH
NUMBER 7'S *JUSTICE BEAVER*...
...IS FORGED FROM A NEW ALLOY KNOWN AS *KONGOTAN*. BLADE LENGTH: 245 CM. WEIGHT: 77 KG.
THE ODACHI LONG SWORD HAS EXISTED SINCE THE KAMA-KURA PERIOD, BUT FEW HAVE MAS-TERED IT.
FOR ONE THING, IT'S HEAVY.
AND UNLIKE POLE ARMS, YOU GRIP THE END, WHICH RESULTS IN POOR BAL-ANCE.
THUS, SOME OF THOSE WHO MASTER IT...
...ARE BRAWNY.

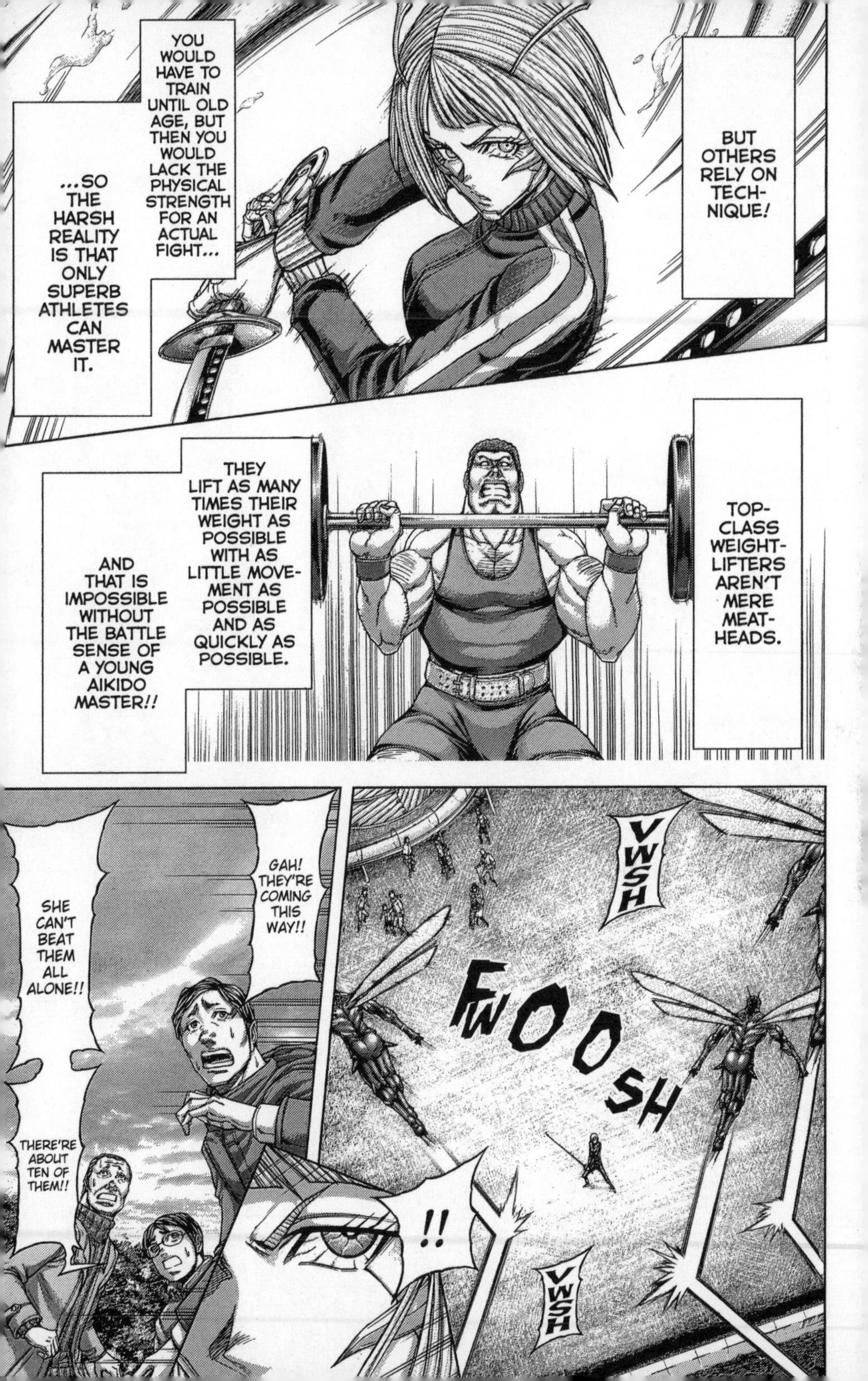

BUT OTHERS RELY ON TECH-NIQUE!
YOU WOULD HAVE TO TRAIN UNTIL OLD AGE, BUT THEN YOU WOULD LACK THE PHYSICAL STRENGTH FOR AN ACTUAL FIGHT...
...SO THE HARSH REALITY IS THAT ONLY SUPERB ATHLETES CAN MASTER IT.
TOP-CLASS WEIGHT-LIFTERS AREN'T MERE MEAT-HEADS.
THEY LIFT AS MANY TIMES THEIR WEIGHT AS POSSIBLE WITH AS LITTLE MOVE-MENT AS POSSIBLE AND AS QUICKLY AS POSSIBLE.
AND THAT IS IMPOSSIBLE WITHOUT THE BATTLE SENSE OF A YOUNG AIKIDO MASTER!!
VWSH
FWOOSH
!!
VWSH
GAH! THEY'RE COMING THIS WAY!!
SHE CAN'T BEAT THEM ALL ALONE!!
THERE'RE ABOUT TEN OF THEM!!

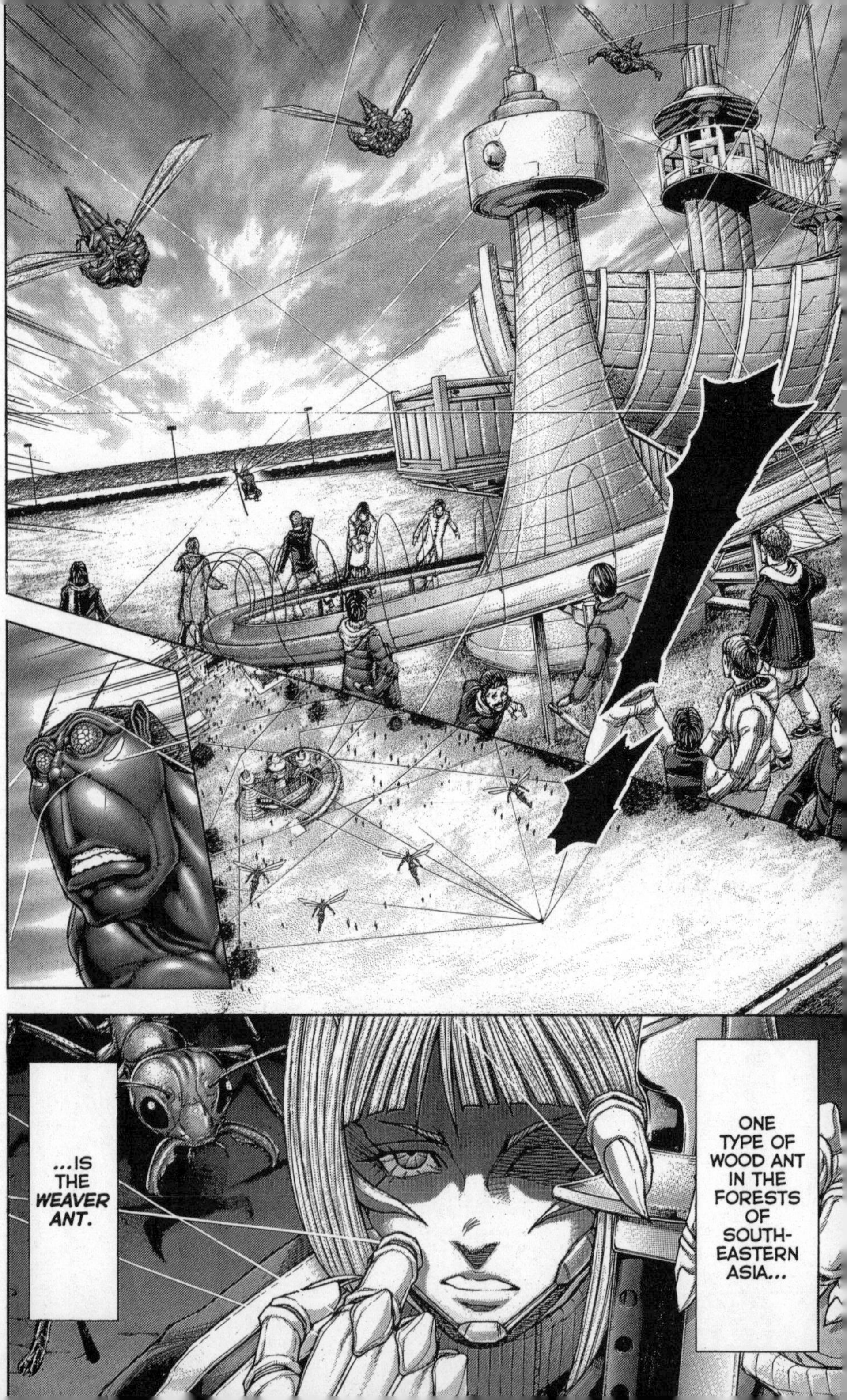
ONE TYPE OF WOOD ANT IN THE FORESTS OF SOUTH-EASTERN ASIA...
...IS THE *WEAVER ANT*.

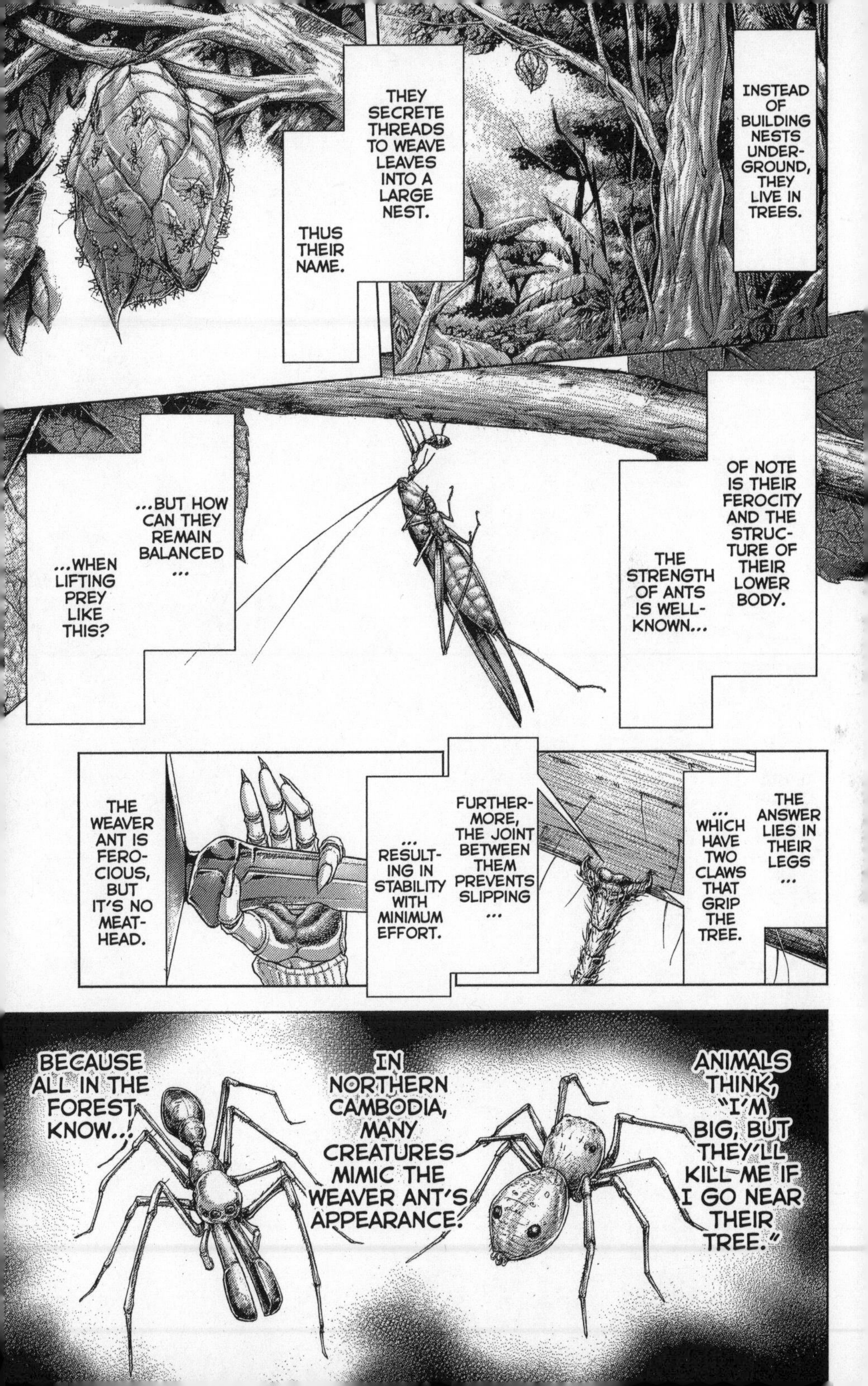
INSTEAD OF BUILDING NESTS UNDERGROUND, THEY LIVE IN TREES.
THEY SECRETE THREADS TO WEAVE LEAVES INTO A LARGE NEST.
THUS THEIR NAME.
OF NOTE IS THEIR FEROCITY AND THE STRUCTURE OF THEIR LOWER BODY.
THE STRENGTH OF ANTS IS WELL-KNOWN...
...BUT HOW CAN THEY REMAIN BALANCED...
...WHEN LIFTING PREY LIKE THIS?
THE ANSWER LIES IN THEIR LEGS...
...WHICH HAVE TWO CLAWS THAT GRIP THE TREE.
FURTHERMORE, THE JOINT BETWEEN THEM PREVENTS SLIPPING...
...RESULTING IN STABILITY WITH MINIMUM EFFORT.
THE WEAVER ANT IS FEROCIOUS, BUT IT'S NO MEATHEAD.
ANIMALS THINK, "I'M BIG, BUT THEY'LL KILL ME IF I GO NEAR THEIR TREE."
IN NORTHERN CAMBODIA, MANY CREATURES MIMIC THE WEAVER ANT'S APPEARANCE.
BECAUSE ALL IN THE FOREST KNOW...!

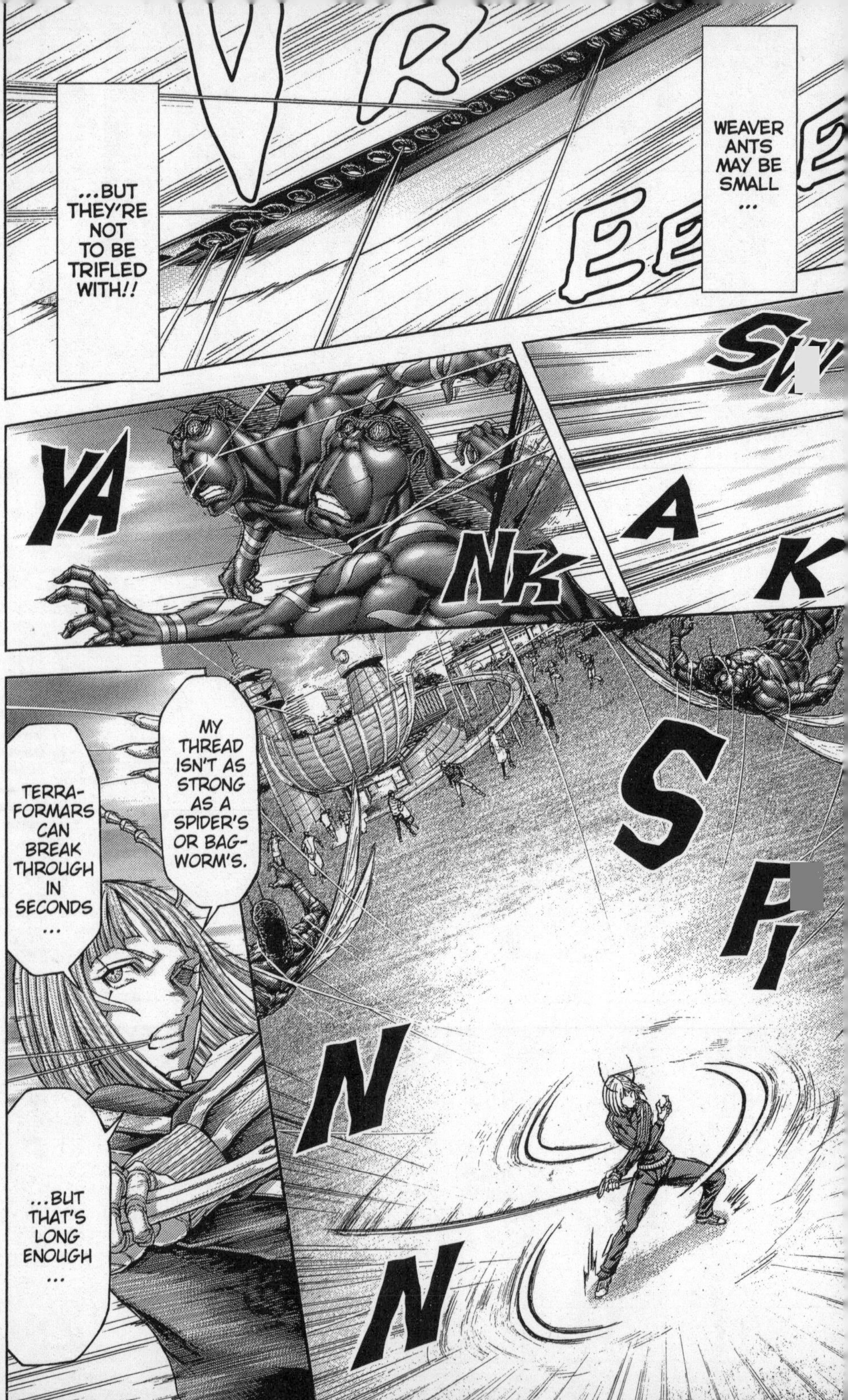
WEAVER ANTS MAY BE SMALL ...
...BUT THEY'RE NOT TO BE TRIFLED WITH!!
VR
EEE
SW
A K
YA
NK
MY THREAD ISN'T AS STRONG AS A SPIDER'S OR BAG-WORM'S.
TERRA-FORMARS CAN BREAK THROUGH IN SECONDS ...
S
PI
N
N
...BUT THAT'S LONG ENOUGH ...

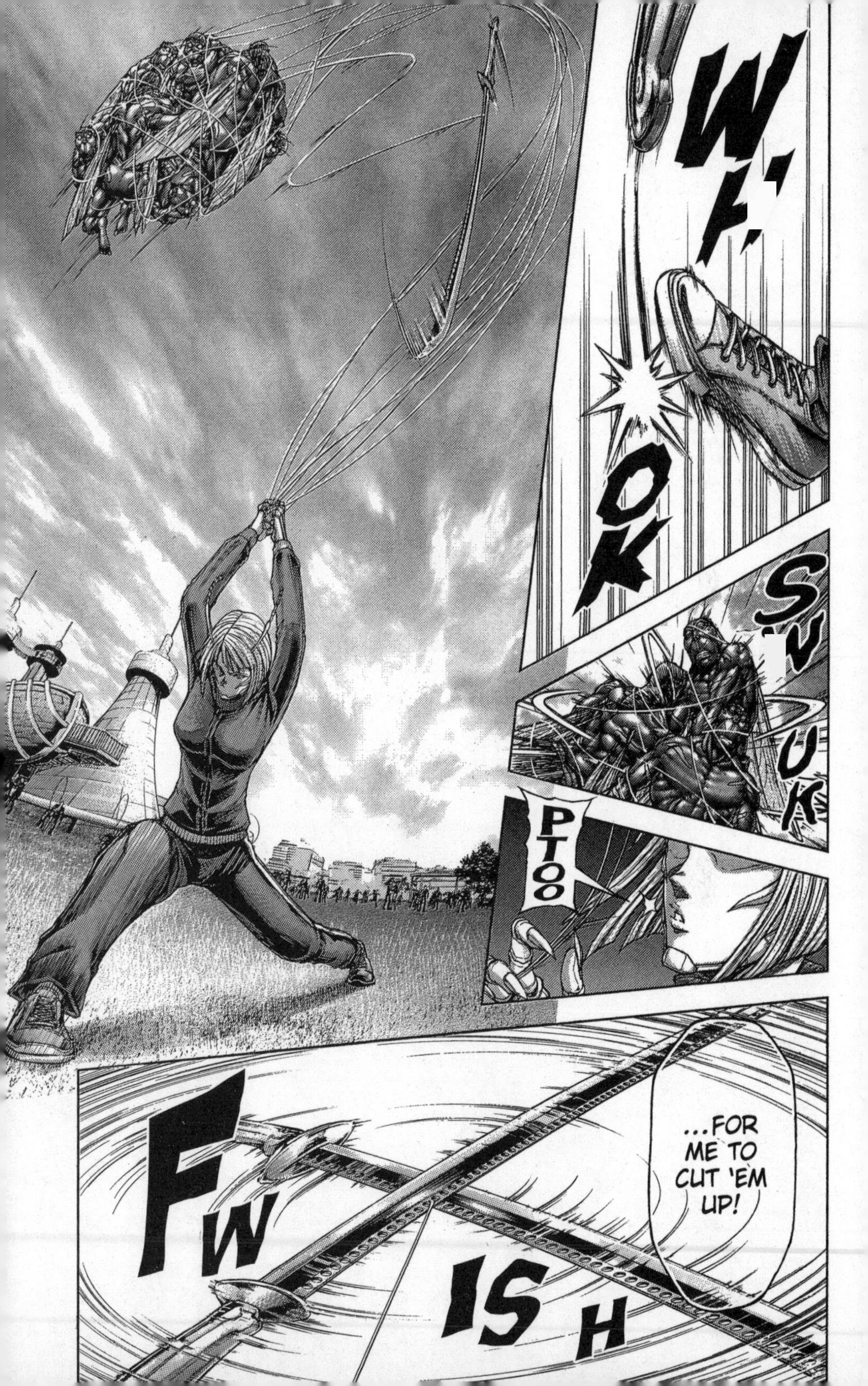
WHOK
PTOO
...FOR ME TO CUT 'EM UP!
FWISH

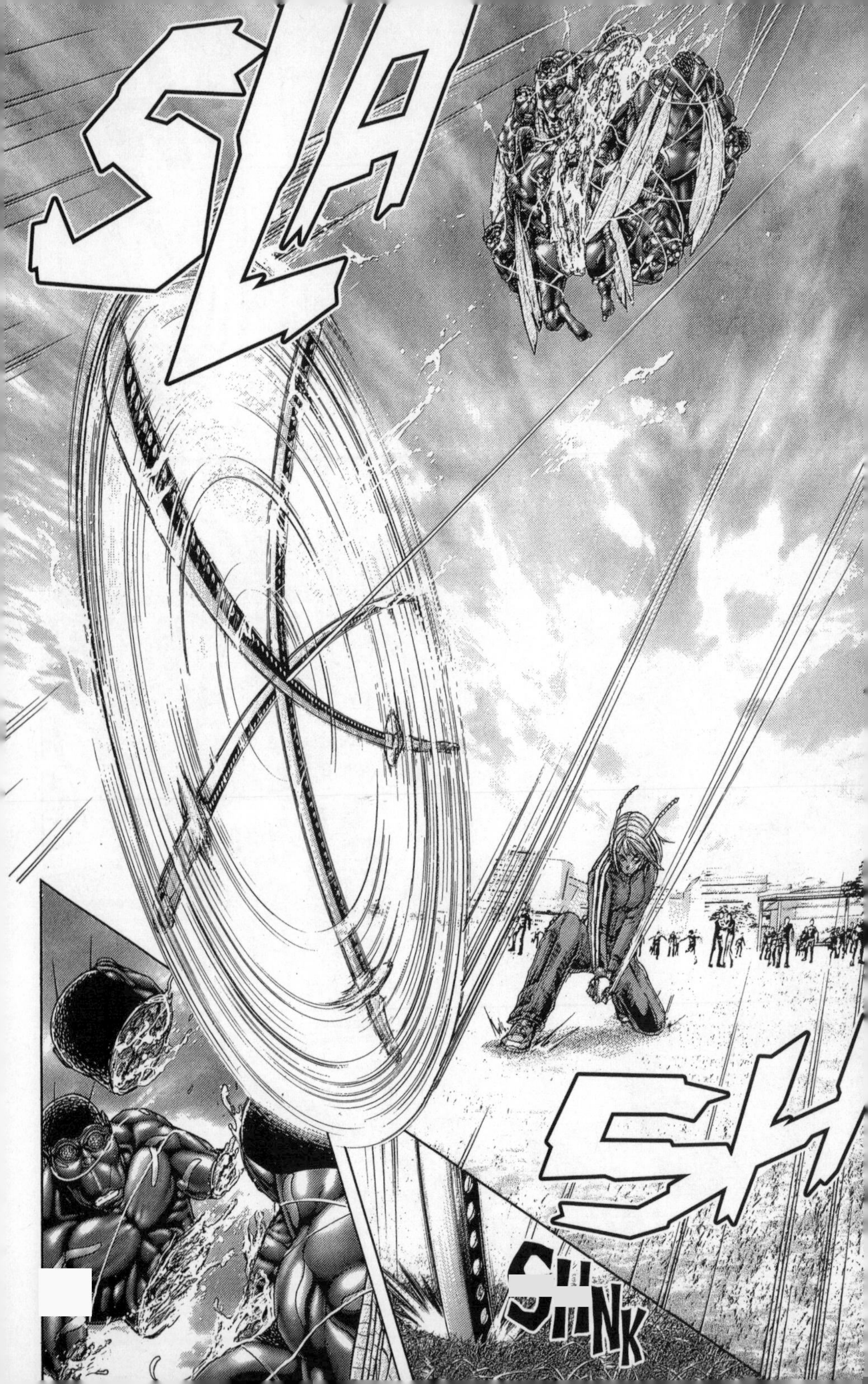
SLA
SH
SHINK

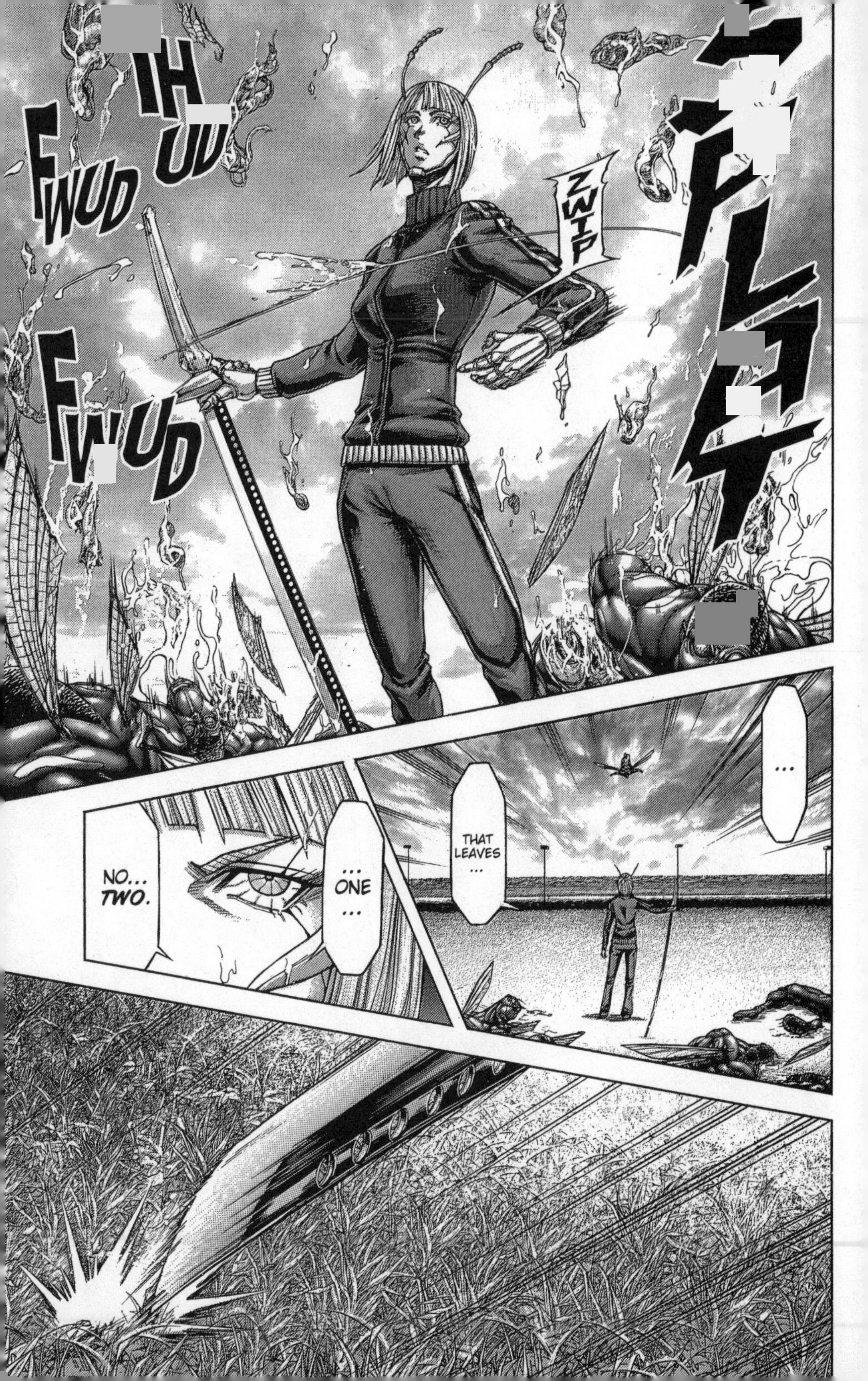
ZWIP
FWUD
FWUD
...
THAT LEAVES ...
... ONE ...
NO... TWO.

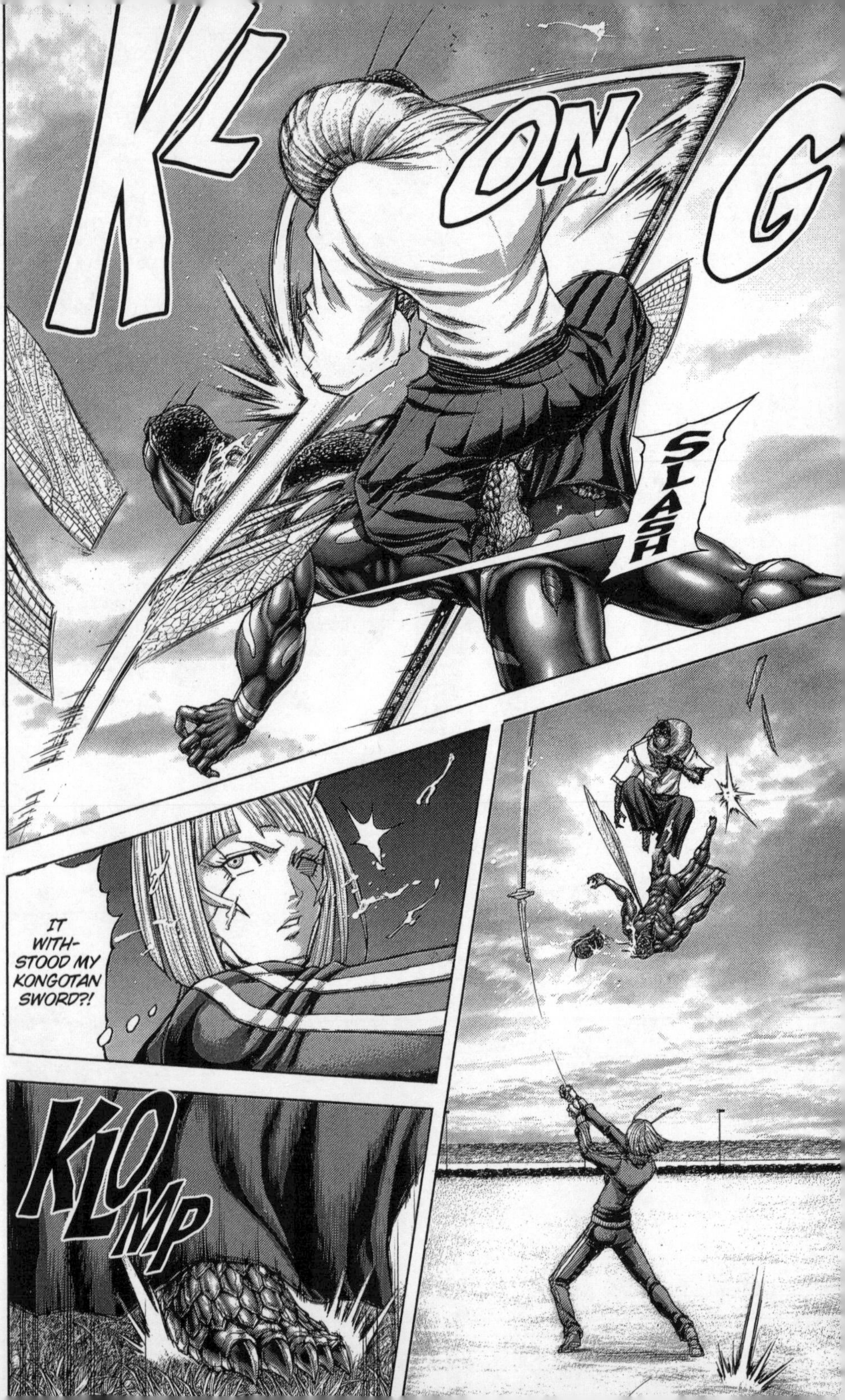
KLONG
SLASH
IT WITH-STOOD MY KONGOTAN SWORD?!
KLOMP

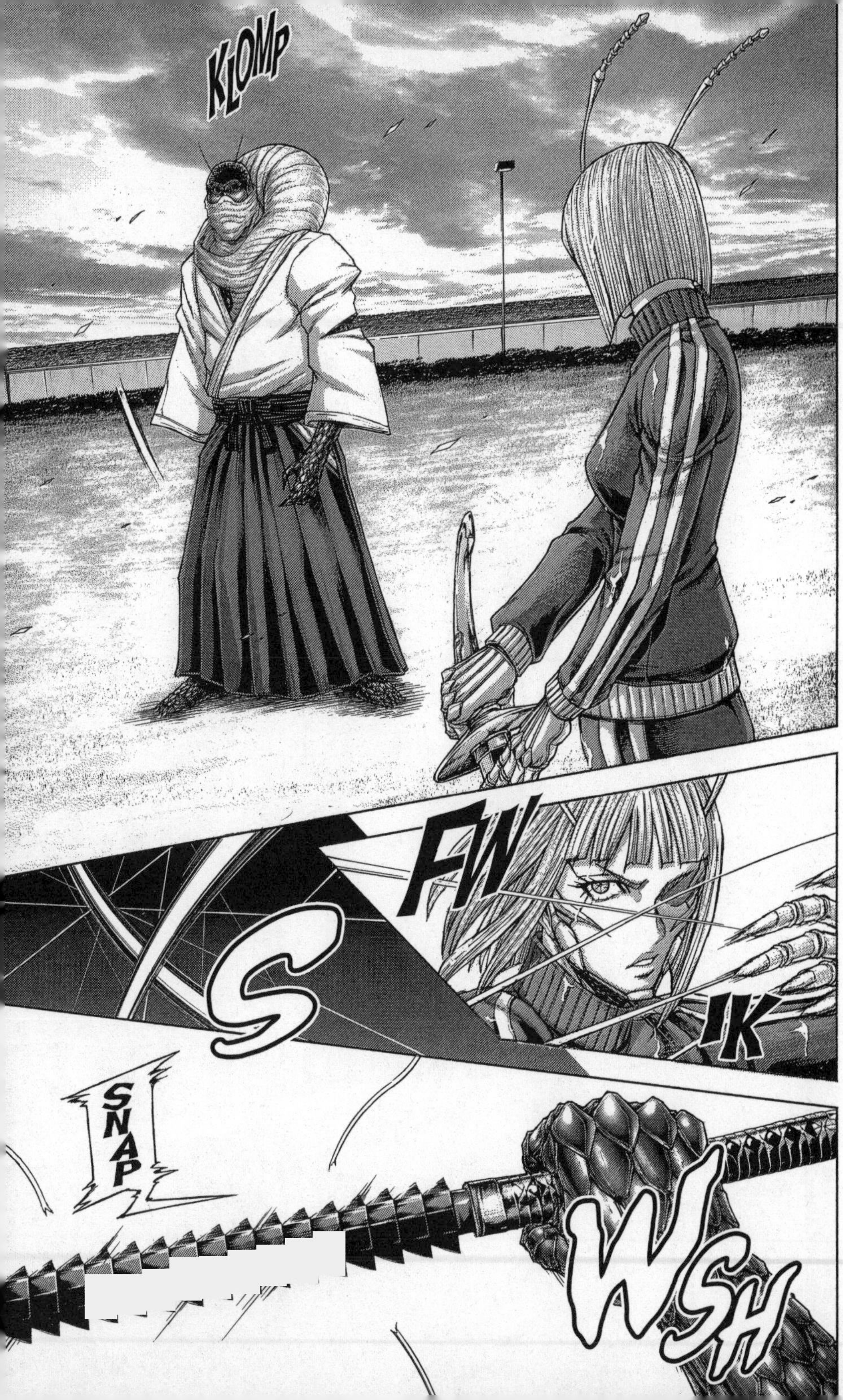
KLOMP
FW
S
IK
WSH
SNAP

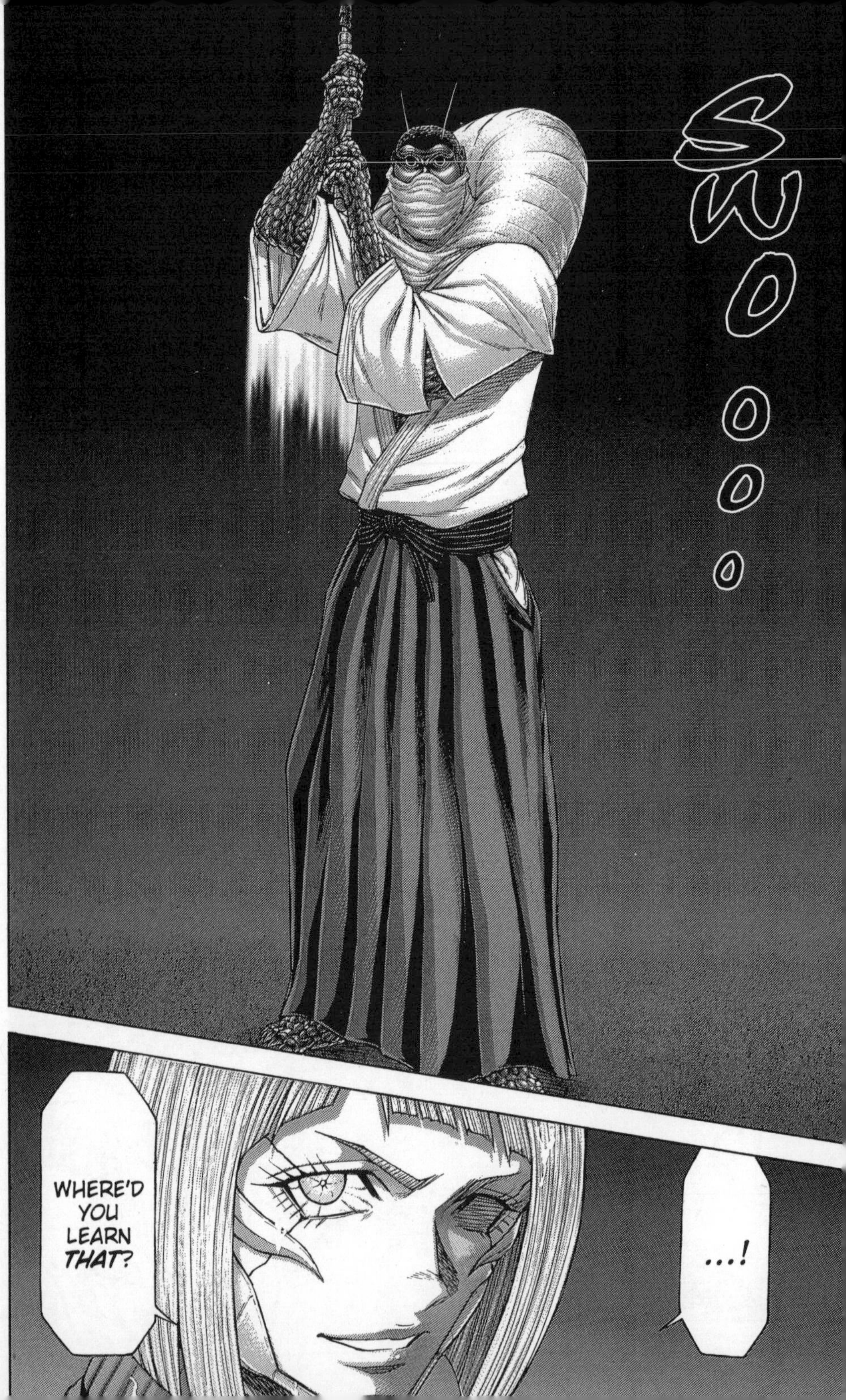
SWOOOOO
...!
WHERE'D YOU LEARN *THAT?*

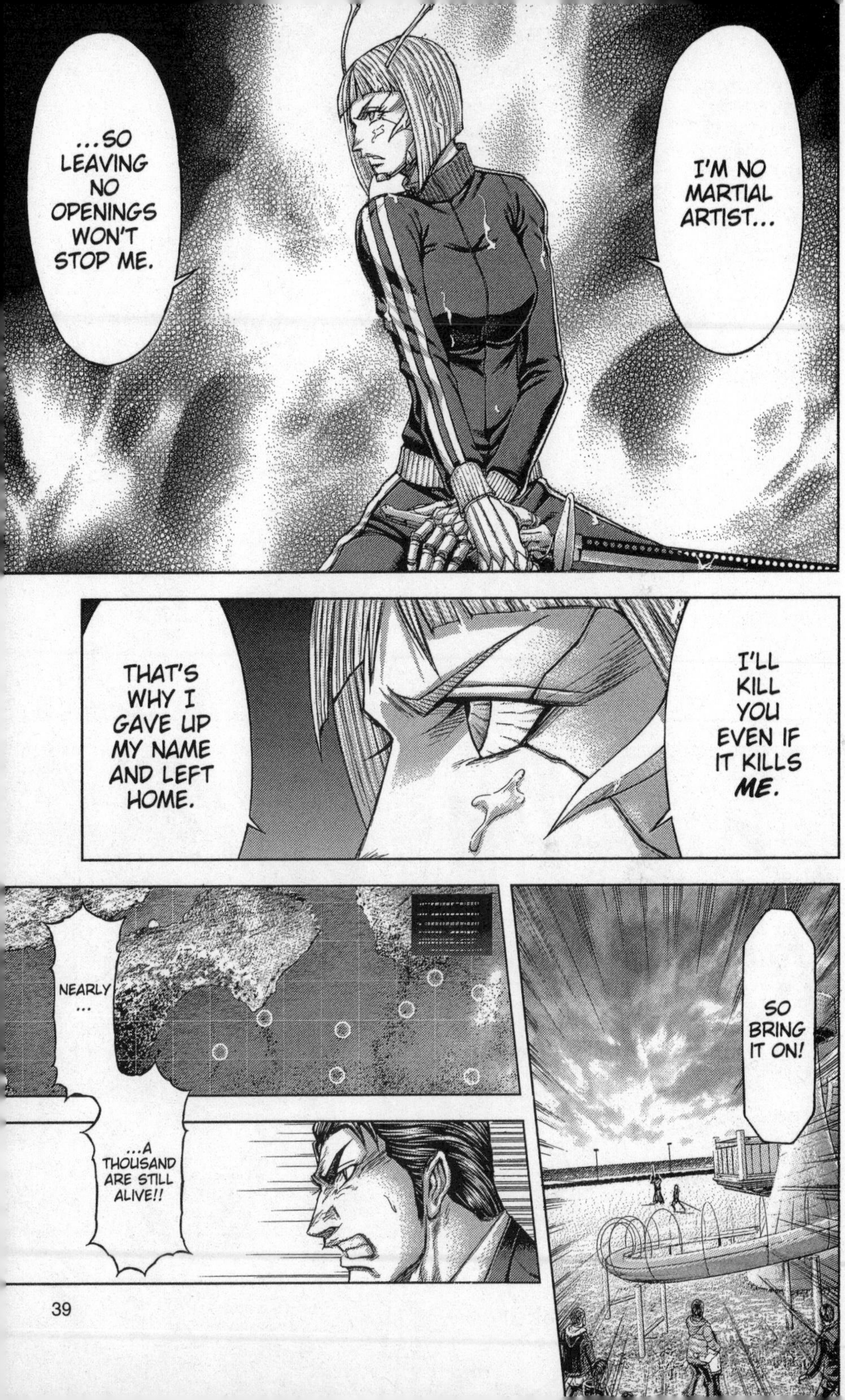

I'M NO MARTIAL ARTIST...
...SO LEAVING NO OPENINGS WON'T STOP ME.
I'LL KILL YOU EVEN IF IT KILLS ME.
THAT'S WHY I GAVE UP MY NAME AND LEFT HOME.
SO BRING IT ON!
NEARLY...
...A THOUSAND ARE STILL ALIVE!!

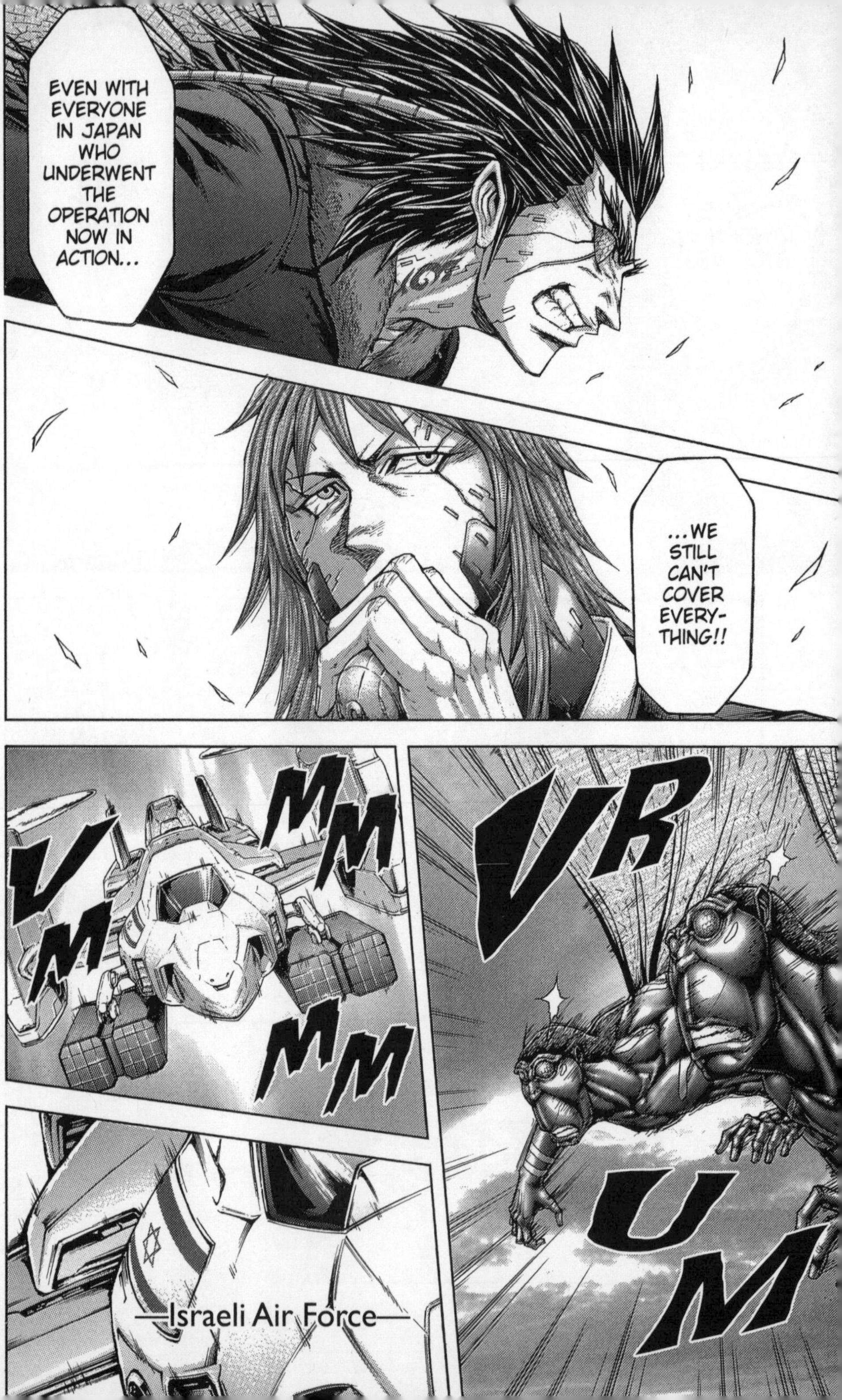
EVEN WITH EVERYONE IN JAPAN WHO UNDERWENT THE OPERATION NOW IN ACTION...
...WE STILL CAN'T COVER EVERY-THING!!
VRUM
VMMMMM
—Israeli Air Force—

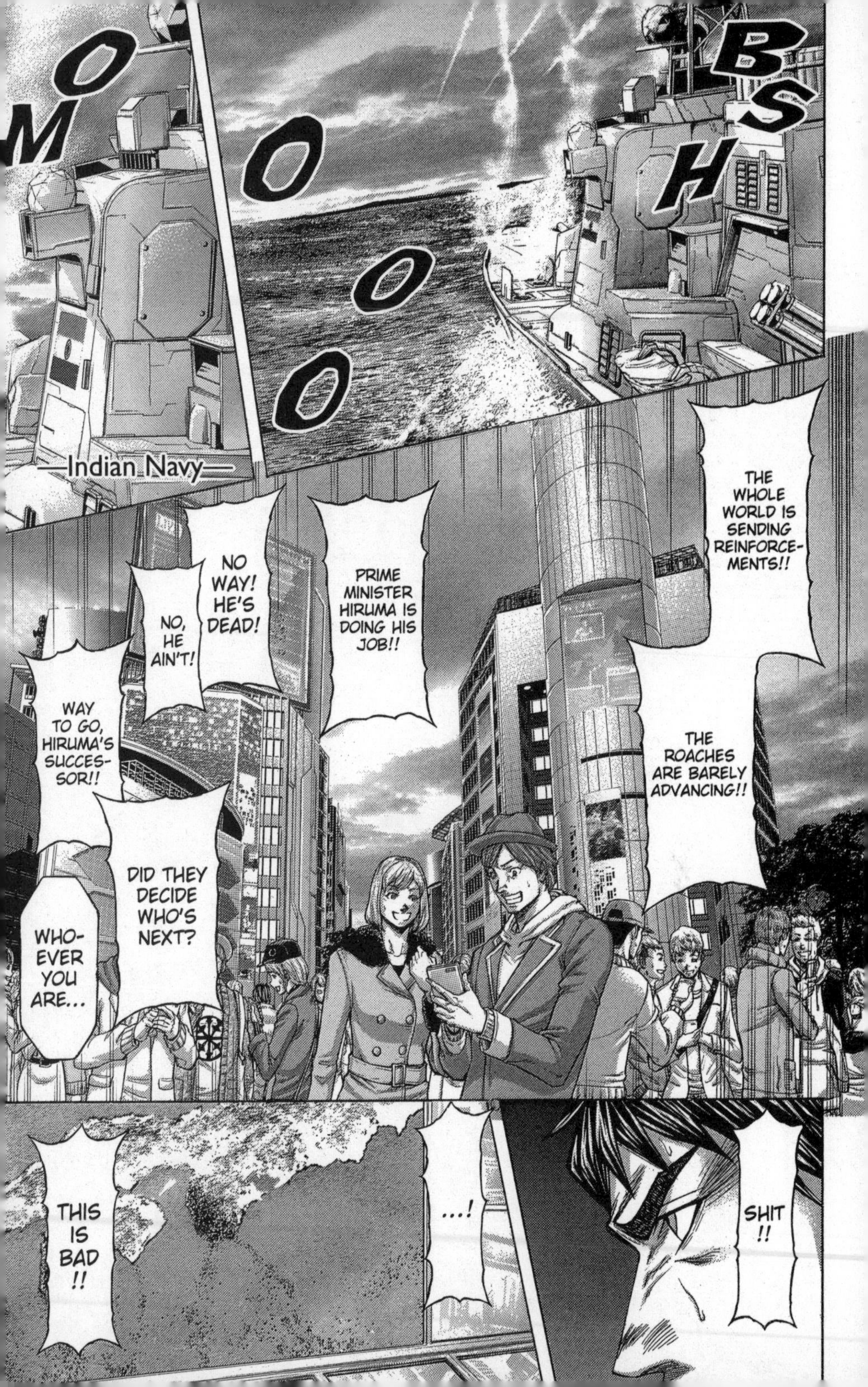
BSH
MOOOOO
—Indian Navy—
THE WHOLE WORLD IS SENDING REINFORCEMENTS!!
THE ROACHES ARE BARELY ADVANCING!!
PRIME MINISTER HIRUMA IS DOING HIS JOB!!
NO WAY! HE'S DEAD!
NO, HE AIN'T!
WAY TO GO, HIRUMA'S SUCCESSOR!!
DID THEY DECIDE WHO'S NEXT?
WHOEVER YOU ARE...
SHIT!!
...!
THIS IS BAD!!

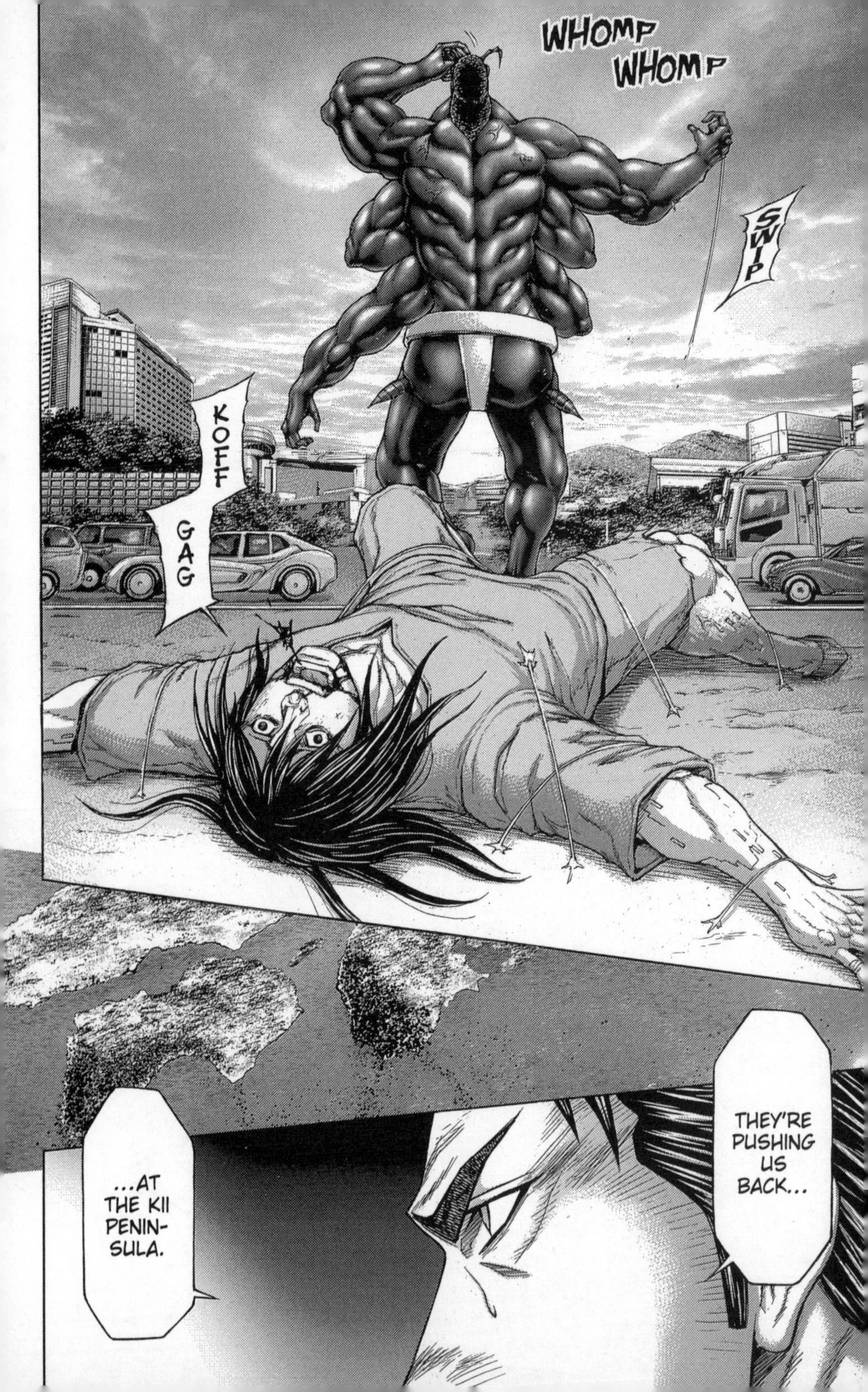
WHOMP WHOMP
SWIP
KOFF GAG
THEY'RE PUSHING US BACK...
...AT THE KII PENIN-SULA.

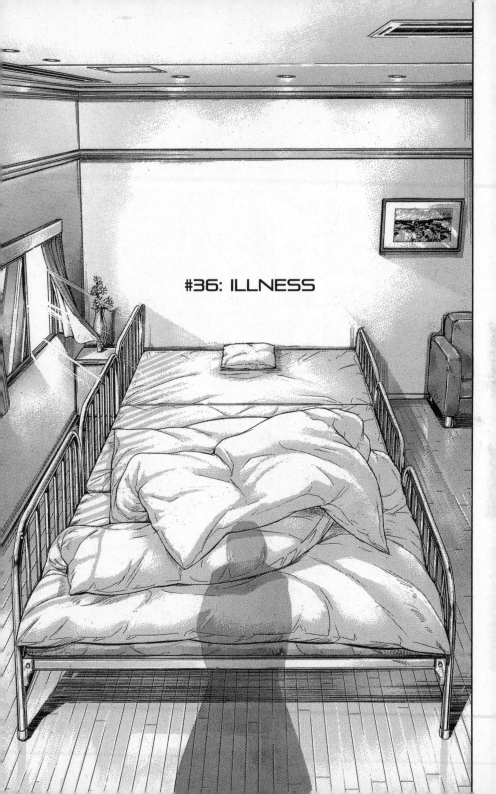

#36: ILLNESS

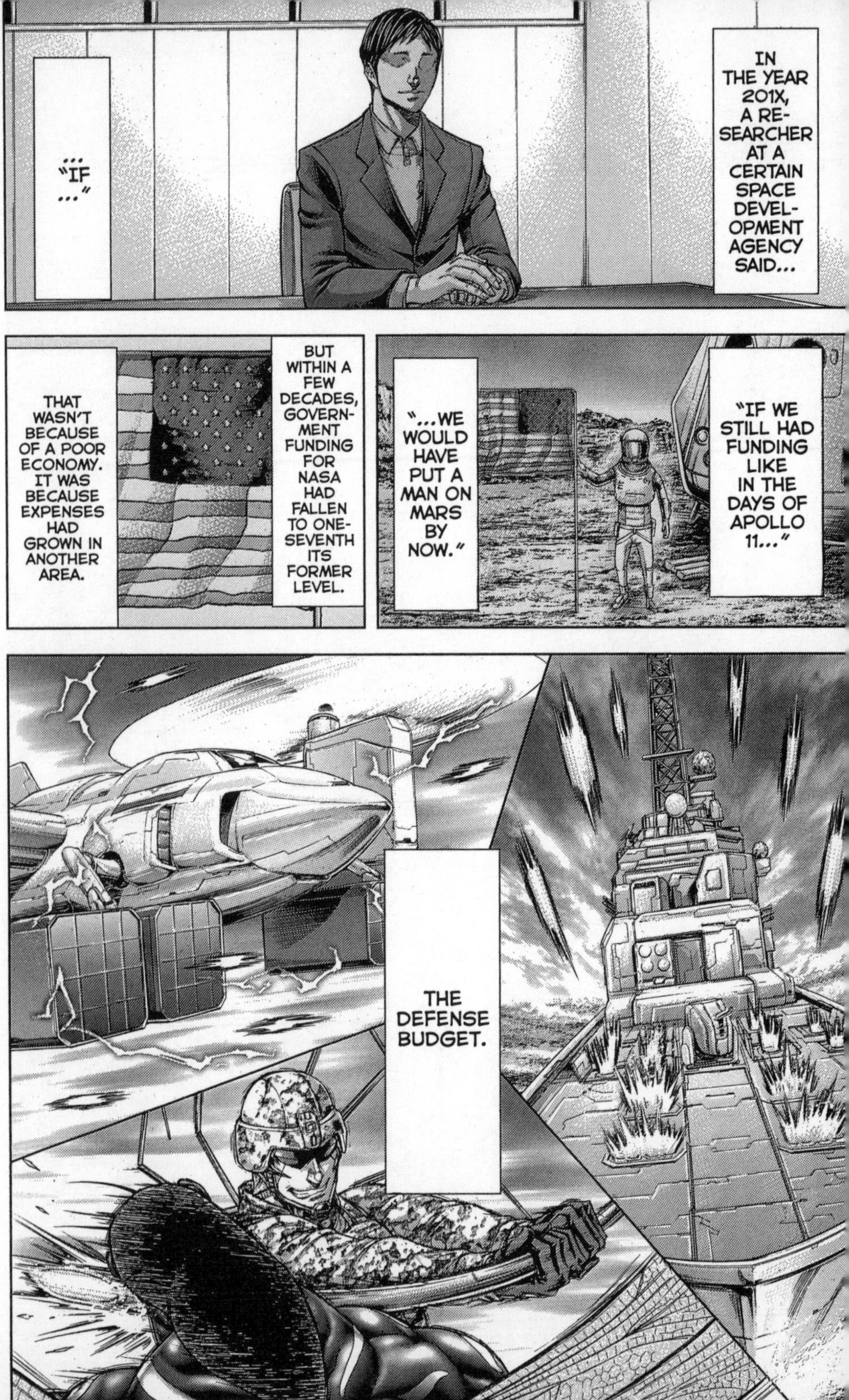
IN THE YEAR 201X, A RESEARCHER AT A CERTAIN SPACE DEVELOPMENT AGENCY SAID...
..."IF..."
"IF WE STILL HAD FUNDING LIKE IN THE DAYS OF APOLLO 11..."
"...WE WOULD HAVE PUT A MAN ON MARS BY NOW."
BUT WITHIN A FEW DECADES, GOVERNMENT FUNDING FOR NASA HAD FALLEN TO ONE-SEVENTH ITS FORMER LEVEL.
THAT WASN'T BECAUSE OF A POOR ECONOMY. IT WAS BECAUSE EXPENSES HAD GROWN IN ANOTHER AREA.
THE DEFENSE BUDGET.

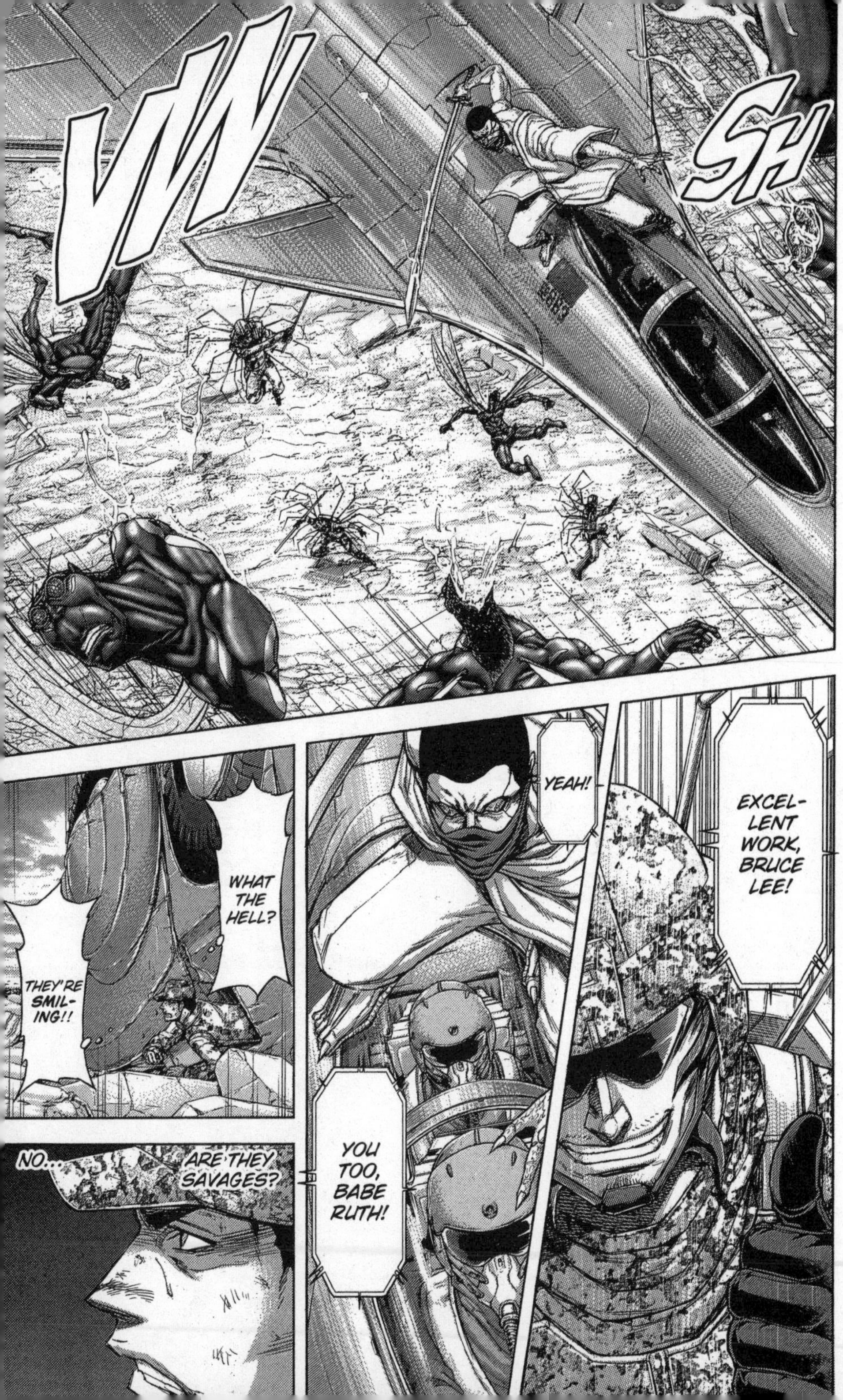
SH
VVN
EXCEL-LENT WORK, BRUCE LEE!
YEAH!
YOU TOO, BABE RUTH!
WHAT THE HELL?
THEY'RE SMIL-ING!!
NO...
ARE THEY SAVAGES?

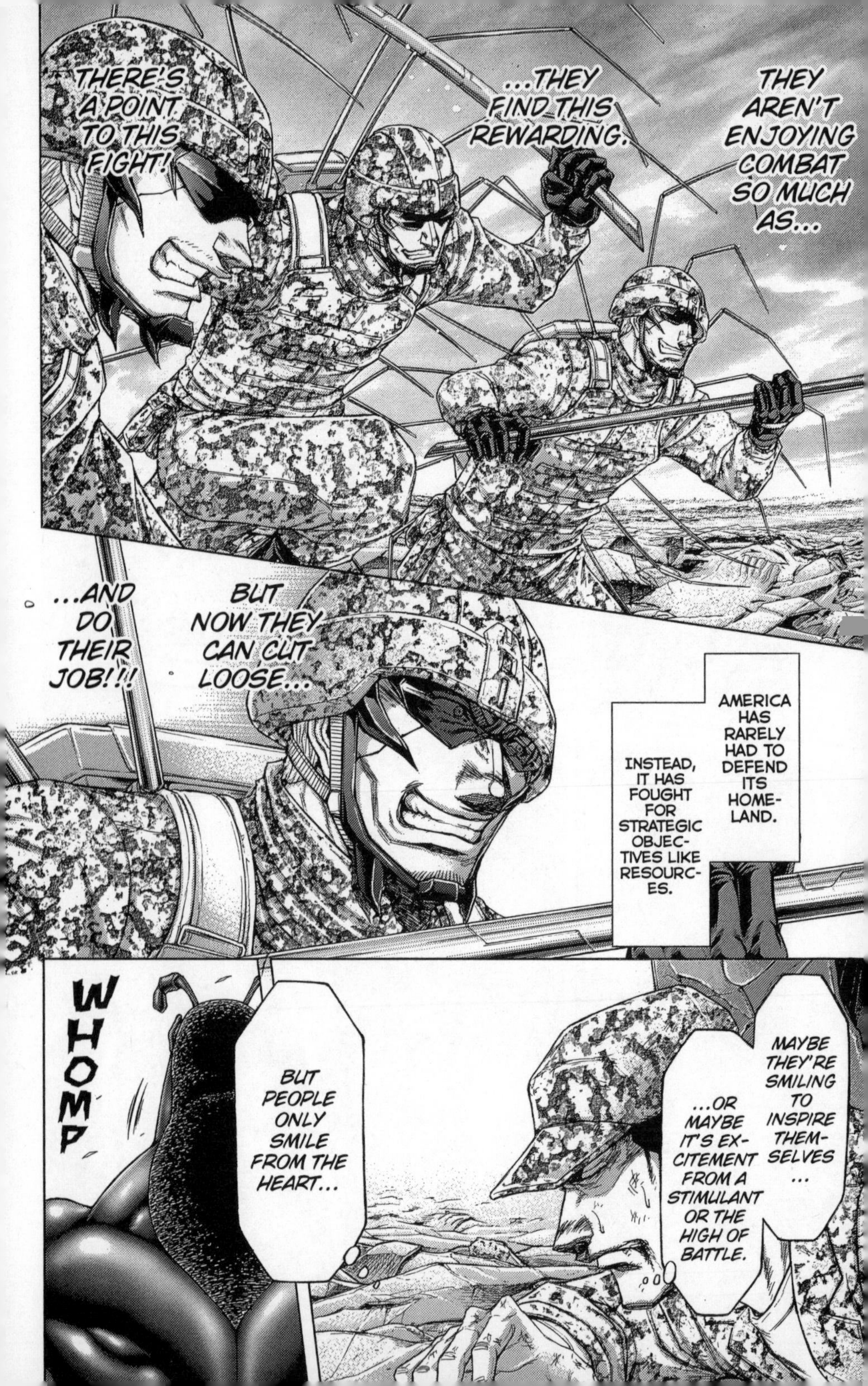
THEY AREN'T ENJOYING COMBAT SO MUCH AS...
...THEY FIND THIS REWARDING.
THERE'S A POINT TO THIS FIGHT!
AMERICA HAS RARELY HAD TO DEFEND ITS HOMELAND.
INSTEAD, IT HAS FOUGHT FOR STRATEGIC OBJECTIVES LIKE RESOURCES.
BUT NOW THEY CAN CUT LOOSE...
...AND DO THEIR JOB!!!
MAYBE THEY'RE SMILING TO INSPIRE THEMSELVES...
...OR MAYBE IT'S EXCITEMENT FROM A STIMULANT OR THE HIGH OF BATTLE.
BUT PEOPLE ONLY SMILE FROM THE HEART...
WHOMP

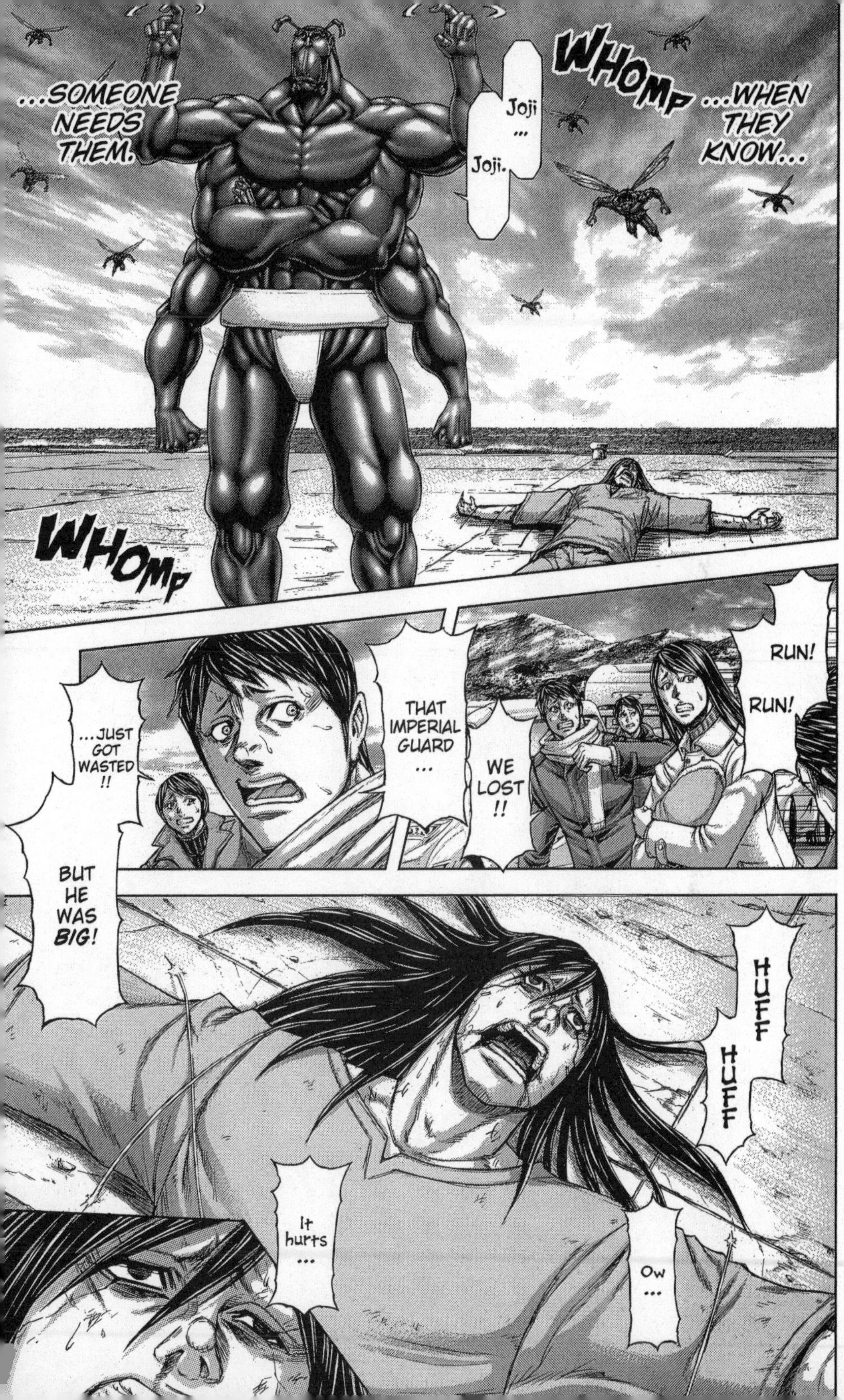
...WHEN THEY KNOW...
WHOMP
Joji ... Joji.
...SOMEONE NEEDS THEM.
WHOMP
RUN!
RUN!
WE LOST !!
THAT IMPERIAL GUARD ...
...JUST GOT WASTED !!
BUT HE WAS BIG!
HUFF HUFF
Ow ...
It hurts ...

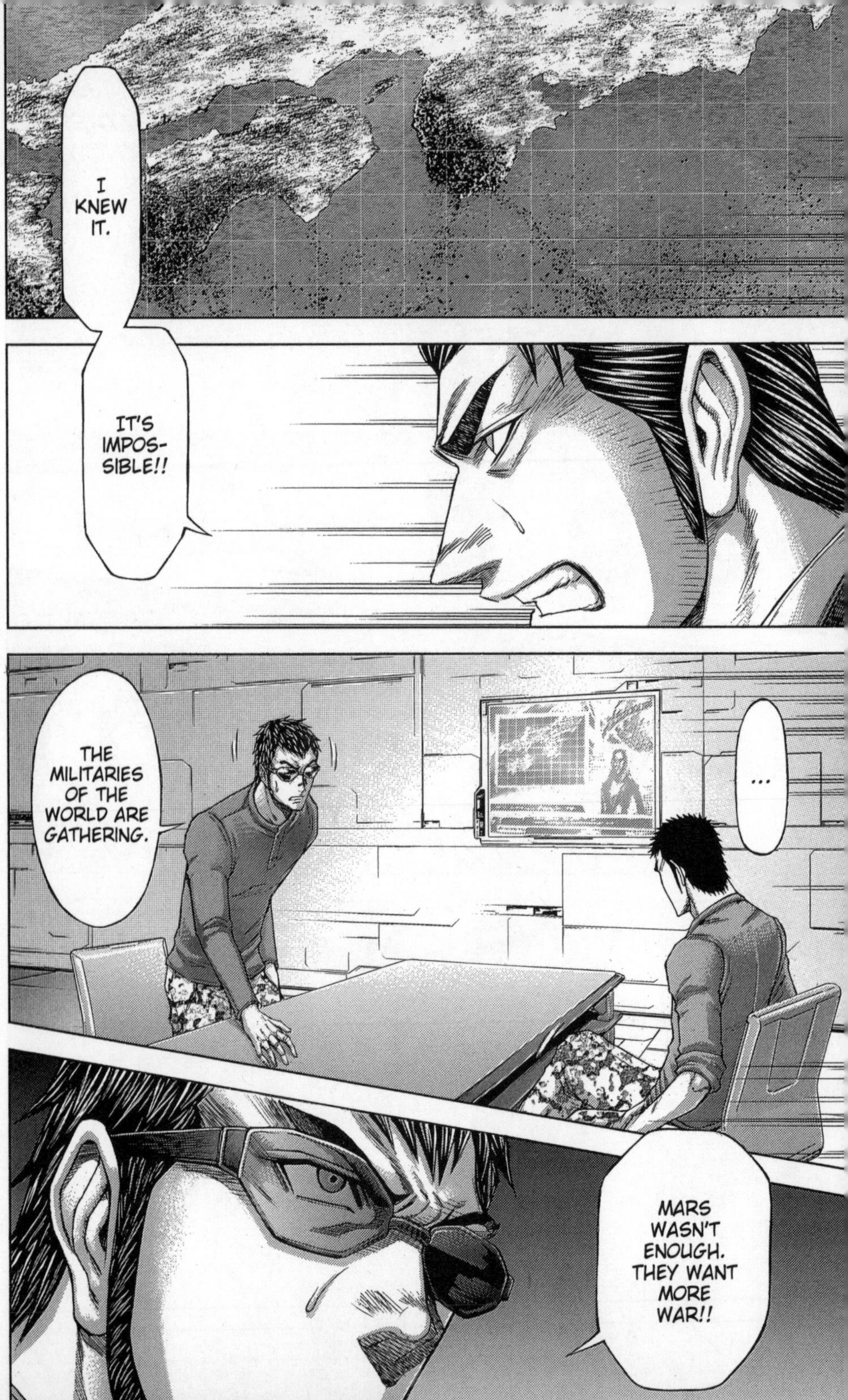
I KNEW IT.
IT'S IMPOSSIBLE!!
...
THE MILITARIES OF THE WORLD ARE GATHERING.
MARS WASN'T ENOUGH. THEY WANT MORE WAR!!

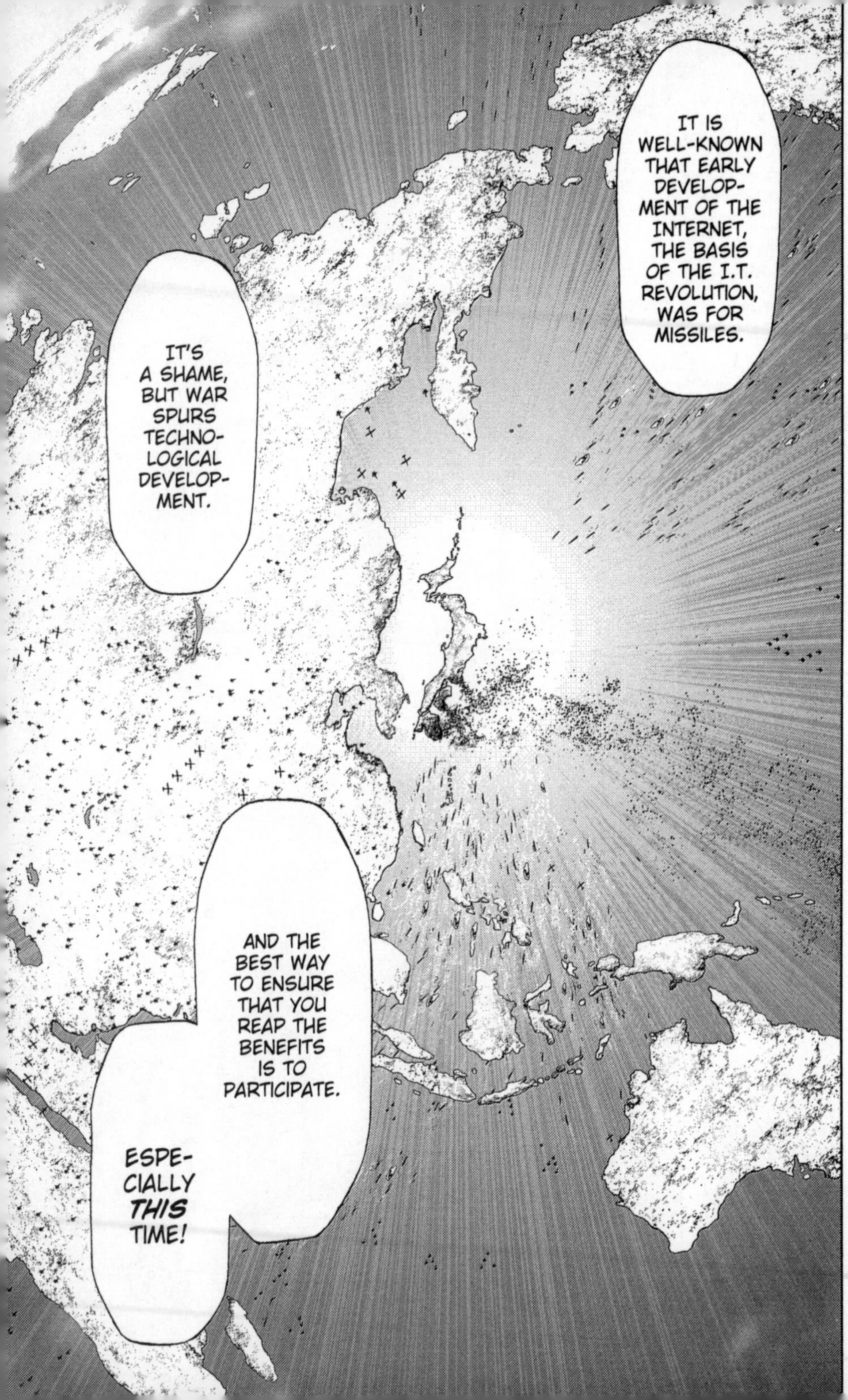
IT IS WELL-KNOWN THAT EARLY DEVELOPMENT OF THE INTERNET, THE BASIS OF THE I.T. REVOLUTION, WAS FOR MISSILES.
IT'S A SHAME, BUT WAR SPURS TECHNOLOGICAL DEVELOPMENT.
AND THE BEST WAY TO ENSURE THAT YOU REAP THE BENEFITS IS TO PARTICIPATE.
ESPECIALLY *THIS* TIME!

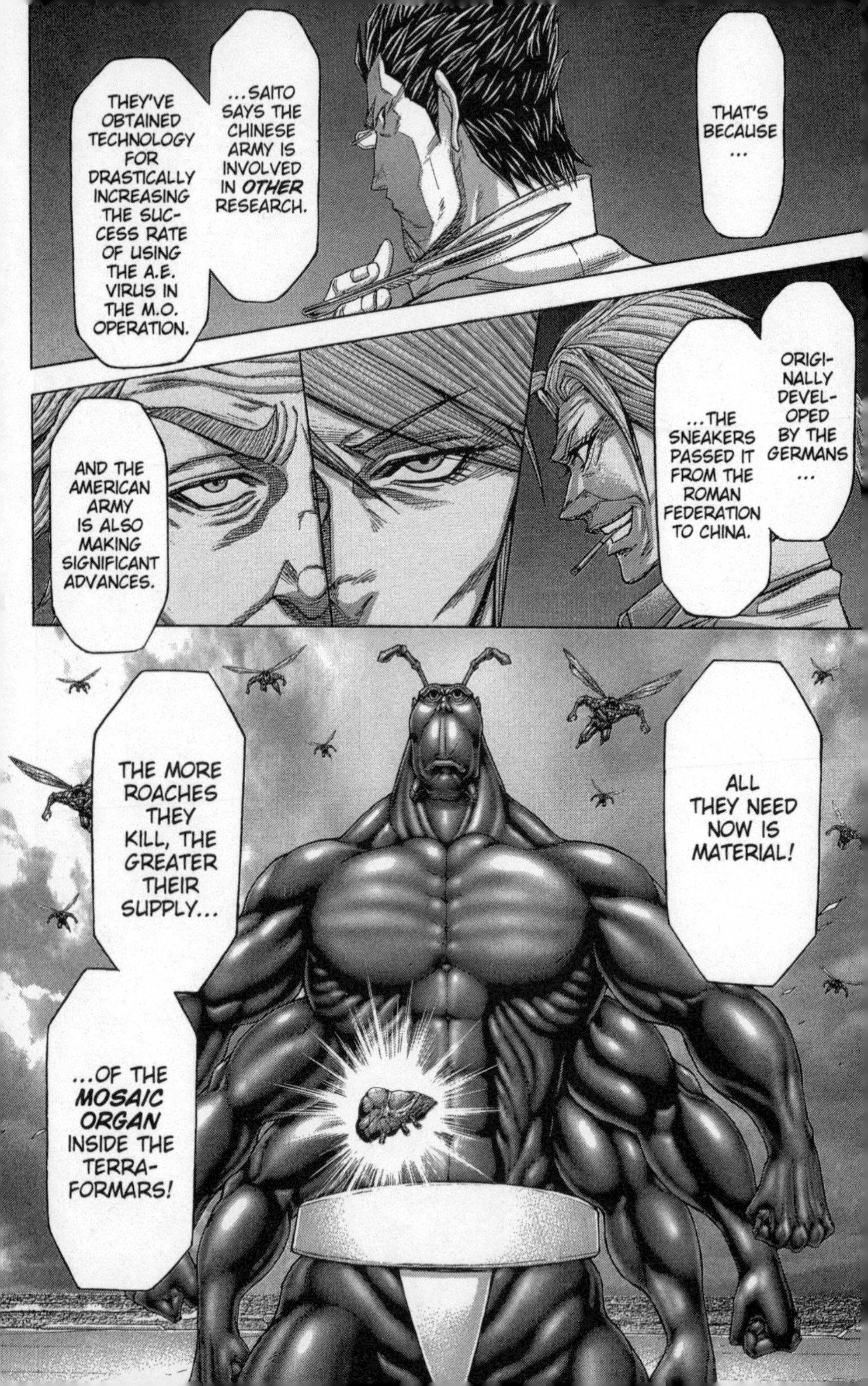
THAT'S BECAUSE...
...SAITO SAYS THE CHINESE ARMY IS INVOLVED IN *OTHER* RESEARCH.
THEY'VE OBTAINED TECHNOLOGY FOR DRASTICALLY INCREASING THE SUCCESS RATE OF USING THE A.E. VIRUS IN THE M.O. OPERATION.
ORIGINALLY DEVELOPED BY THE GERMANS...
...THE SNEAKERS PASSED IT FROM THE ROMAN FEDERATION TO CHINA.
AND THE AMERICAN ARMY IS ALSO MAKING SIGNIFICANT ADVANCES.
ALL THEY NEED NOW IS MATERIAL!
THE MORE ROACHES THEY KILL, THE GREATER THEIR SUPPLY...
...OF THE ***MOSAIC ORGAN*** INSIDE THE TERRAFORMARS!

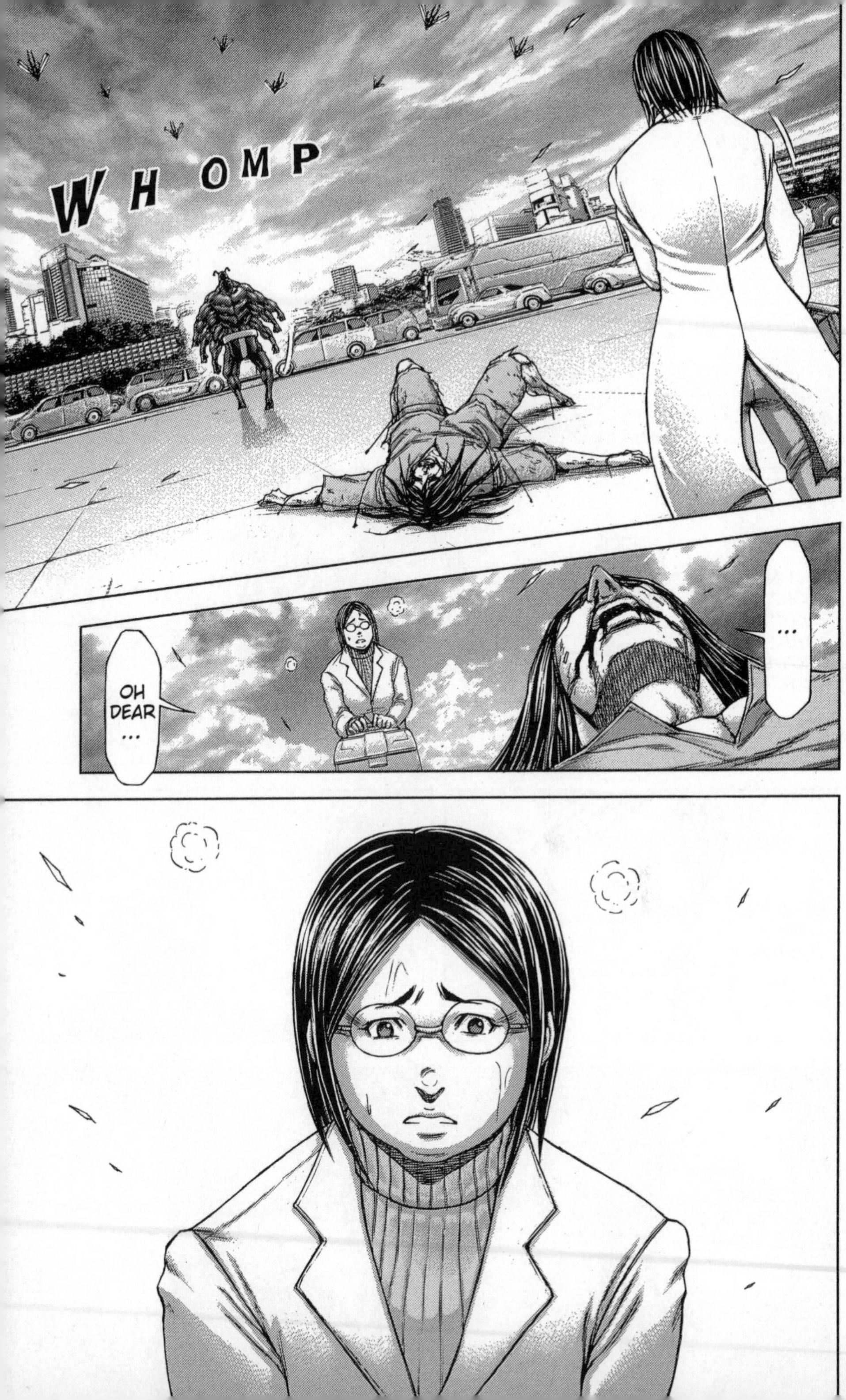
WHOMP
...
OH DEAR ...

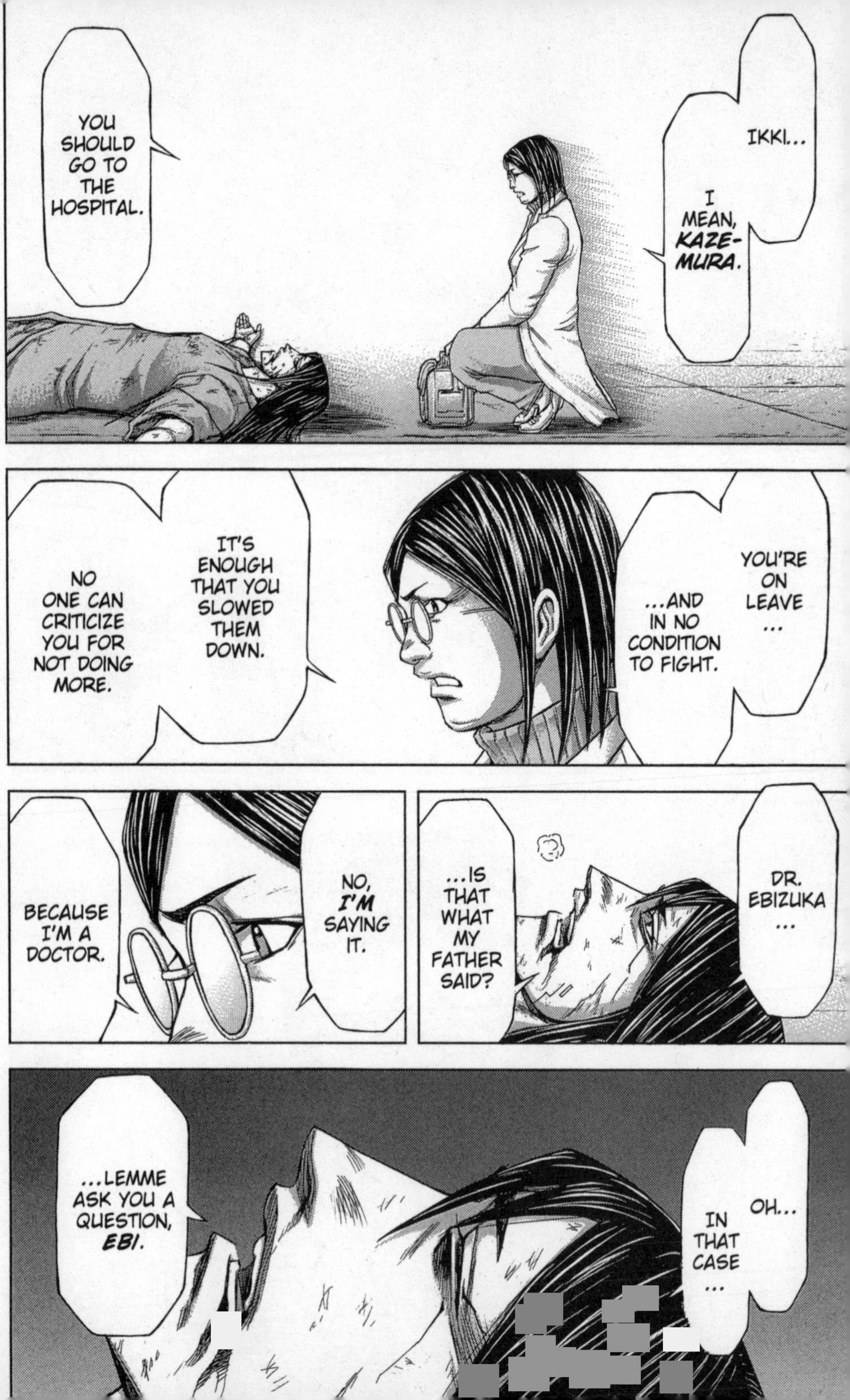
IKKI...
I MEAN, *KAZE-MURA*.
YOU SHOULD GO TO THE HOSPITAL.
YOU'RE ON LEAVE...
...AND IN NO CONDITION TO FIGHT.
IT'S ENOUGH THAT YOU SLOWED THEM DOWN.
NO ONE CAN CRITICIZE YOU FOR NOT DOING MORE.
DR. EBIZUKA...
...IS THAT WHAT MY FATHER SAID?
NO, *I'M* SAYING IT.
BECAUSE I'M A DOCTOR.
OH...
IN THAT CASE...
...LEMME ASK YOU A QUESTION, *EBI*.

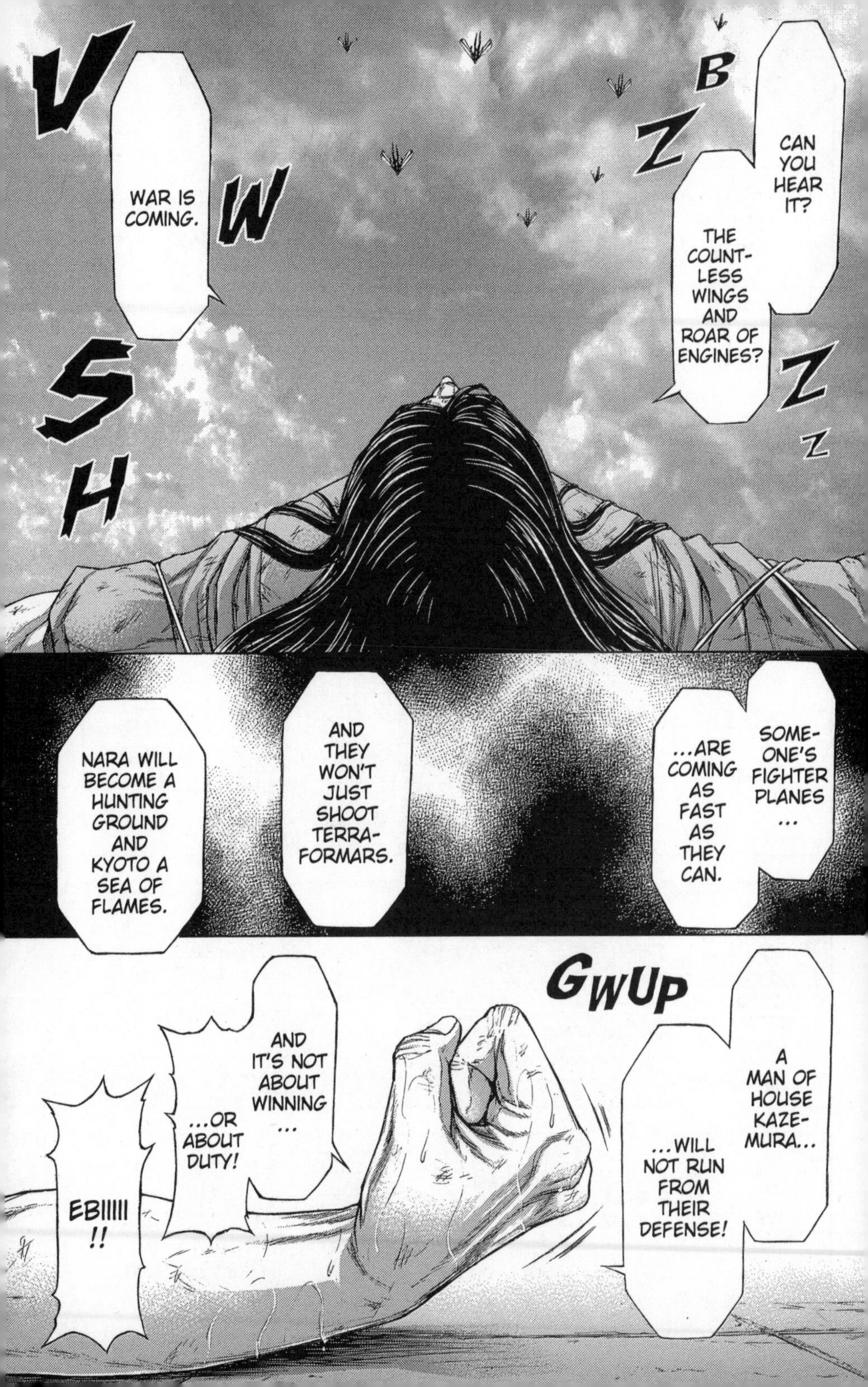
BZZZ
CAN YOU HEAR IT?
THE COUNT-LESS WINGS AND ROAR OF ENGINES?
VWSH
WAR IS COMING.
SOME-ONE'S FIGHTER PLANES...
...ARE COMING AS FAST AS THEY CAN.
AND THEY WON'T JUST SHOOT TERRA-FORMARS.
NARA WILL BECOME A HUNTING GROUND AND KYOTO A SEA OF FLAMES.
A MAN OF HOUSE KAZE-MURA...
...WILL NOT RUN FROM THEIR DEFENSE!
GWUP
AND IT'S NOT ABOUT WINNING...
...OR ABOUT DUTY!
EBIIIII!!

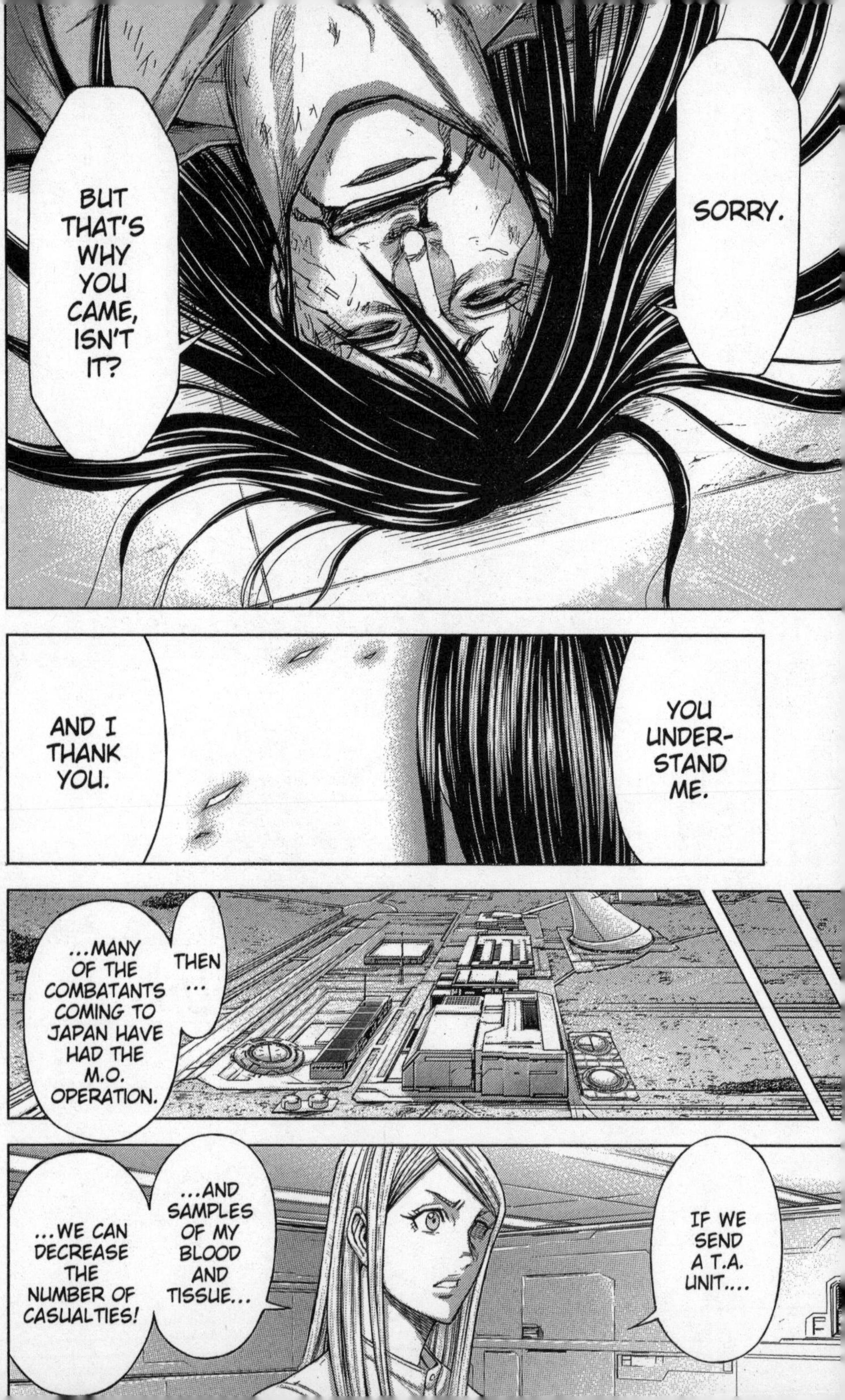
SORRY.
BUT THAT'S WHY YOU CAME, ISN'T IT?
YOU UNDER-STAND ME.
AND I THANK YOU.
THEN ...
...MANY OF THE COMBATANTS COMING TO JAPAN HAVE HAD THE M.O. OPERATION.
IF WE SEND A T.A. UNIT....
...AND SAMPLES OF MY BLOOD AND TISSUE...
...WE CAN DECREASE THE NUMBER OF CASUALTIES!

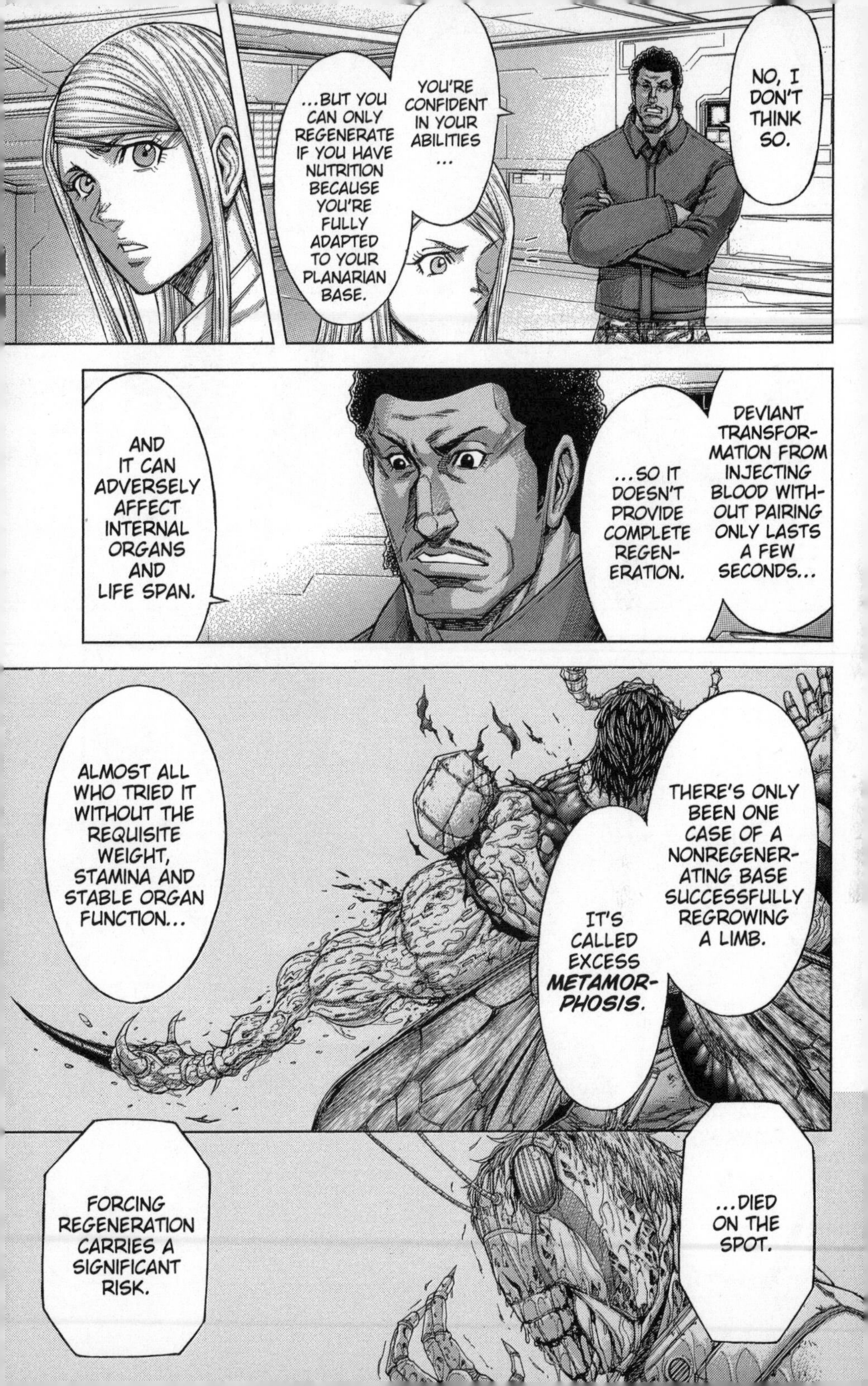
NO, I DON'T THINK SO.
YOU'RE CONFIDENT IN YOUR ABILITIES...
...BUT YOU CAN ONLY REGENERATE IF YOU HAVE NUTRITION BECAUSE YOU'RE FULLY ADAPTED TO YOUR PLANARIAN BASE.
DEVIANT TRANSFORMATION FROM INJECTING BLOOD WITHOUT PAIRING ONLY LASTS A FEW SECONDS...
...SO IT DOESN'T PROVIDE COMPLETE REGENERATION.
AND IT CAN ADVERSELY AFFECT INTERNAL ORGANS AND LIFE SPAN.
THERE'S ONLY BEEN ONE CASE OF A NONREGENERATING BASE SUCCESSFULLY REGROWING A LIMB.
IT'S CALLED EXCESS ***METAMORPHOSIS***.
ALMOST ALL WHO TRIED IT WITHOUT THE REQUISITE WEIGHT, STAMINA AND STABLE ORGAN FUNCTION...
...DIED ON THE SPOT.
FORCING REGENERATION CARRIES A SIGNIFICANT RISK.

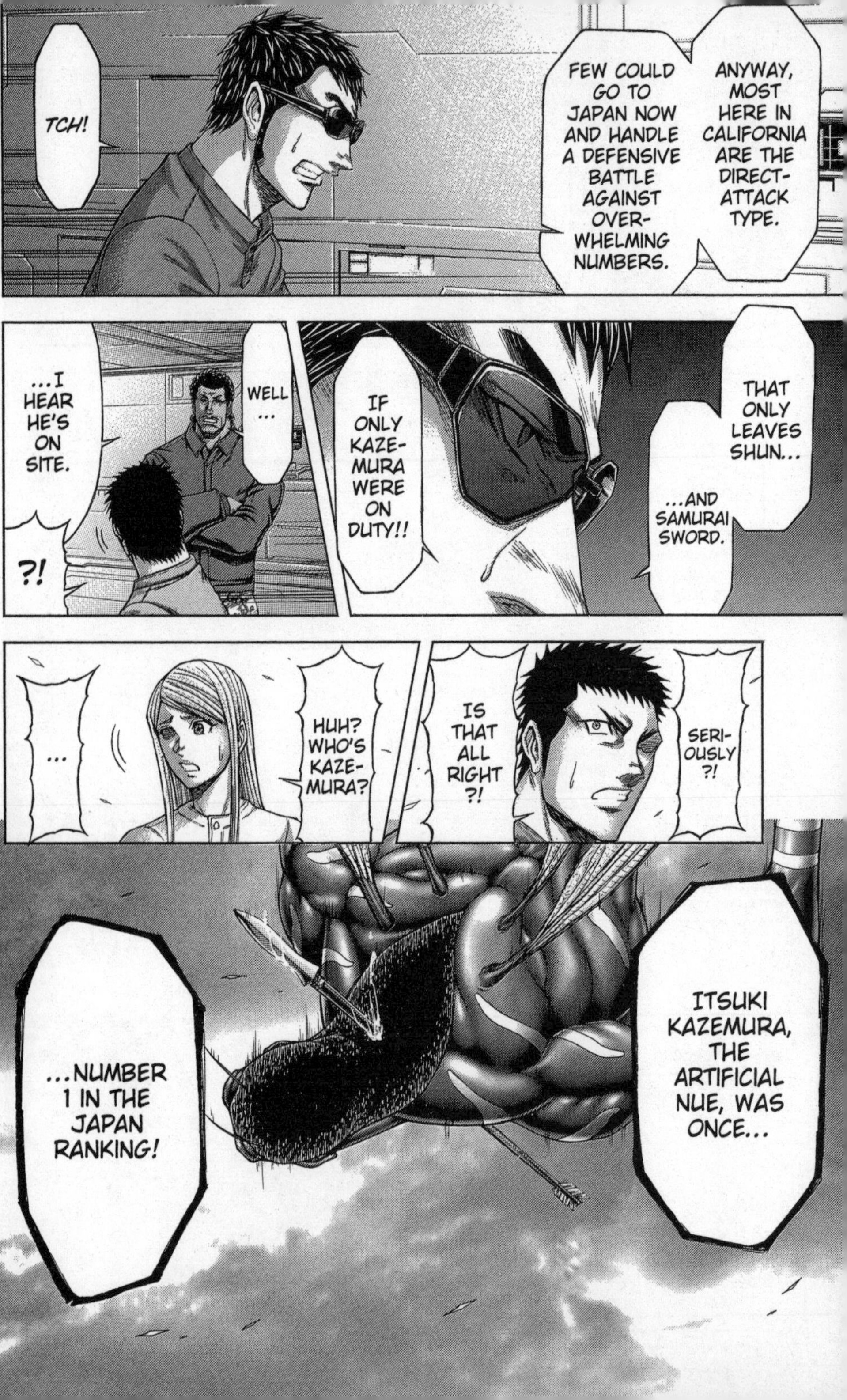
ANYWAY, MOST HERE IN CALIFORNIA ARE THE DIRECT-ATTACK TYPE.
FEW COULD GO TO JAPAN NOW AND HANDLE A DEFENSIVE BATTLE AGAINST OVER-WHELMING NUMBERS.
TCH!
THAT ONLY LEAVES SHUN...
...AND SAMURAI SWORD.
IF ONLY KAZE-MURA WERE ON DUTY!!
WELL...
...I HEAR HE'S ON SITE.
?!
SERI-OUSLY?!
IS THAT ALL RIGHT?!
HUH? WHO'S KAZE-MURA?
...
ITSUKI KAZEMURA, THE ARTIFICIAL NUE, WAS ONCE...
...NUMBER 1 IN THE JAPAN RANKING!

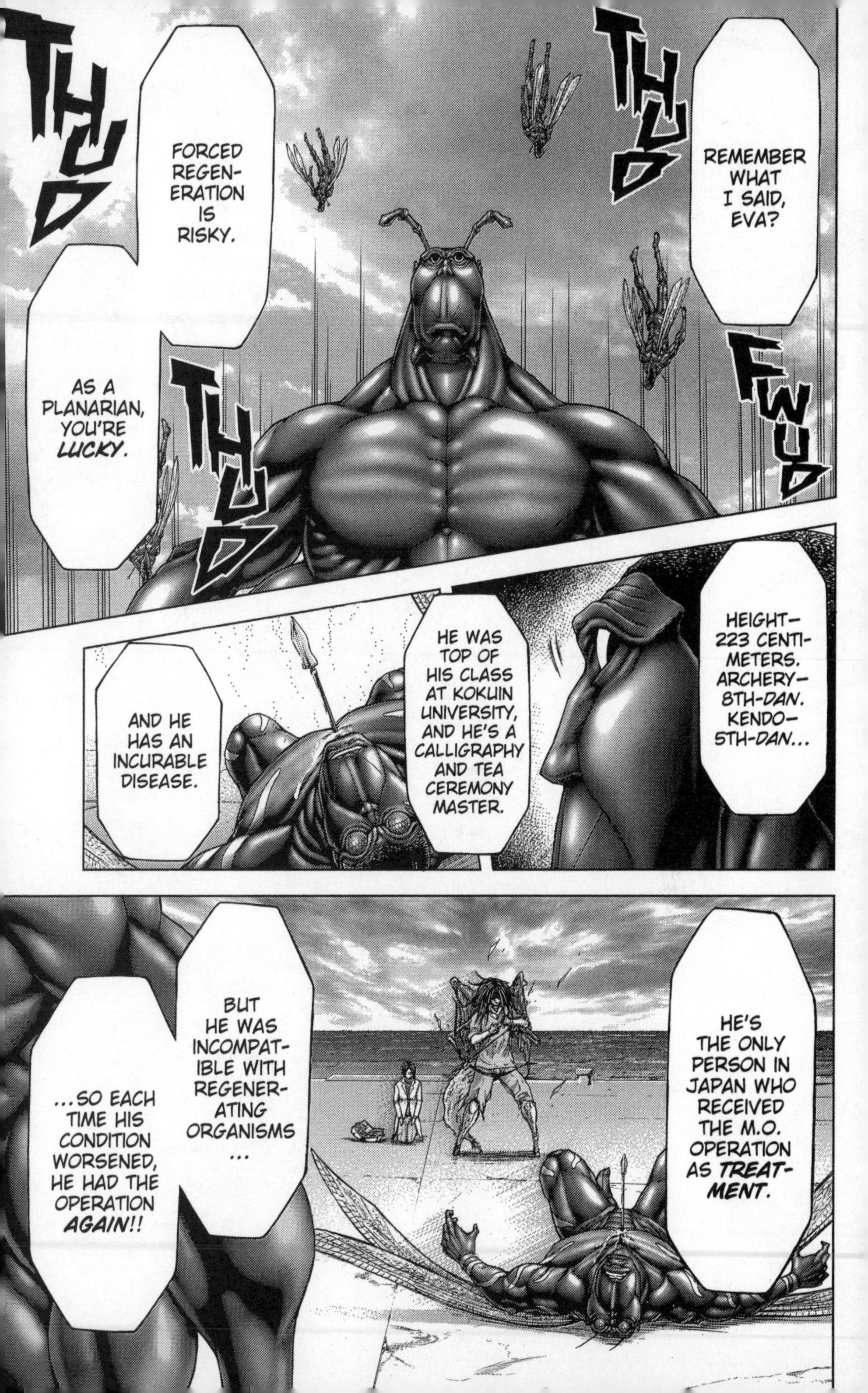
THUD
REMEMBER WHAT I SAID, EVA?
FORCED REGEN-ERATION IS RISKY.
THUD
FWUD
THUD
AS A PLANARIAN, YOU'RE *LUCKY*.
HEIGHT— 223 CENTI-METERS. ARCHERY— 8TH-*DAN*. KENDO— 5TH-*DAN*...
HE WAS TOP OF HIS CLASS AT KOKUIN UNIVERSITY, AND HE'S A CALLIGRAPHY AND TEA CEREMONY MASTER.
AND HE HAS AN INCURABLE DISEASE.
HE'S THE ONLY PERSON IN JAPAN WHO RECEIVED THE M.O. OPERATION AS *TREAT-MENT*.
BUT HE WAS INCOMPAT-IBLE WITH REGENER-ATING ORGANISMS...
...SO EACH TIME HIS CONDITION WORSENED, HE HAD THE OPERATION *AGAIN*!!

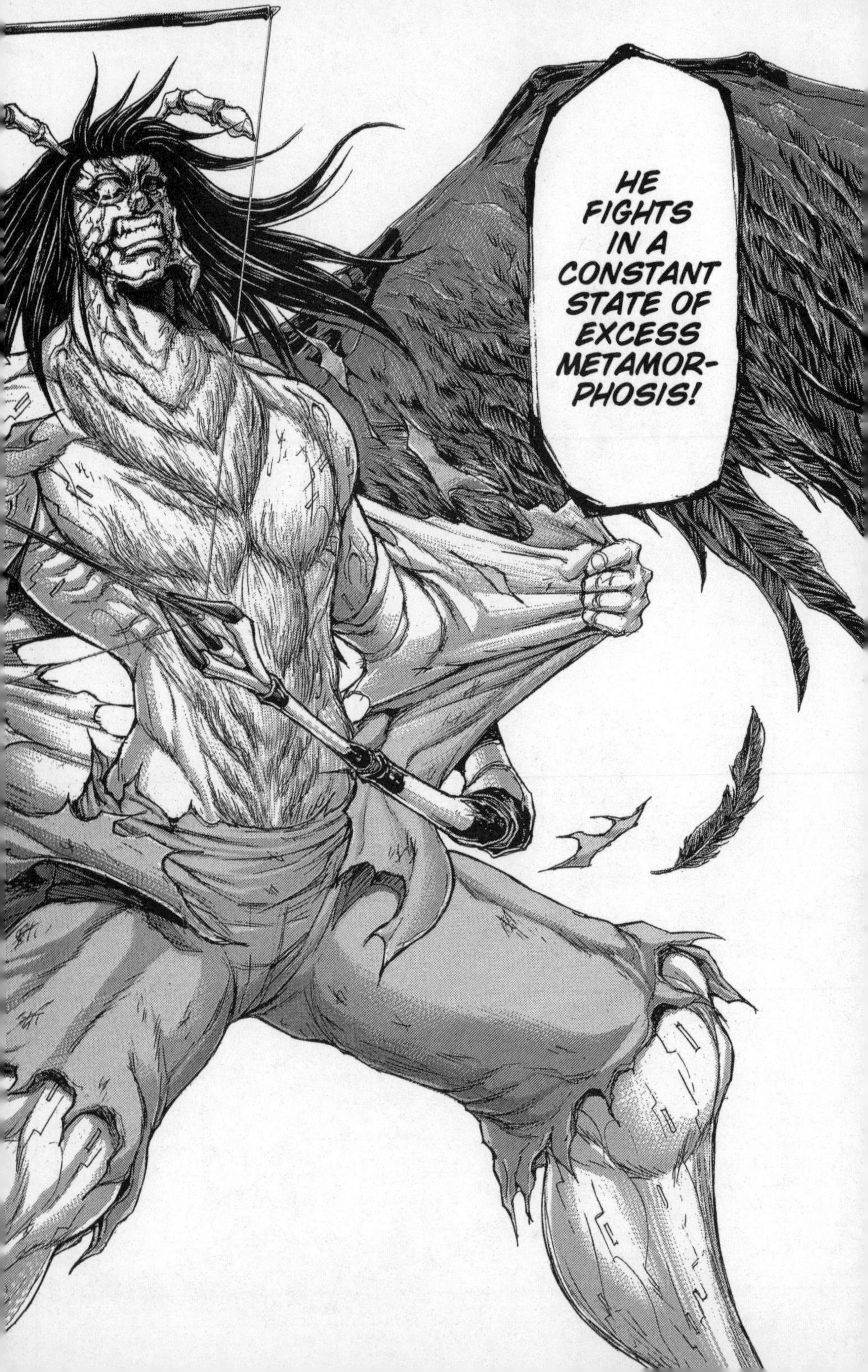
HE FIGHTS IN A CONSTANT STATE OF EXCESS METAMOR-PHOSIS!

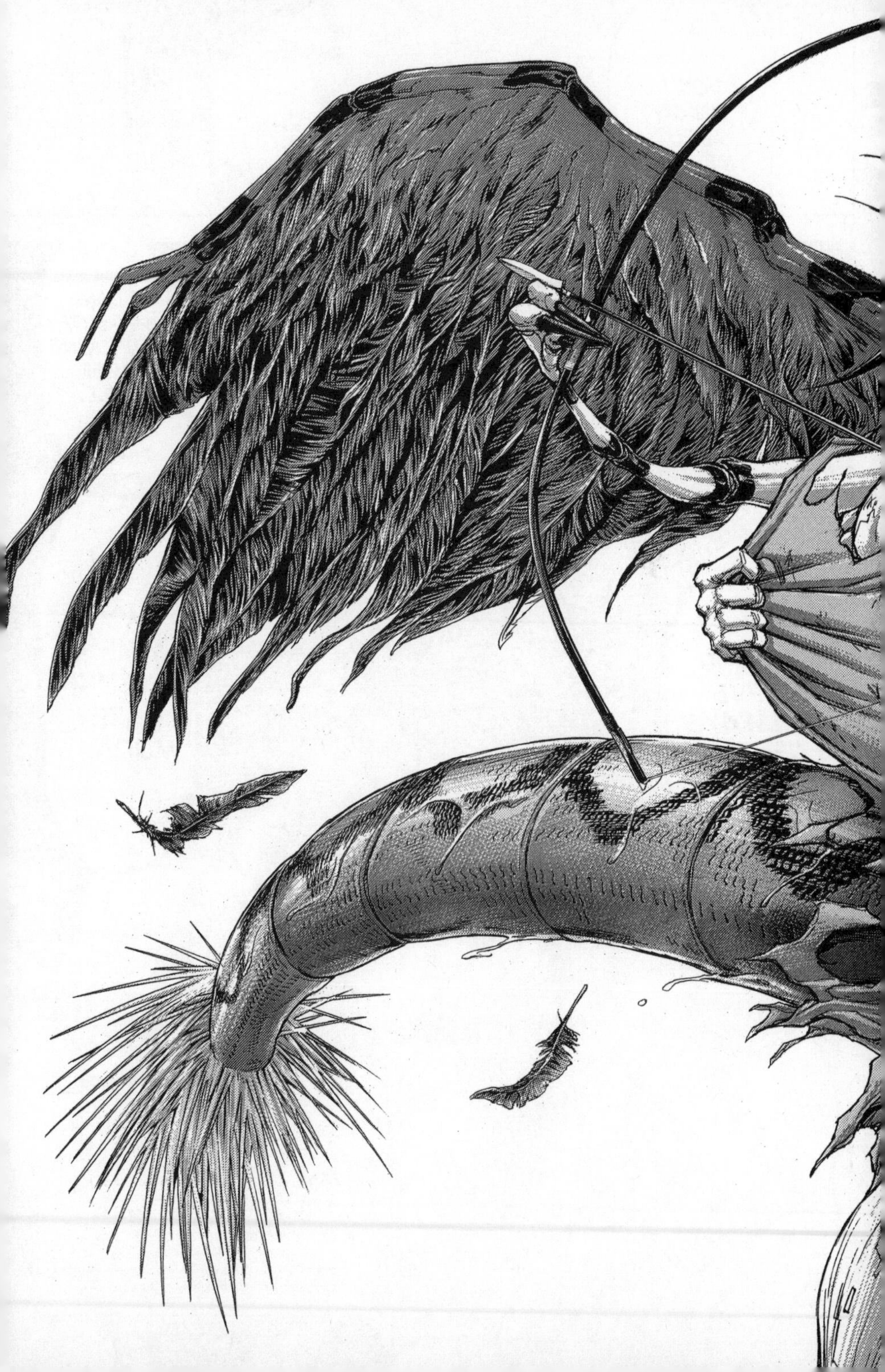

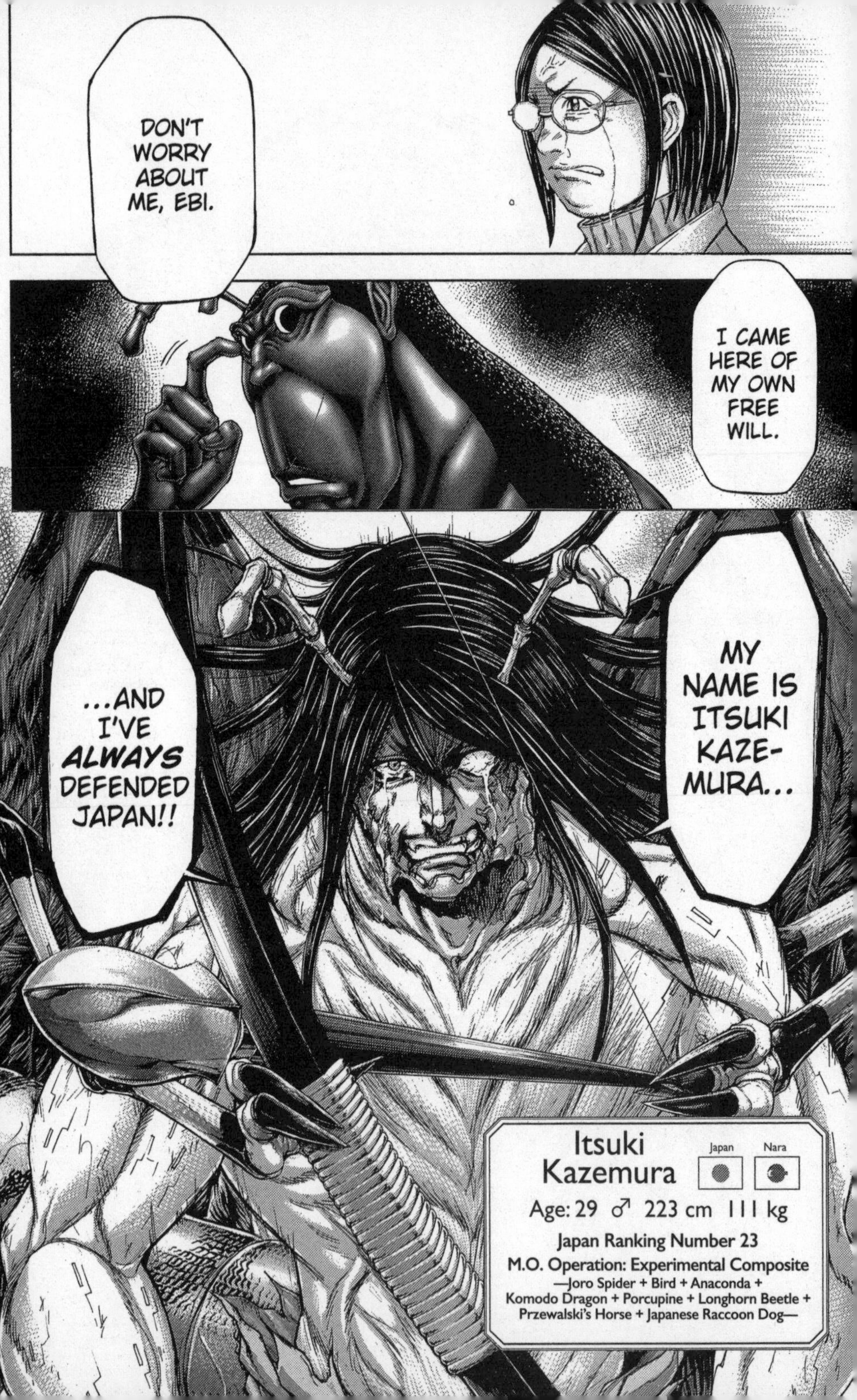
DON'T WORRY ABOUT ME, EBI.
I CAME HERE OF MY OWN FREE WILL.
MY NAME IS ITSUKI KAZEMURA...
...AND I'VE *ALWAYS* DEFENDED JAPAN!!
Itsuki Kazemura
Japan
Nara
Age: 29 ♂ 223 cm 111 kg
Japan Ranking Number 23
M.O. Operation: Experimental Composite
—Joro Spider + Bird + Anaconda + Komodo Dragon + Porcupine + Longhorn Beetle + Przewalski's Horse + Japanese Raccoon Dog—

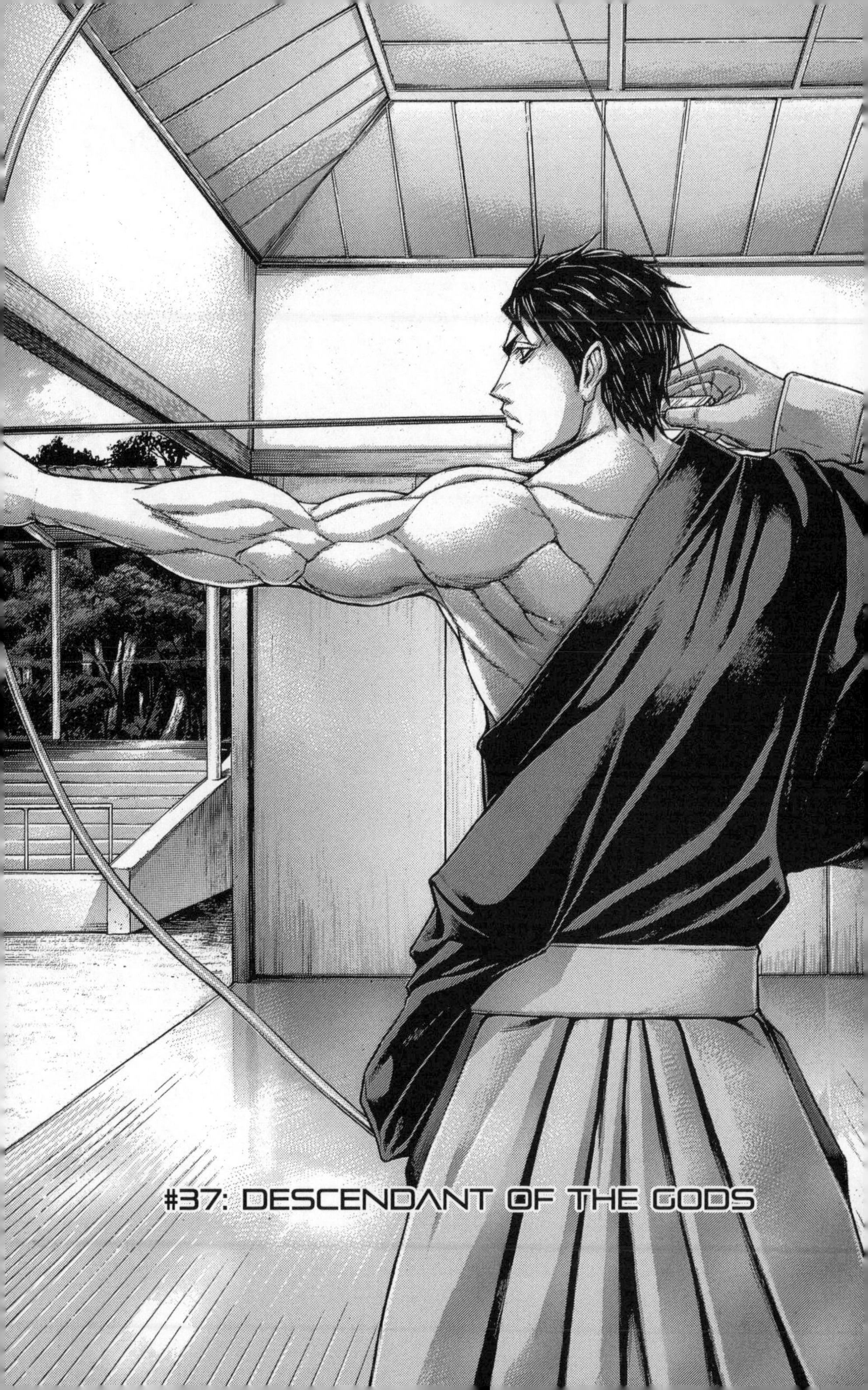
#37: DESCENDANT OF THE GODS

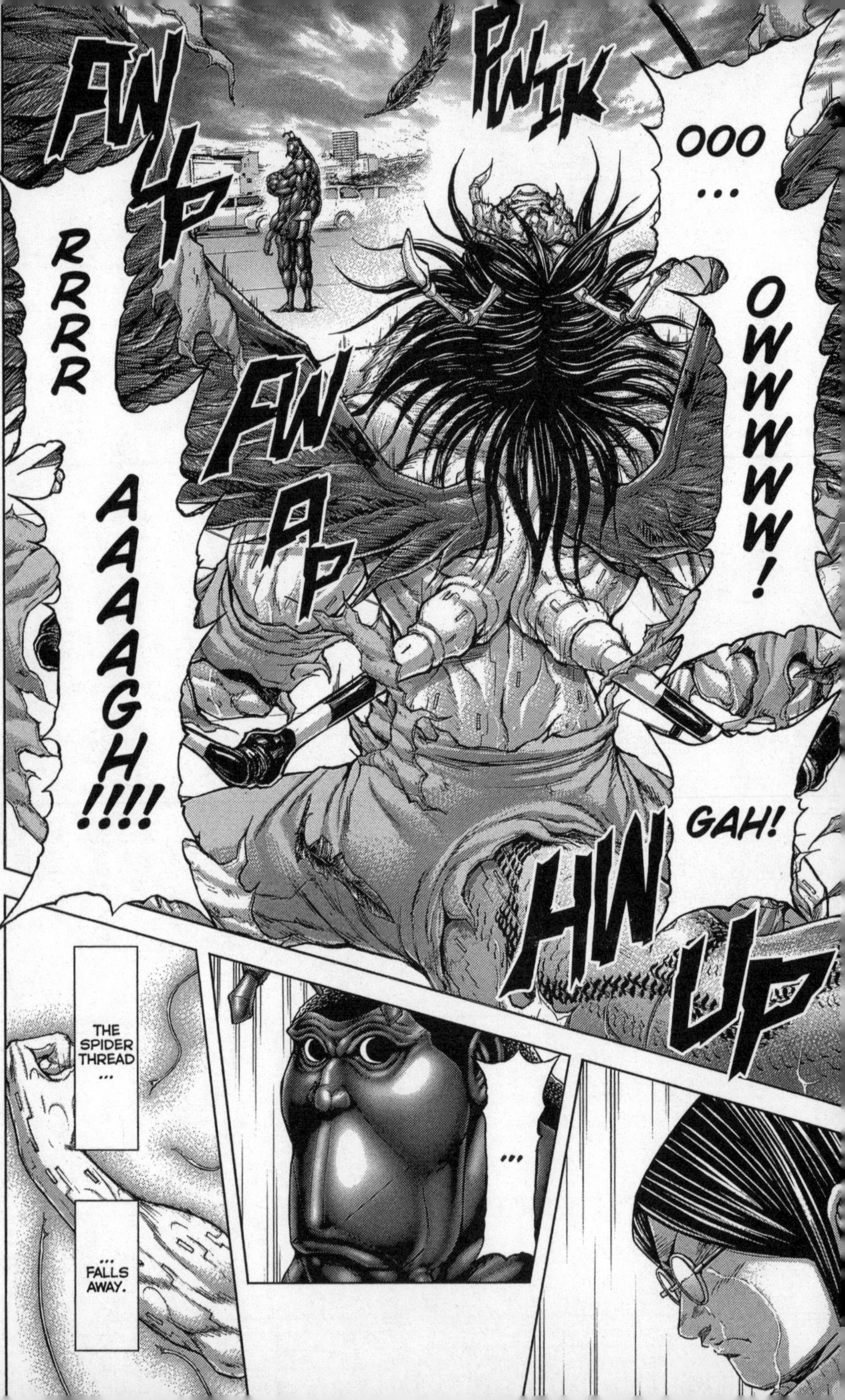
OOO... OWWWWWW!
PWIK
FWUP
RRRR AAAAAGH!!!!
FWAP
GAH!
HWUP
...
THE SPIDER THREAD ...
... FALLS AWAY.

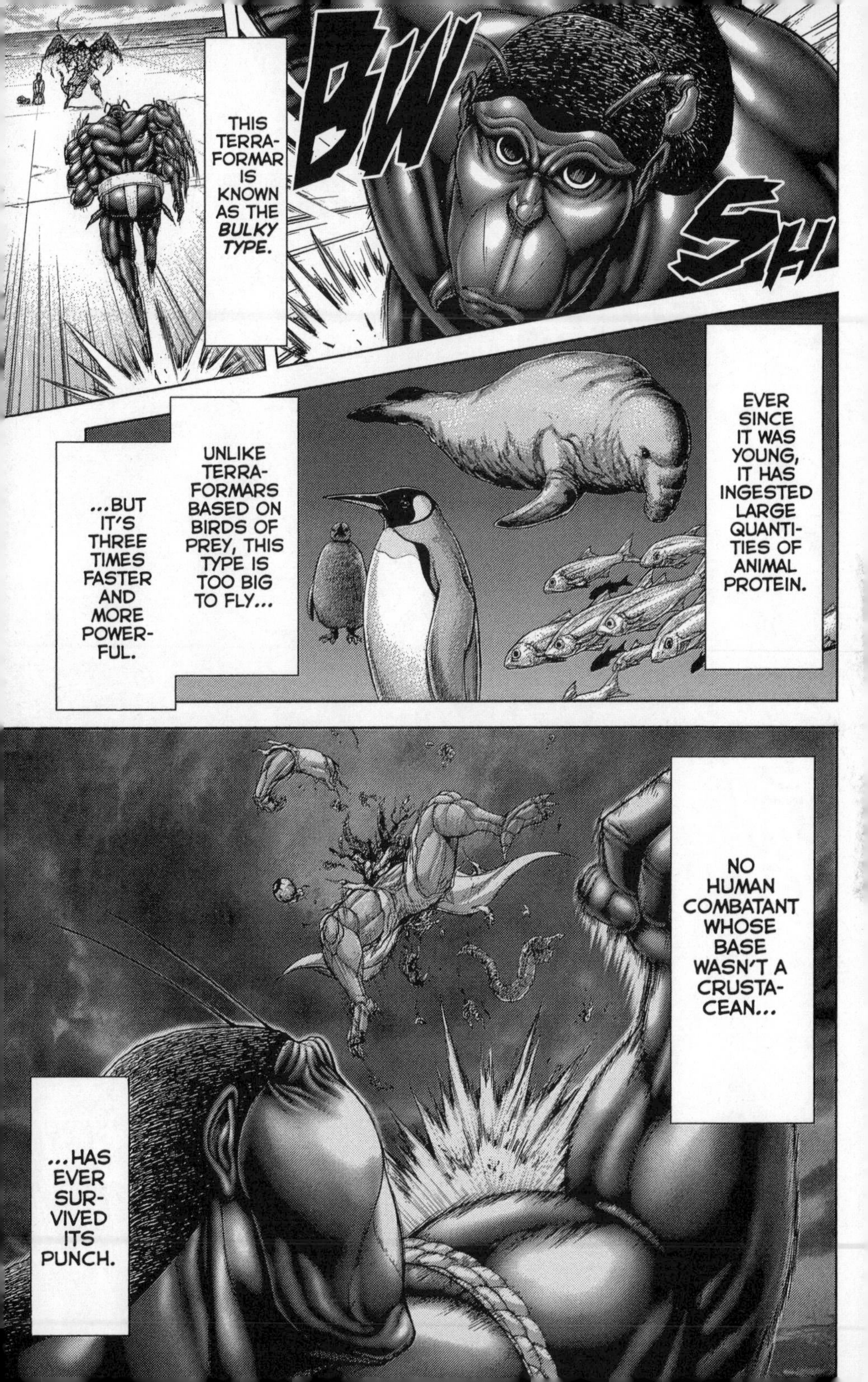
BW
SH
THIS TERRAFORMAR IS KNOWN AS THE *BULKY TYPE*.
EVER SINCE IT WAS YOUNG, IT HAS INGESTED LARGE QUANTITIES OF ANIMAL PROTEIN.
UNLIKE TERRAFORMARS BASED ON BIRDS OF PREY, THIS TYPE IS TOO BIG TO FLY...
...BUT IT'S THREE TIMES FASTER AND MORE POWERFUL.
NO HUMAN COMBATANT WHOSE BASE WASN'T A CRUSTACEAN...
...HAS EVER SURVIVED ITS PUNCH.

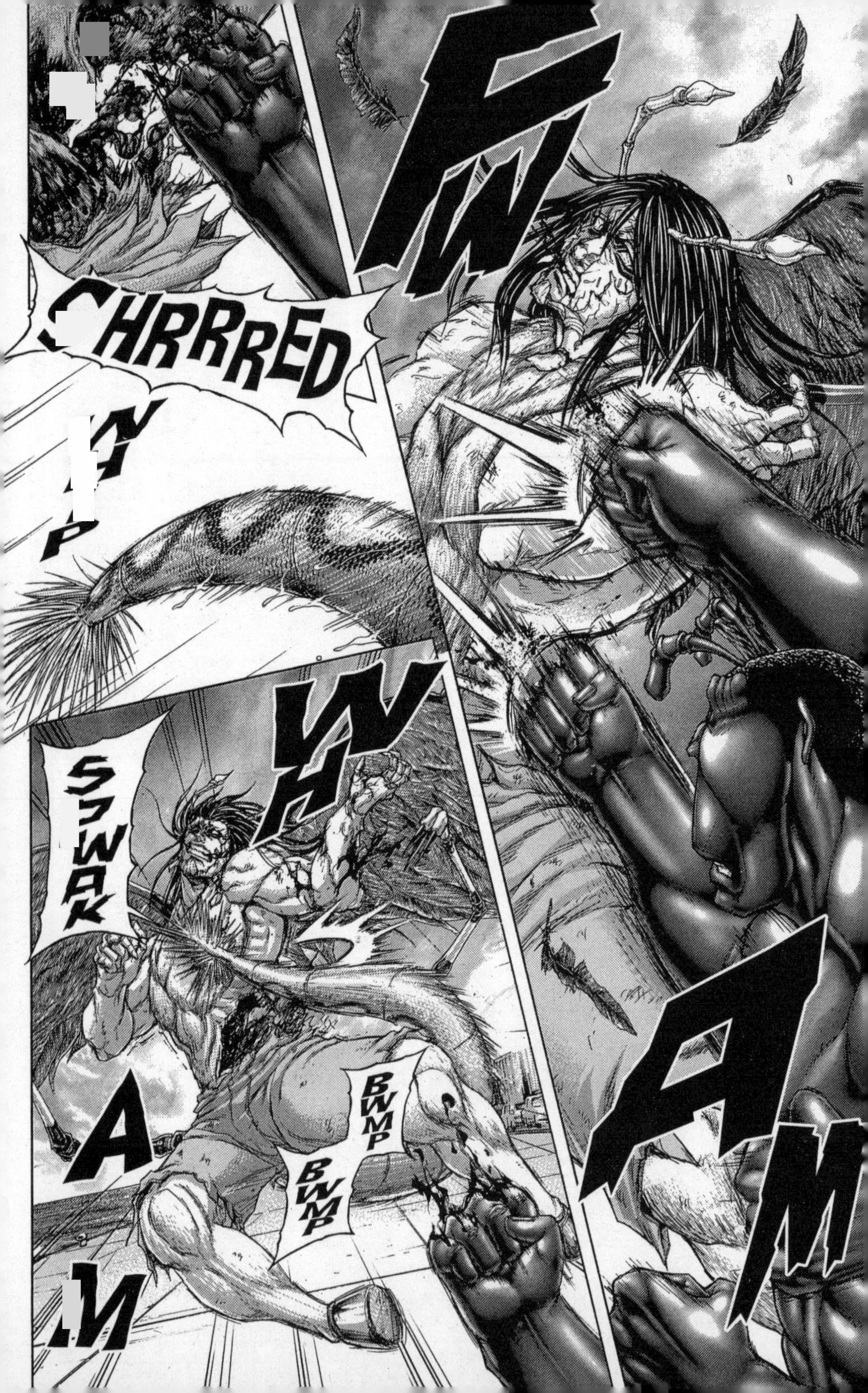
CHRRRED
WHAM
BWMP
BWMP

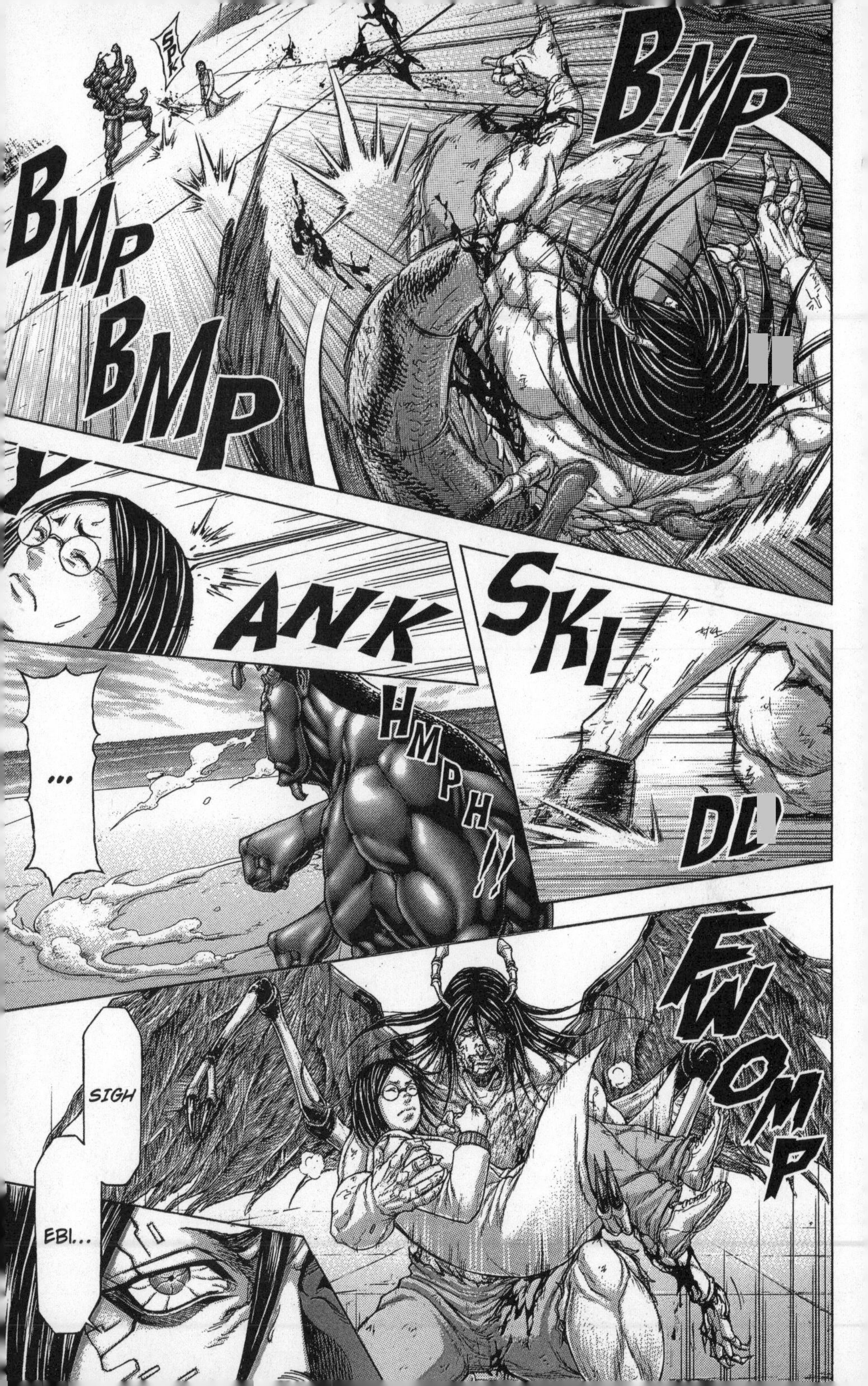
BMP
SPK
BMP
BMP
BMP
SKI
DD
ANK
HMPH!!
...
FWOMP
SIGH
EBI...

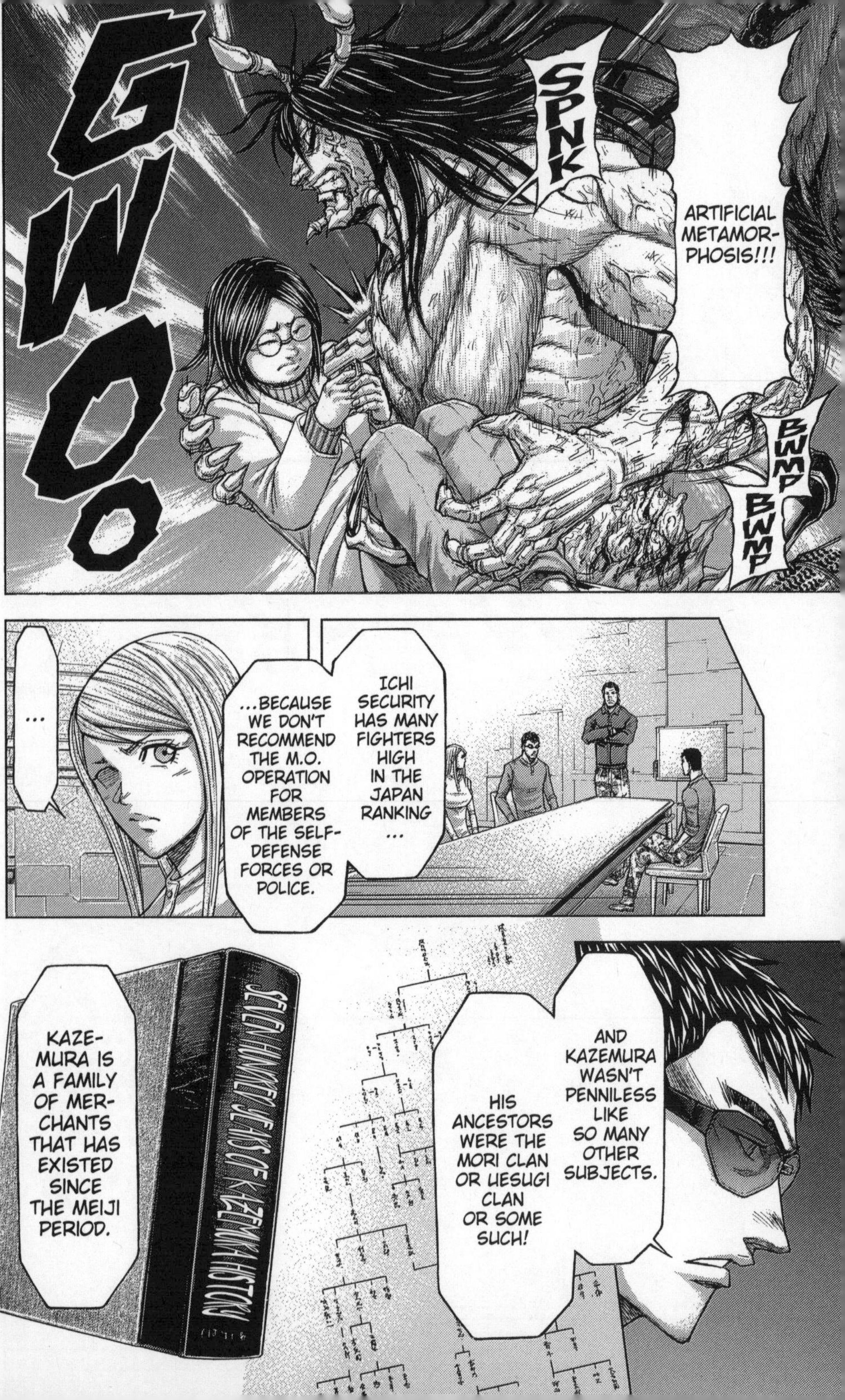
ARTIFICIAL METAMORPHOSIS!!!
BWMP BWMP
SPNK
GWOO
ICHI SECURITY HAS MANY FIGHTERS HIGH IN THE JAPAN RANKING ...
...BECAUSE WE DON'T RECOMMEND THE M.O. OPERATION FOR MEMBERS OF THE SELF-DEFENSE FORCES OR POLICE.
...
AND KAZEMURA WASN'T PENNILESS LIKE SO MANY OTHER SUBJECTS.
HIS ANCESTORS WERE THE MORI CLAN OR UESUGI CLAN OR SOME SUCH!
KAZEMURA IS A FAMILY OF MERCHANTS THAT HAS EXISTED SINCE THE MEIJI PERIOD.
SEVEN HUNDRED YEARS OF KAZEMURA HISTORY

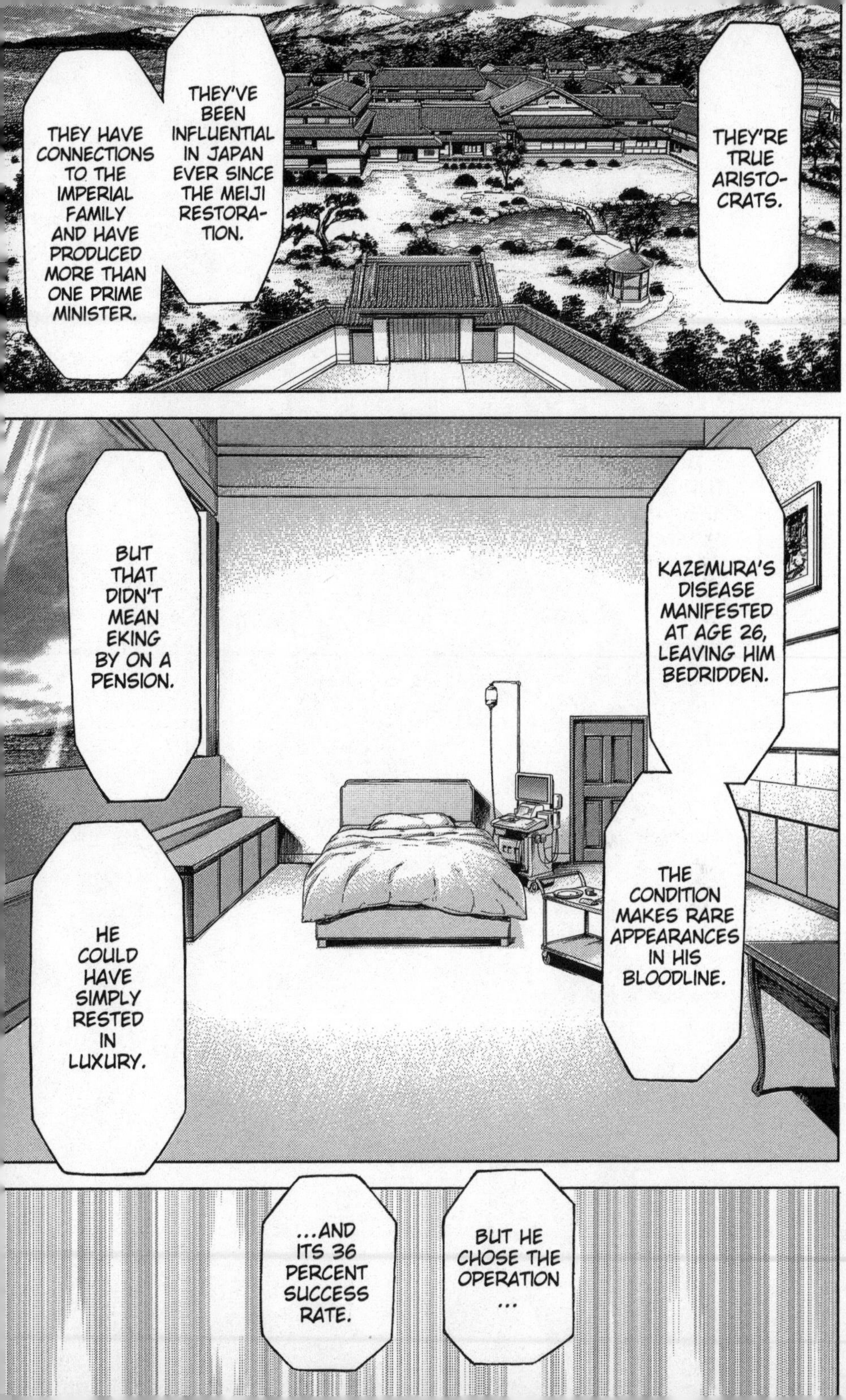
THEY'RE TRUE ARISTO-CRATS.
THEY'VE BEEN INFLUENTIAL IN JAPAN EVER SINCE THE MEIJI RESTORA-TION.
THEY HAVE CONNECTIONS TO THE IMPERIAL FAMILY AND HAVE PRODUCED MORE THAN ONE PRIME MINISTER.
KAZEMURA'S DISEASE MANIFESTED AT AGE 26, LEAVING HIM BEDRIDDEN.
THE CONDITION MAKES RARE APPEARANCES IN HIS BLOODLINE.
BUT THAT DIDN'T MEAN EKING BY ON A PENSION.
HE COULD HAVE SIMPLY RESTED IN LUXURY.
BUT HE CHOSE THE OPERATION ...
...AND ITS 36 PERCENT SUCCESS RATE.

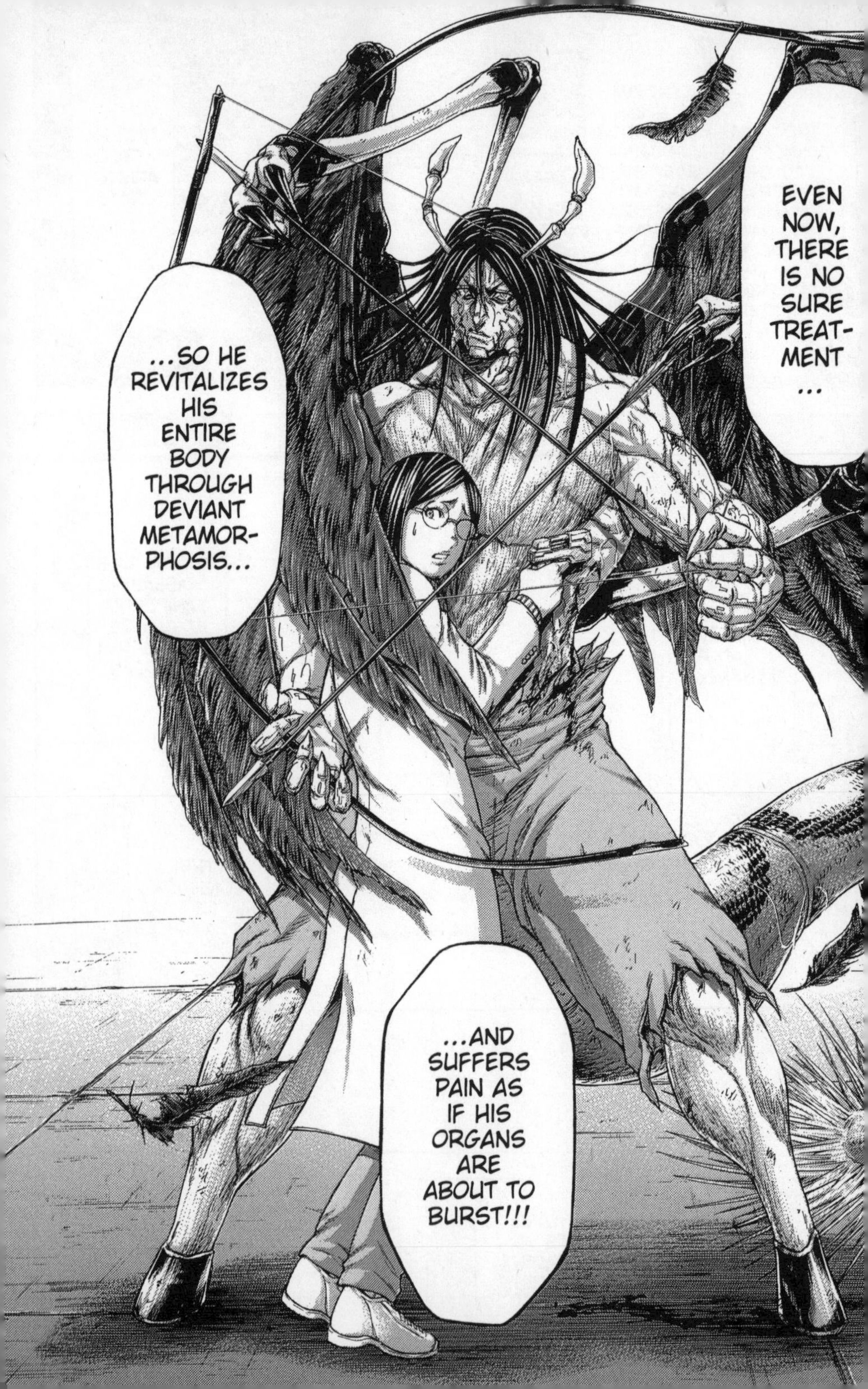
EVEN NOW, THERE IS NO SURE TREATMENT...
...SO HE REVITALIZES HIS ENTIRE BODY THROUGH DEVIANT METAMORPHOSIS...
...AND SUFFERS PAIN AS IF HIS ORGANS ARE ABOUT TO BURST!!!

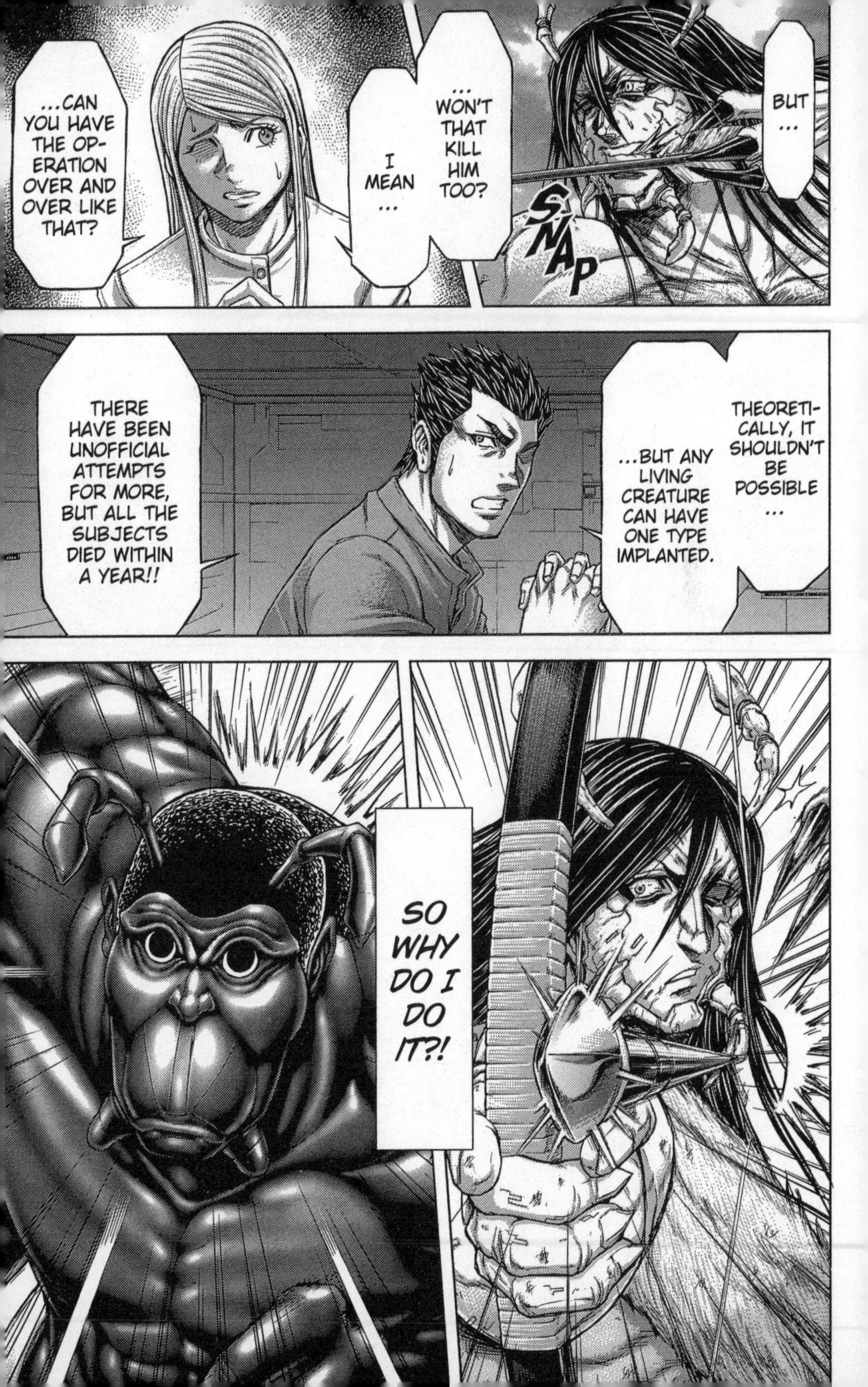
BUT ...
SNAP
... WON'T THAT KILL HIM TOO?
I MEAN ...
...CAN YOU HAVE THE OPERATION OVER AND OVER LIKE THAT?
THEORETICALLY, IT SHOULDN'T BE POSSIBLE ...
...BUT ANY LIVING CREATURE CAN HAVE ONE TYPE IMPLANTED.
THERE HAVE BEEN UNOFFICIAL ATTEMPTS FOR MORE, BUT ALL THE SUBJECTS DIED WITHIN A YEAR!!
SO WHY DO I DO IT?!

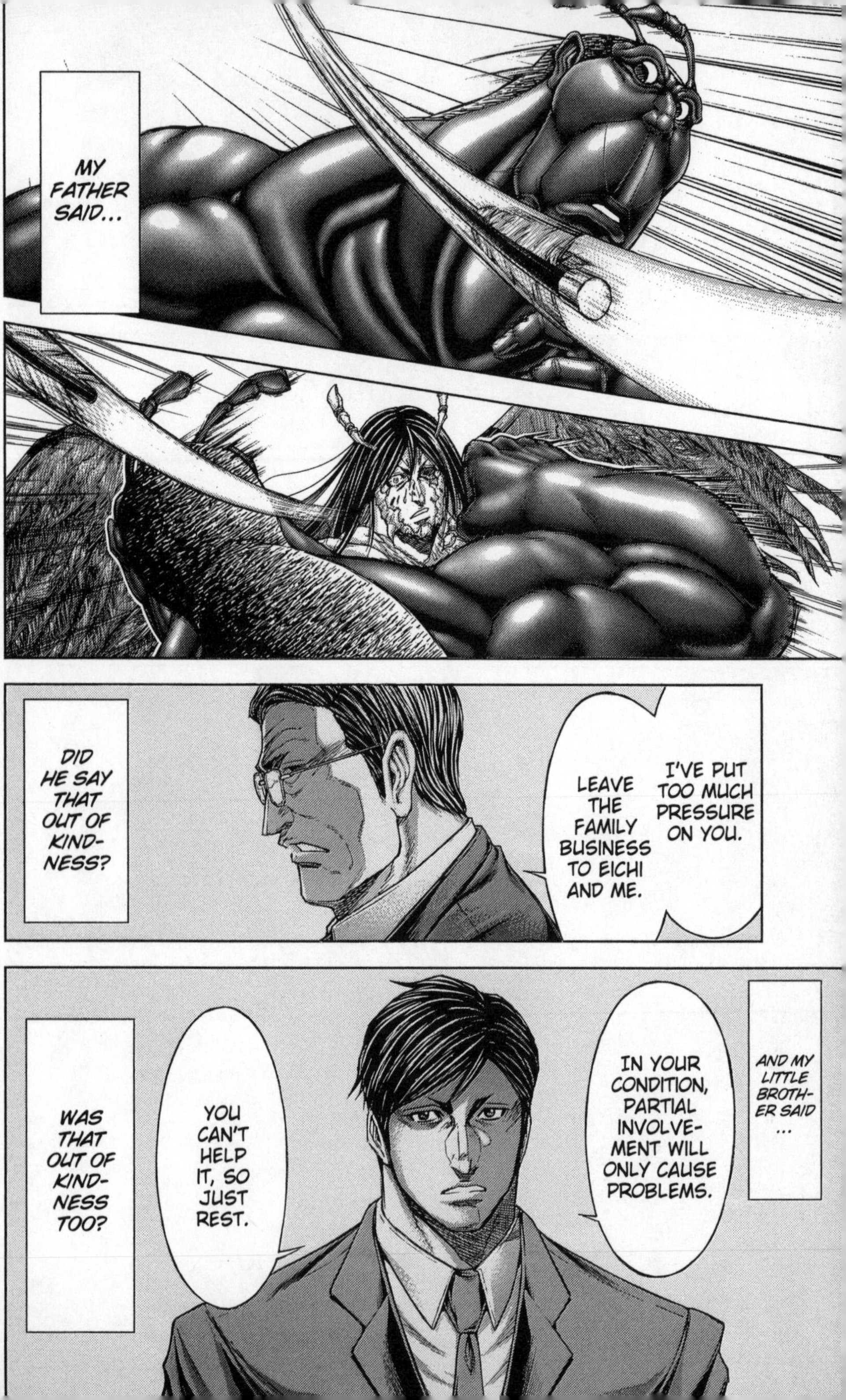
MY FATHER SAID...
I'VE PUT TOO MUCH PRESSURE ON YOU.
LEAVE THE FAMILY BUSINESS TO EICHI AND ME.
DID HE SAY THAT OUT OF KIND-NESS?
AND MY LITTLE BROTH-ER SAID...
IN YOUR CONDITION, PARTIAL INVOLVE-MENT WILL ONLY CAUSE PROBLEMS.
YOU CAN'T HELP IT, SO JUST REST.
WAS THAT OUT OF KIND-NESS TOO?

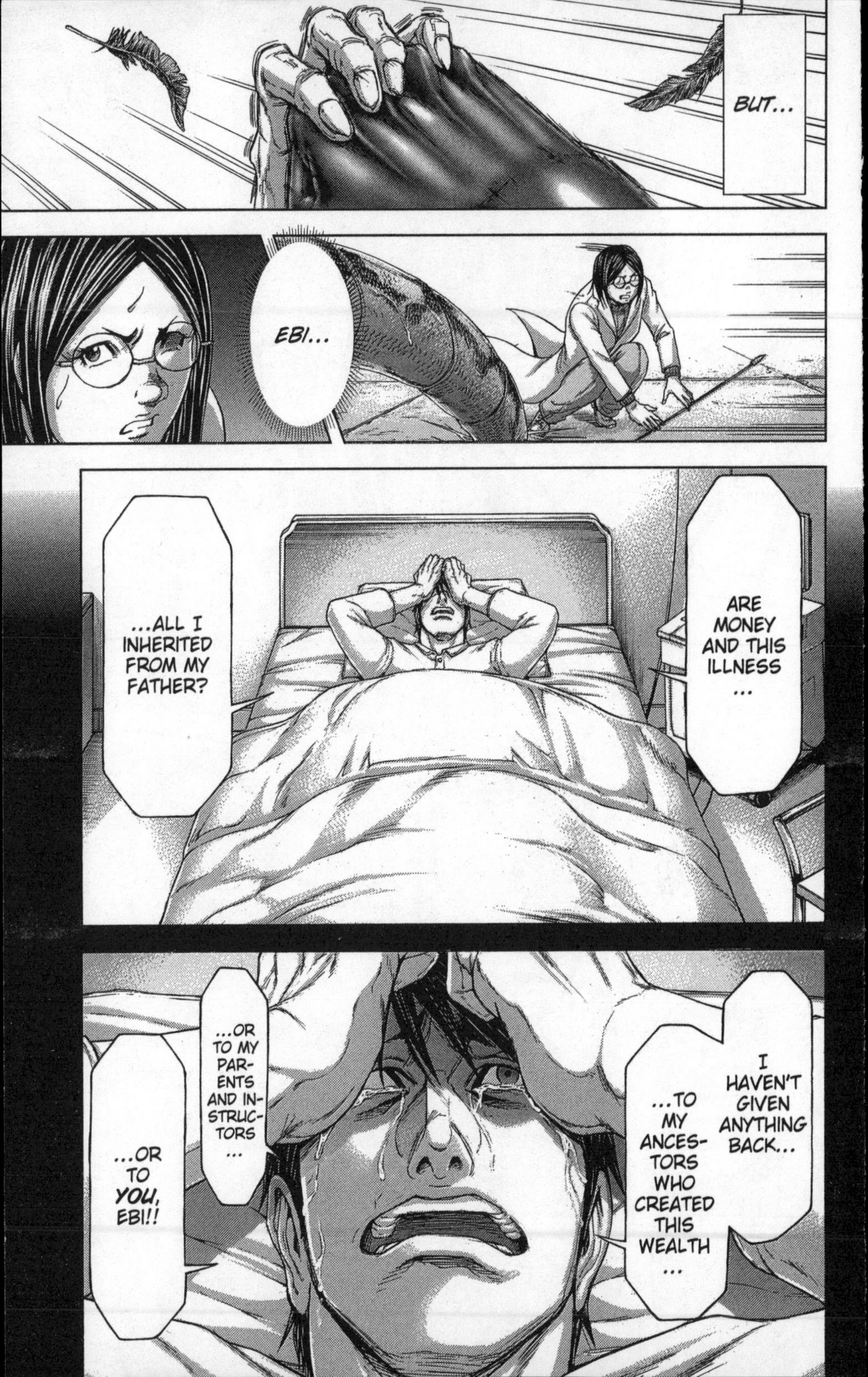
BUT...
EBI...
ARE MONEY AND THIS ILLNESS ...
...ALL I INHERITED FROM MY FATHER?
I HAVEN'T GIVEN ANYTHING BACK...
...TO MY ANCES-TORS WHO CREATED THIS WEALTH ...
...OR TO MY PAR-ENTS AND IN-STRUC-TORS ...
...OR TO *YOU*, EBI!!

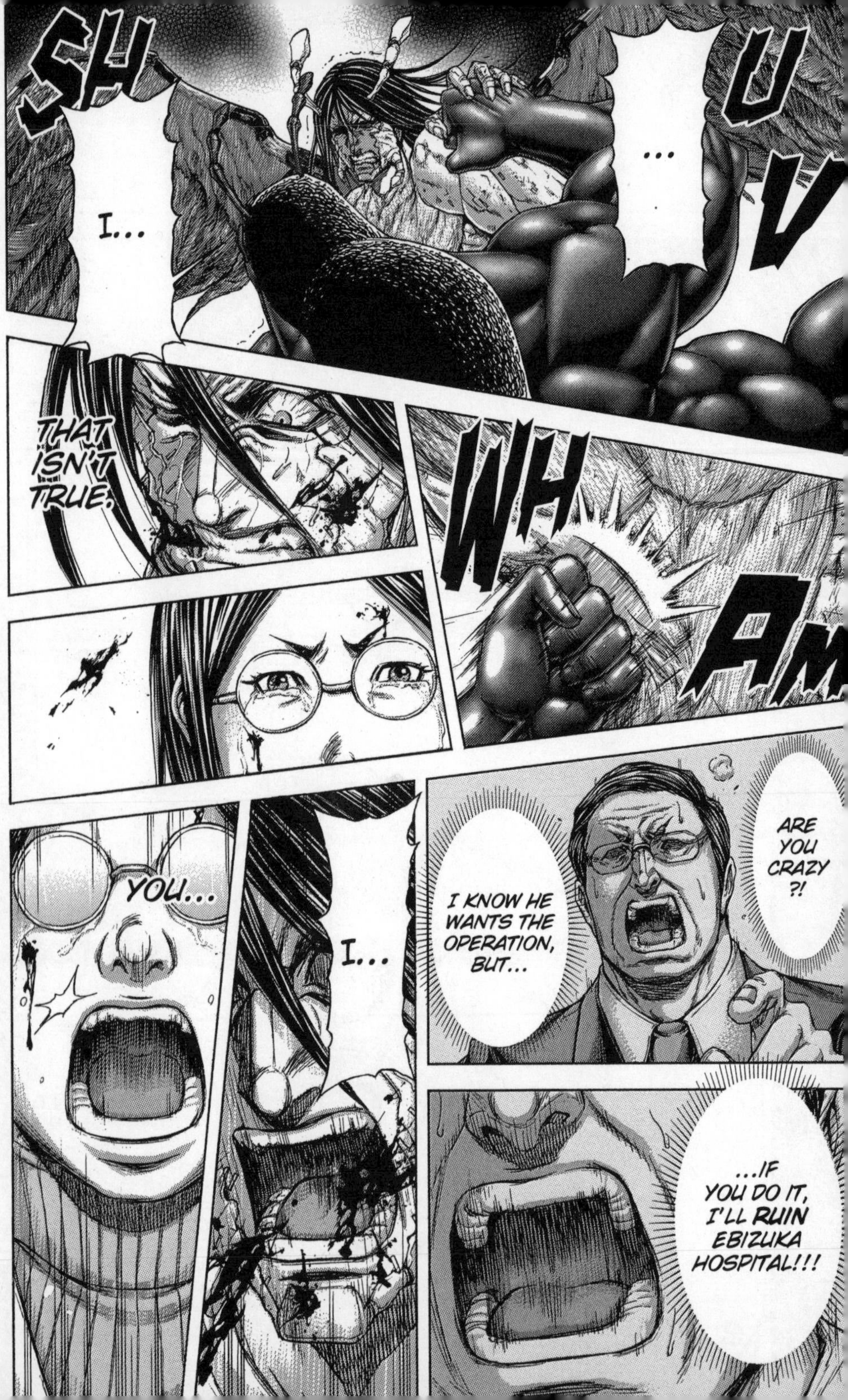
UV
...
SH
I...
WH
AM
THAT ISN'T TRUE.
ARE YOU CRAZY?!
I KNOW HE WANTS THE OPERATION, BUT...
...IF YOU DO IT, I'LL RUIN EBIZUKA HOSPITAL!!!
I...
YOU...

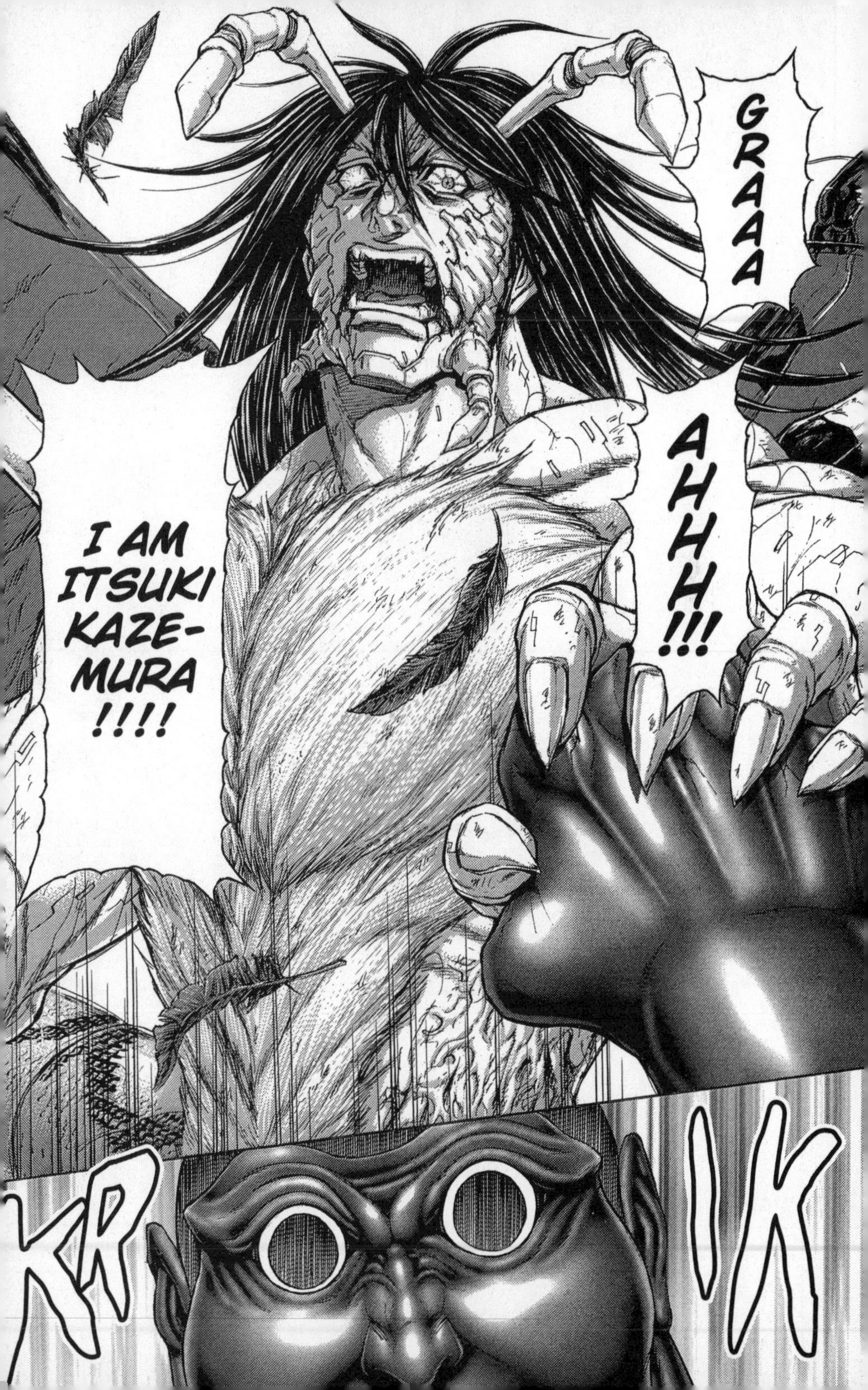
GRAAAA
AHHHH!!!
I AM ITSUKI KAZE-MURA!!!!
KR IK

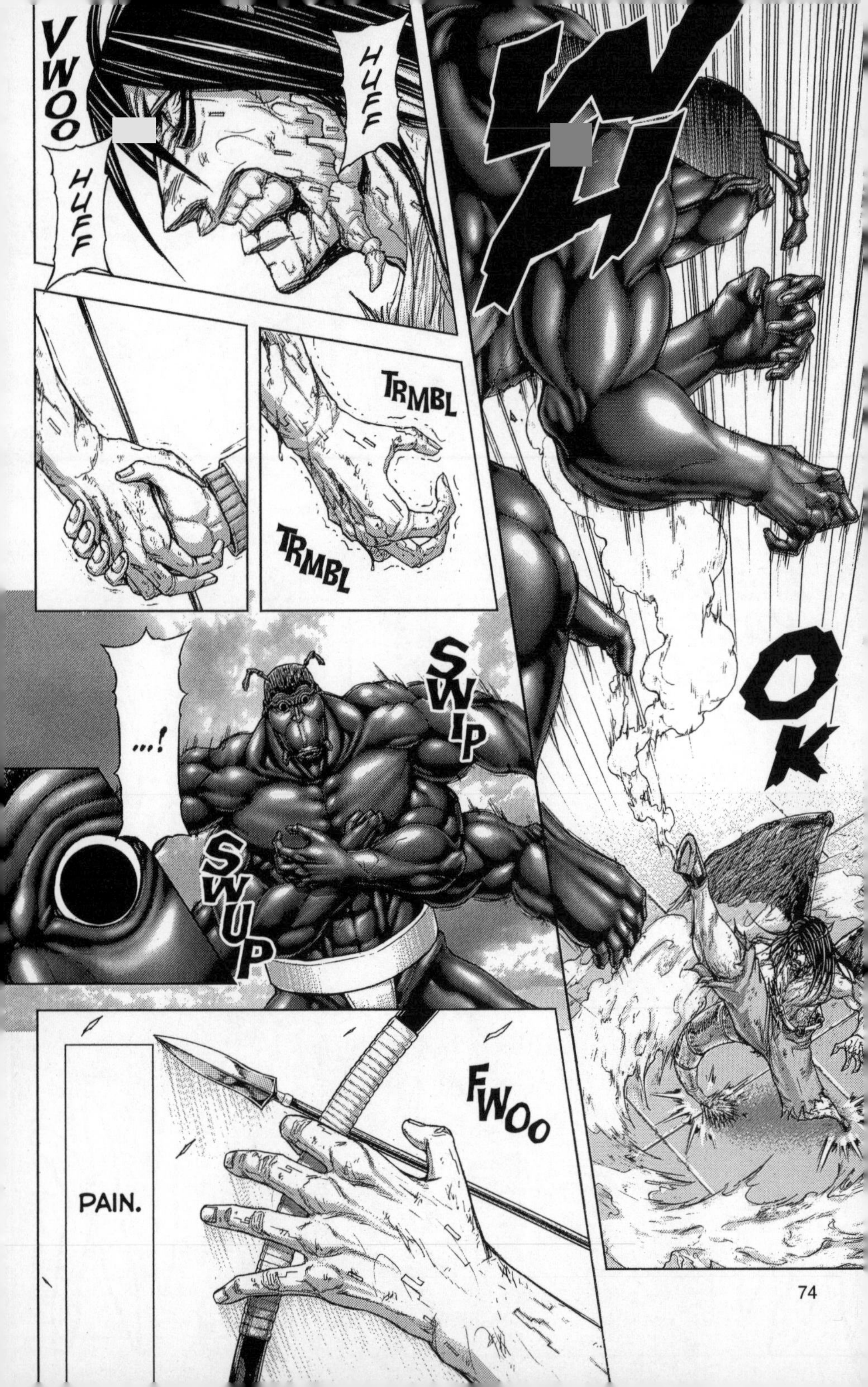
O K
VWOO
HUFF
HUFF
TRMBL
TRMBL
...!
SWIP
SWUP
FWOO
PAIN.

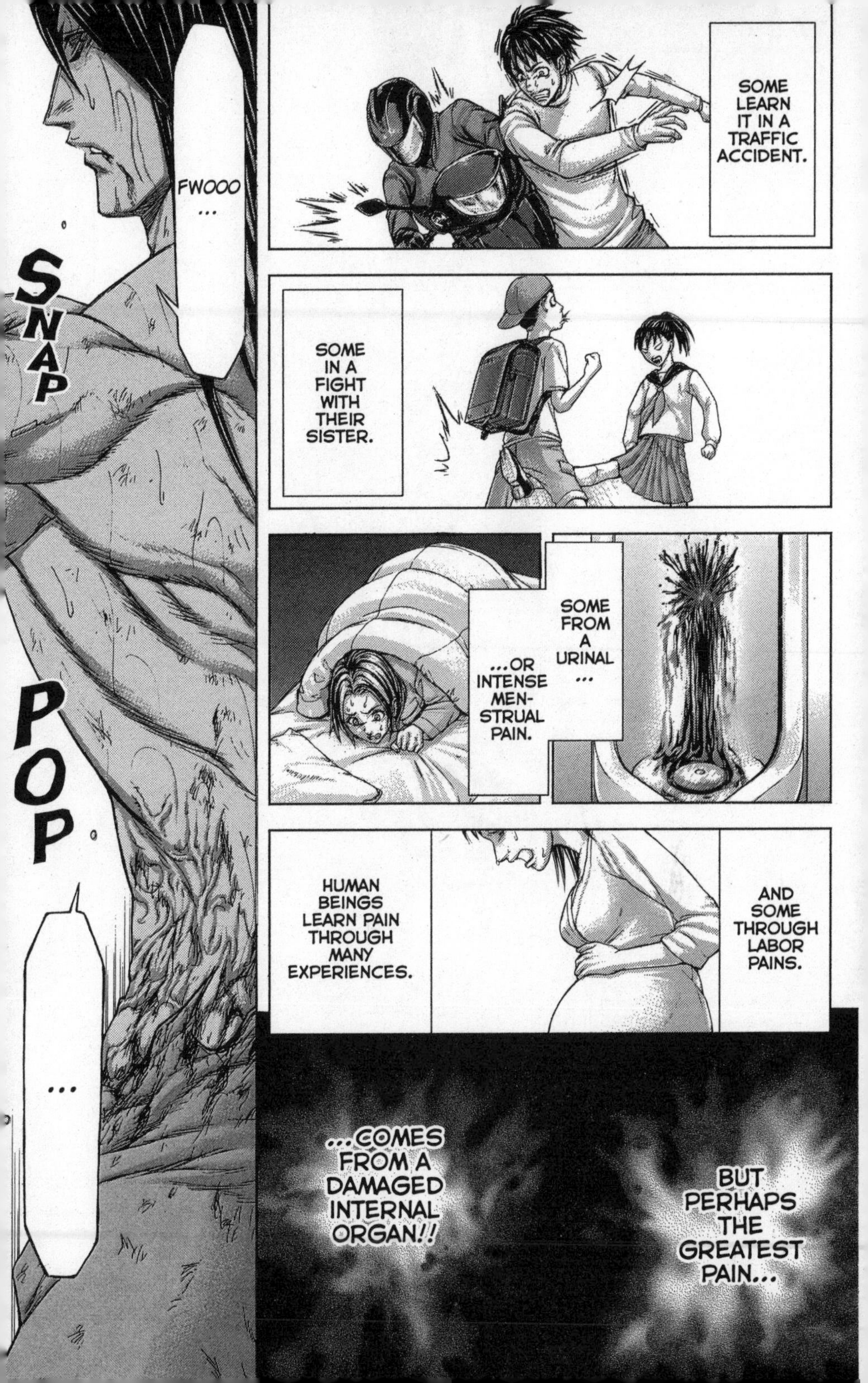
SOME LEARN IT IN A TRAFFIC ACCIDENT.
SOME IN A FIGHT WITH THEIR SISTER.
SOME FROM A URINAL...
...OR INTENSE MEN-STRUAL PAIN.
AND SOME THROUGH LABOR PAINS.
HUMAN BEINGS LEARN PAIN THROUGH MANY EXPERIENCES.
BUT PERHAPS THE GREATEST PAIN...
...COMES FROM A DAMAGED INTERNAL ORGAN!!
FWOOO...
SNAP
POP
...

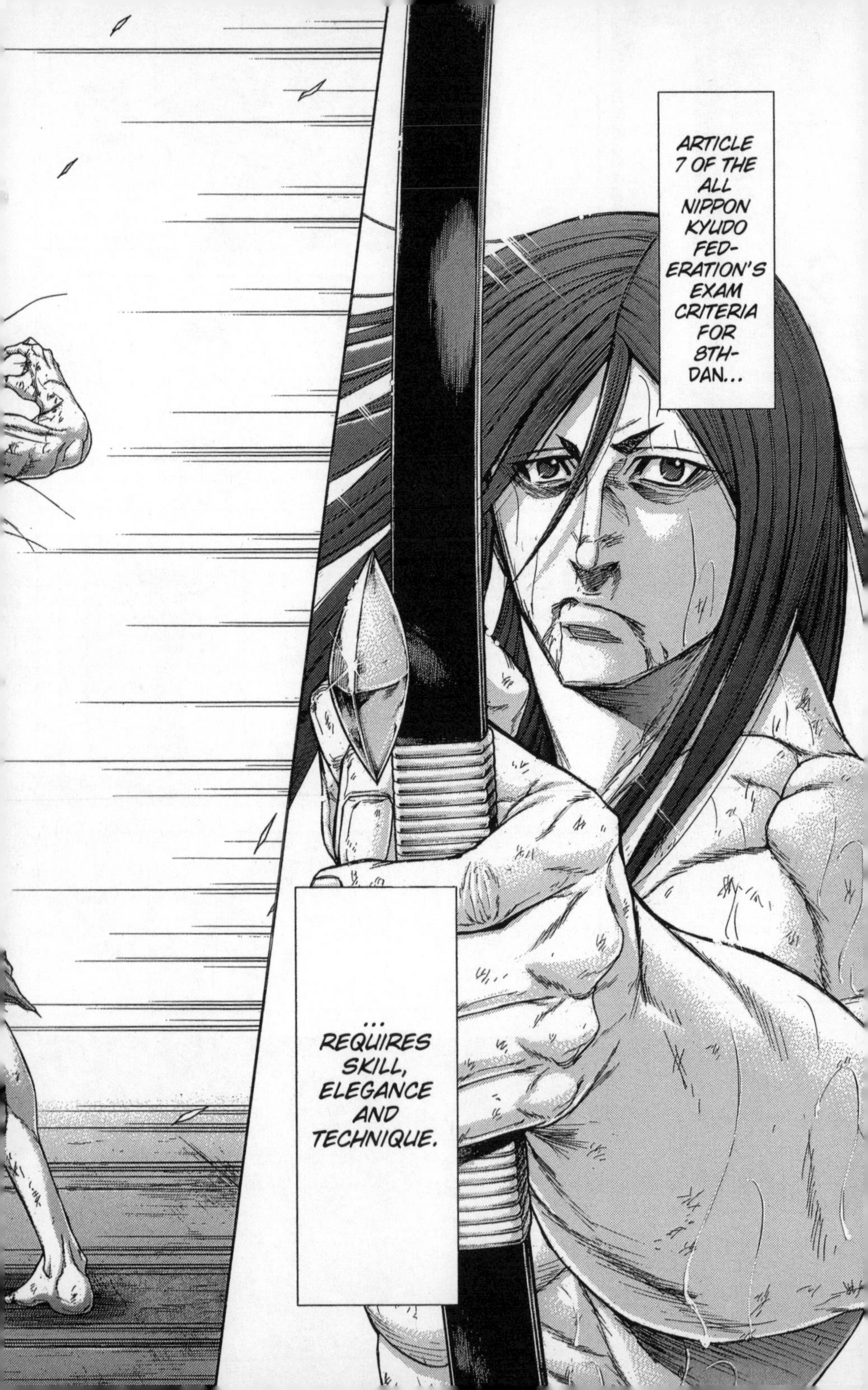
ARTICLE 7 OF THE ALL NIPPON KYUDO FED-ERATION'S EXAM CRITERIA FOR 8TH-DAN...
...REQUIRES SKILL, ELEGANCE AND TECHNIQUE.

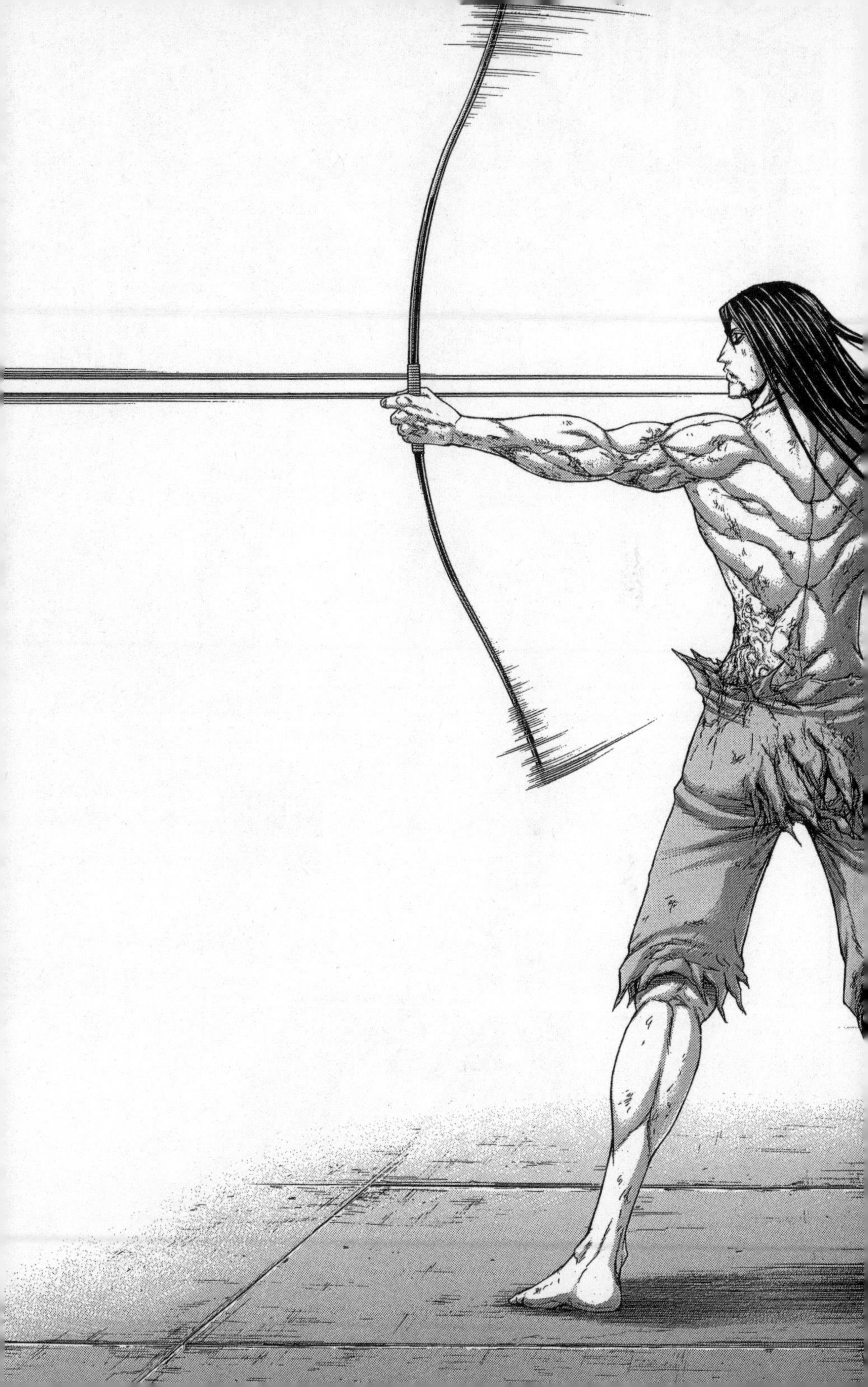

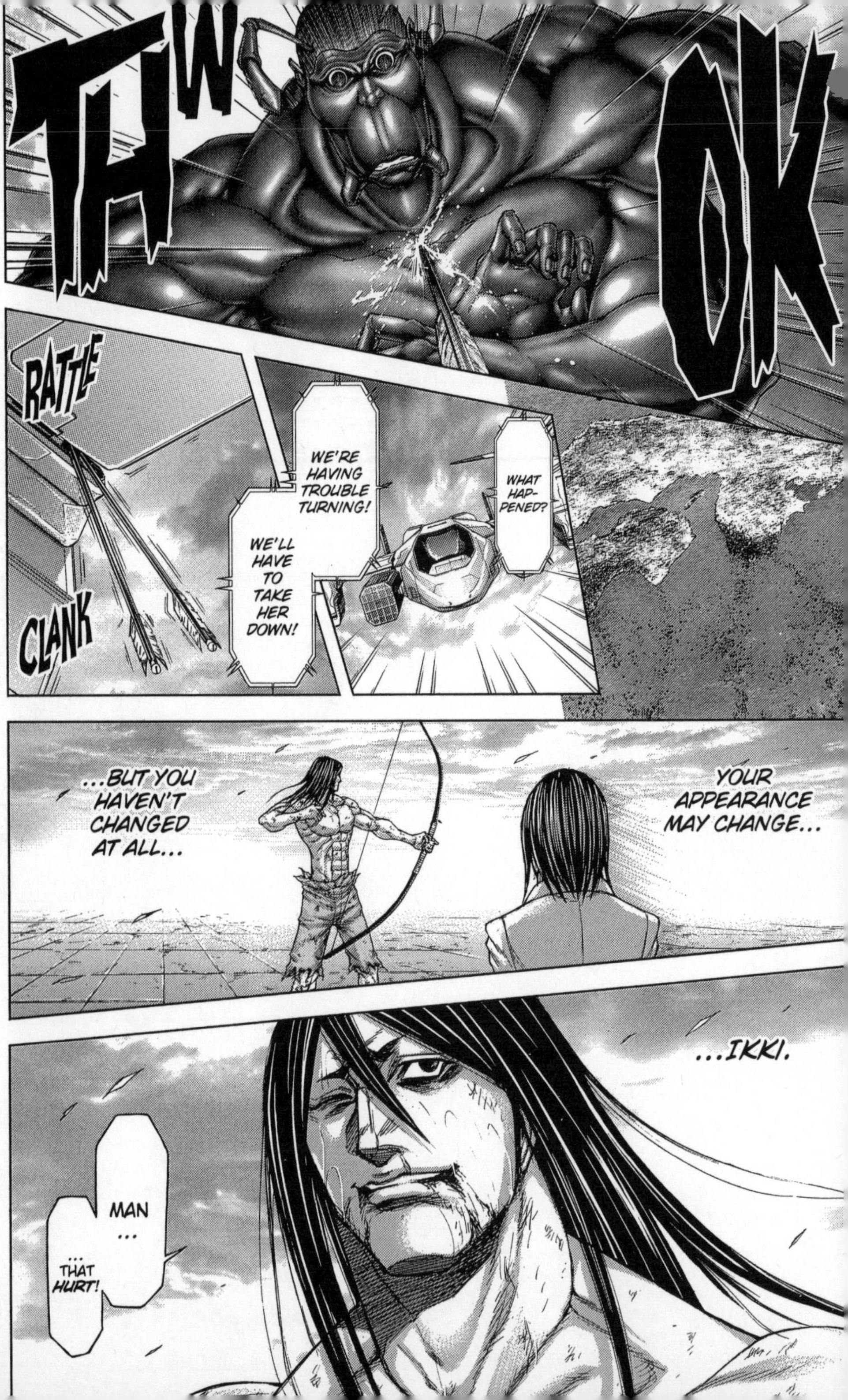
THWOK
WHAT HAPPENED?
WE'RE HAVING TROUBLE TURNING!
WE'LL HAVE TO TAKE HER DOWN!
RATTLE
CLANK
YOUR APPEARANCE MAY CHANGE...
...BUT YOU HAVEN'T CHANGED AT ALL...
...IKKI.
MAN ...
... THAT HURT!

Two Surprisingly (?) Close Coworkers

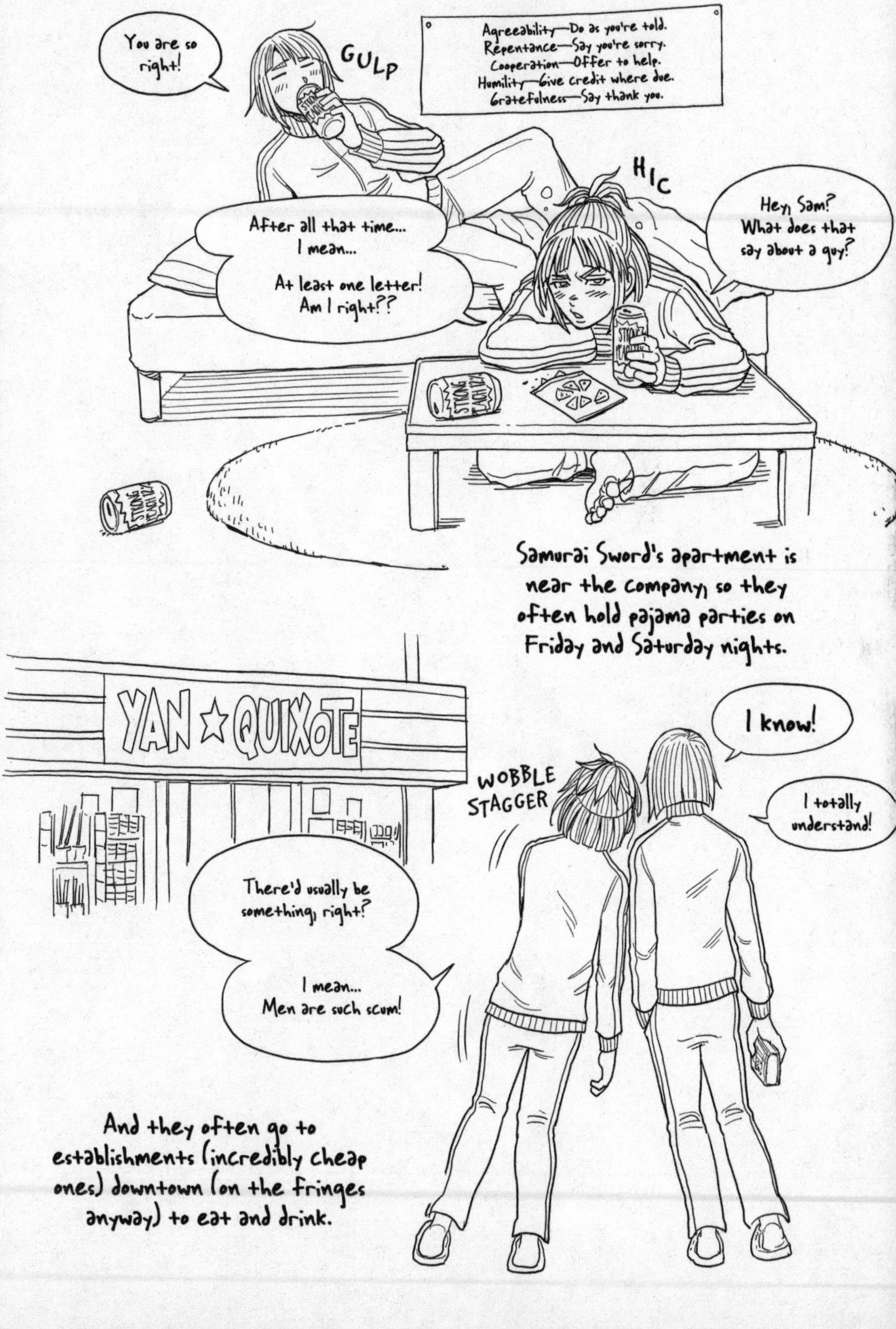
Agreeability—Do as you're told.
Repentance—Say you're sorry.
Cooperation—Offer to help.
Humility—Give credit where due.
Gratefulness—Say thank you.
Hey, Sam? What does that say about a guy?
HIC
After all that time... I mean... At least one letter! Am I right??
You are so right!
GULP
STRONG PEACH 12%
Samurai Sword's apartment is near the company, so they often hold pajama parties on Friday and Saturday nights.
I know!
I totally understand!
WOBBLE STAGGER
There'd usually be something, right? I mean... Men are such scum!
YAN ☆ QUIXOTE
And they often go to establishments (incredibly cheap ones) downtown (on the fringes anyway) to eat and drink.

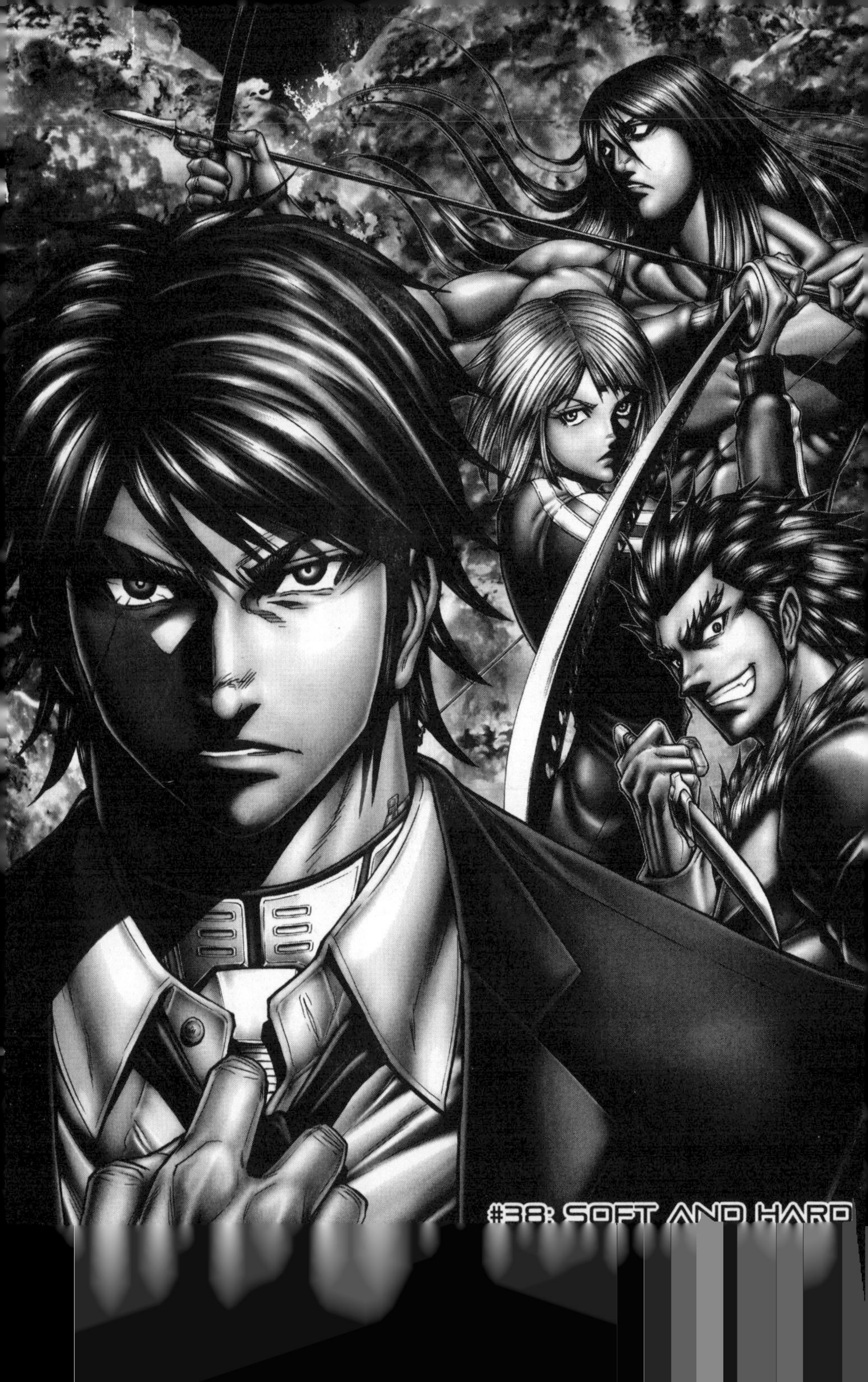
#38: SOFT AND HARD

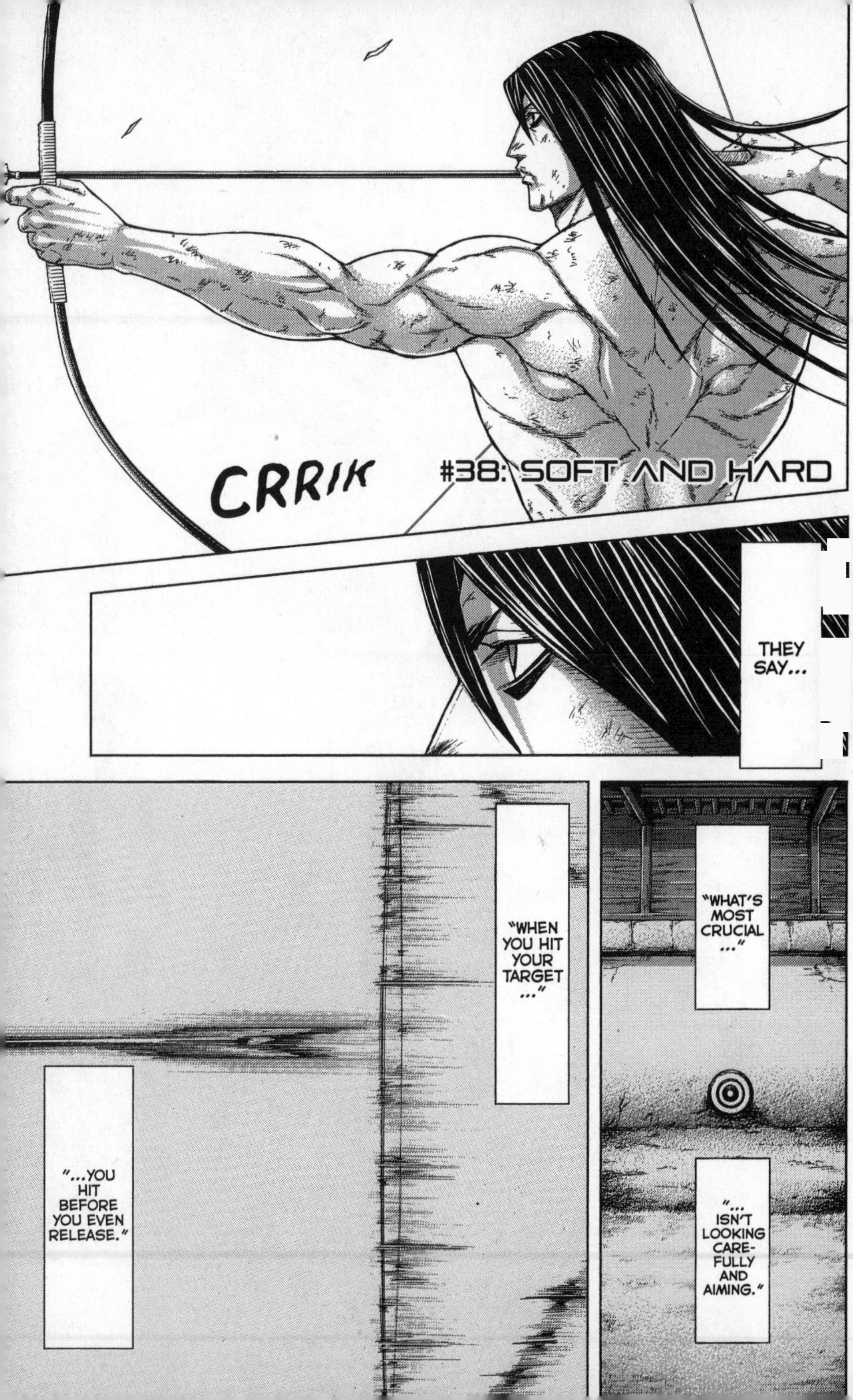
#38: SOFT AND HARD
CRRIK
THEY SAY...
"WHAT'S MOST CRUCIAL..."
"...ISN'T LOOKING CARE-FULLY AND AIMING."
"WHEN YOU HIT YOUR TARGET..."
"...YOU HIT BEFORE YOU EVEN RELEASE."

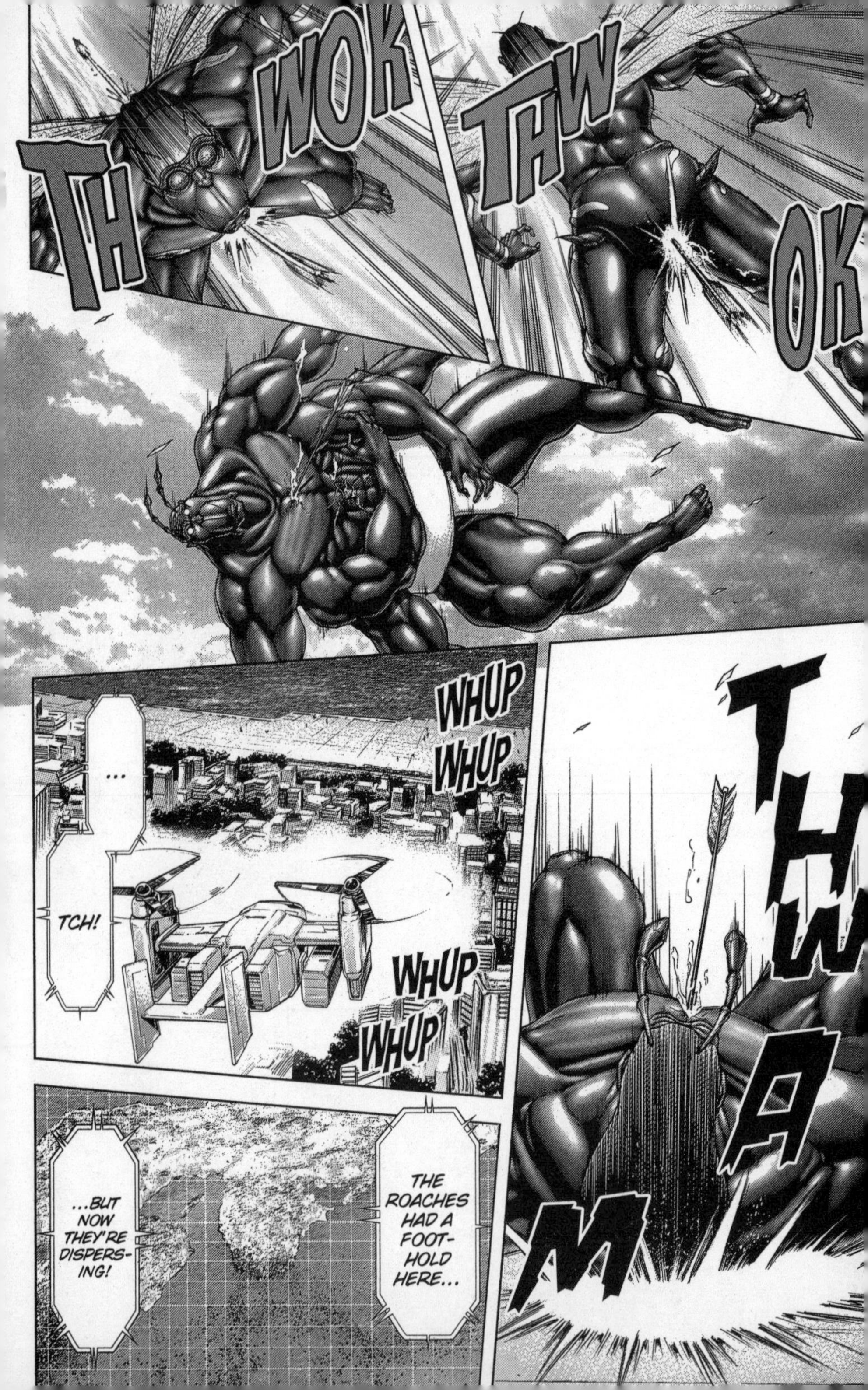
THW
OK
TH
WOK
THWAM
WHUP WHUP
...
TCH!
WHUP WHUP
THE ROACHES HAD A FOOTHOLD HERE...
...BUT NOW THEY'RE DISPERSING!

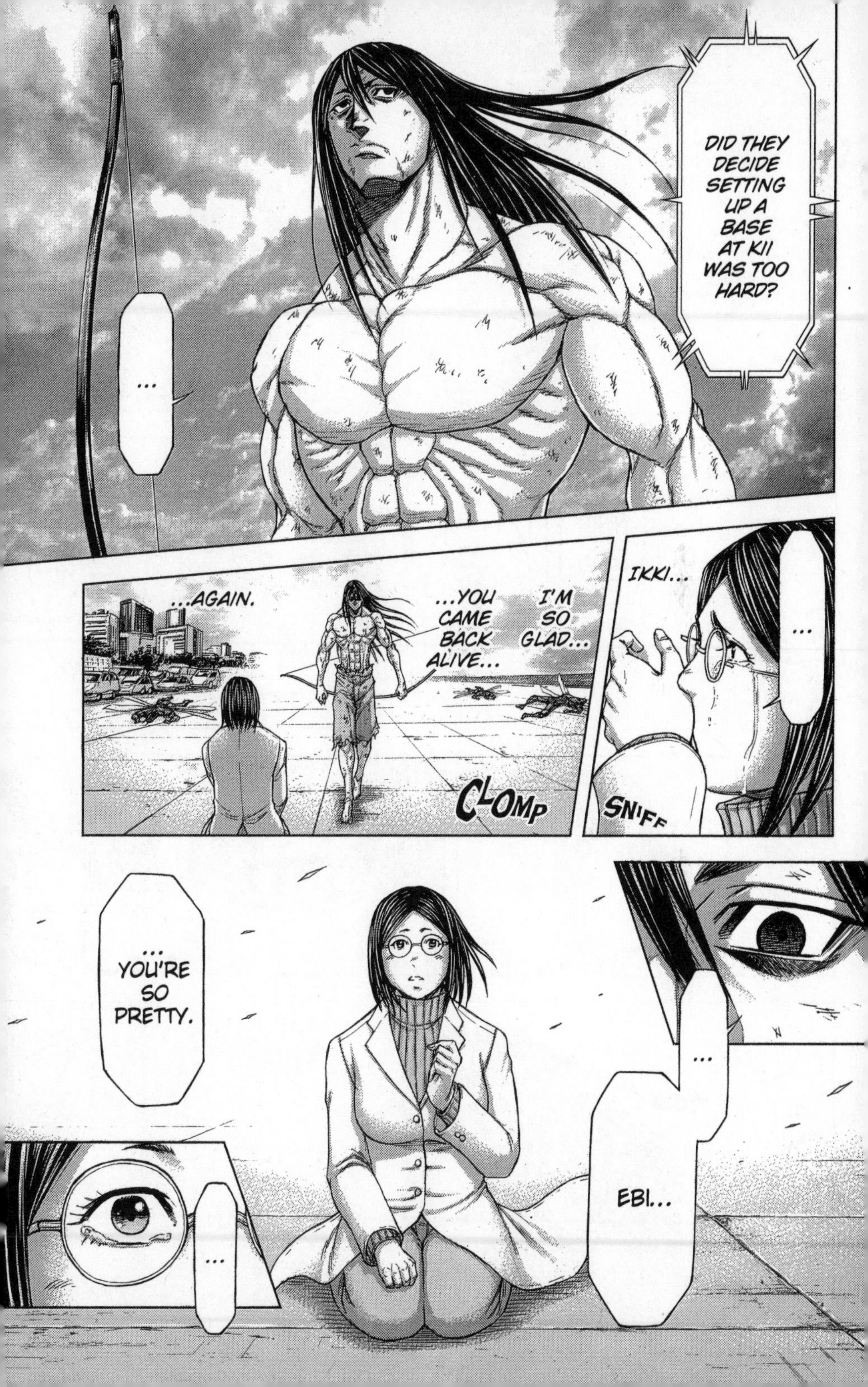

DID THEY DECIDE SETTING UP A BASE AT KII WAS TOO HARD?
...
IKKI...
...
SNIFF
I'M SO GLAD...
...YOU CAME BACK ALIVE...
...AGAIN.
CLOMP
...
EBI...
... YOU'RE SO PRETTY.
...

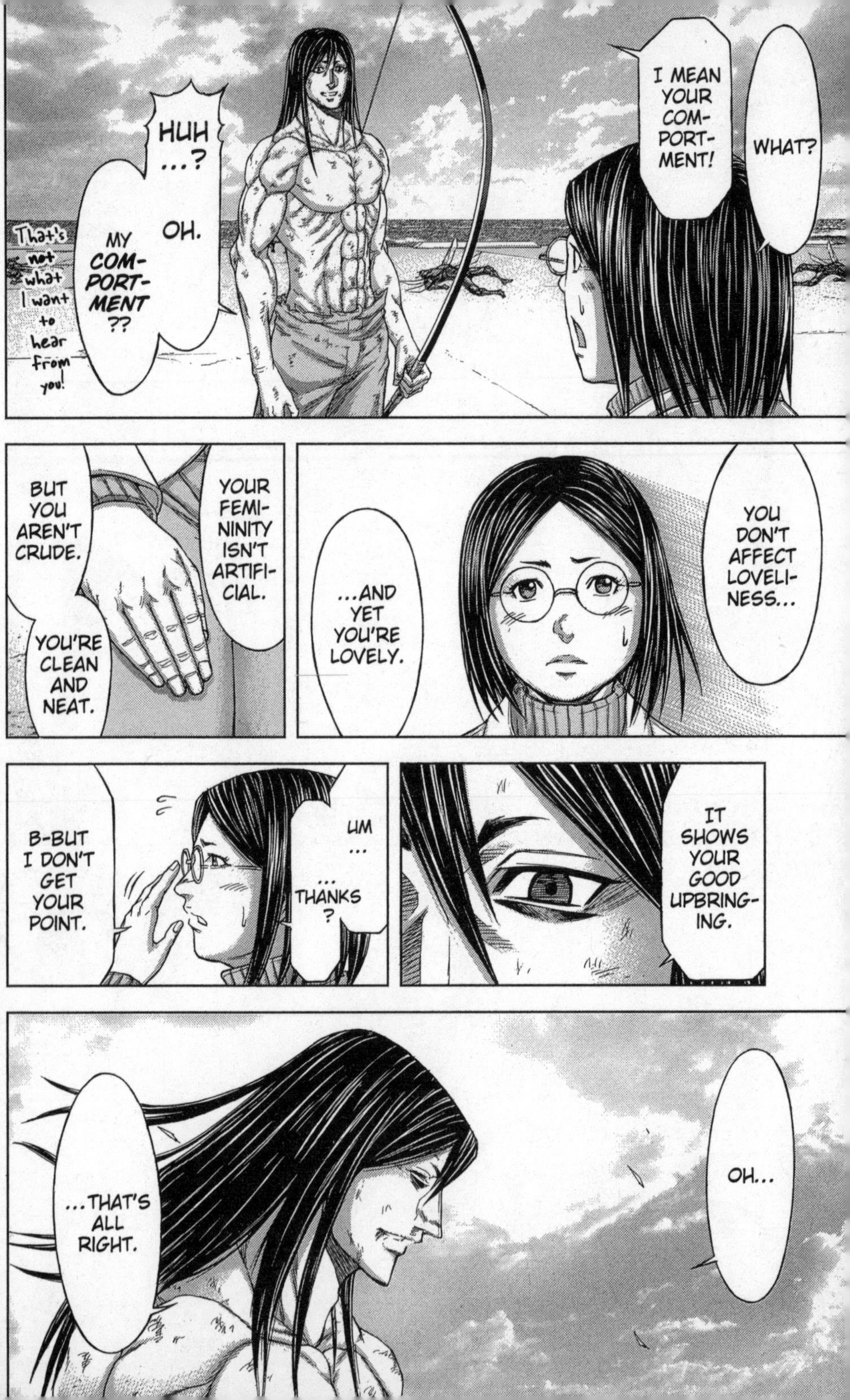
WHAT?
I MEAN YOUR COMPORTMENT!
HUH...? OH.
MY COMPORTMENT??
That's not what I want to hear from you!
YOU DON'T AFFECT LOVELINESS...
...AND YET YOU'RE LOVELY.
YOUR FEMININITY ISN'T ARTIFICIAL.
BUT YOU AREN'T CRUDE.
YOU'RE CLEAN AND NEAT.
IT SHOWS YOUR GOOD UPBRINGING.
UM... ...THANKS?
B-BUT I DON'T GET YOUR POINT.
OH...
...THAT'S ALL RIGHT.

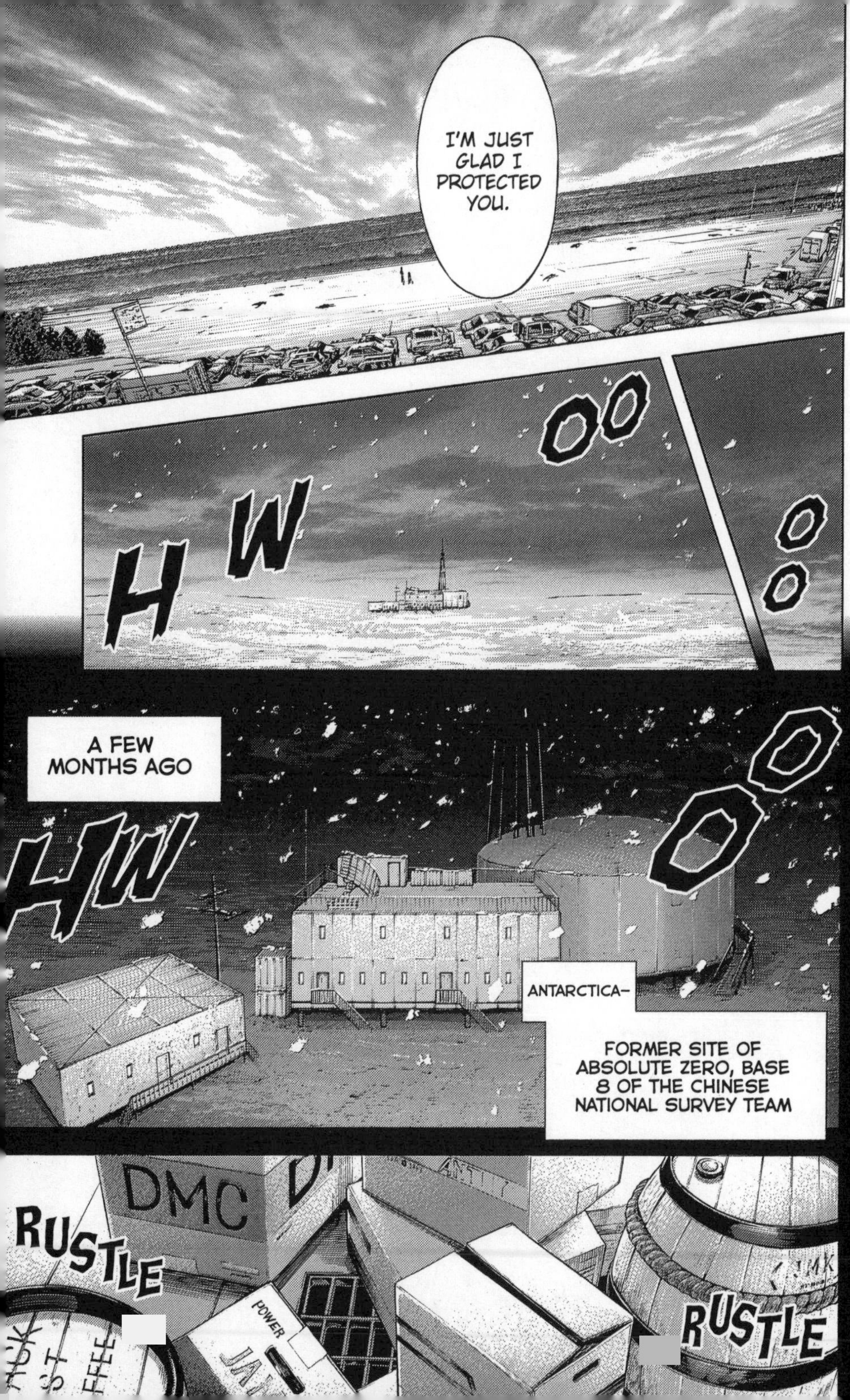
I'M JUST GLAD I PROTECTED YOU.
HWOOO
A FEW MONTHS AGO
HWOOO
ANTARCTICA—
FORMER SITE OF ABSOLUTE ZERO, BASE 8 OF THE CHINESE NATIONAL SURVEY TEAM
RUSTLE
DMC
POWER
RUSTLE

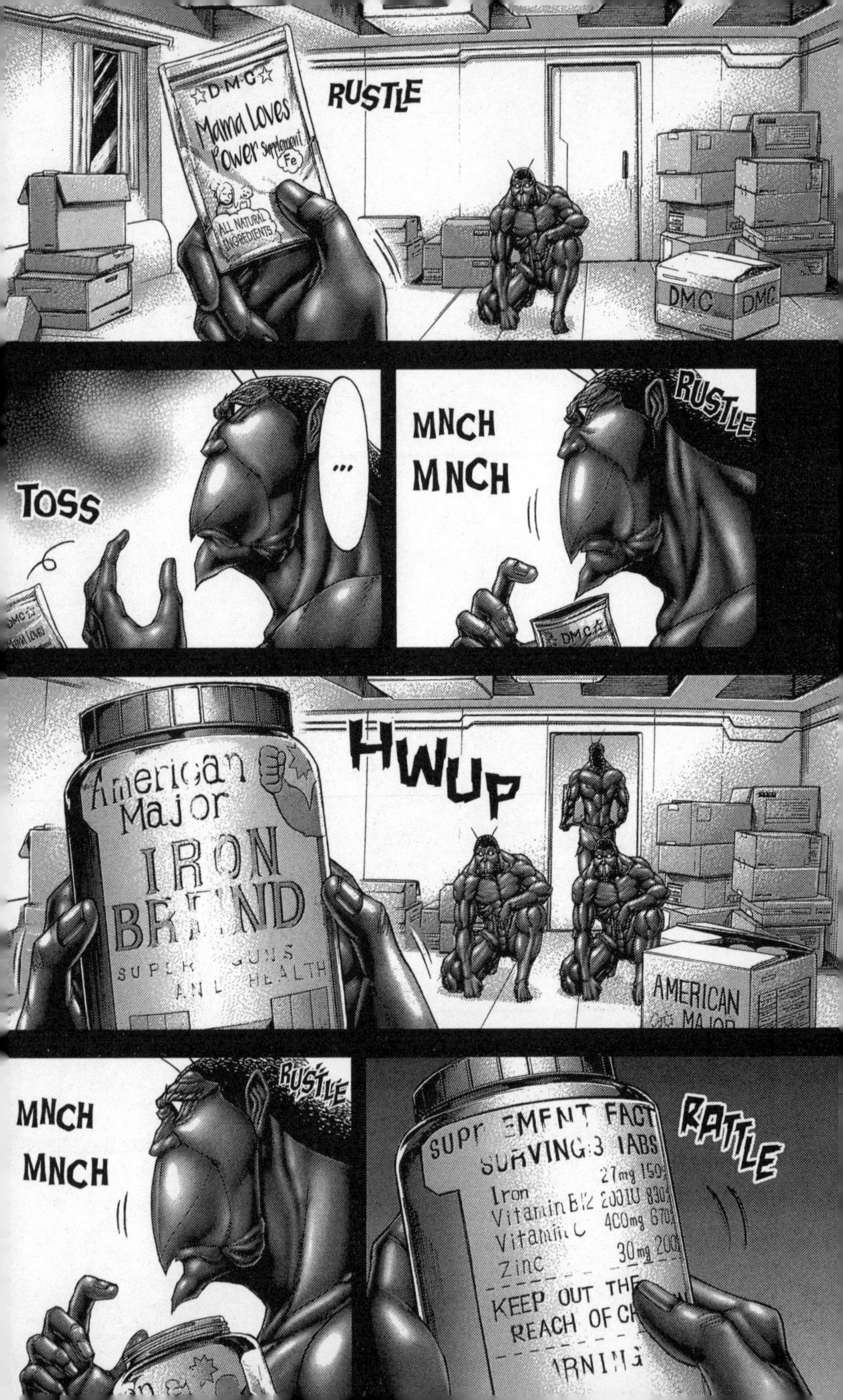

☆DMC☆
Mama Loves Power
Supplement
Fe
ALL NATURAL INGREDIENTS
RUSTLE
DMC
DMC
RUSTLE
MNCH
MNCH
DMC
...
TOSS
DMC
Mama Loves
HWUP
American Major
IRON
AMERICAN
RATTLE
Iron
27mg
Zinc
30mg
KEEP OUT THE
REACH OF C
RUSTLE
MNCH
MNCH

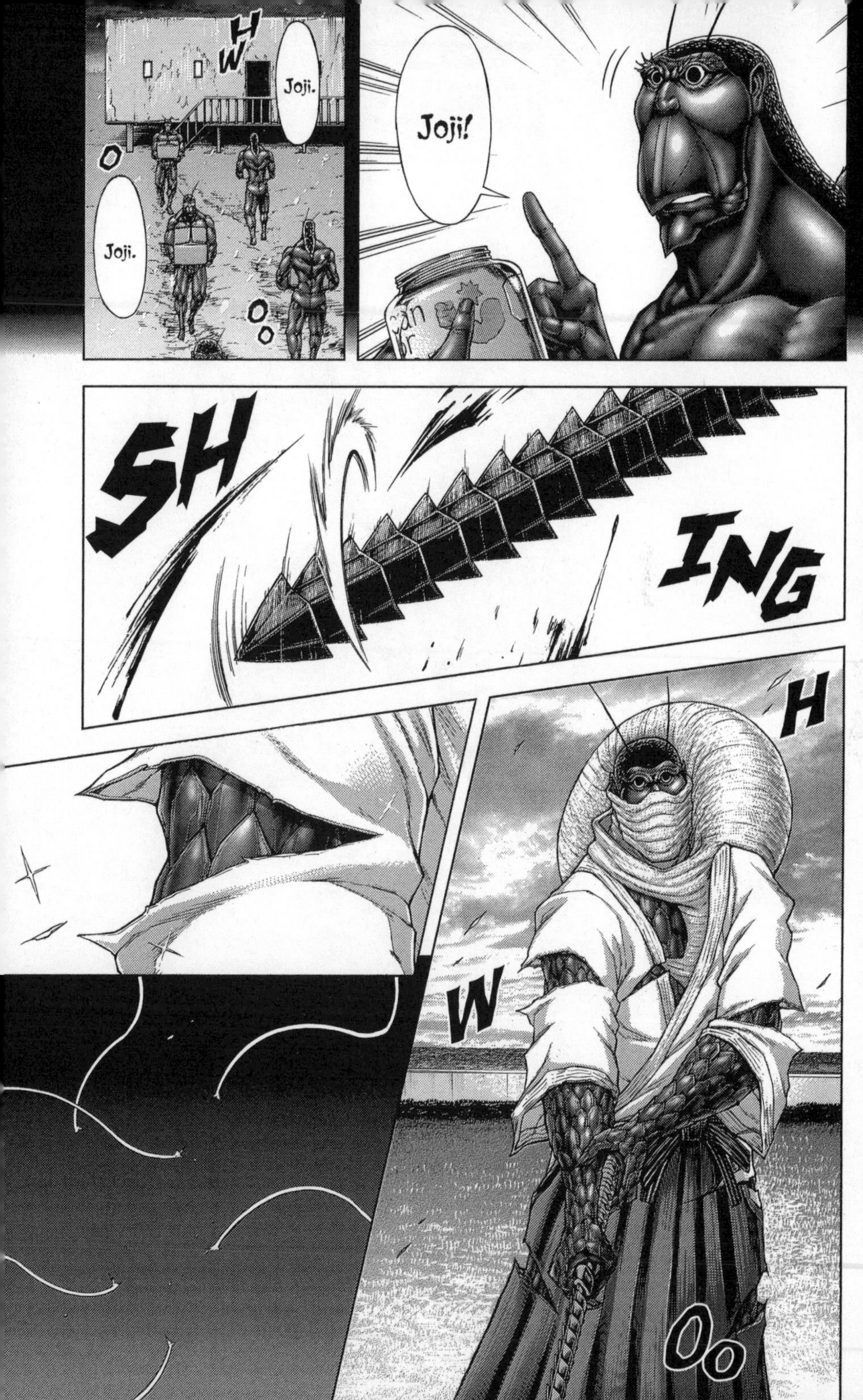
Joji!
Joji.
WH
Joji.
O
O
O
SH
ING
H
W
OO

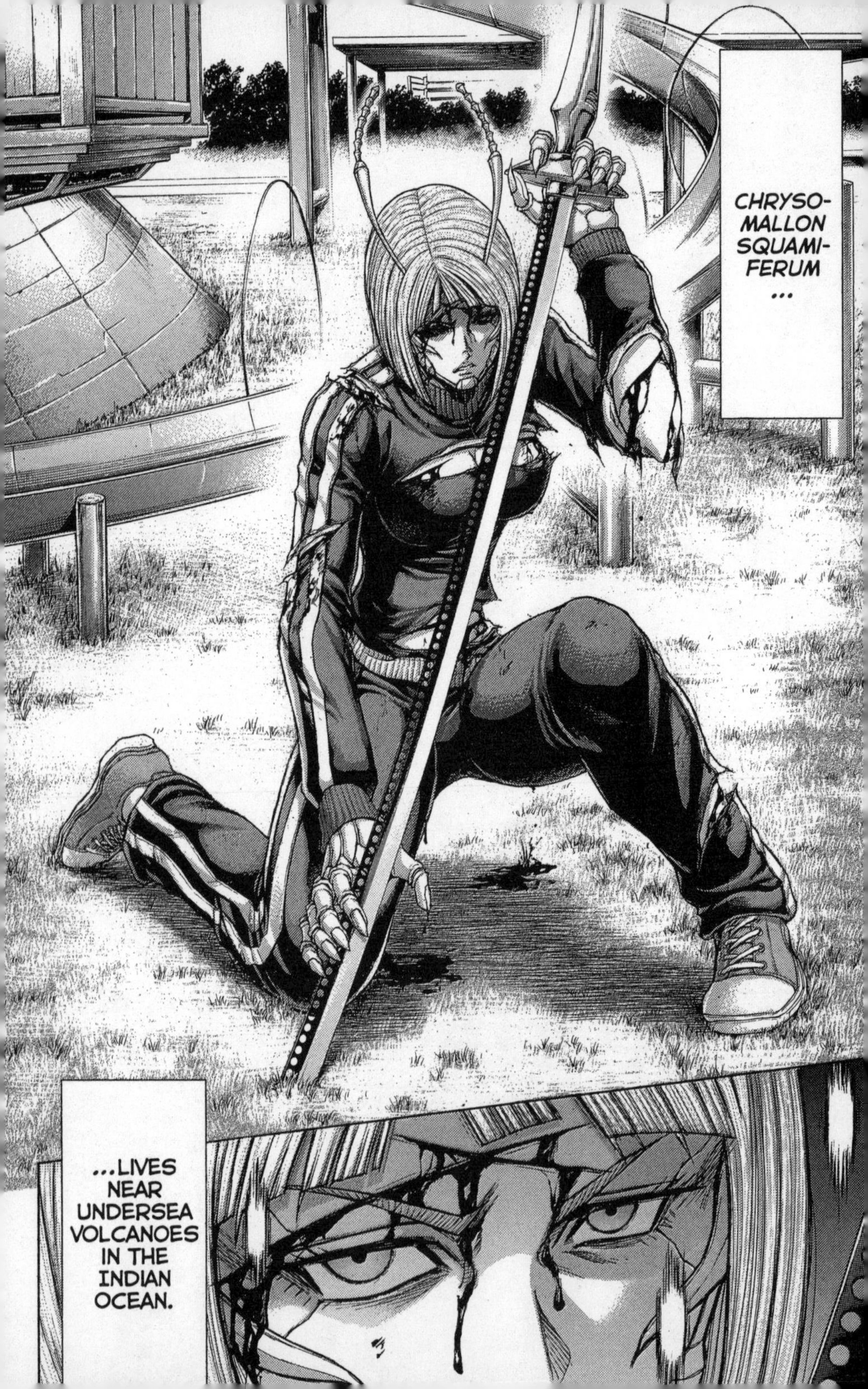
CHRYSO-
MALLON
SQUAMI-
FERUM
...
...LIVES
NEAR
UNDERSEA
VOLCANOES
IN THE
INDIAN
OCEAN.

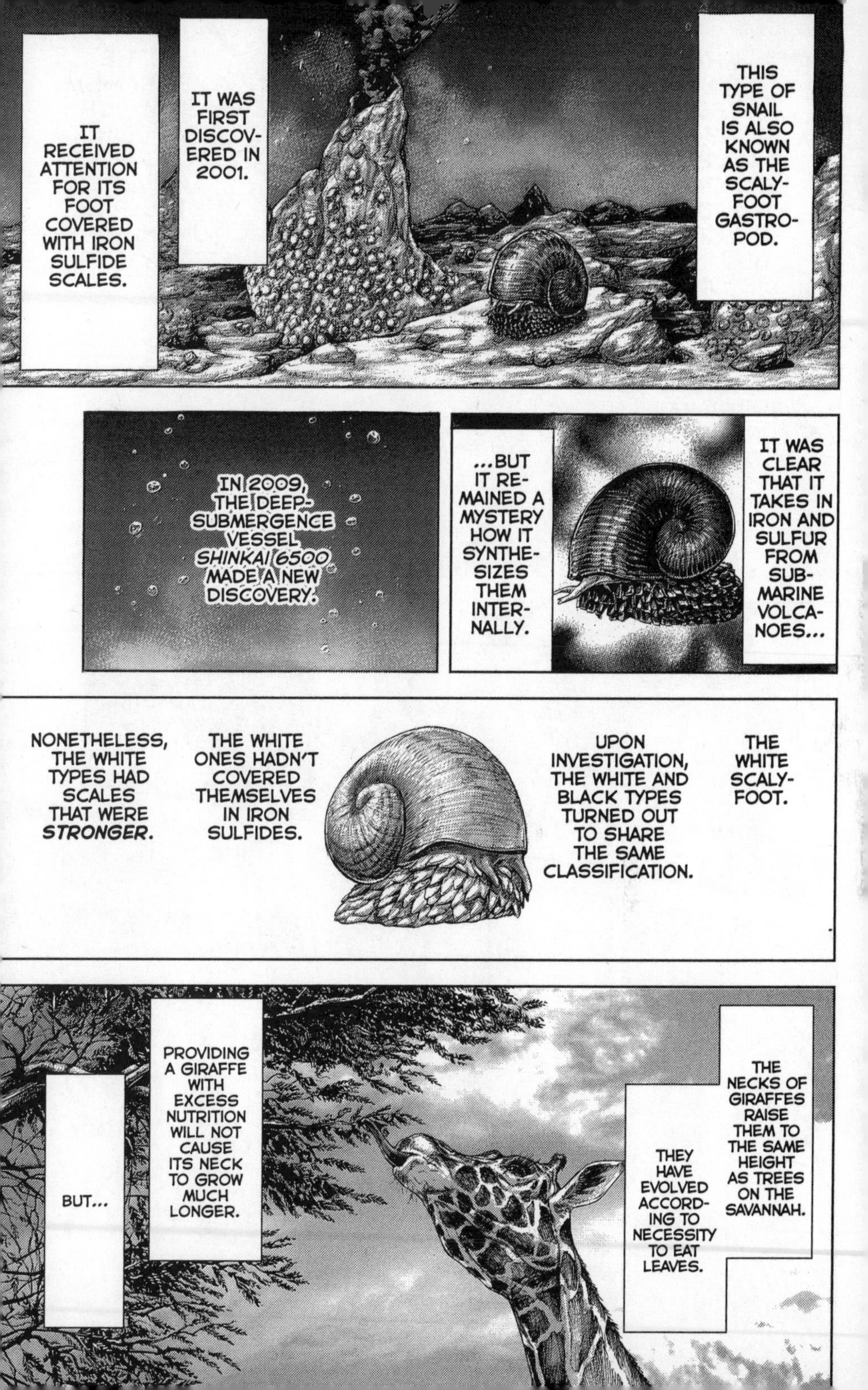
THIS TYPE OF SNAIL IS ALSO KNOWN AS THE SCALY-FOOT GASTROPOD.
IT WAS FIRST DISCOVERED IN 2001.
IT RECEIVED ATTENTION FOR ITS FOOT COVERED WITH IRON SULFIDE SCALES.
IT WAS CLEAR THAT IT TAKES IN IRON AND SULFUR FROM SUBMARINE VOLCANOES...
...BUT IT REMAINED A MYSTERY HOW IT SYNTHESIZES THEM INTERNALLY.
IN 2009, THE DEEP-SUBMERGENCE VESSEL *SHINKAI 6500* MADE A NEW DISCOVERY.
THE WHITE SCALY-FOOT.
UPON INVESTIGATION, THE WHITE AND BLACK TYPES TURNED OUT TO SHARE THE SAME CLASSIFICATION.
THE WHITE ONES HADN'T COVERED THEMSELVES IN IRON SULFIDES.
NONETHELESS, THE WHITE TYPES HAD SCALES THAT WERE ***STRONGER***.
THE NECKS OF GIRAFFES RAISE THEM TO THE SAME HEIGHT AS TREES ON THE SAVANNAH.
THEY HAVE EVOLVED ACCORDING TO NECESSITY TO EAT LEAVES.
PROVIDING A GIRAFFE WITH EXCESS NUTRITION WILL NOT CAUSE ITS NECK TO GROW MUCH LONGER.
BUT...

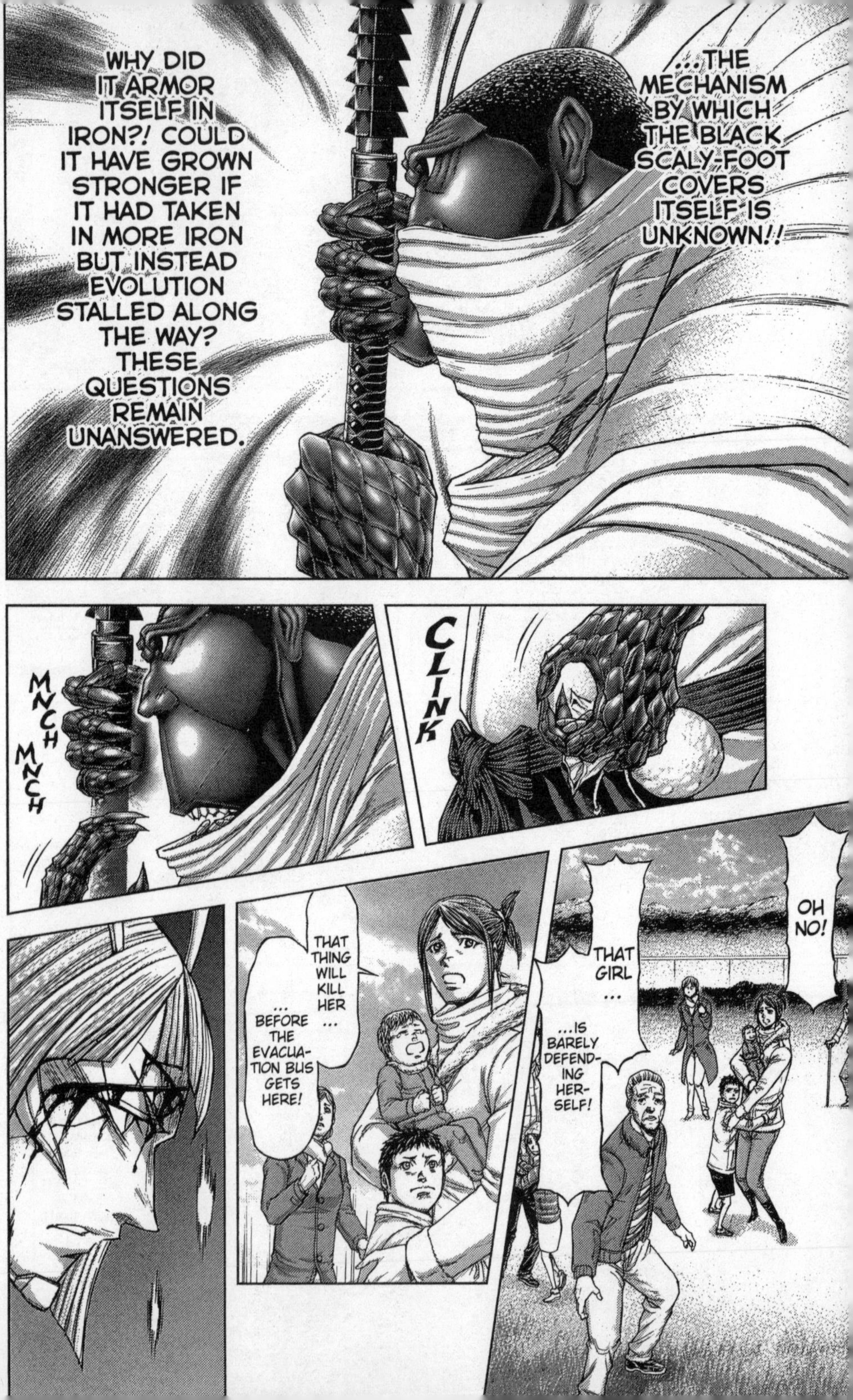
...THE MECHANISM BY WHICH THE BLACK SCALY-FOOT COVERS ITSELF IS UNKNOWN!!
WHY DID IT ARMOR ITSELF IN IRON?! COULD IT HAVE GROWN STRONGER IF IT HAD TAKEN IN MORE IRON BUT INSTEAD EVOLUTION STALLED ALONG THE WAY? THESE QUESTIONS REMAIN UNANSWERED.
CLINK
MNCH MNCH
OH NO!
THAT GIRL...
...IS BARELY DEFENDING HERSELF!
THAT THING WILL KILL HER...
...BEFORE THE EVACUATION BUS GETS HERE!

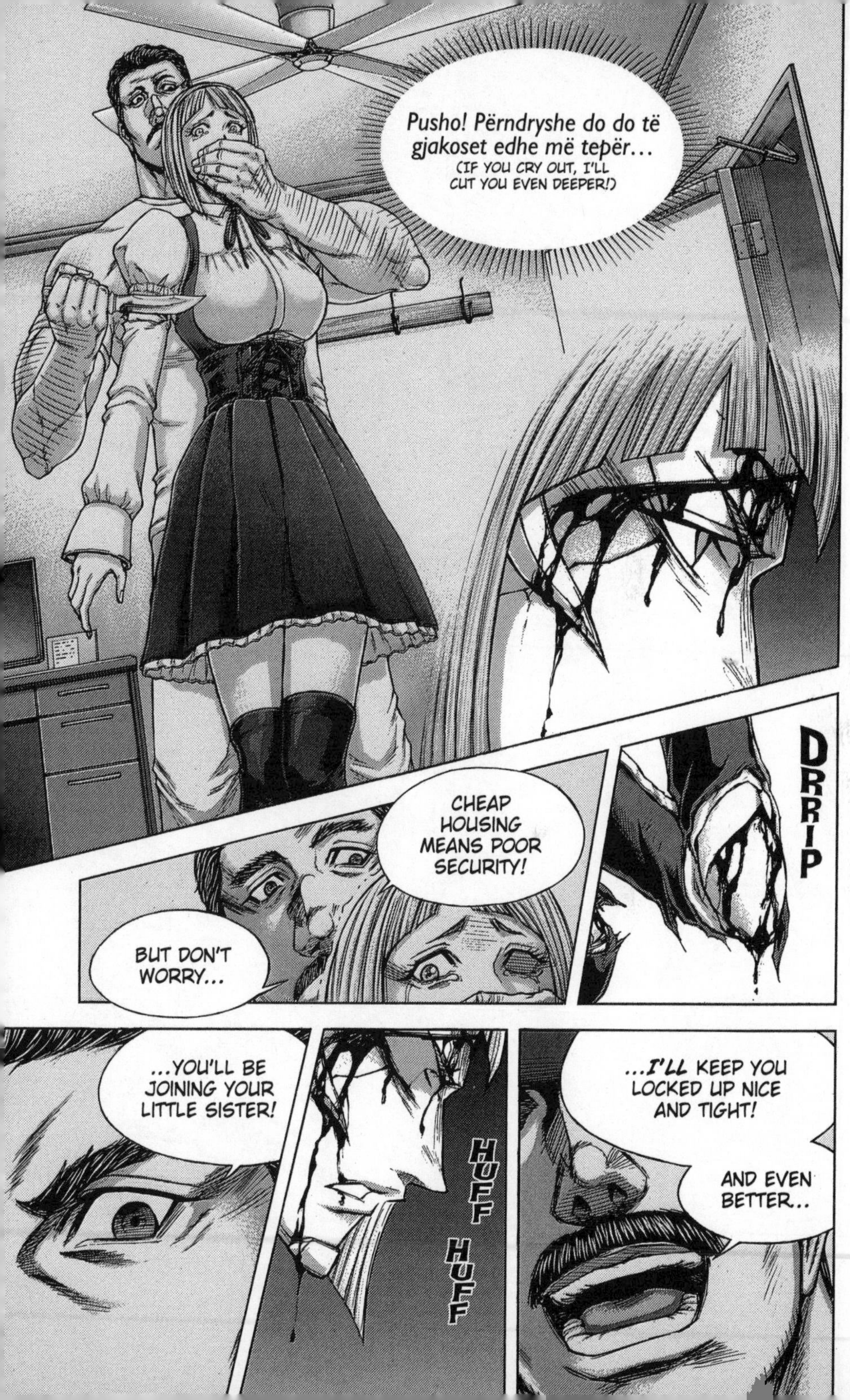
Pusho! Përndryshe do do të gjakoset edhe më tepër…
(IF YOU CRY OUT, I'LL CUT YOU EVEN DEEPER!)
CHEAP HOUSING MEANS POOR SECURITY!
BUT DON'T WORRY…
DRRIP
…YOU'LL BE JOINING YOUR LITTLE SISTER!
HUFF HUFF
…I'LL KEEP YOU LOCKED UP NICE AND TIGHT!
AND EVEN BETTER..

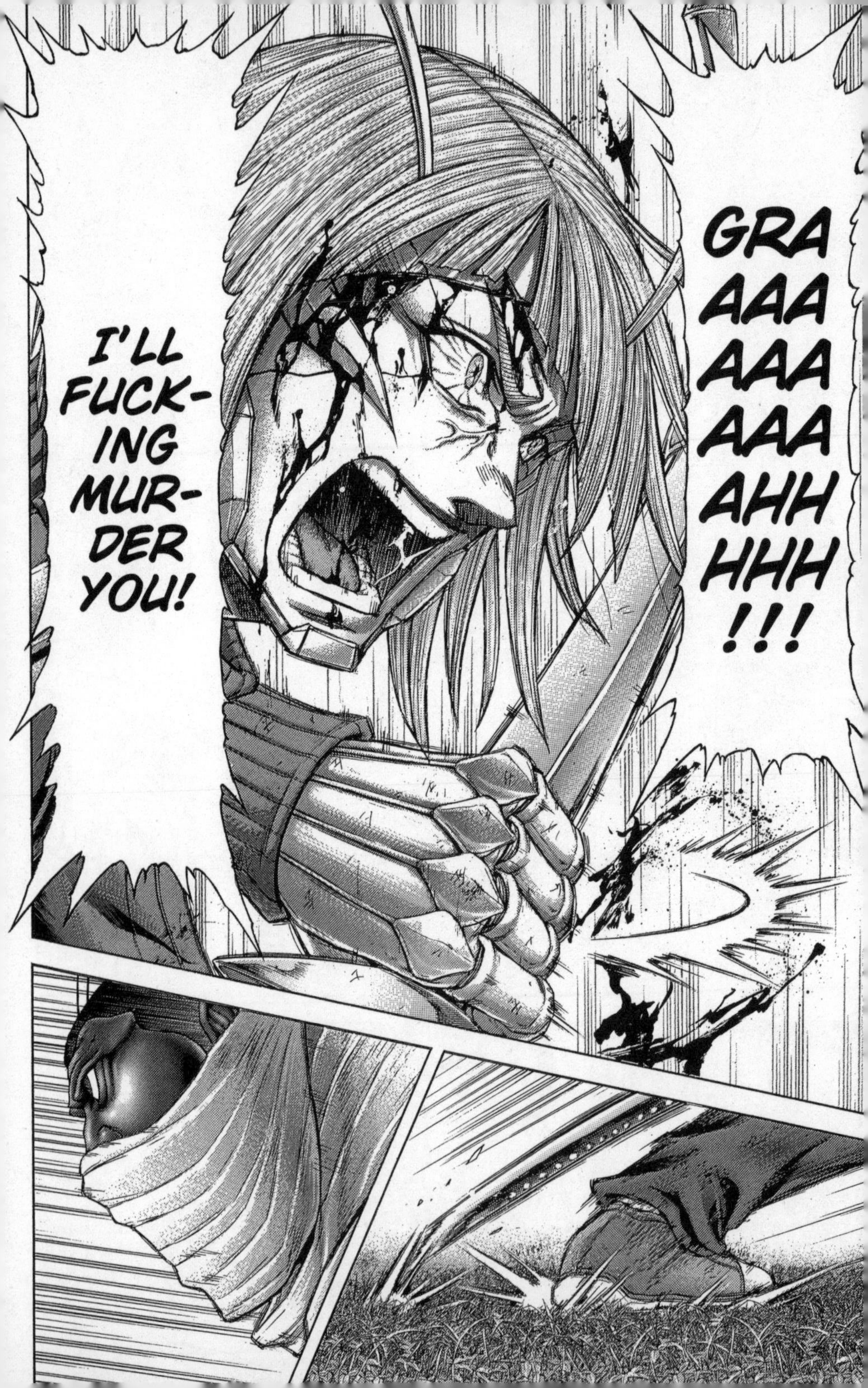
GRAAAAAAAAAAAAHHHHH!!!
I'LL FUCKING MURDER YOU!

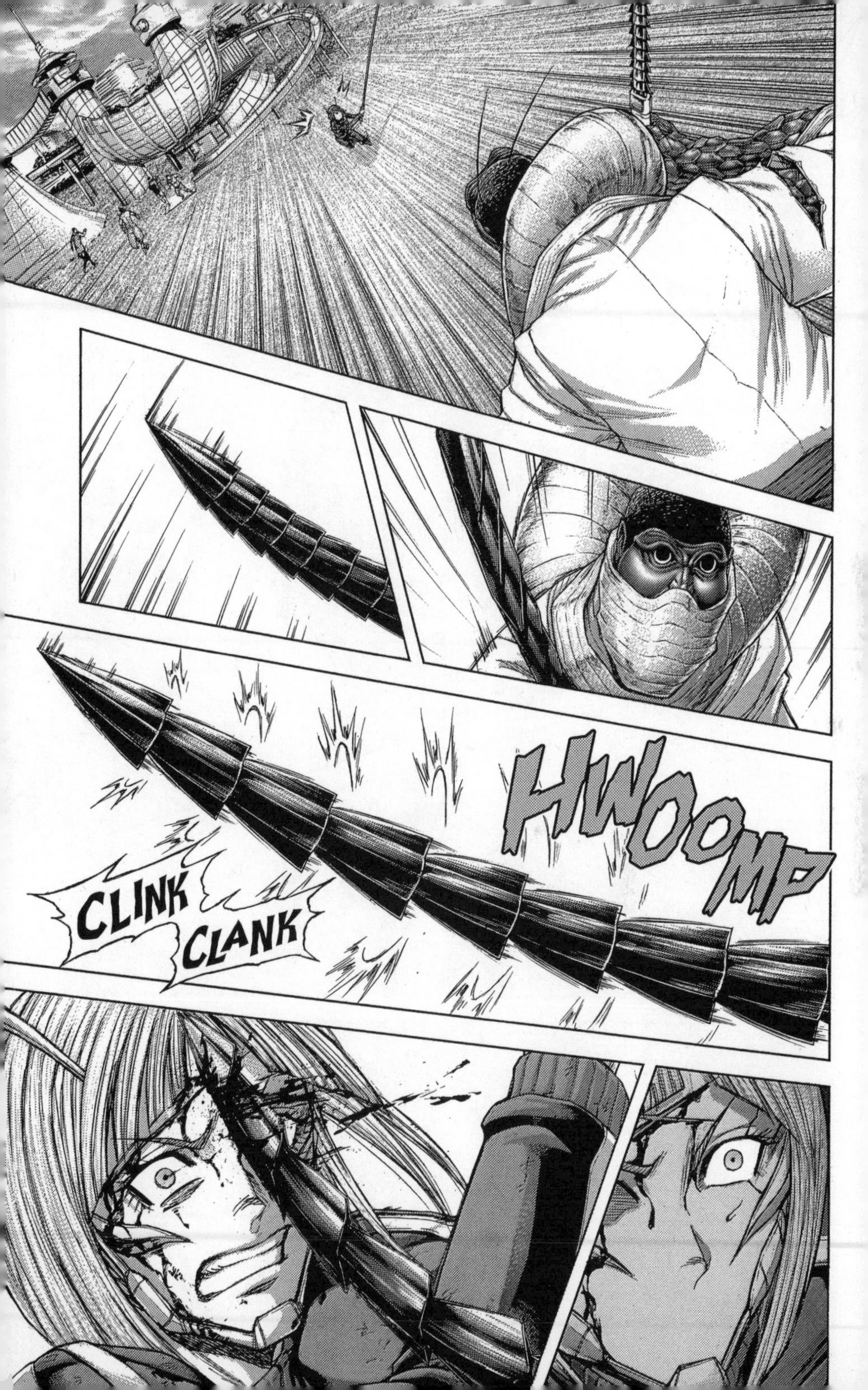
HWOOMP
CLINK
CLANK

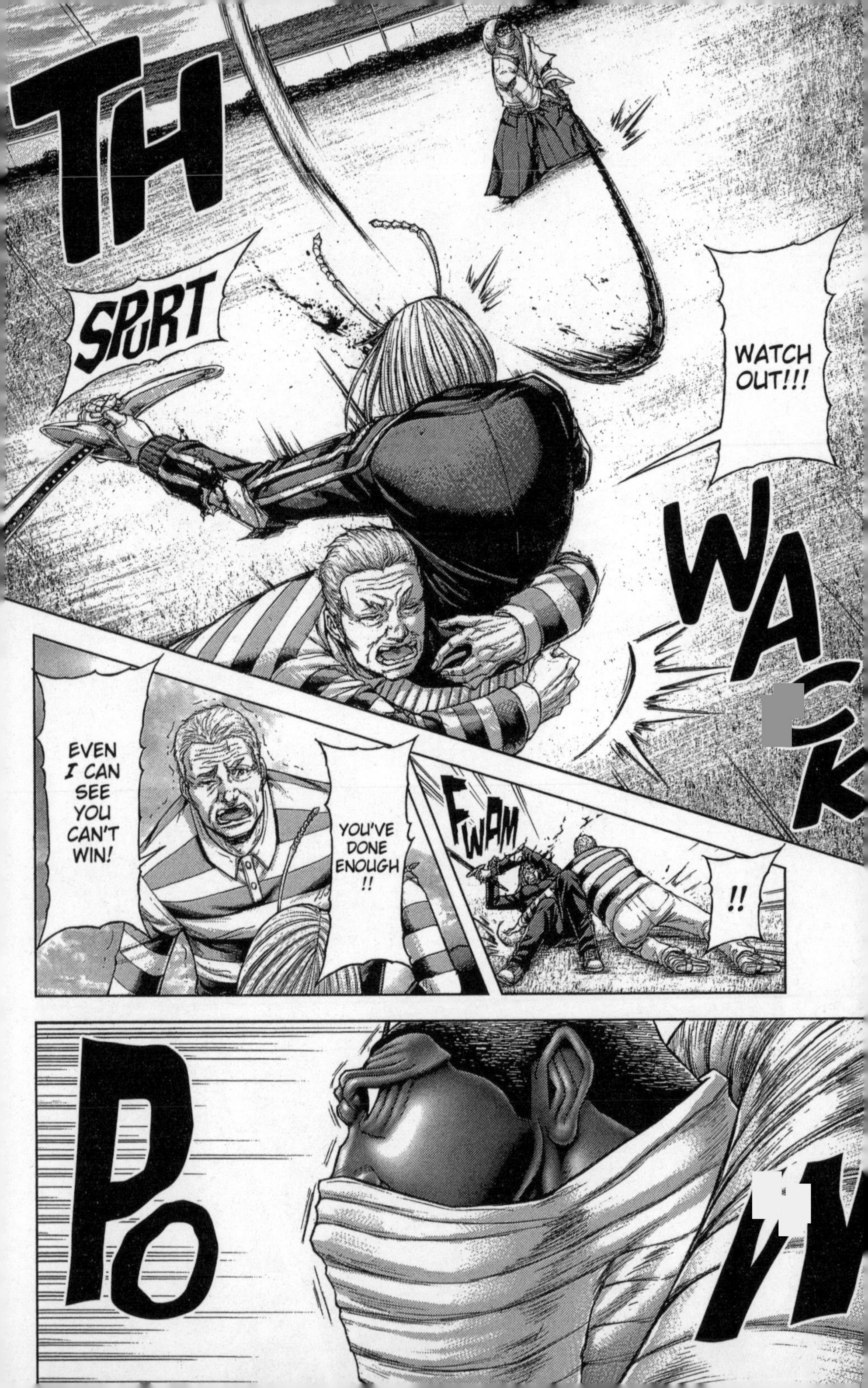
TH
SPURT
WATCH OUT!!!
WACK
FWAM
!!
YOU'VE DONE ENOUGH!!
EVEN I CAN SEE YOU CAN'T WIN!
POW

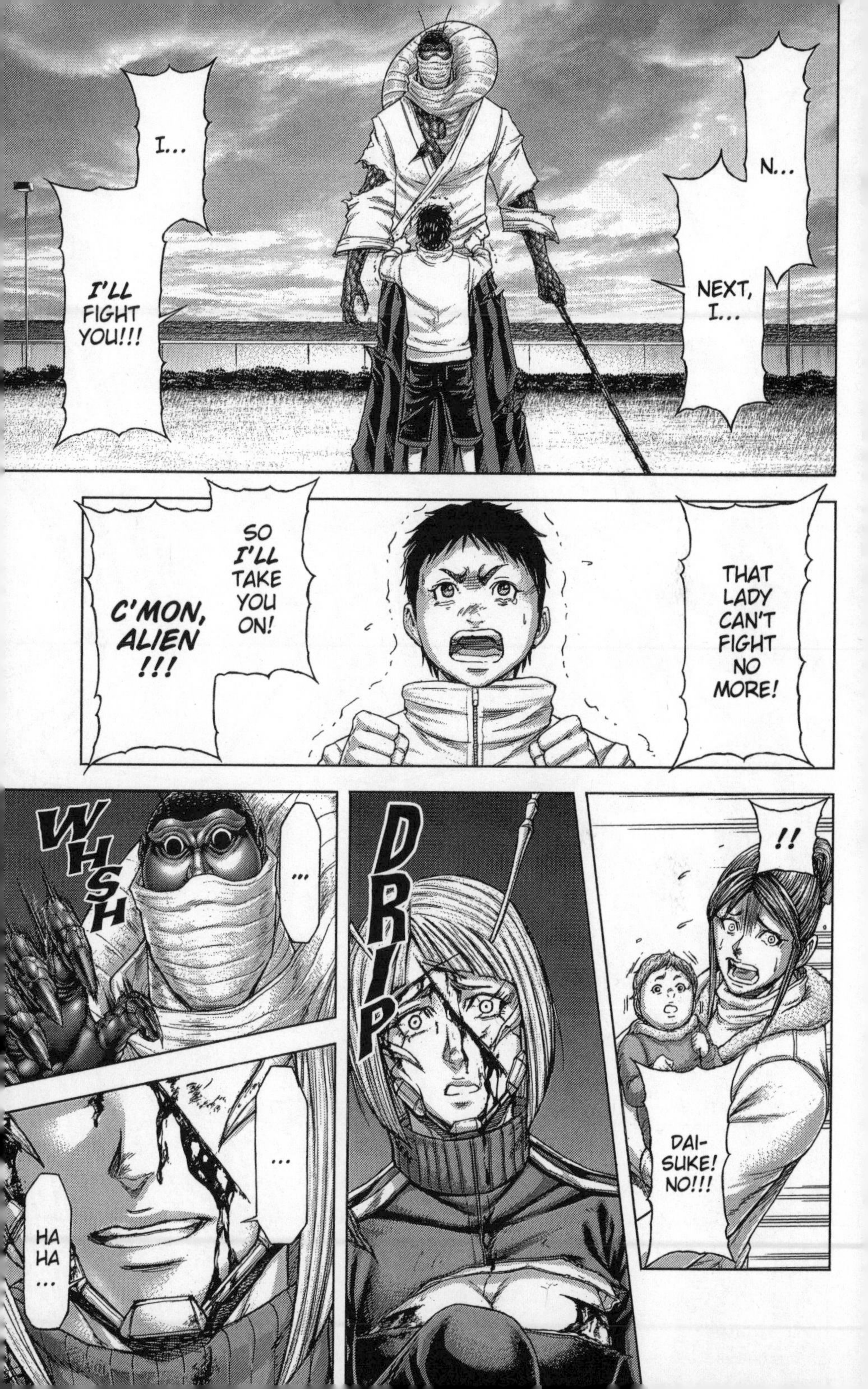
N...
NEXT, I...
I...
I'LL FIGHT YOU!!!
THAT LADY CAN'T FIGHT NO MORE!
SO I'LL TAKE YOU ON!
C'MON, ALIEN!!!
!!
DAI-SUKE! NO!!!
DRIP
WHSH
...
...
HA HA ...

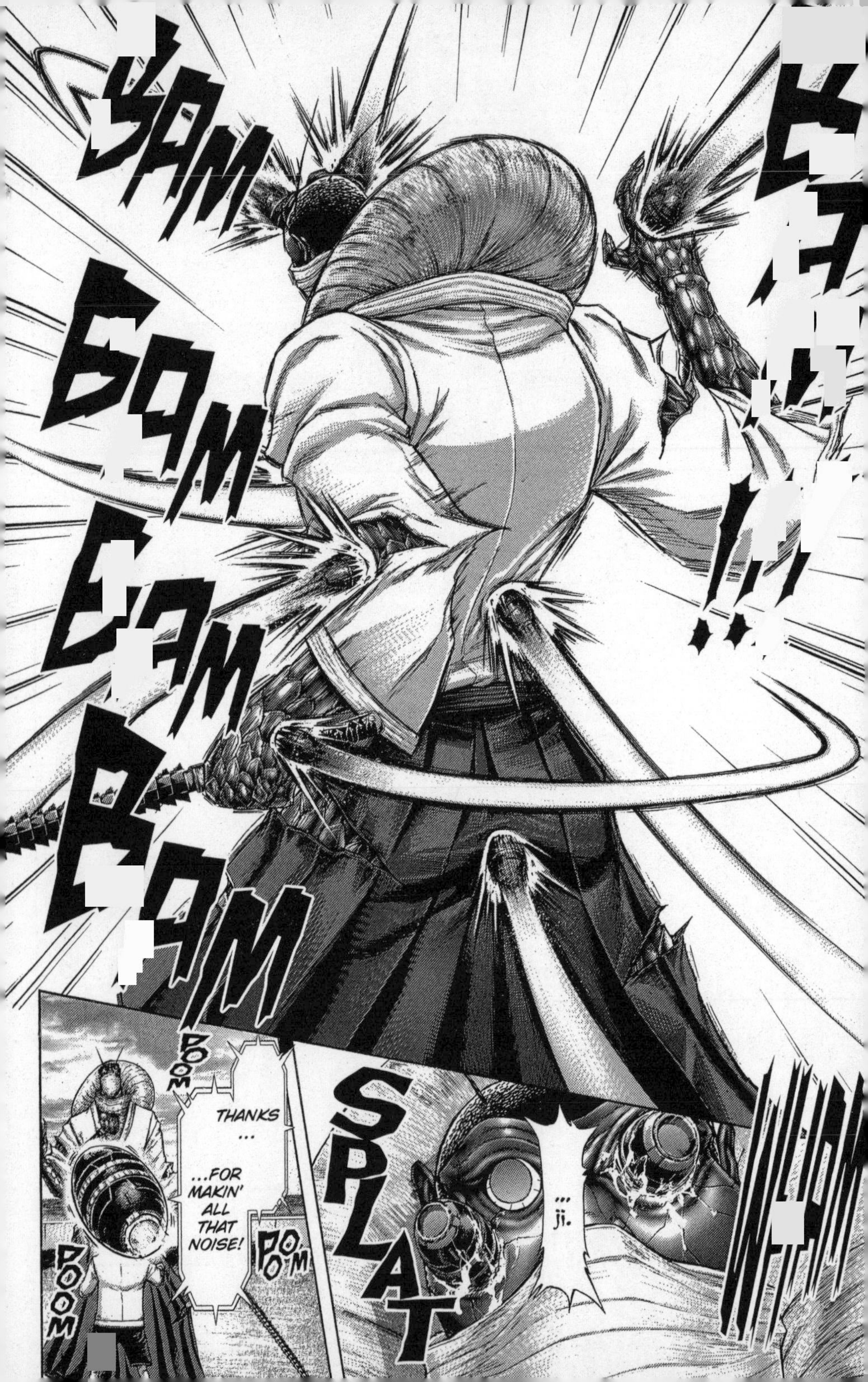
BAM
BAM
BAM
BAM
BAM
...ji.
SPLAT
THANKS ...
...FOR MAKIN' ALL THAT NOISE!
POOM
POOM
POOM

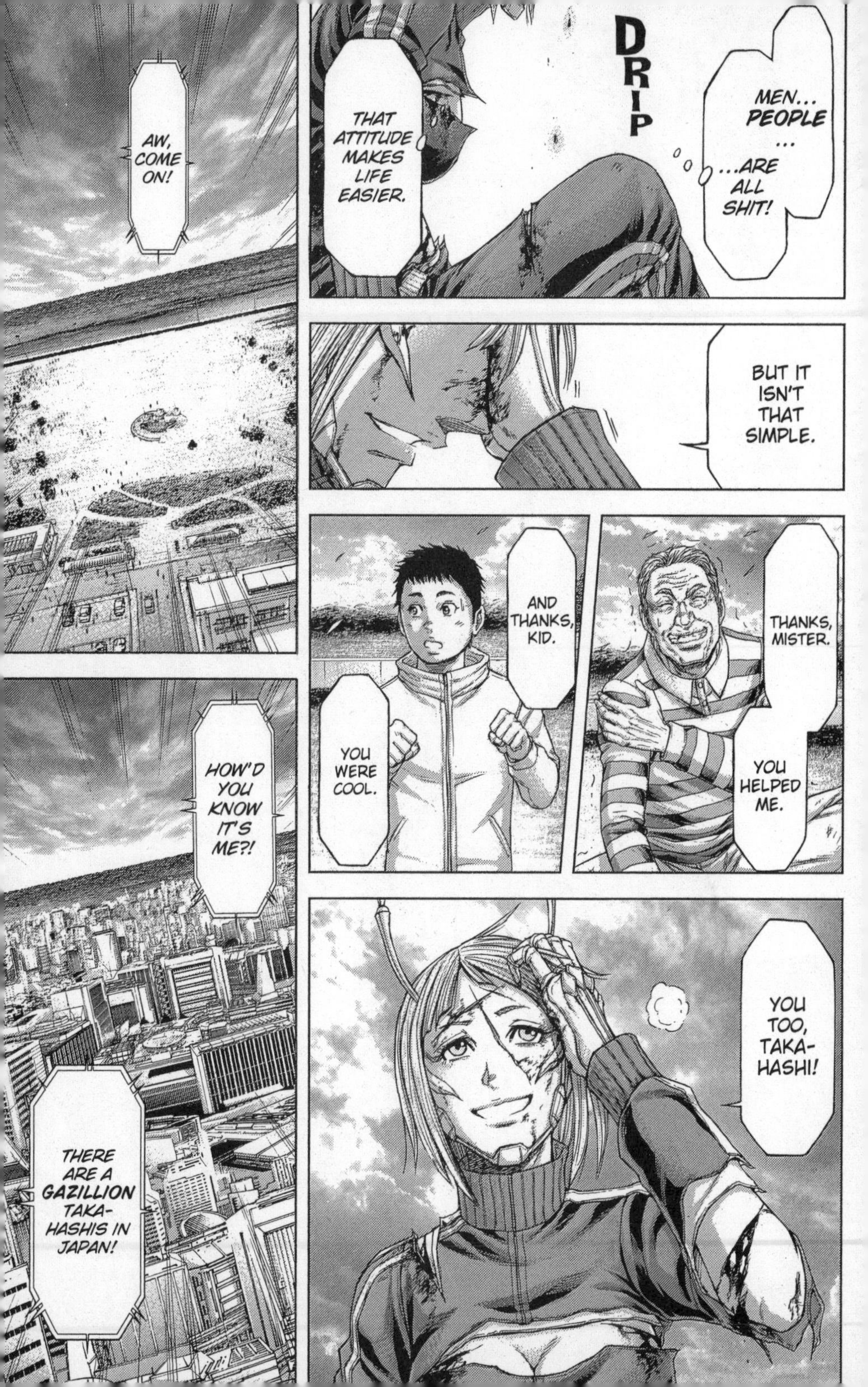
MEN... PEOPLE ... ...ARE ALL SHIT!
DRIP
THAT ATTITUDE MAKES LIFE EASIER.
BUT IT ISN'T THAT SIMPLE.
THANKS, MISTER.
YOU HELPED ME.
AND THANKS, KID.
YOU WERE COOL.
YOU TOO, TAKA-HASHI!
AW, COME ON!
HOW'D YOU KNOW IT'S ME?!
THERE ARE A GAZILLION TAKA-HASHIS IN JAPAN!

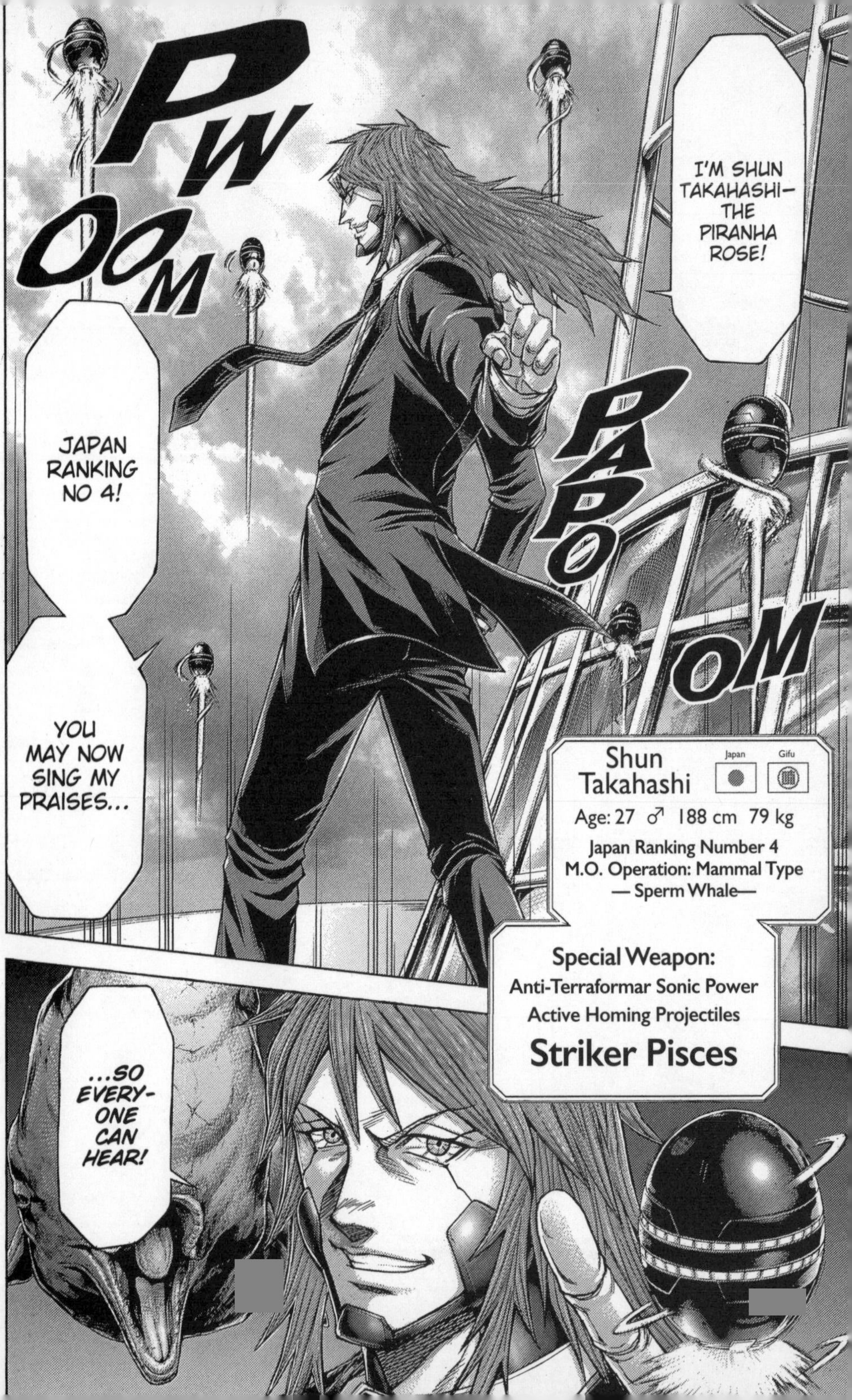
I'M SHUN TAKAHASHI—THE PIRANHA ROSE!
PWOOM
PADOOM
JAPAN RANKING NO 4!
YOU MAY NOW SING MY PRAISES...
Shun Takahashi
Japan
Gifu
Age: 27 ♂ 188 cm 79 kg
Japan Ranking Number 4
M.O. Operation: Mammal Type
— Sperm Whale—
Special Weapon:
Anti-Terraformar Sonic Power
Active Homing Projectiles
Striker Pisces
...SO EVERYONE CAN HEAR!

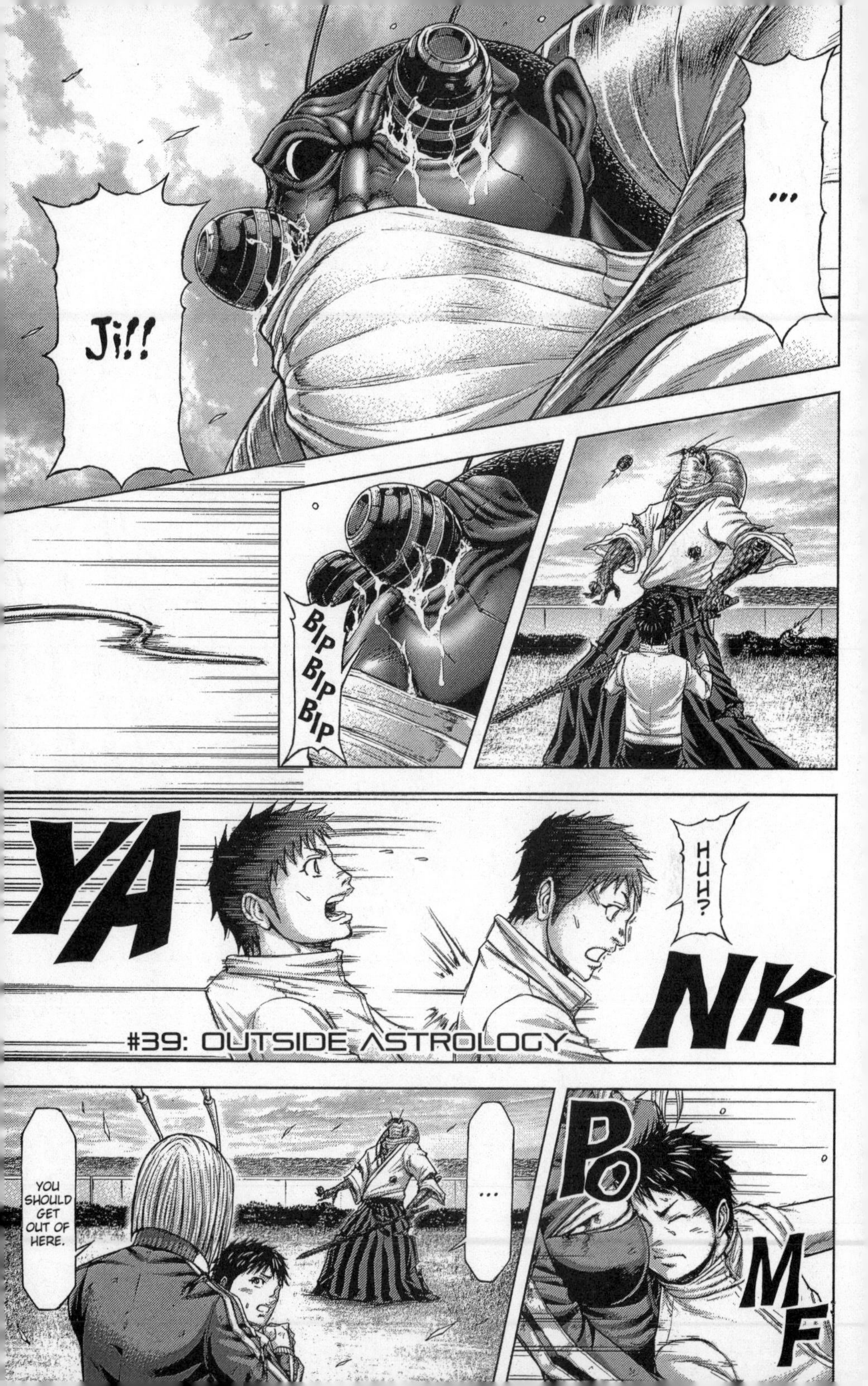
...
Ji!!
BIP BIP BIP
HUH?
YANK
#39: OUTSIDE ASTROLOGY
BOMF
...
YOU SHOULD GET OUT OF HERE.

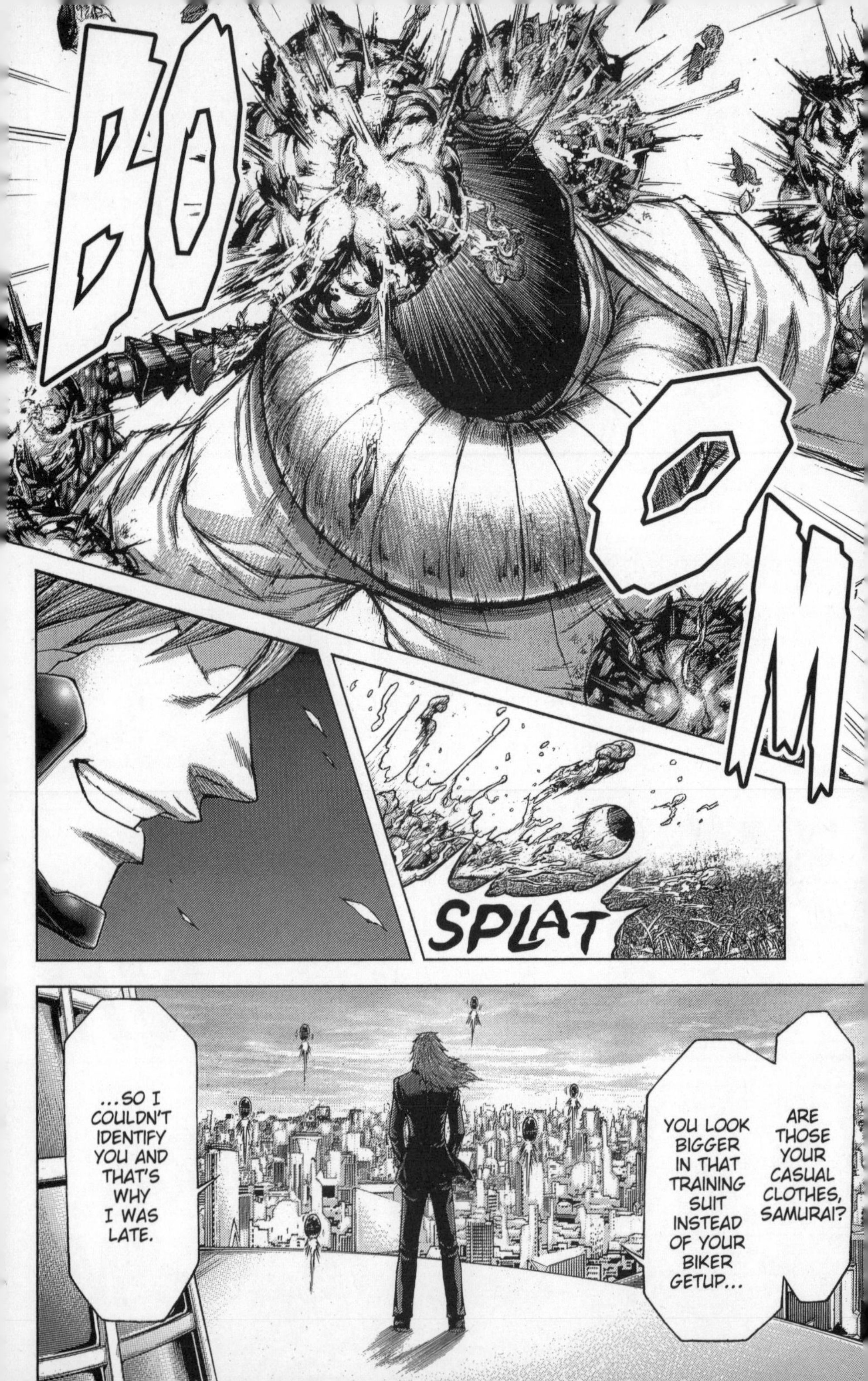
BOOM
SPLAT
ARE THOSE YOUR CASUAL CLOTHES, SAMURAI?
YOU LOOK BIGGER IN THAT TRAINING SUIT INSTEAD OF YOUR BIKER GETUP...
...SO I COULDN'T IDENTIFY YOU AND THAT'S WHY I WAS LATE.

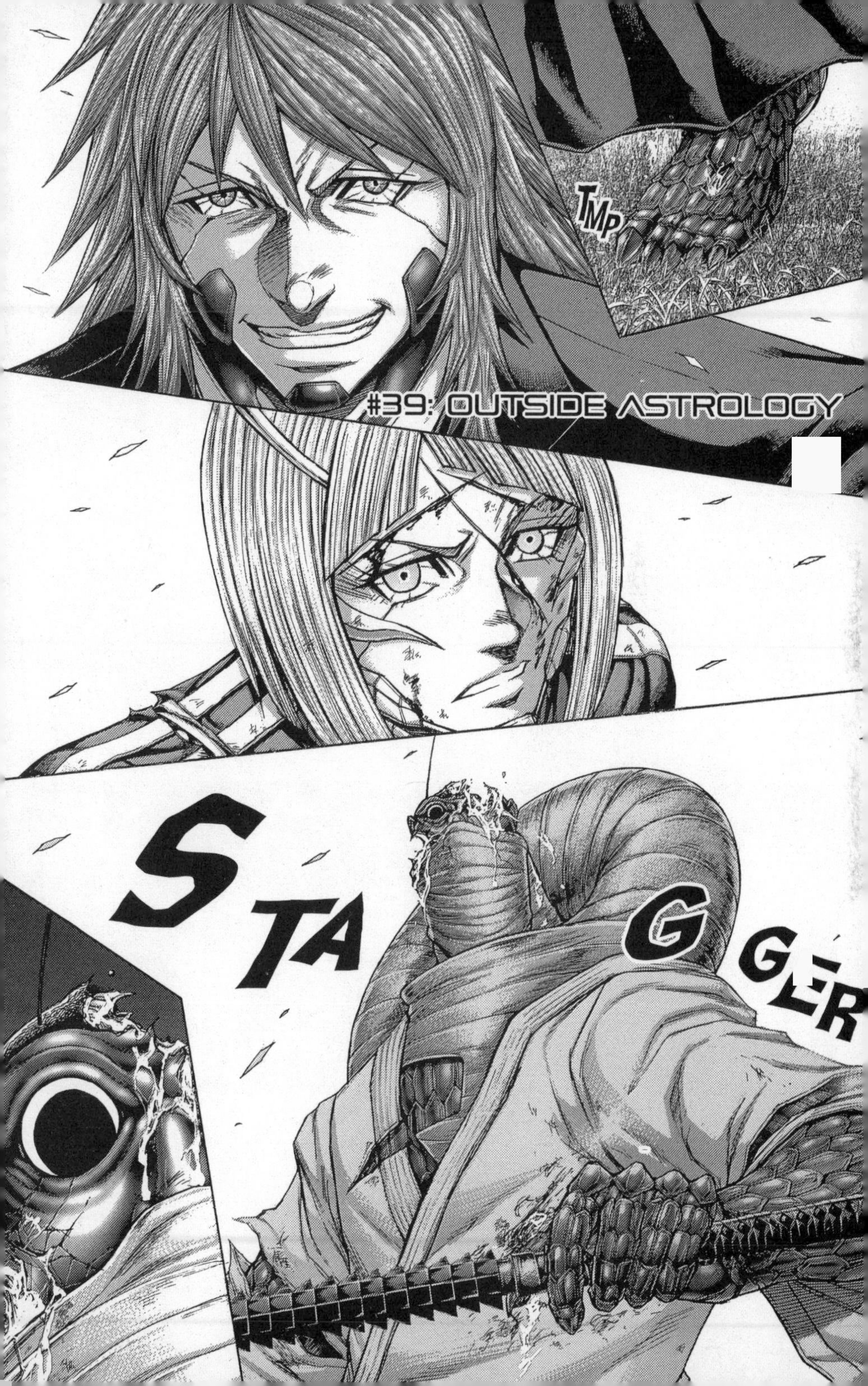
TMP
#39: OUTSIDE ASTROLOGY
STAGGER

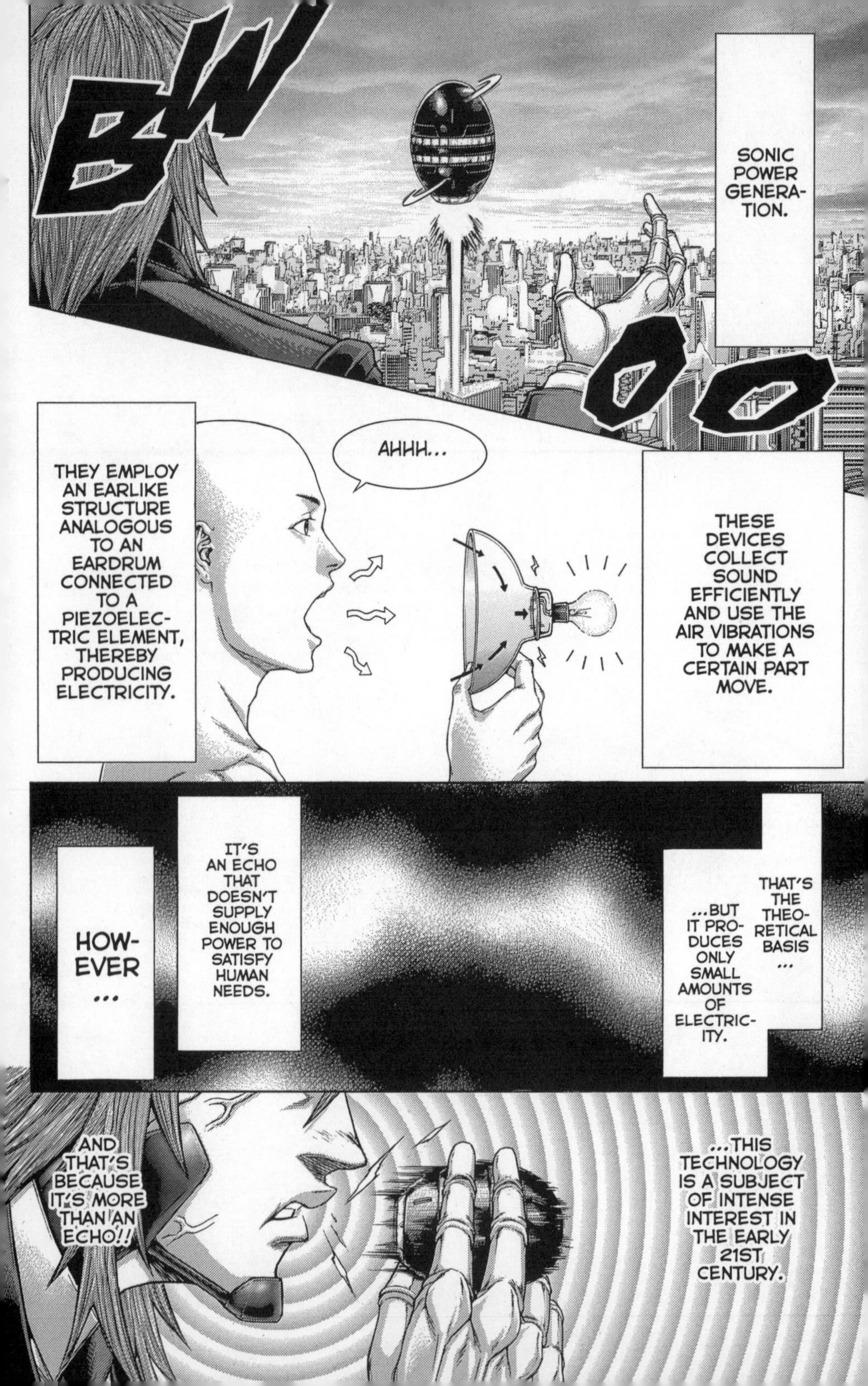
SONIC POWER GENERATION.
BWOO
THESE DEVICES COLLECT SOUND EFFICIENTLY AND USE THE AIR VIBRATIONS TO MAKE A CERTAIN PART MOVE.
AHHH...
THEY EMPLOY AN EARLIKE STRUCTURE ANALOGOUS TO AN EARDRUM CONNECTED TO A PIEZOELECTRIC ELEMENT, THEREBY PRODUCING ELECTRICITY.
THAT'S THE THEORETICAL BASIS...
...BUT IT PRODUCES ONLY SMALL AMOUNTS OF ELECTRICITY.
IT'S AN ECHO THAT DOESN'T SUPPLY ENOUGH POWER TO SATISFY HUMAN NEEDS.
HOWEVER...
...THIS TECHNOLOGY IS A SUBJECT OF INTENSE INTEREST IN THE EARLY 21ST CENTURY.
AND THAT'S BECAUSE IT'S MORE THAN AN ECHO!!

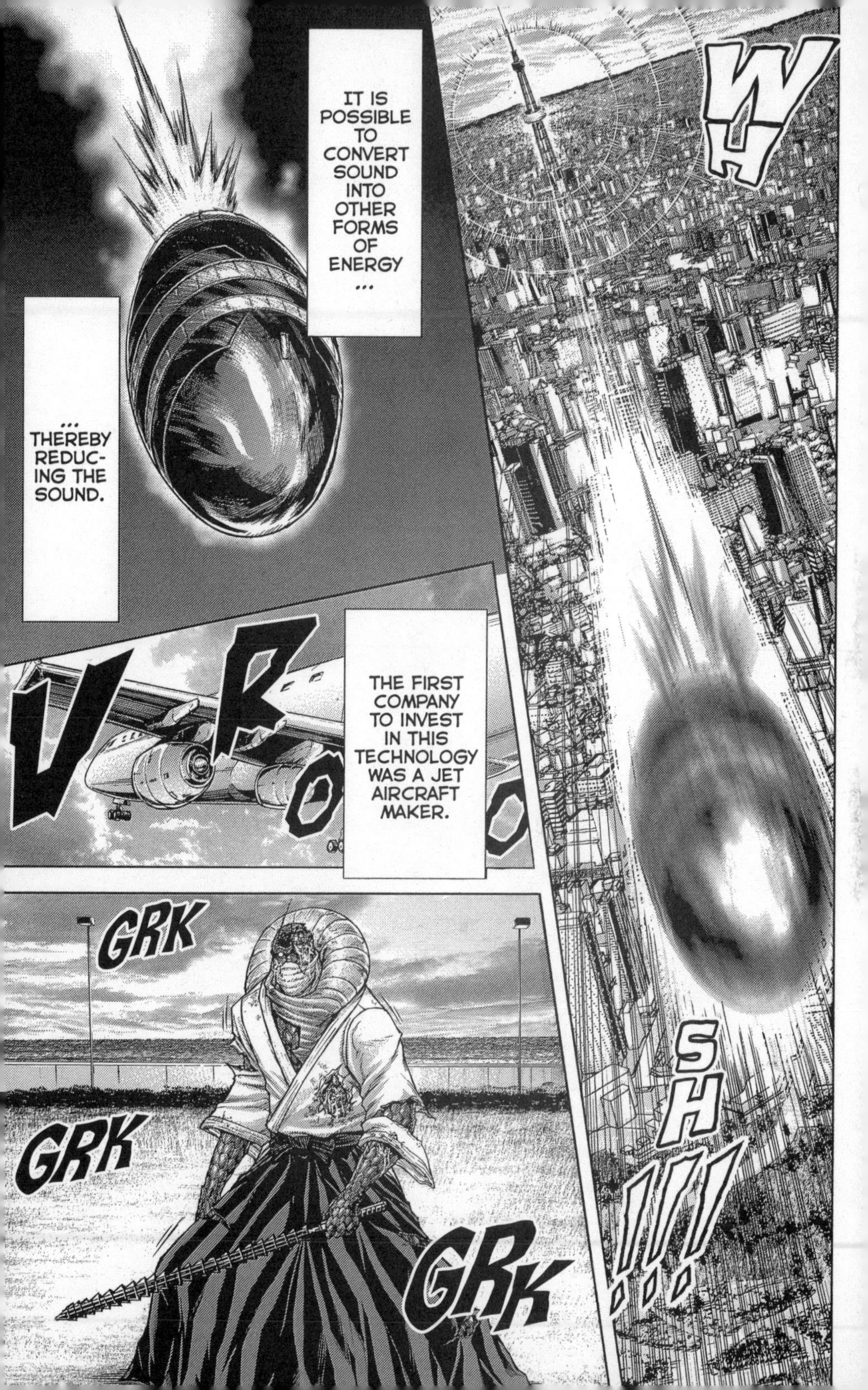
WH
SH!!!
IT IS POSSIBLE TO CONVERT SOUND INTO OTHER FORMS OF ENERGY...
...THEREBY REDUC-ING THE SOUND.
THE FIRST COMPANY TO INVEST IN THIS TECHNOLOGY WAS A JET AIRCRAFT MAKER.
VROOO
GRK
GRK
GRK

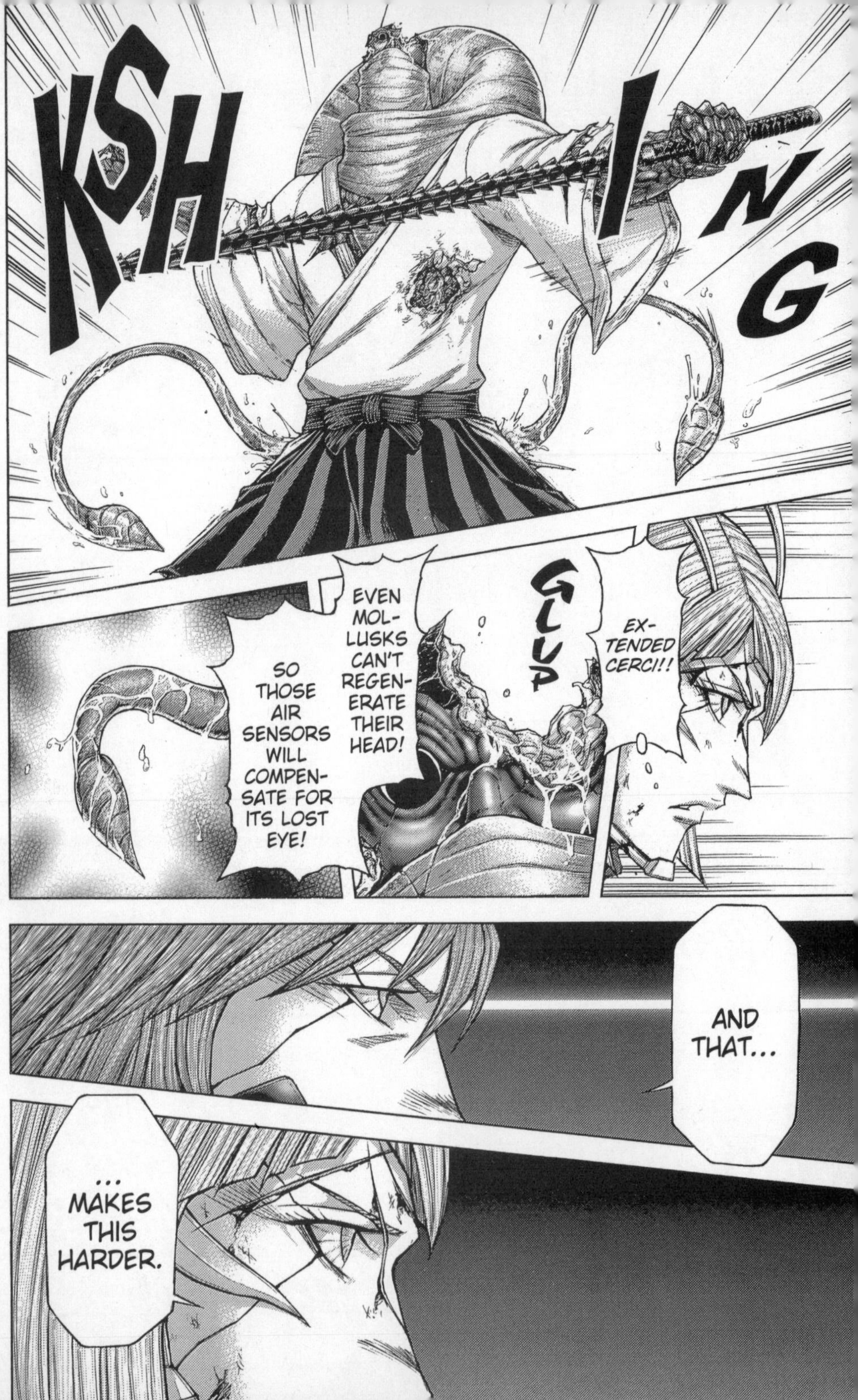
KSHING
EXTENDED CERCI!!
GLUP
EVEN MOLLUSKS CAN'T REGENERATE THEIR HEAD!
SO THOSE AIR SENSORS WILL COMPENSATE FOR ITS LOST EYE!
AND THAT...
...MAKES THIS HARDER.

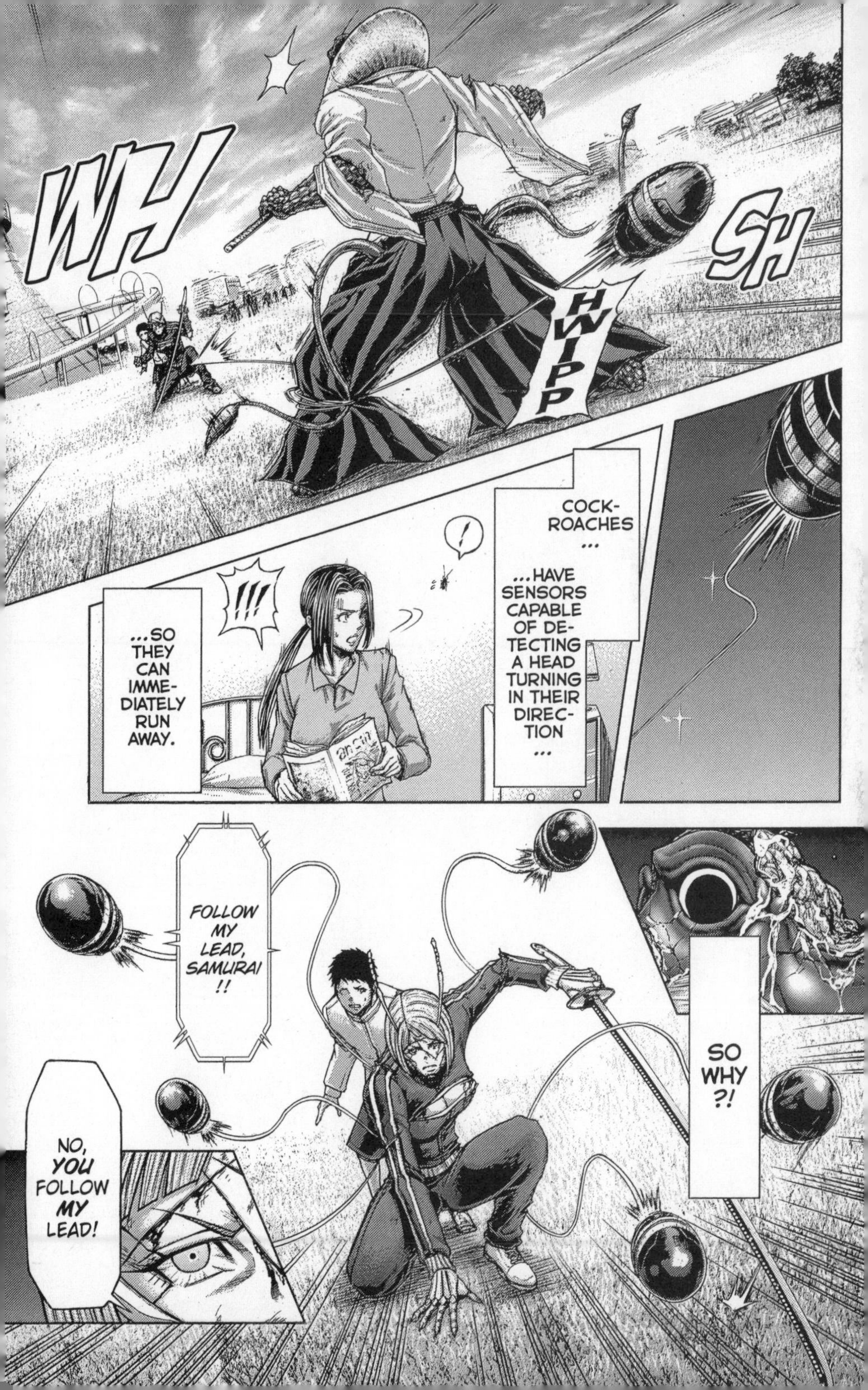
WH
SH
HWIPP
COCK-ROACHES...
...HAVE SENSORS CAPABLE OF DE-TECTING A HEAD TURNING IN THEIR DIREC-TION...
!
!!!
...SO THEY CAN IMME-DIATELY RUN AWAY.
SO WHY?!
FOLLOW MY LEAD, SAMURAI!!
NO, *YOU* FOLLOW *MY* LEAD!

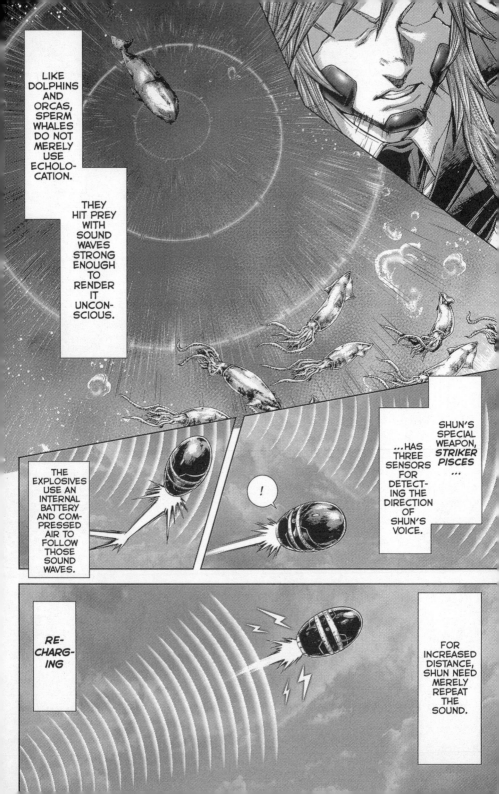

LIKE DOLPHINS AND ORCAS, SPERM WHALES DO NOT MERELY USE ECHOLOCATION.

THEY HIT PREY WITH SOUND WAVES STRONG ENOUGH TO RENDER IT UNCONSCIOUS.

SHUN'S SPECIAL WEAPON, *STRIKER PISCES* ...

...HAS THREE SENSORS FOR DETECTING THE DIRECTION OF SHUN'S VOICE.

!

THE EXPLOSIVES USE AN INTERNAL BATTERY AND COMPRESSED AIR TO FOLLOW THOSE SOUND WAVES.

RE-CHARG-ING

FOR INCREASED DISTANCE, SHUN NEED MERELY REPEAT THE SOUND.

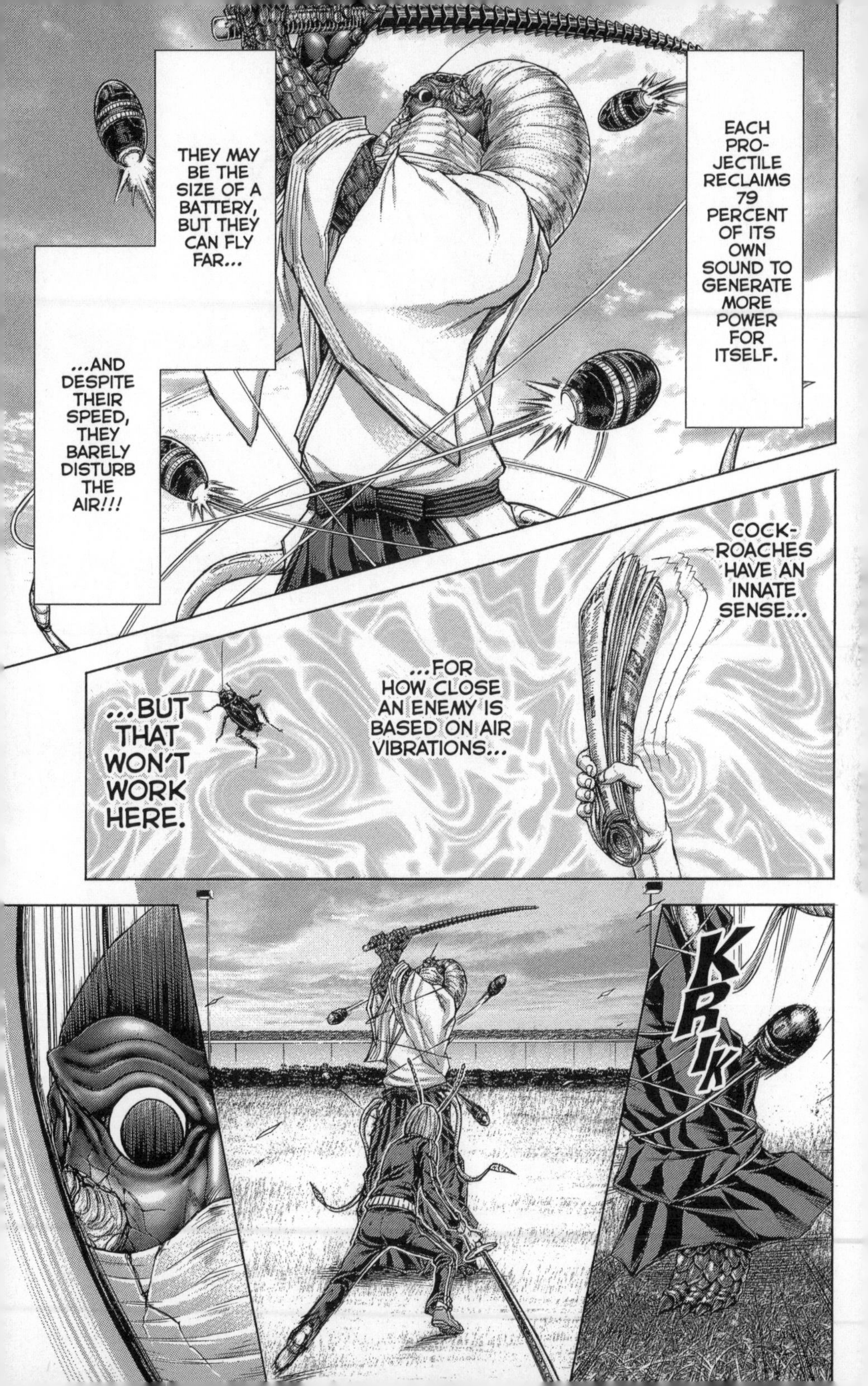
EACH PRO-JECTILE RECLAIMS 79 PERCENT OF ITS OWN SOUND TO GENERATE MORE POWER FOR ITSELF.
THEY MAY BE THE SIZE OF A BATTERY, BUT THEY CAN FLY FAR...
...AND DESPITE THEIR SPEED, THEY BARELY DISTURB THE AIR!!!
COCK-ROACHES HAVE AN INNATE SENSE...
...FOR HOW CLOSE AN ENEMY IS BASED ON AIR VIBRATIONS...
...BUT THAT WON'T WORK HERE.
KRIK

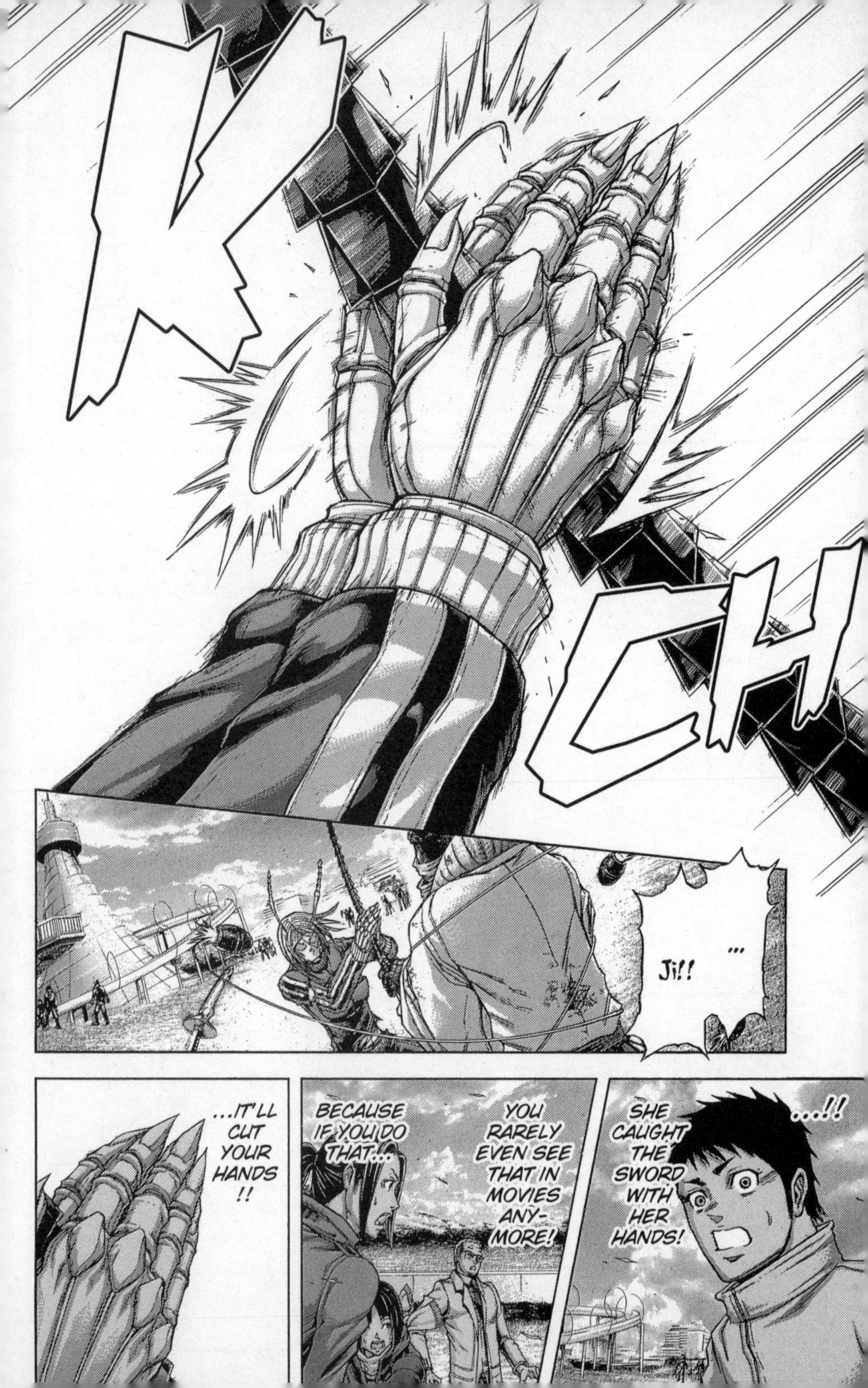
KCH
...
Ji!!
...!!
SHE CAUGHT THE SWORD WITH HER HANDS!
YOU RARELY EVEN SEE THAT IN MOVIES ANY-MORE!
BECAUSE IF YOU DO THAT...
...IT'LL CUT YOUR HANDS!!

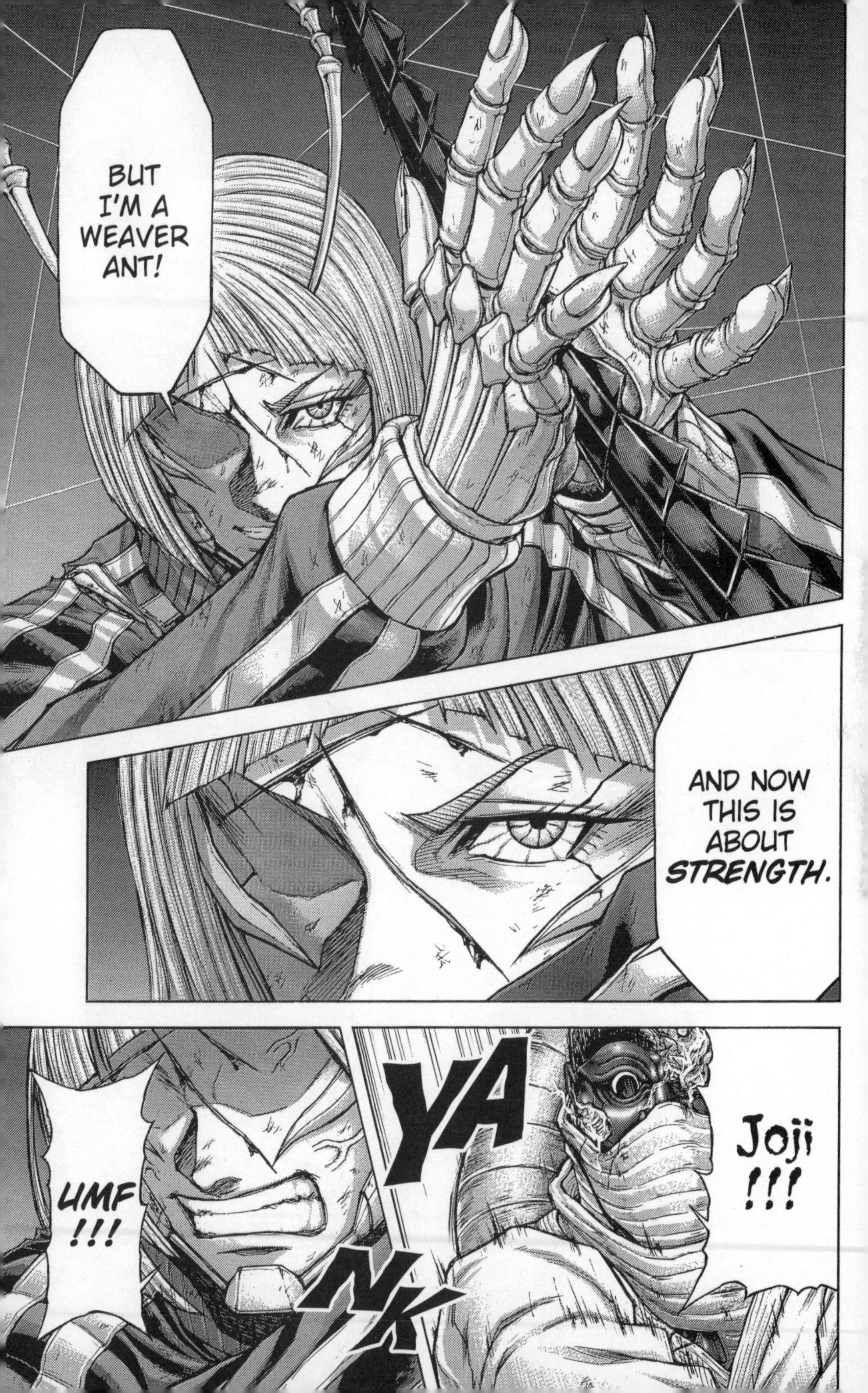
BUT I'M A WEAVER ANT!
AND NOW THIS IS ABOUT STRENGTH.
Joji !!!
YA
NK
UMF !!!

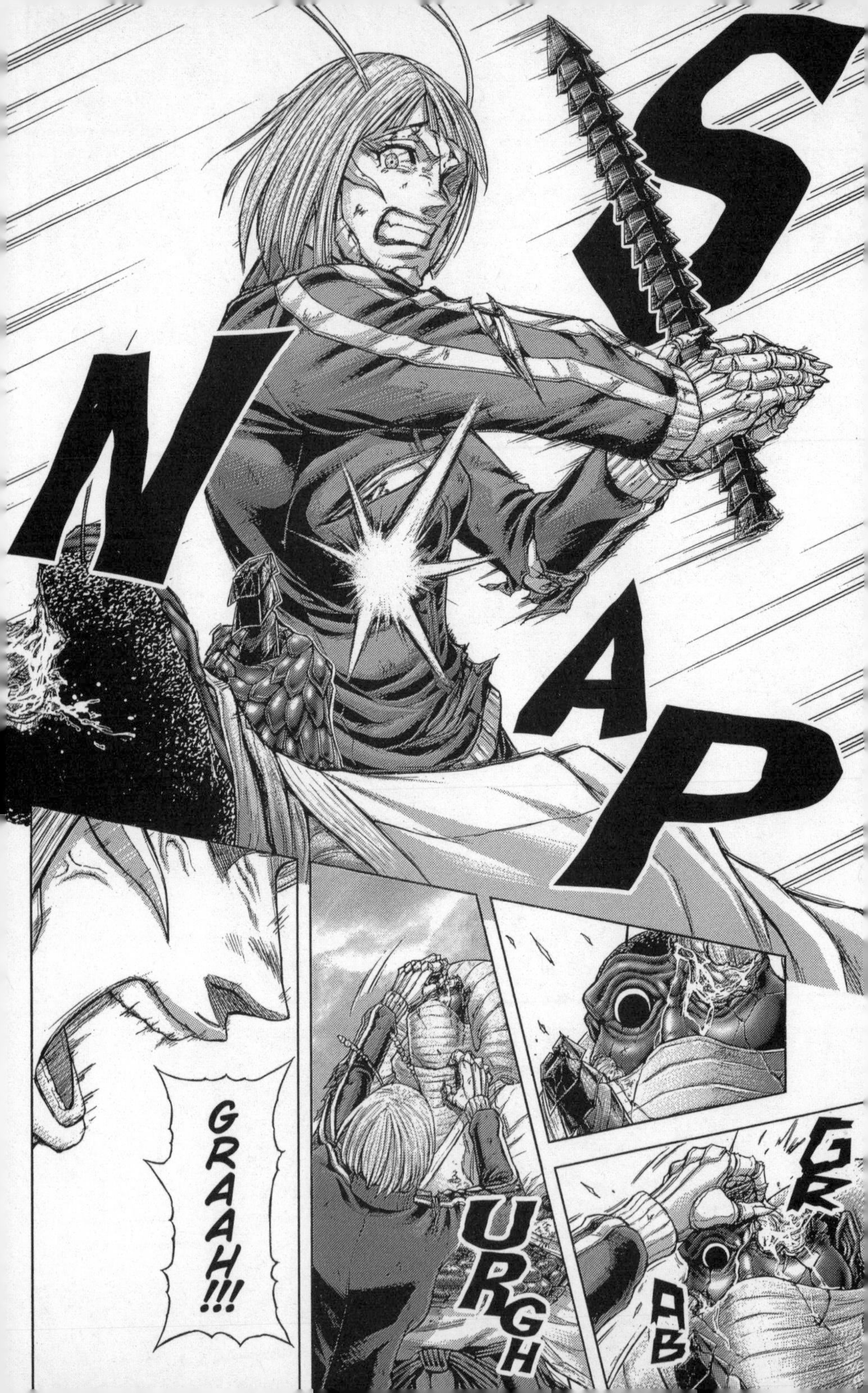
SNAP
GRAB
URGH
GRAAAH!!!

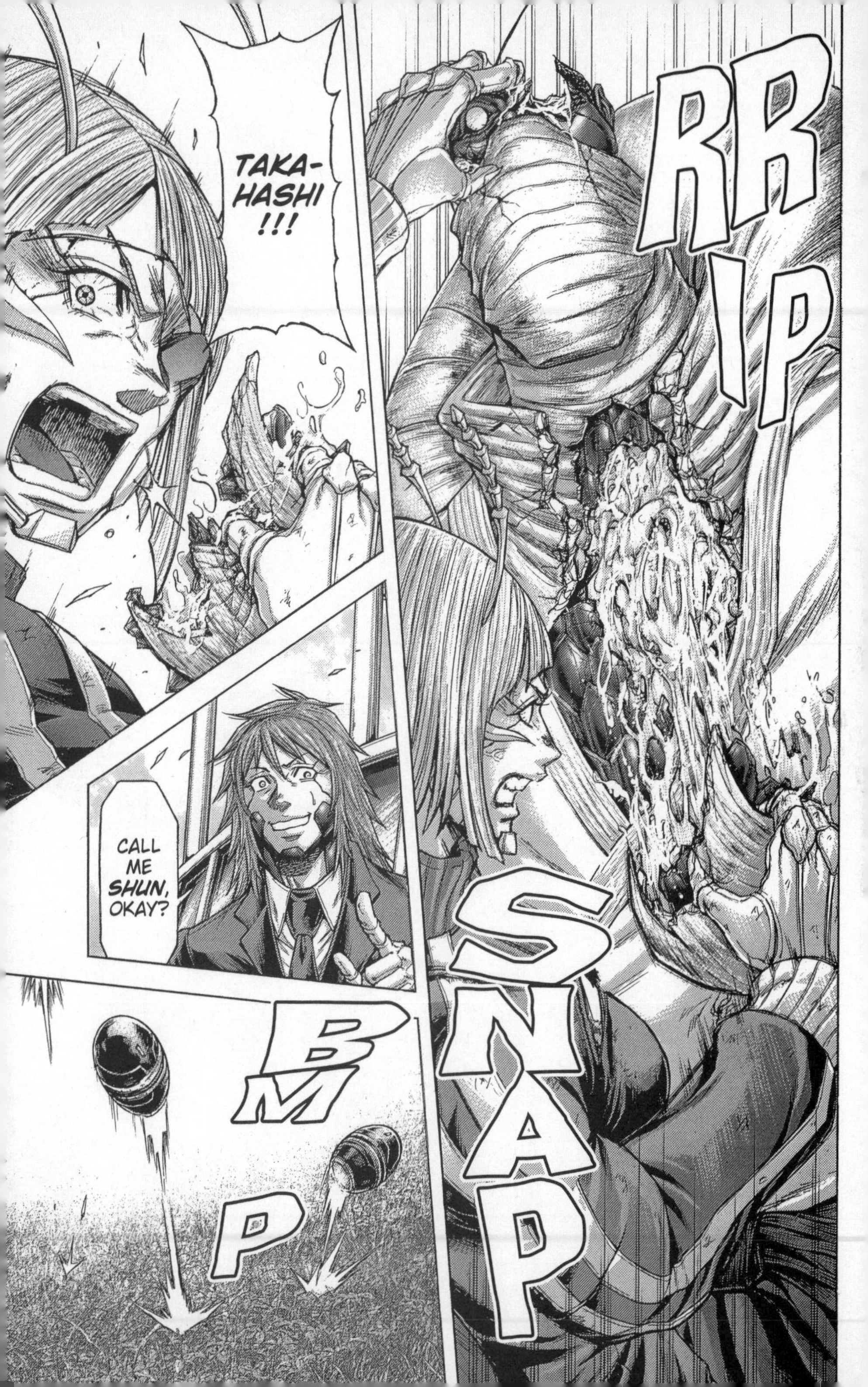
RRIP
SNAP
TAKA-HASHI!!!
CALL ME SHUN, OKAY?
BMP

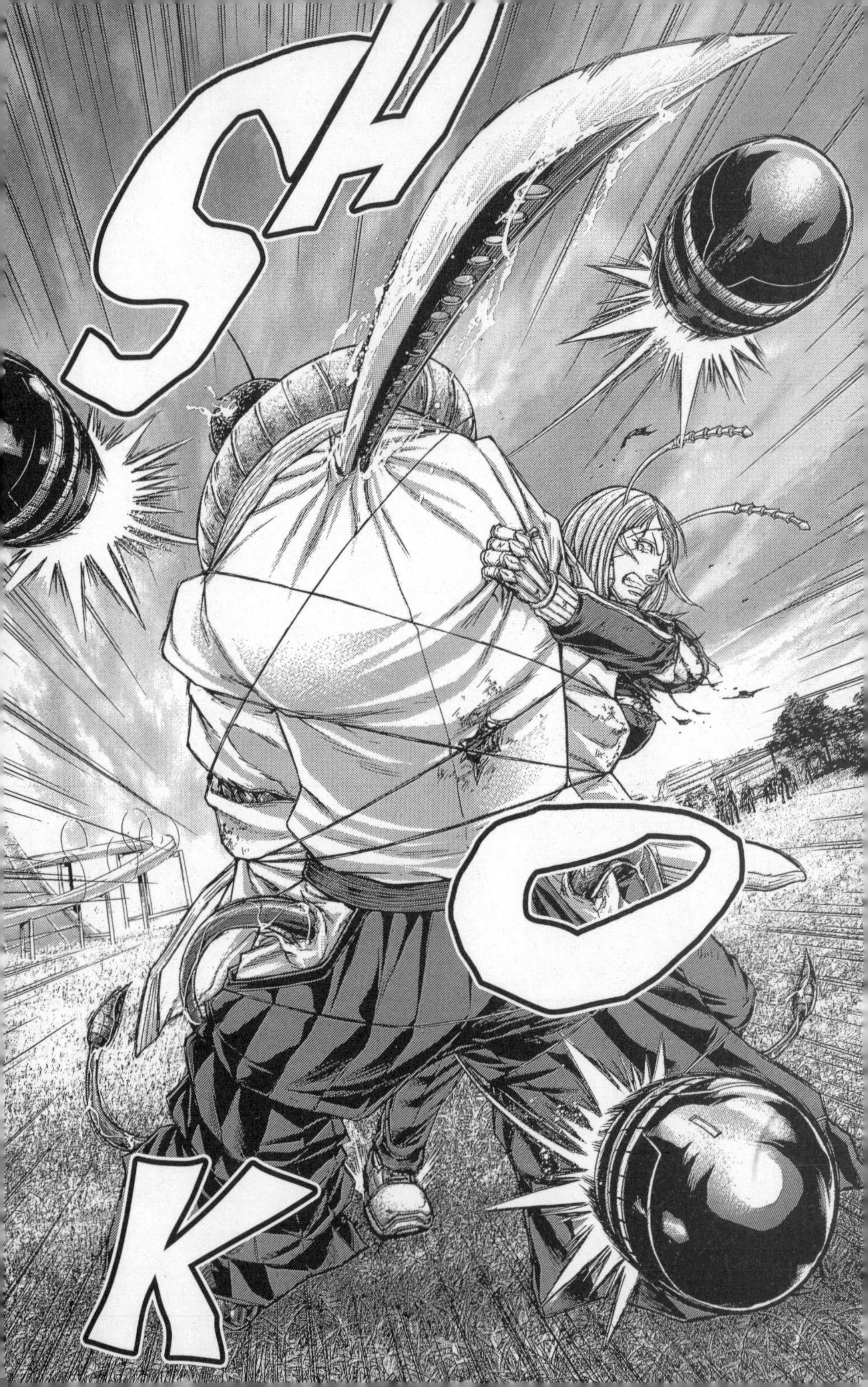
SHOOK

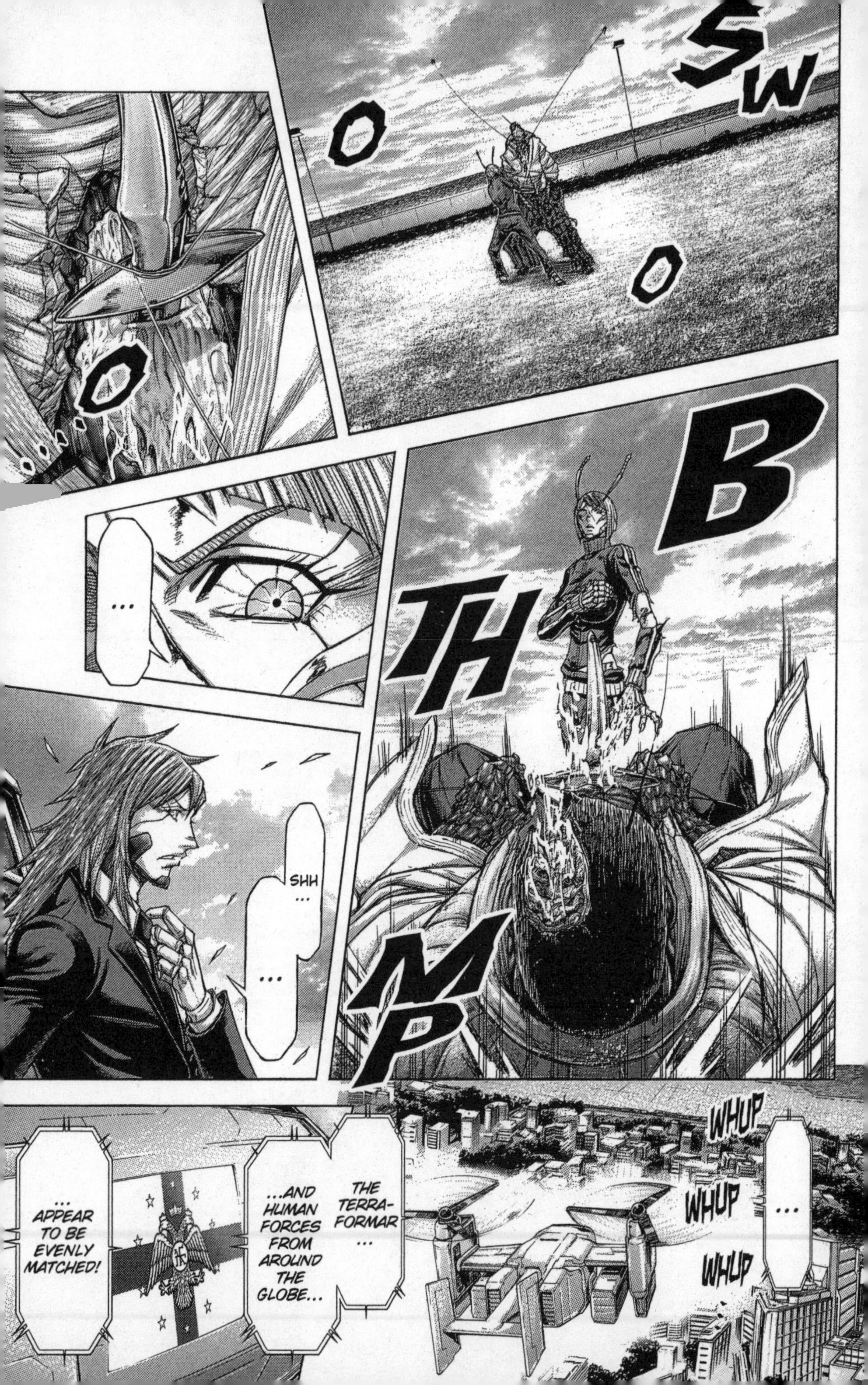
SW
O
O
O . . .
B
TH
M
P
...
SHH ...
...
WHUP
WHUP
WHUP
...
THE TERRA-FORMAR ...
...AND HUMAN FORCES FROM AROUND THE GLOBE...
... APPEAR TO BE EVENLY MATCHED!

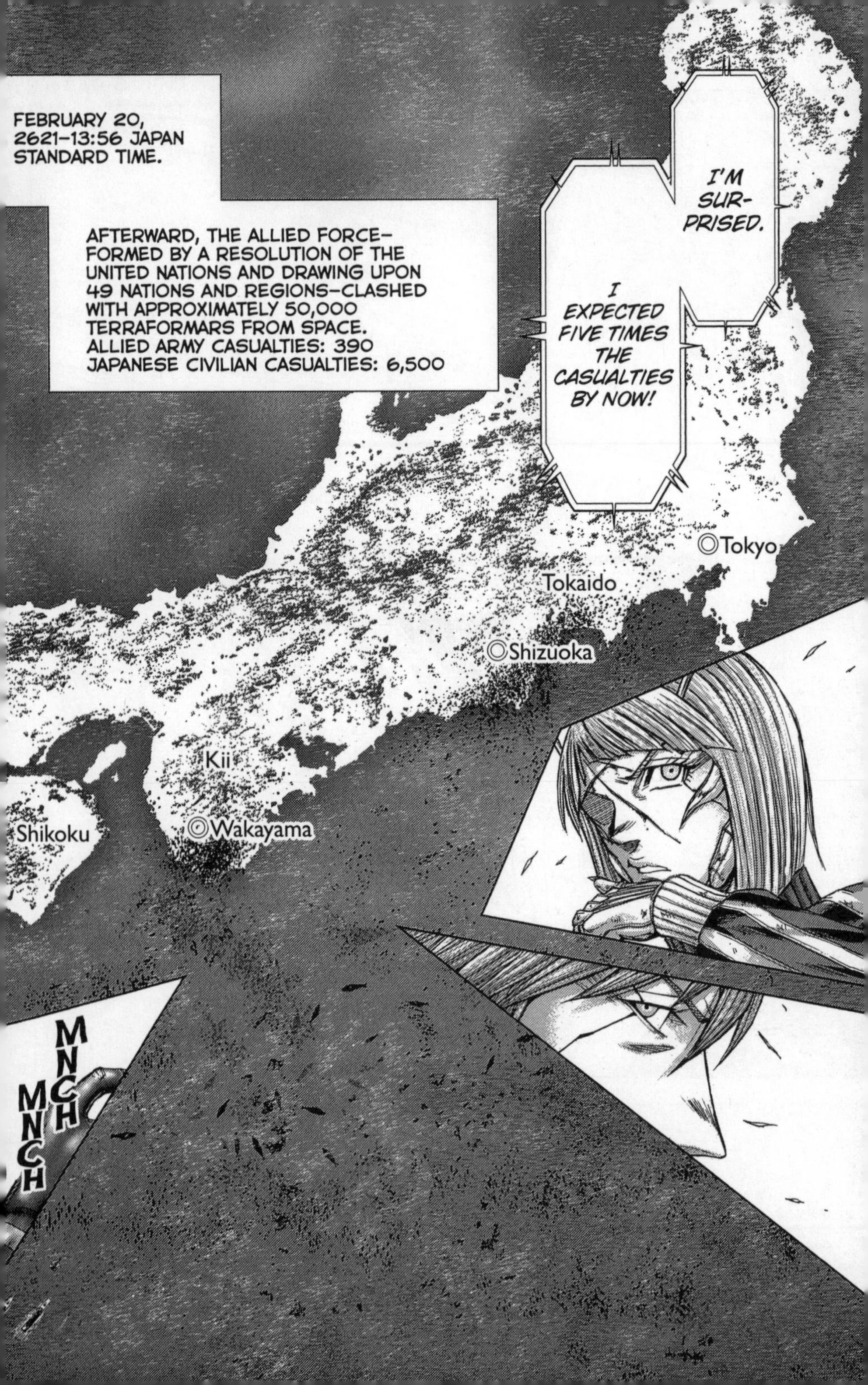
I'M SURPRISED.
I EXPECTED FIVE TIMES THE CASUALTIES BY NOW!
FEBRUARY 20, 2621–13:56 JAPAN STANDARD TIME.
AFTERWARD, THE ALLIED FORCE–FORMED BY A RESOLUTION OF THE UNITED NATIONS AND DRAWING UPON 49 NATIONS AND REGIONS–CLASHED WITH APPROXIMATELY 50,000 TERRAFORMARS FROM SPACE.
ALLIED ARMY CASUALTIES: 390
JAPANESE CIVILIAN CASUALTIES: 6,500
Tokyo
Tokaido
Shizuoka
Kii
Wakayama
Shikoku
MNCH MNCH

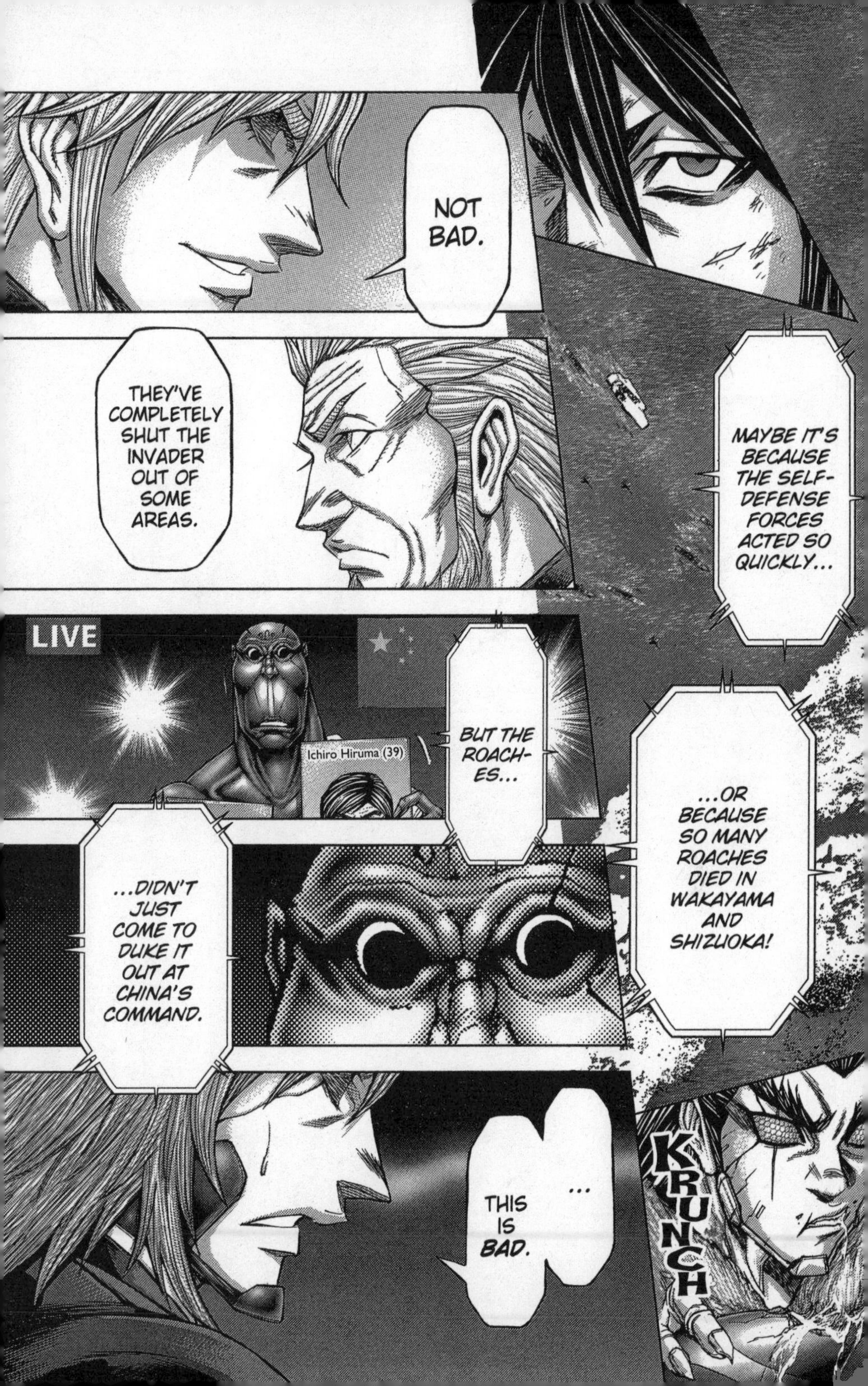
NOT BAD.
THEY'VE COMPLETELY SHUT THE INVADER OUT OF SOME AREAS.
MAYBE IT'S BECAUSE THE SELF-DEFENSE FORCES ACTED SO QUICKLY...
...OR BECAUSE SO MANY ROACHES DIED IN WAKAYAMA AND SHIZUOKA!
LIVE
Ichiro Hiruma (39)
BUT THE ROACH-ES...
...DIDN'T JUST COME TO DUKE IT OUT AT CHINA'S COMMAND.
KRUNCH
...
THIS IS BAD.

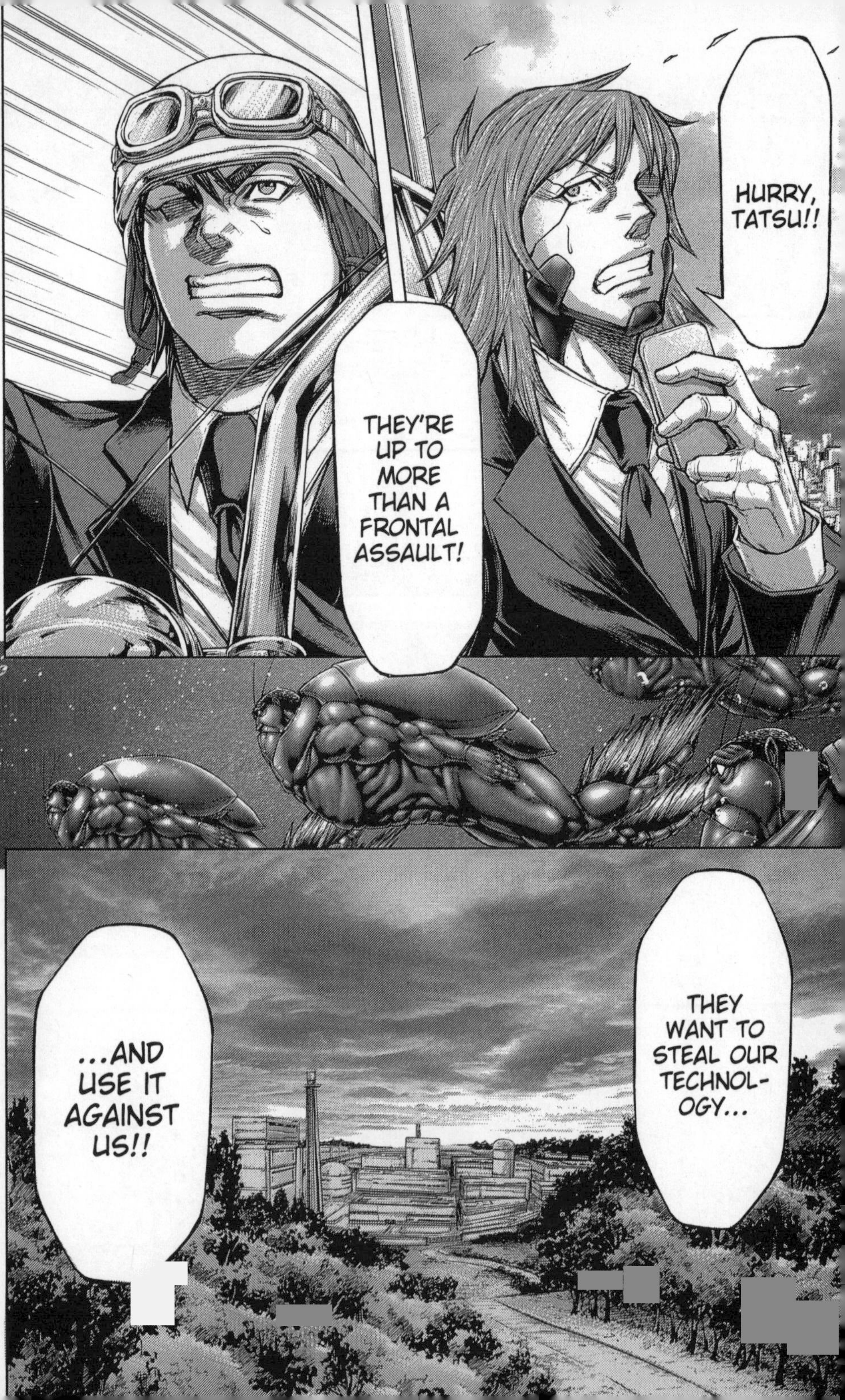
HURRY, TATSU!!
THEY'RE UP TO MORE THAN A FRONTAL ASSAULT!
THEY WANT TO STEAL OUR TECHNOL-OGY...
...AND USE IT AGAINST US!!

TERRA FORMARS

character

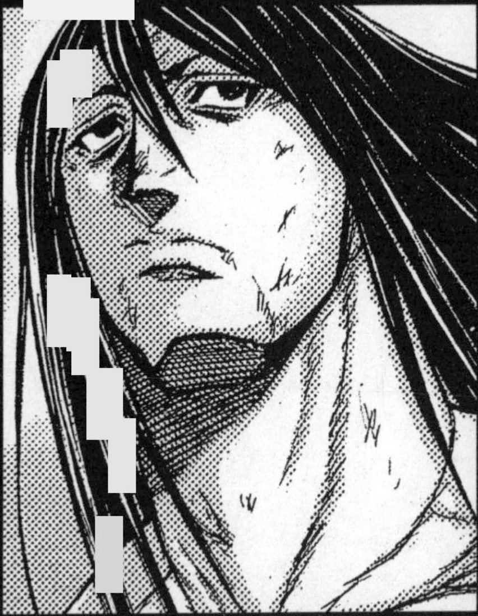

Itsuki Kazemura ♂

Nara 29 yrs. 223 cm 111 kg

Favorite Foods: Meat and wine
Dislikes: Too much shaving cream making it difficult to shave
Eye Color: Black Blood Type: O
DOB: April 26 (Taurus)
Recent source of joy: See end of volume.

Born into one of Japan's top three business families, one with venerable ancestry. Strictly speaking, the main family is descended from a warrior baron, and Itsuki is in a branch of that family. Most of the close branches are powerful in politics and business, with strong interconnections. He was quick to distinguish himself as an imperial guard, but an illness caused him to gradually lose control of his muscles. He had a wife, but the onset of his illness led to their separation.

There were no previous instances of a single person receiving multiple M.O. Operations, and it was thought to be impossible. The only explanation for Itsuki's survival is his incredible constitution and mental fortitude. Bow draw weight: 200 kilograms.

Moeko Ebizuka ♀

Nara [illegible]0 yrs. 155 cm 55 kg

Favorite Foods: White rice, pickles, strawberries
Dislikes: Expensive parking with machines that only accept small bills
Eye Color: Light brown Blood Type: B
DOB: Januar[illegible] Capricorn)
Skill: See end[illegible]lume.

[illegible]e youngest daughter of a family that owns a large hospital [illegible] Nara. She is a surgeon able to perform the M.O. Operation, [illegible]ich only certain physicians are capable of learning.

Due to the relationship between their families and the proximity of their schools, she is old friends with Itsuki. He has jokingly mentioned getting married, but she knows that can never be anything but a joke. The Kazemura family was opposed to Itsuki's M.O. Operation, but she's the type who never fails, so the family has yet to disinherit him or cut off support.

When relaxing, she's an E-cup, but she can change her appearance depending on how much she gathers her flab.

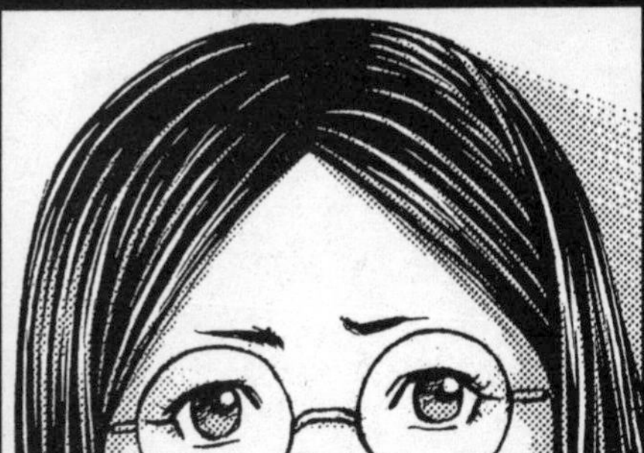

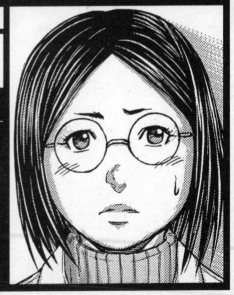

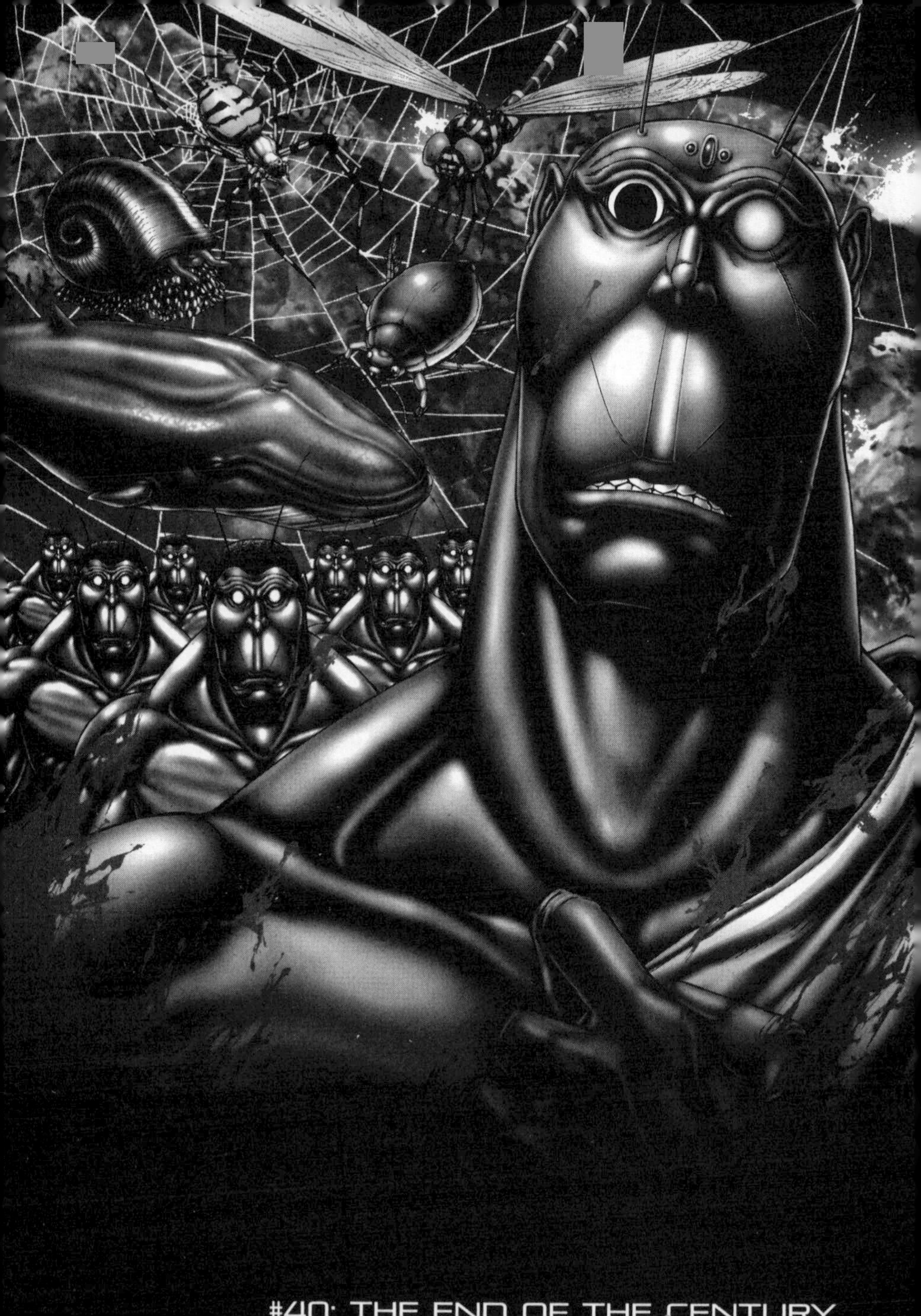

#40: THE END OF THE CENTURY

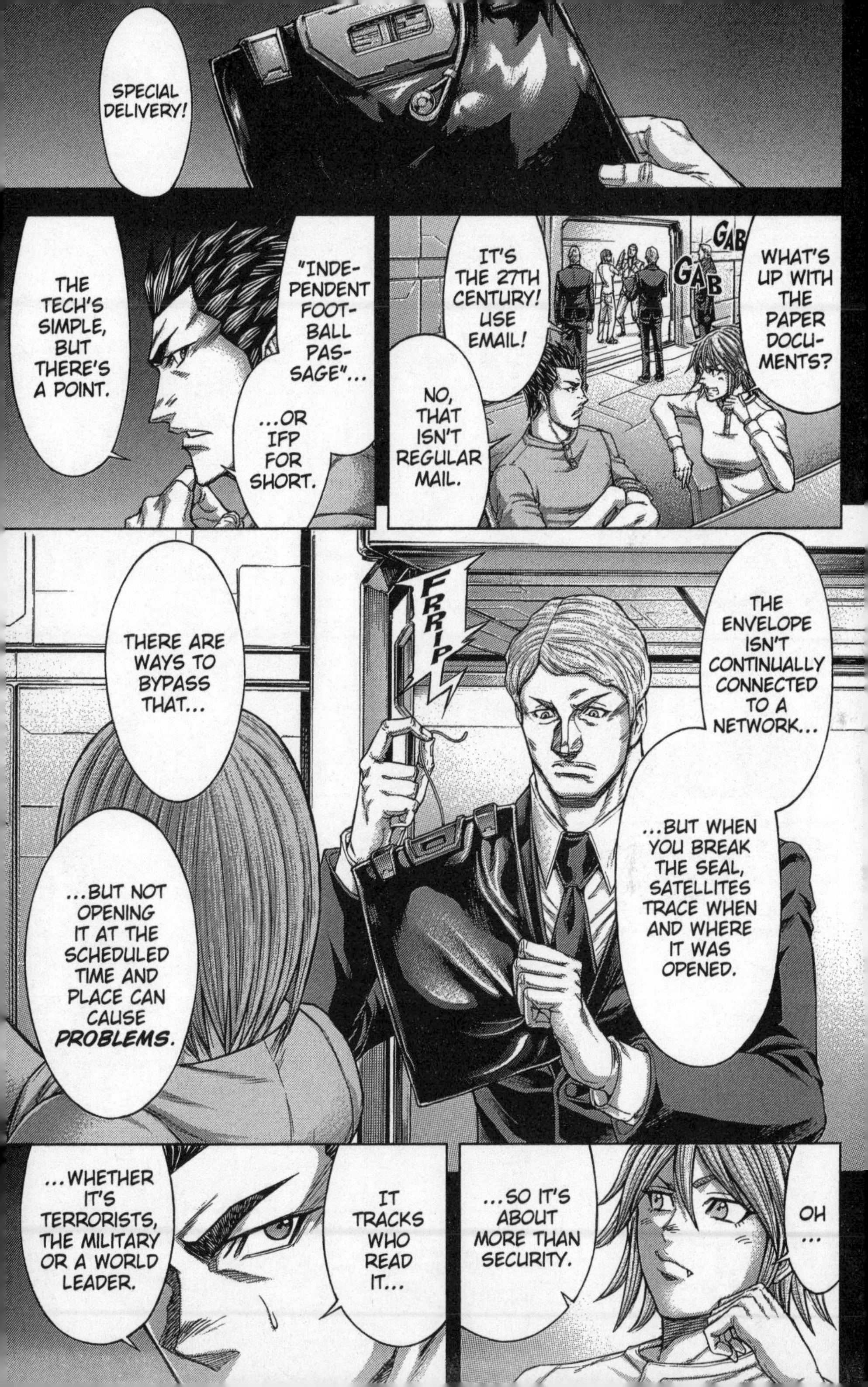
SPECIAL DELIVERY!
WHAT'S UP WITH THE PAPER DOCUMENTS?
GAB
GAB
IT'S THE 27TH CENTURY! USE EMAIL!
NO, THAT ISN'T REGULAR MAIL.
"INDEPENDENT FOOTBALL PASSAGE"...
...OR IFP FOR SHORT.
THE TECH'S SIMPLE, BUT THERE'S A POINT.
THE ENVELOPE ISN'T CONTINUALLY CONNECTED TO A NETWORK...
FRRIP
...BUT WHEN YOU BREAK THE SEAL, SATELLITES TRACE WHEN AND WHERE IT WAS OPENED.
THERE ARE WAYS TO BYPASS THAT...
...BUT NOT OPENING IT AT THE SCHEDULED TIME AND PLACE CAN CAUSE ***PROBLEMS***.
OH...
...SO IT'S ABOUT MORE THAN SECURITY.
IT TRACKS WHO READ IT...
...WHETHER IT'S TERRORISTS, THE MILITARY OR A WORLD LEADER.

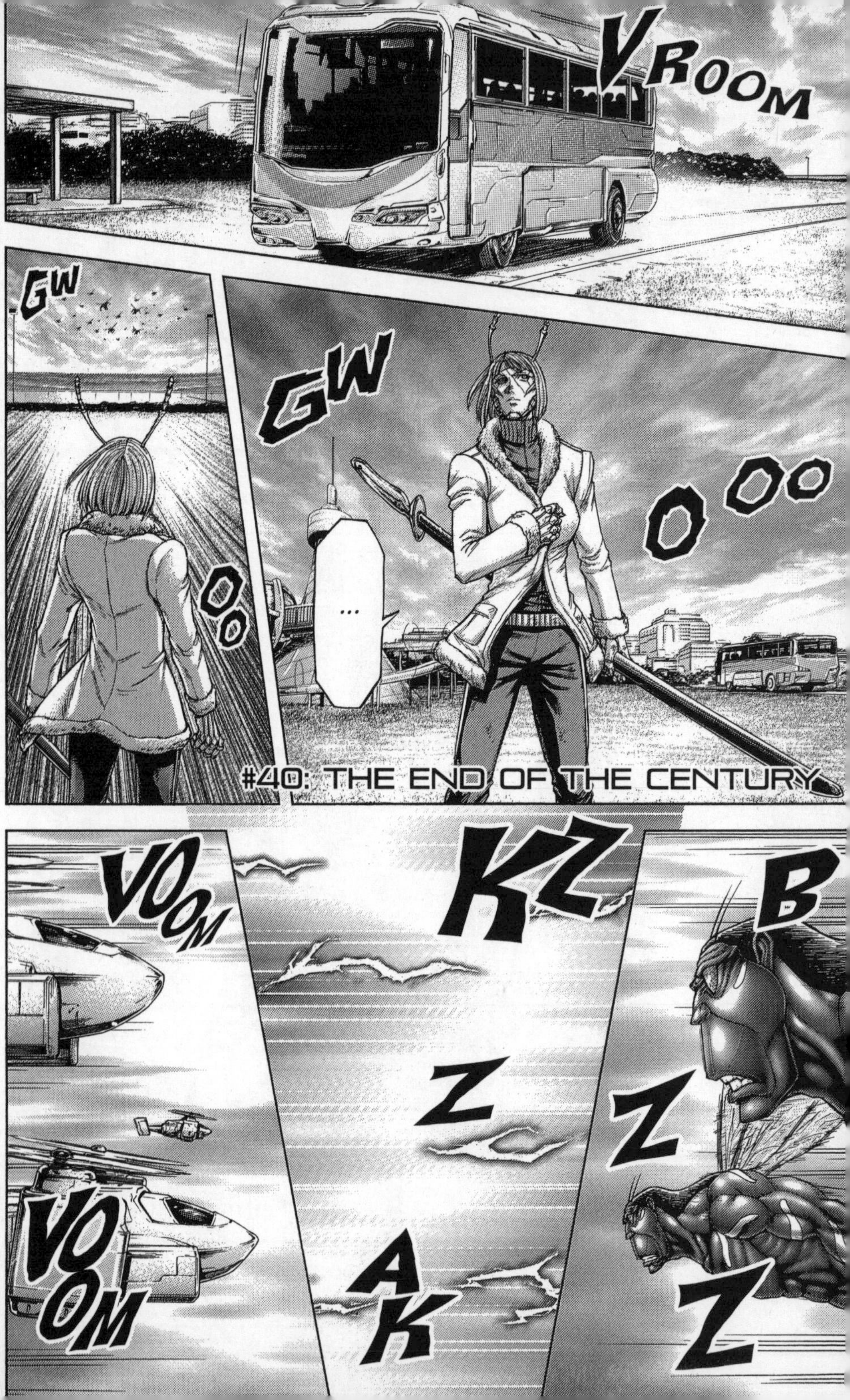
VROOM
GW
OOOO
...
#40: THE END OF THE CENTURY
GW
OO
BZZ
KZZAK
VOOM
VOOM

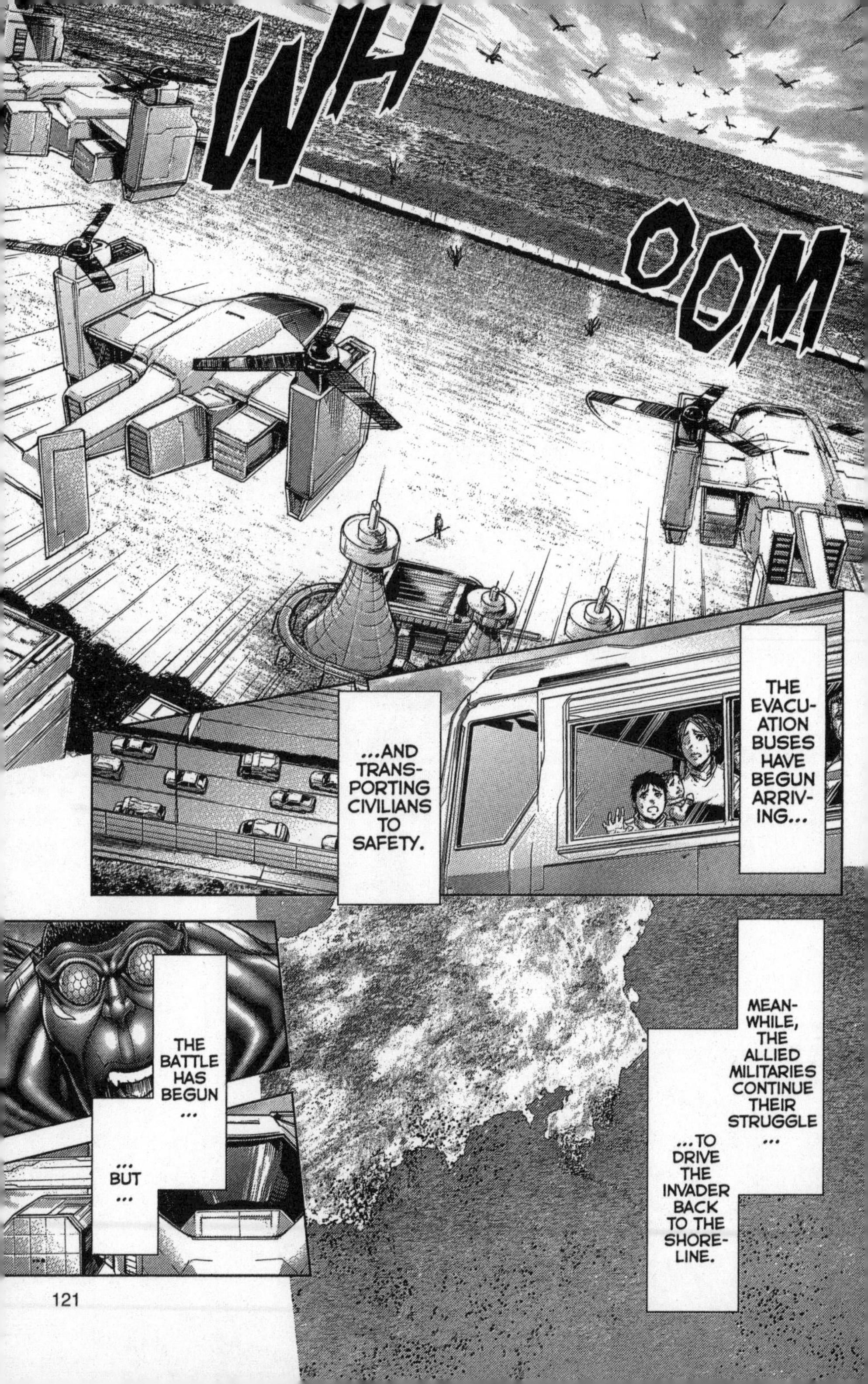
WHOOM
THE EVACUATION BUSES HAVE BEGUN ARRIVING...
...AND TRANSPORTING CIVILIANS TO SAFETY.
MEANWHILE, THE ALLIED MILITARIES CONTINUE THEIR STRUGGLE...
...TO DRIVE THE INVADER BACK TO THE SHORELINE.
THE BATTLE HAS BEGUN...
...BUT...

...HOW WILL IT END?

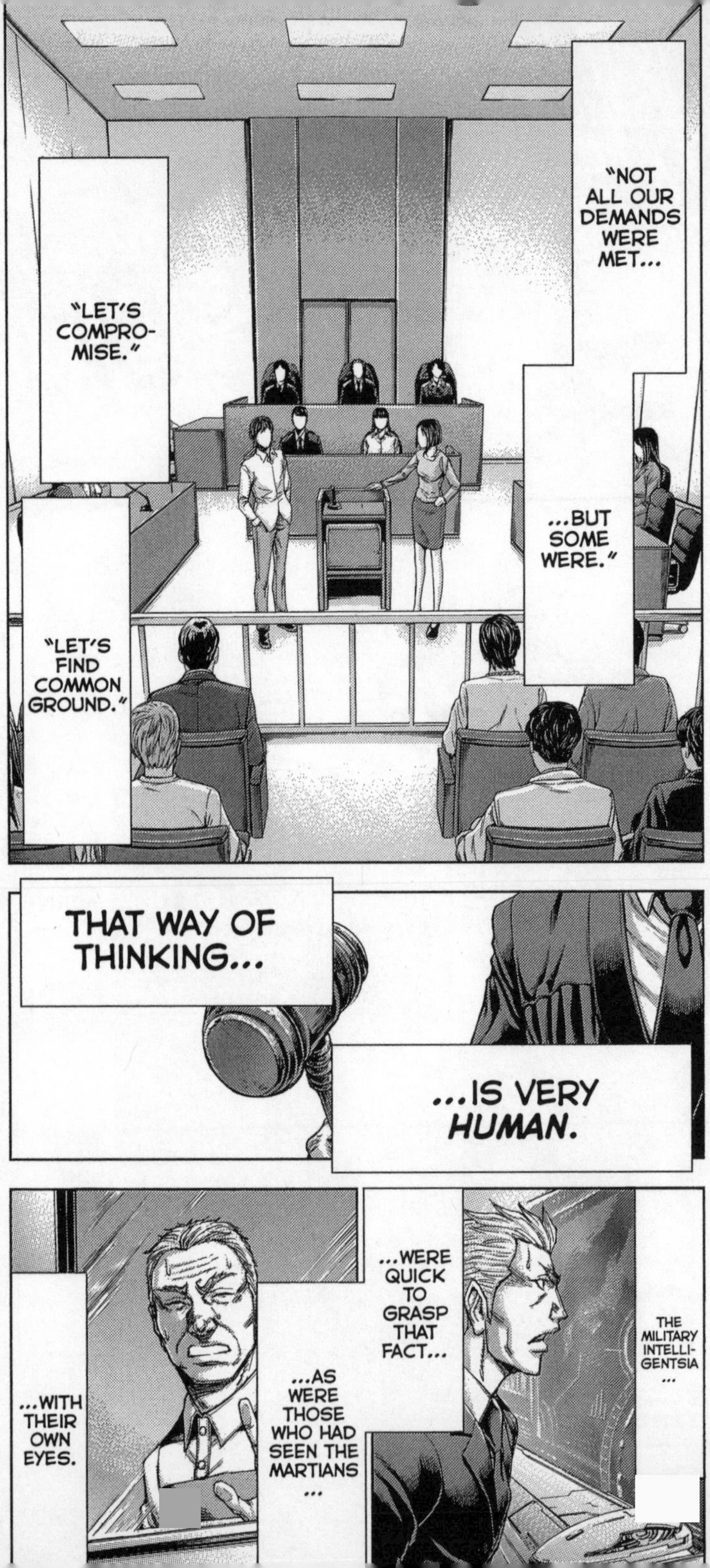
"NOT ALL OUR DEMANDS WERE MET...
...BUT SOME WERE."
"LET'S COMPROMISE."
"LET'S FIND COMMON GROUND."
THAT WAY OF THINKING...
...IS VERY HUMAN.
THE MILITARY INTELLIGENTSIA...
...WERE QUICK TO GRASP THAT FACT...
...AS WERE THOSE WHO HAD SEEN THE MARTIANS...
...WITH THEIR OWN EYES.

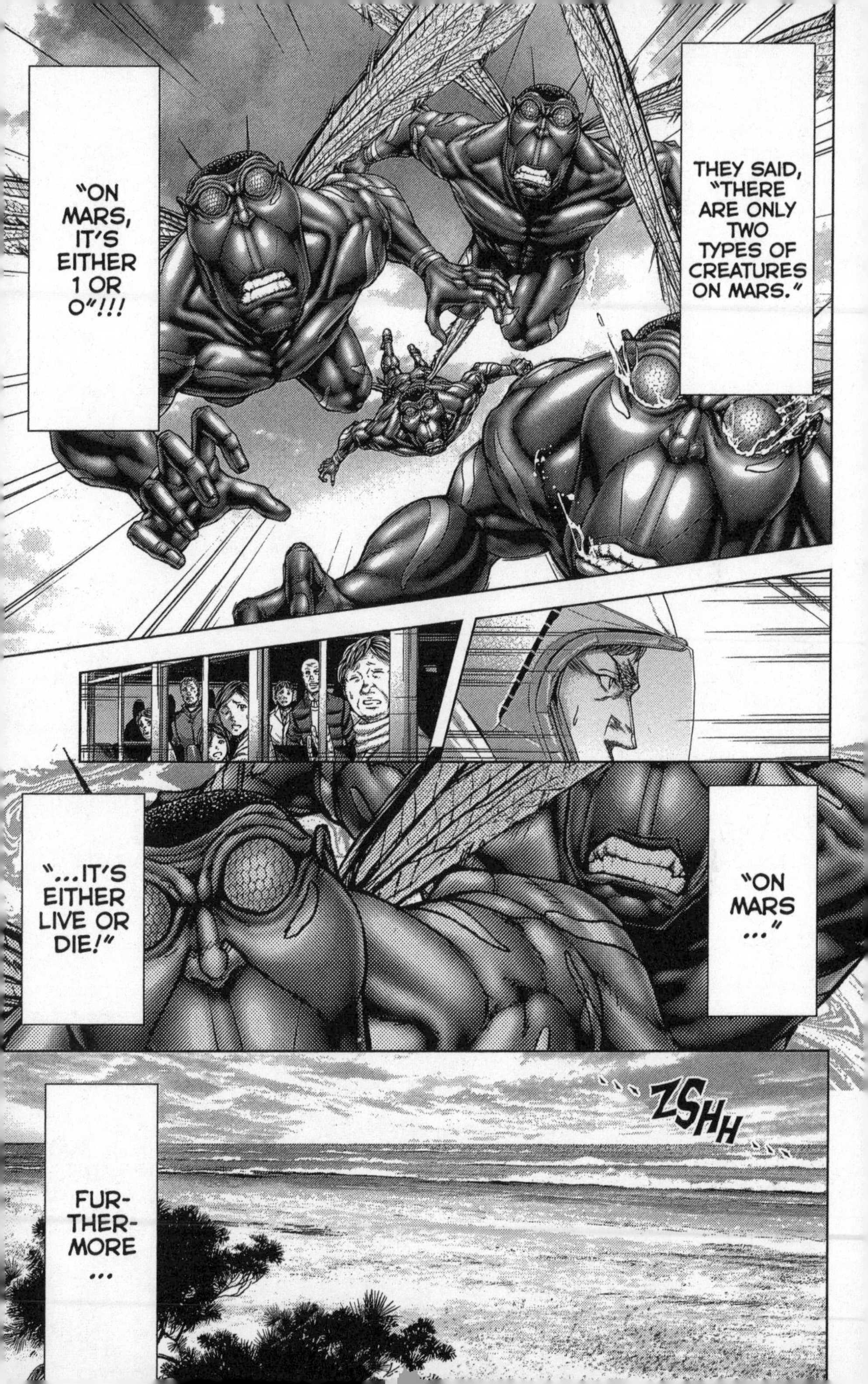
THEY SAID, "THERE ARE ONLY TWO TYPES OF CREATURES ON MARS."
"ON MARS, IT'S EITHER 1 OR 0"!!!
"ON MARS..."
"...IT'S EITHER LIVE OR DIE!"
ZSHH
FUR-THER-MORE...

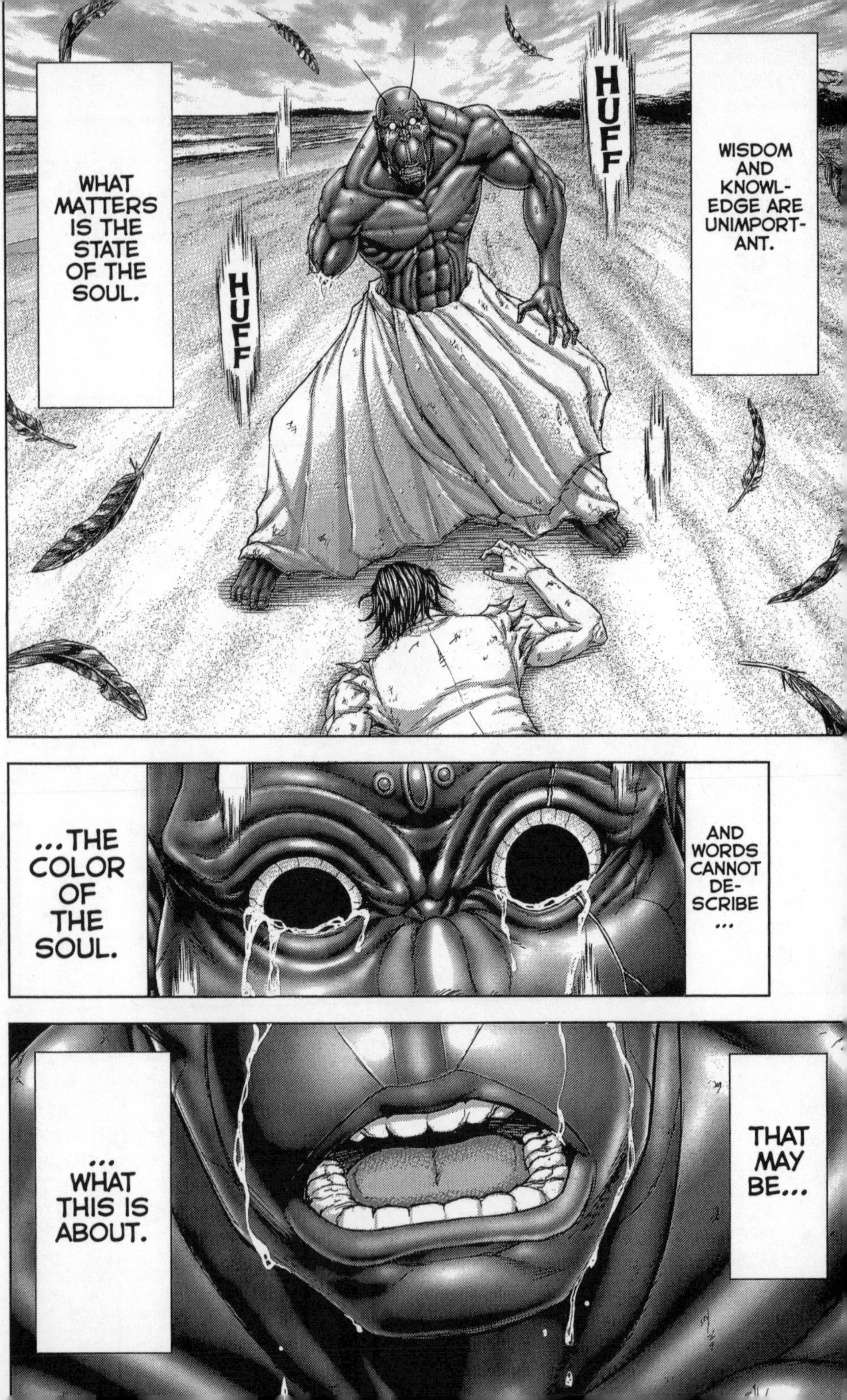
WISDOM AND KNOWLEDGE ARE UNIMPORTANT.
HUFF
HUFF
WHAT MATTERS IS THE STATE OF THE SOUL.
AND WORDS CANNOT DESCRIBE...
...THE COLOR OF THE SOUL.
THAT MAY BE...
...WHAT THIS IS ABOUT.

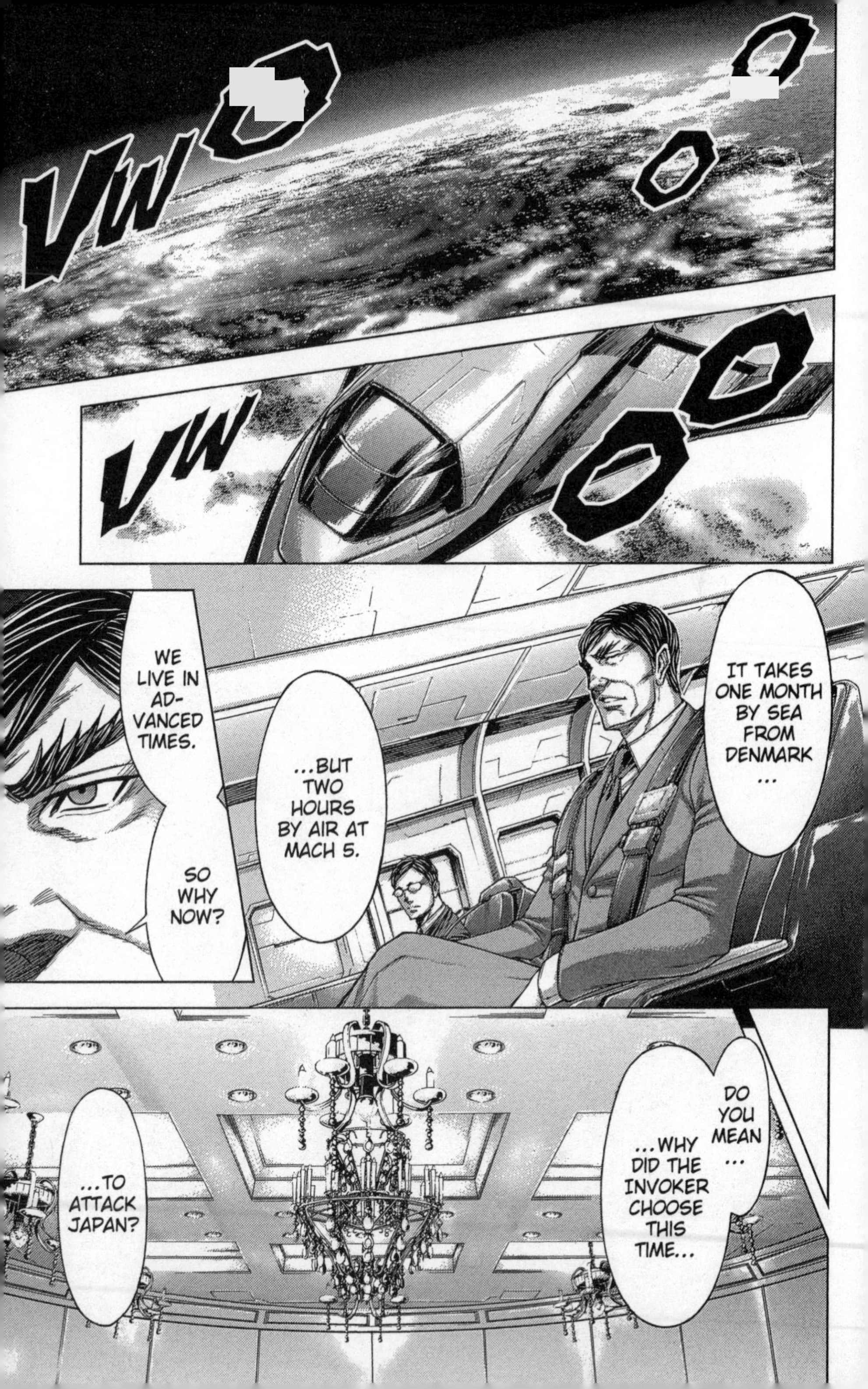
VWOOO
VWOO
IT TAKES ONE MONTH BY SEA FROM DENMARK...
...BUT TWO HOURS BY AIR AT MACH 5.
WE LIVE IN AD-VANCED TIMES.
SO WHY NOW?
DO YOU MEAN...
...WHY DID THE INVOKER CHOOSE THIS TIME...
...TO ATTACK JAPAN?

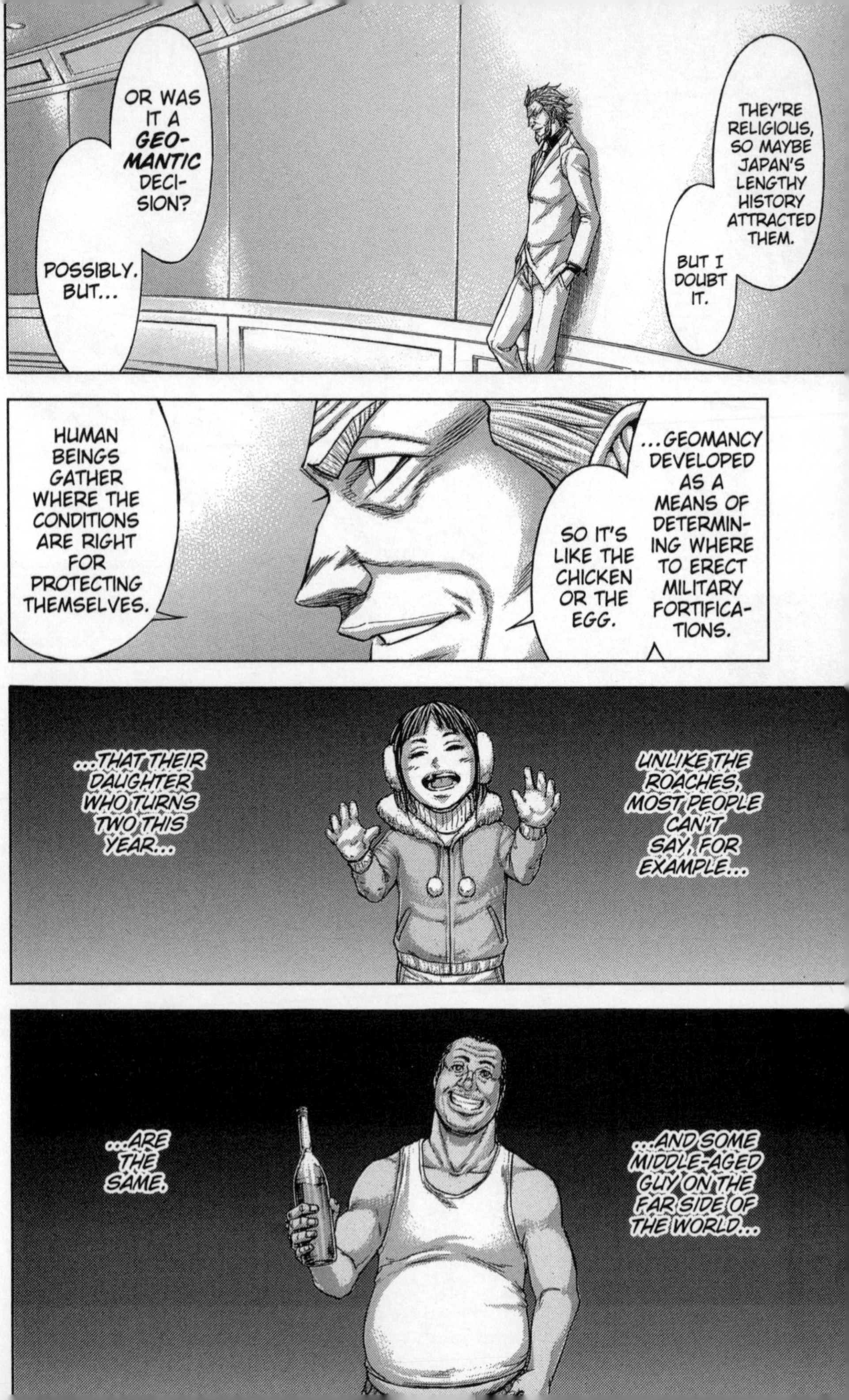
THEY'RE RELIGIOUS, SO MAYBE JAPAN'S LENGTHY HISTORY ATTRACTED THEM.
BUT I DOUBT IT.
OR WAS IT A **GEO-MANTIC** DECI-SION?
POSSIBLY. BUT...
...GEOMANCY DEVELOPED AS A MEANS OF DETERMIN-ING WHERE TO ERECT MILITARY FORTIFICA-TIONS.
SO IT'S LIKE THE CHICKEN OR THE EGG.
HUMAN BEINGS GATHER WHERE THE CONDITIONS ARE RIGHT FOR PROTECTING THEMSELVES.
UNLIKE THE ROACHES, MOST PEOPLE CAN'T SAY, FOR EXAMPLE...
...THAT THEIR DAUGHTER WHO TURNS TWO THIS YEAR...
...AND SOME MIDDLE-AGED GUY ON THE FAR SIDE OF THE WORLD...
...ARE THE SAME.

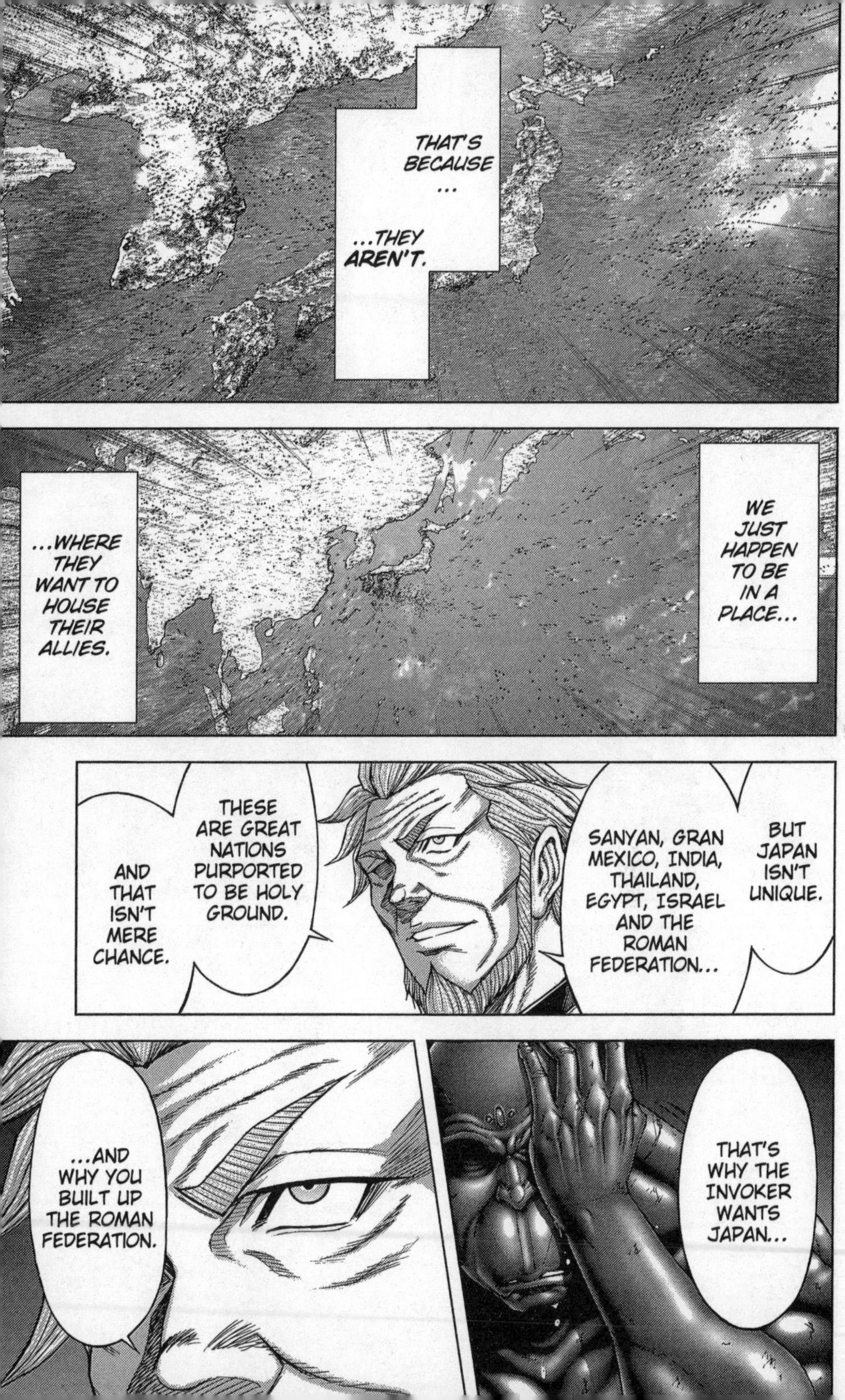
THAT'S BECAUSE ...
...THEY AREN'T.
WE JUST HAPPEN TO BE IN A PLACE...
...WHERE THEY WANT TO HOUSE THEIR ALLIES.
BUT JAPAN ISN'T UNIQUE.
SANYAN, GRAN MEXICO, INDIA, THAILAND, EGYPT, ISRAEL AND THE ROMAN FEDERATION...
THESE ARE GREAT NATIONS PURPORTED TO BE HOLY GROUND.
AND THAT ISN'T MERE CHANCE.
THAT'S WHY THE INVOKER WANTS JAPAN...
...AND WHY YOU BUILT UP THE ROMAN FEDERATION.

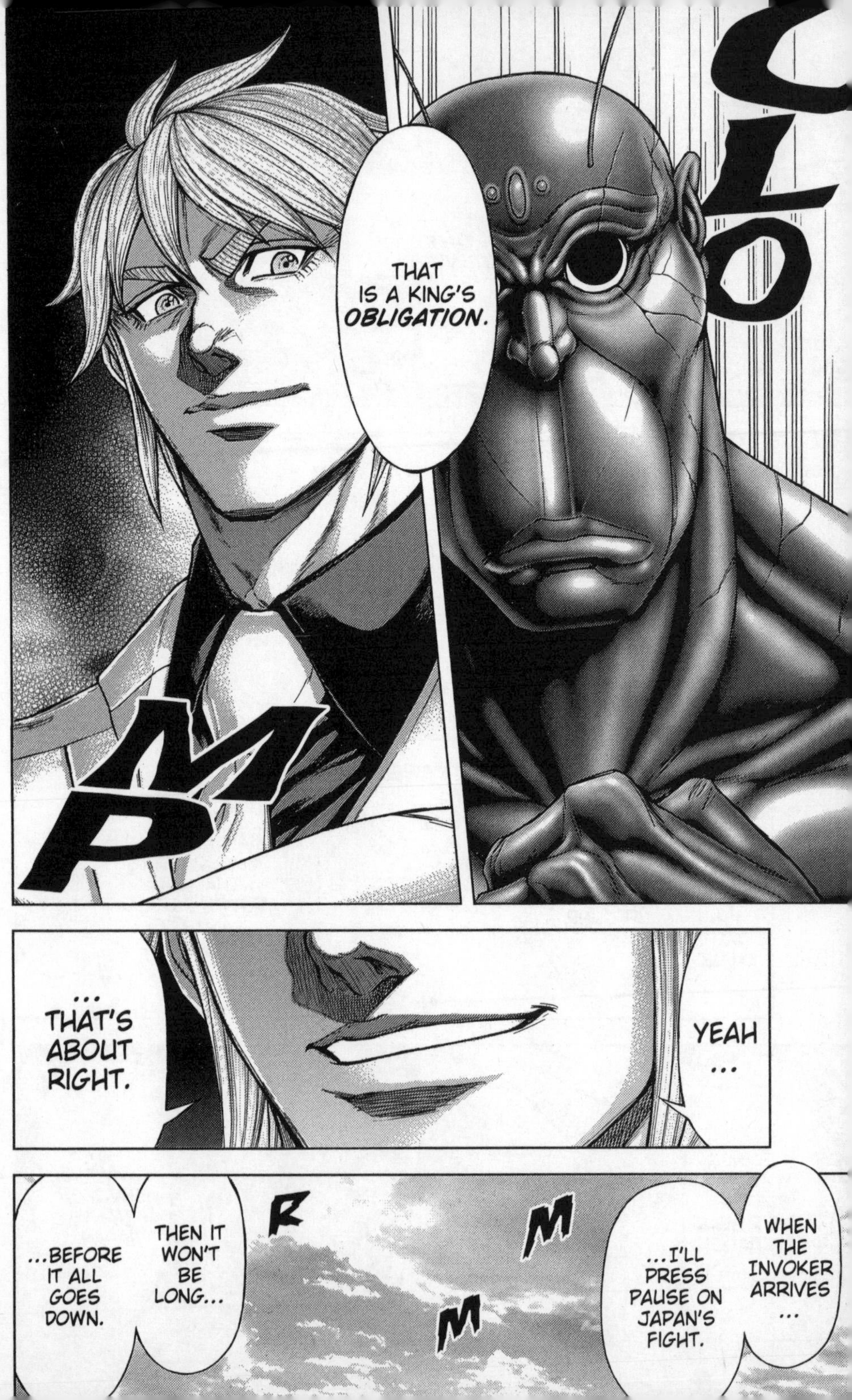

CLO
THAT IS A KING'S *OBLIGATION*.
MP
YEAH ...
... THAT'S ABOUT RIGHT.
WHEN THE INVOKER ARRIVES ...
...I'LL PRESS PAUSE ON JAPAN'S FIGHT.
RMMM
THEN IT WON'T BE LONG...
...BEFORE IT ALL GOES DOWN.

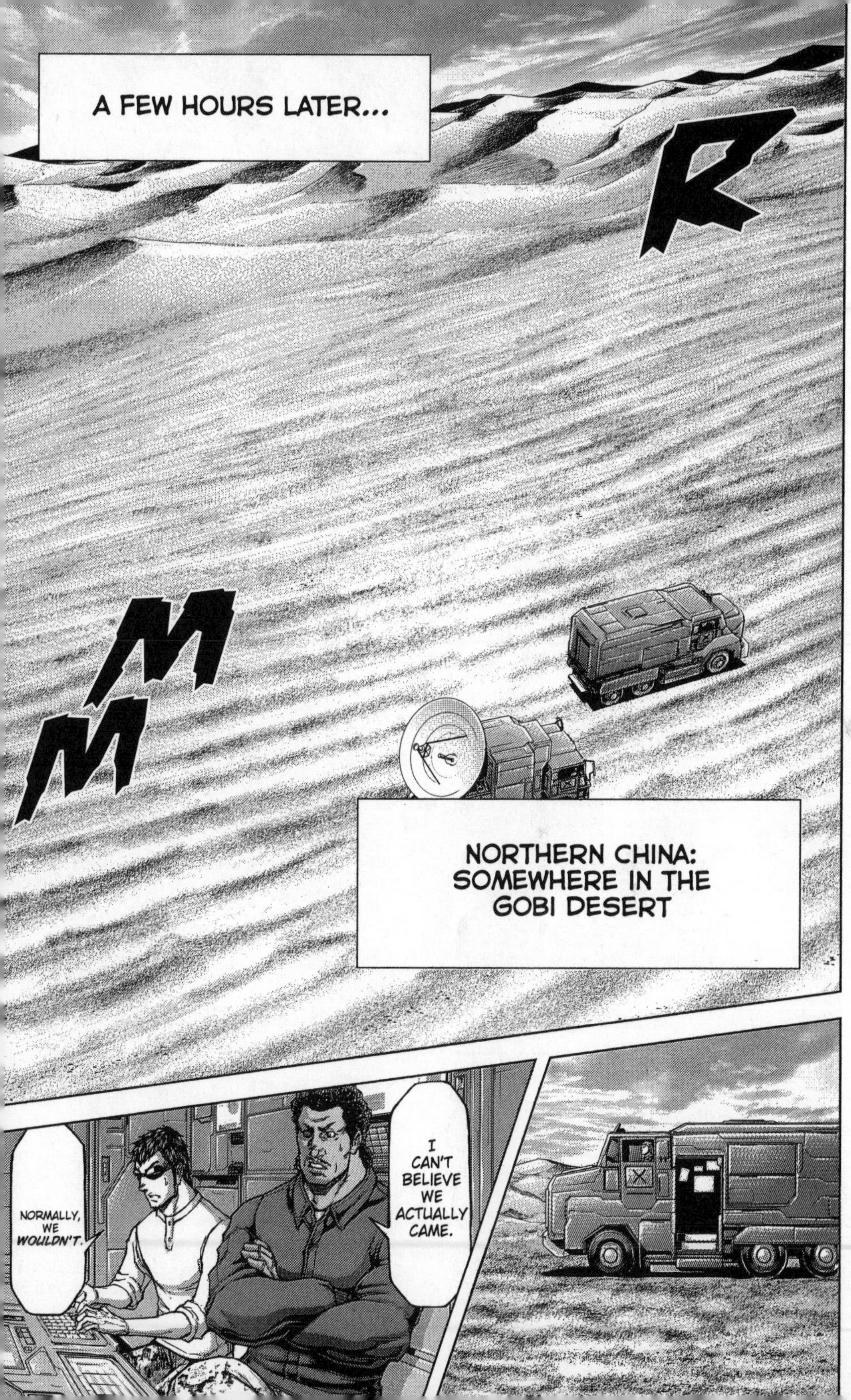

A FEW HOURS LATER...
R
MM
NORTHERN CHINA: SOMEWHERE IN THE GOBI DESERT
I CAN'T BELIEVE WE ACTUALLY CAME.
NORMALLY, WE *WOULDN'T*.

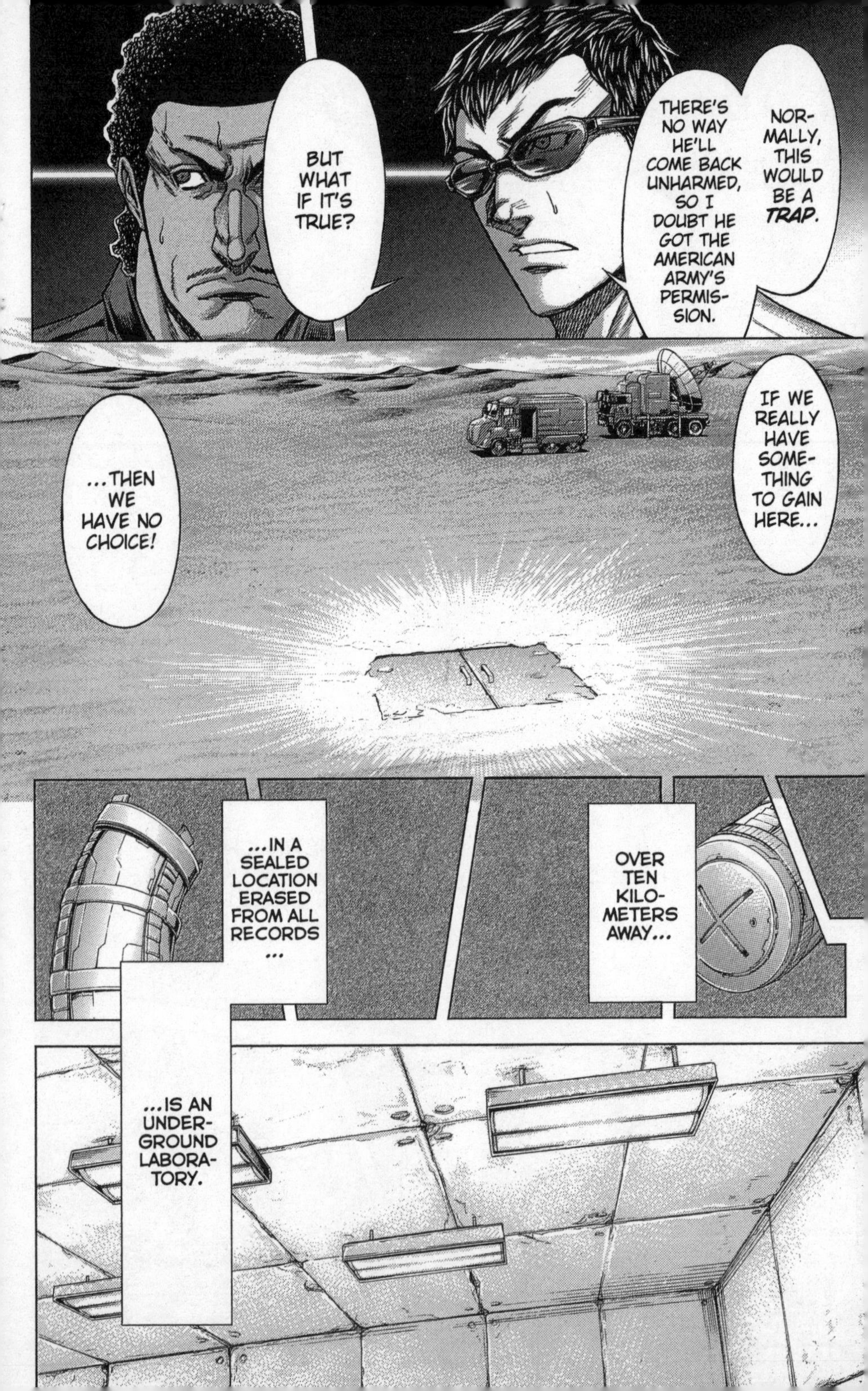
NOR-MALLY, THIS WOULD BE A *TRAP*.
THERE'S NO WAY HE'LL COME BACK UNHARMED, SO I DOUBT HE GOT THE AMERICAN ARMY'S PERMIS-SION.
BUT WHAT IF IT'S TRUE?
IF WE REALLY HAVE SOME-THING TO GAIN HERE...
...THEN WE HAVE NO CHOICE!
OVER TEN KILO-METERS AWAY...
...IN A SEALED LOCATION ERASED FROM ALL RECORDS...
...IS AN UNDER-GROUND LABORA-TORY.

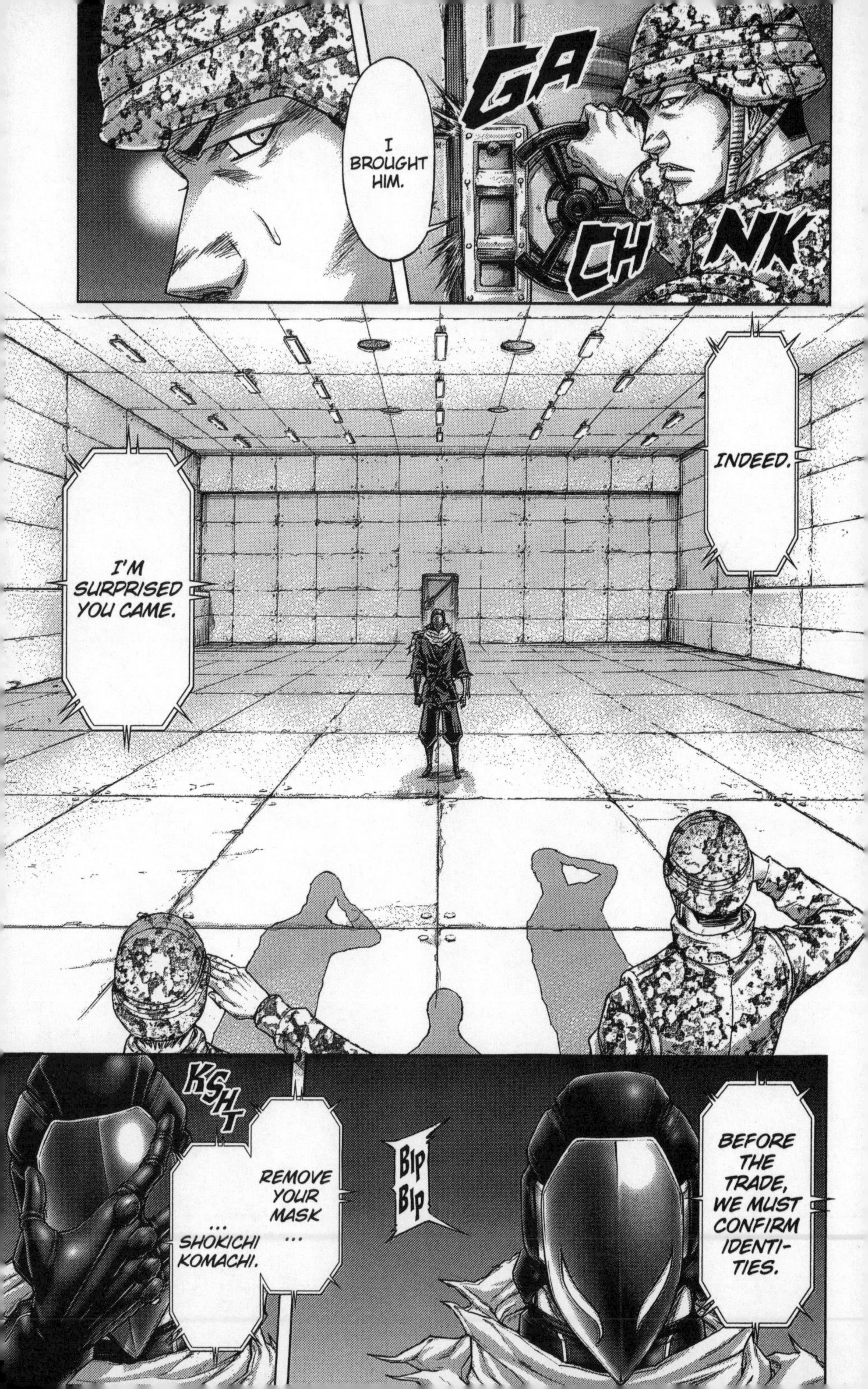
GA CH NK
I BROUGHT HIM.
INDEED.
I'M SURPRISED YOU CAME.
BEFORE THE TRADE, WE MUST CONFIRM IDENTI-TIES.
BIP BIP
REMOVE YOUR MASK ...
... SHOKICHI KOMACHI.
KSHT

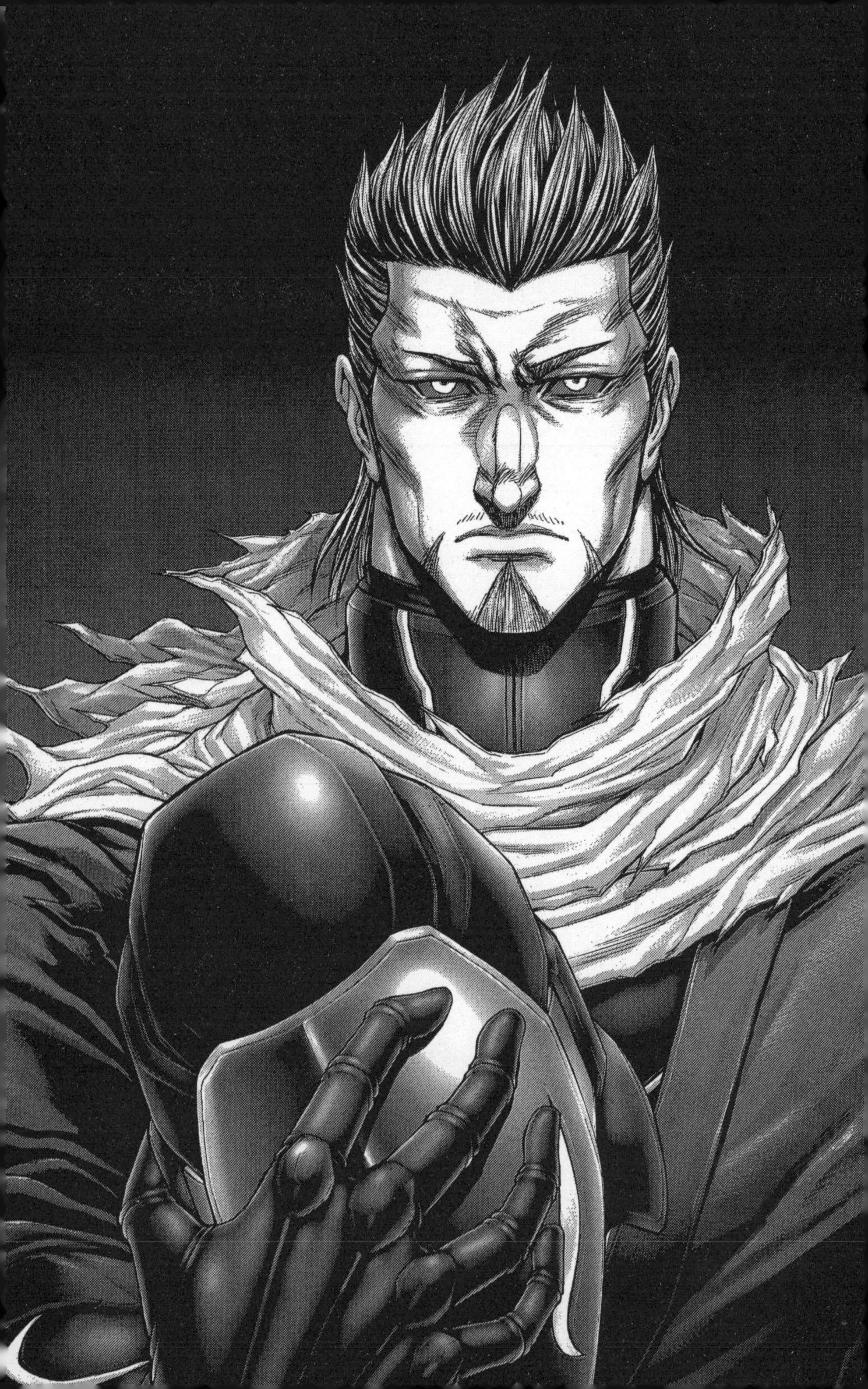

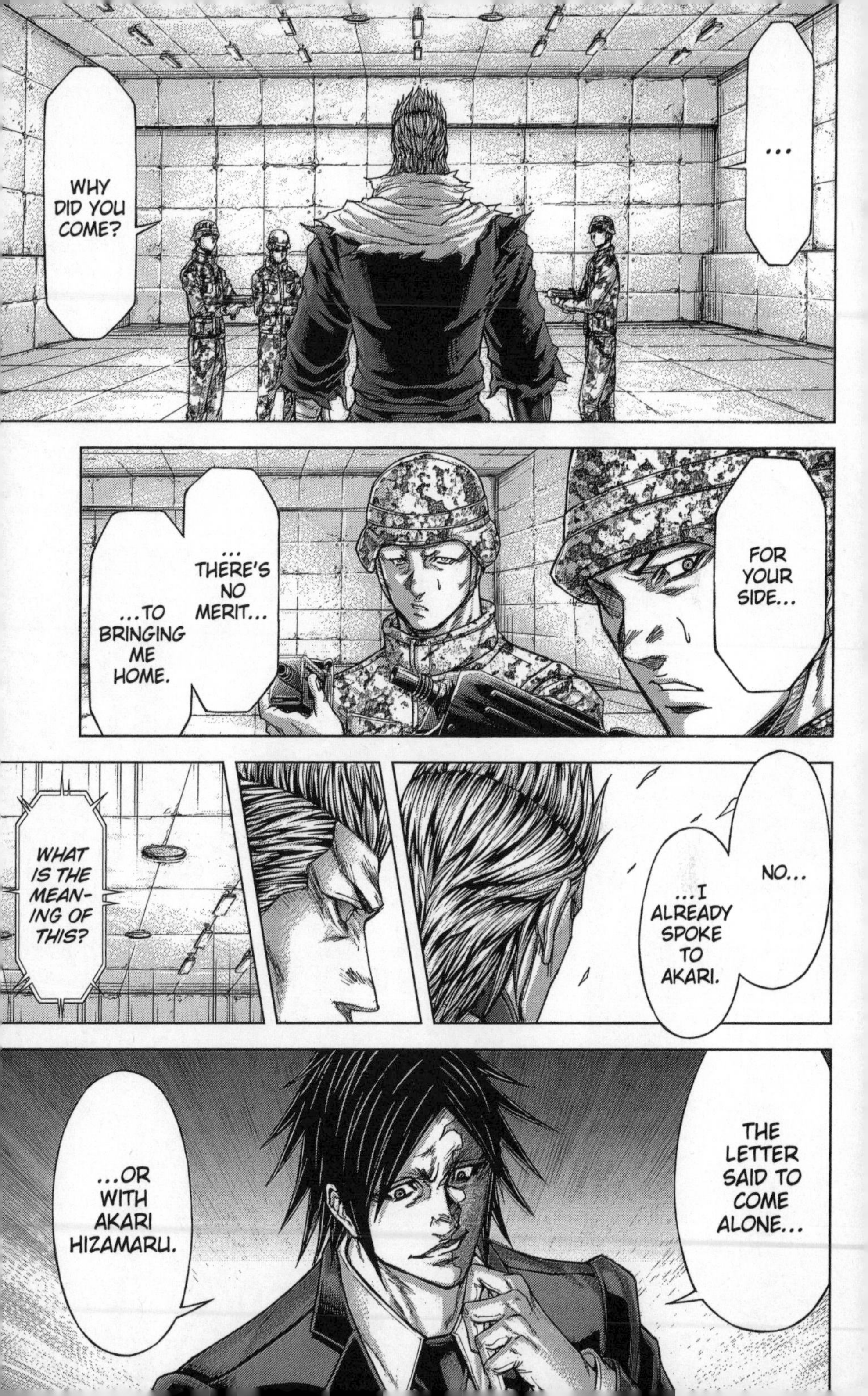
...
WHY DID YOU COME?
FOR YOUR SIDE...
... THERE'S NO MERIT...
...TO BRINGING ME HOME.
NO...
...I ALREADY SPOKE TO AKARI.
WHAT IS THE MEANING OF THIS?
THE LETTER SAID TO COME ALONE...
...OR WITH AKARI HIZAMARU.

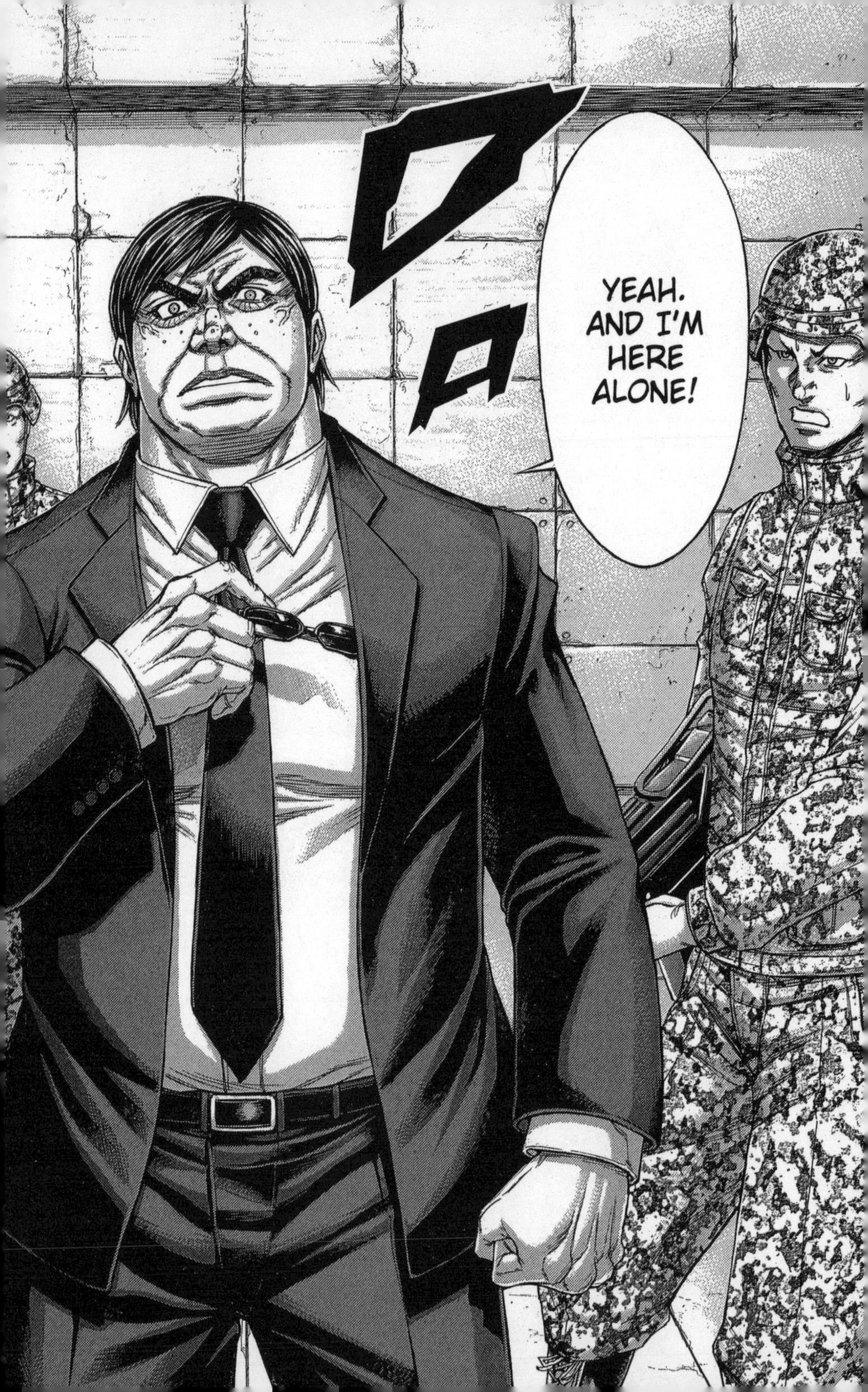
YEAH. AND I'M HERE ALONE!

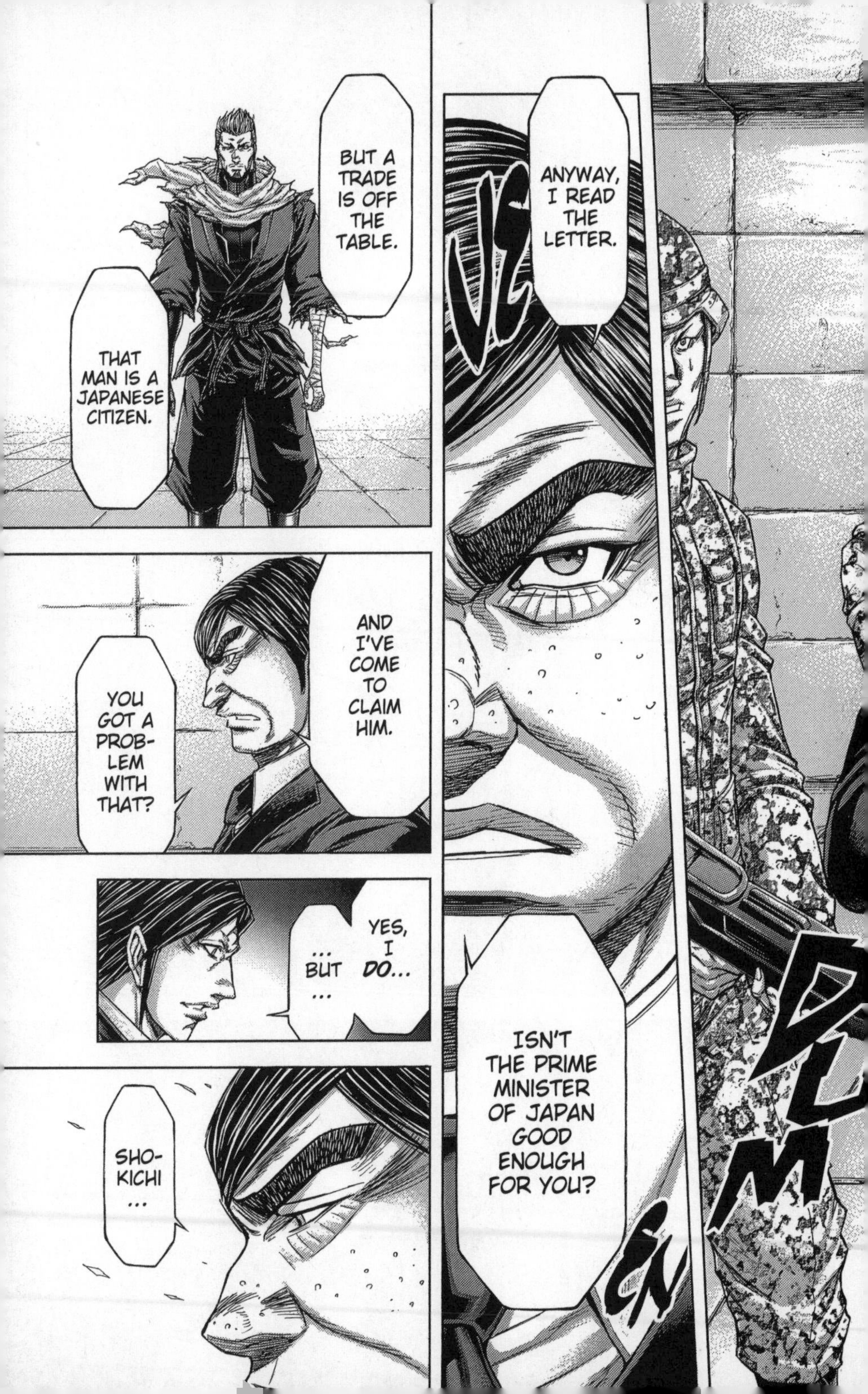
ANYWAY, I READ THE LETTER.
ISN'T THE PRIME MINISTER OF JAPAN GOOD ENOUGH FOR YOU?
BUT A TRADE IS OFF THE TABLE.
THAT MAN IS A JAPANESE CITIZEN.
AND I'VE COME TO CLAIM HIM.
YOU GOT A PROBLEM WITH THAT?
YES, I *DO*...
...BUT...
SHOKICHI...

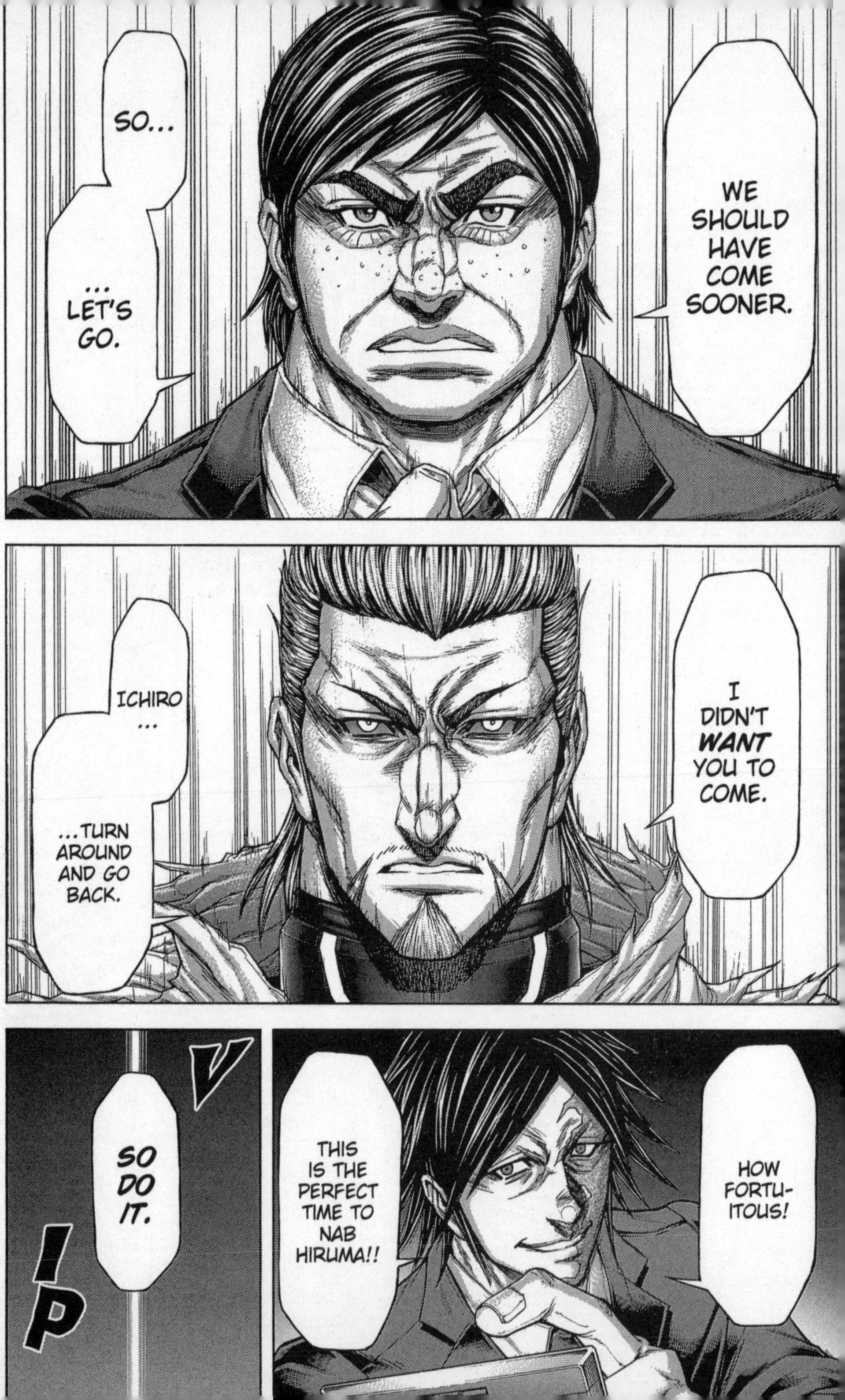
WE SHOULD HAVE COME SOONER.
SO...
...LET'S GO.
I DIDN'T *WANT* YOU TO COME.
ICHIRO...
...TURN AROUND AND GO BACK.
HOW FORTU-ITOUS!
THIS IS THE PERFECT TIME TO NAB HIRUMA!!
V
SO DO IT.
IP

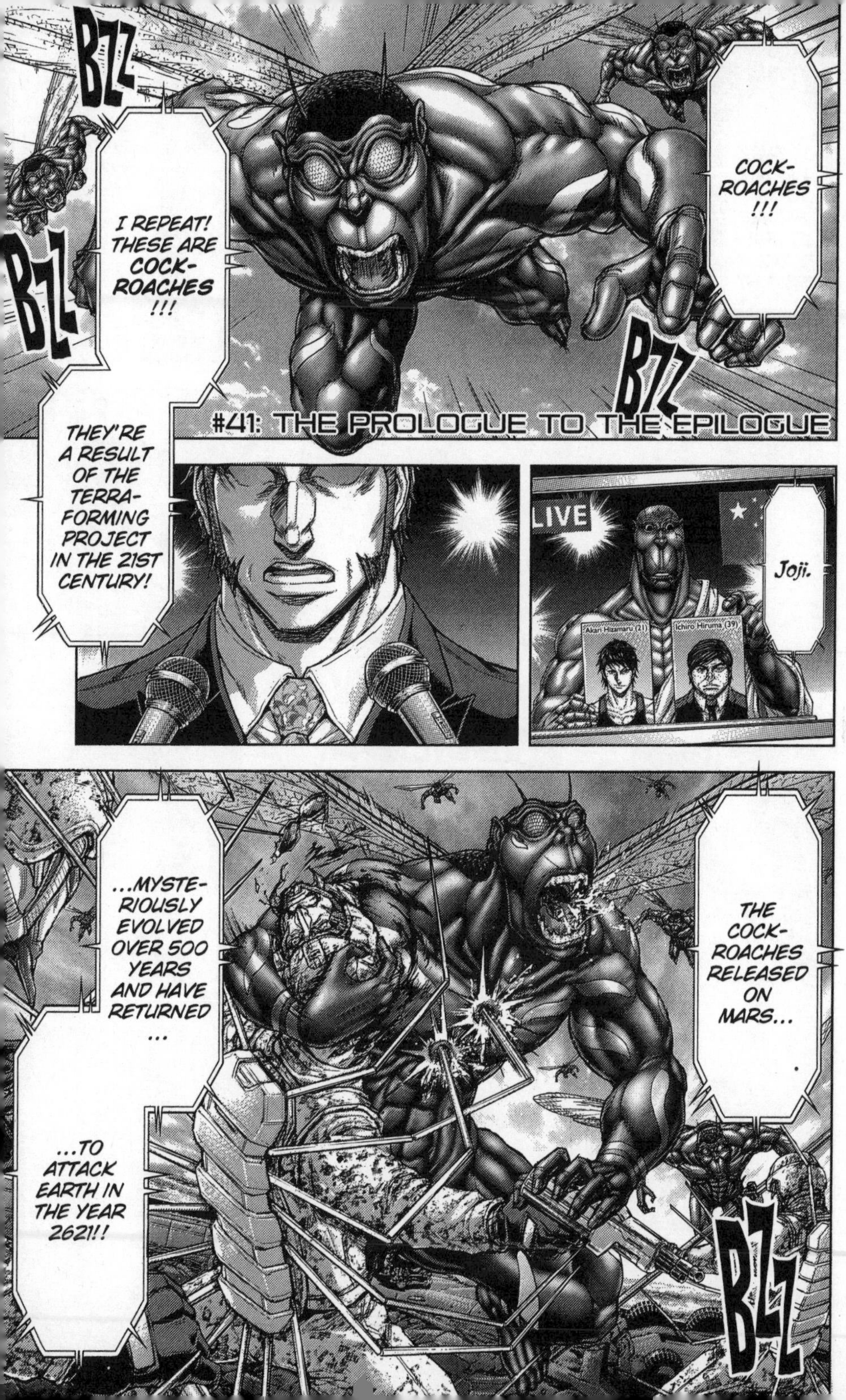
BZZ
COCK-ROACHES!!!
BZZ
I REPEAT! THESE ARE COCK-ROACHES!!!
BZZ
BZZ
#41: THE PROLOGUE TO THE EPILOGUE
LIVE
Akari Hizamaru (21)
Ichiro Hiruma (39)
Joji.
THEY'RE A RESULT OF THE TERRA-FORMING PROJECT IN THE 21ST CENTURY!
THE COCK-ROACHES RELEASED ON MARS...
...MYSTE-RIOUSLY EVOLVED OVER 500 YEARS AND HAVE RETURNED...
...TO ATTACK EARTH IN THE YEAR 2621!!
BZZ

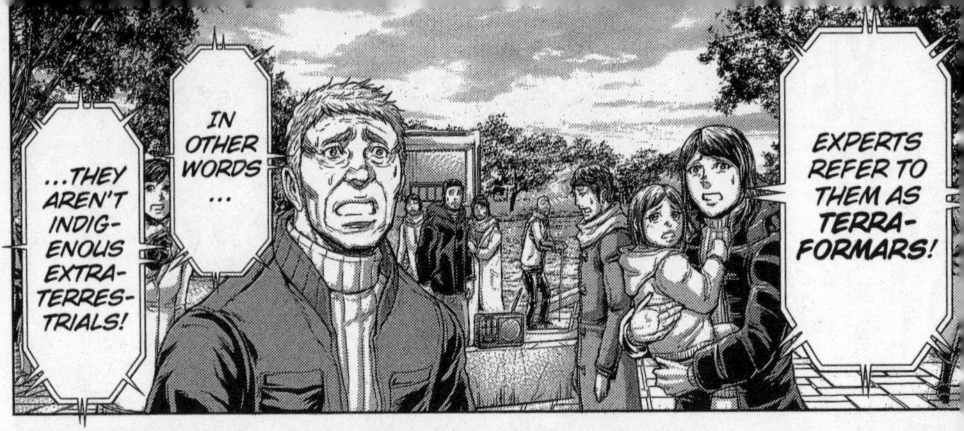
EXPERTS REFER TO THEM AS TERRA-FORMARS!
IN OTHER WORDS...
...THEY AREN'T INDIG-ENOUS EXTRA-TERRES-TRIALS!
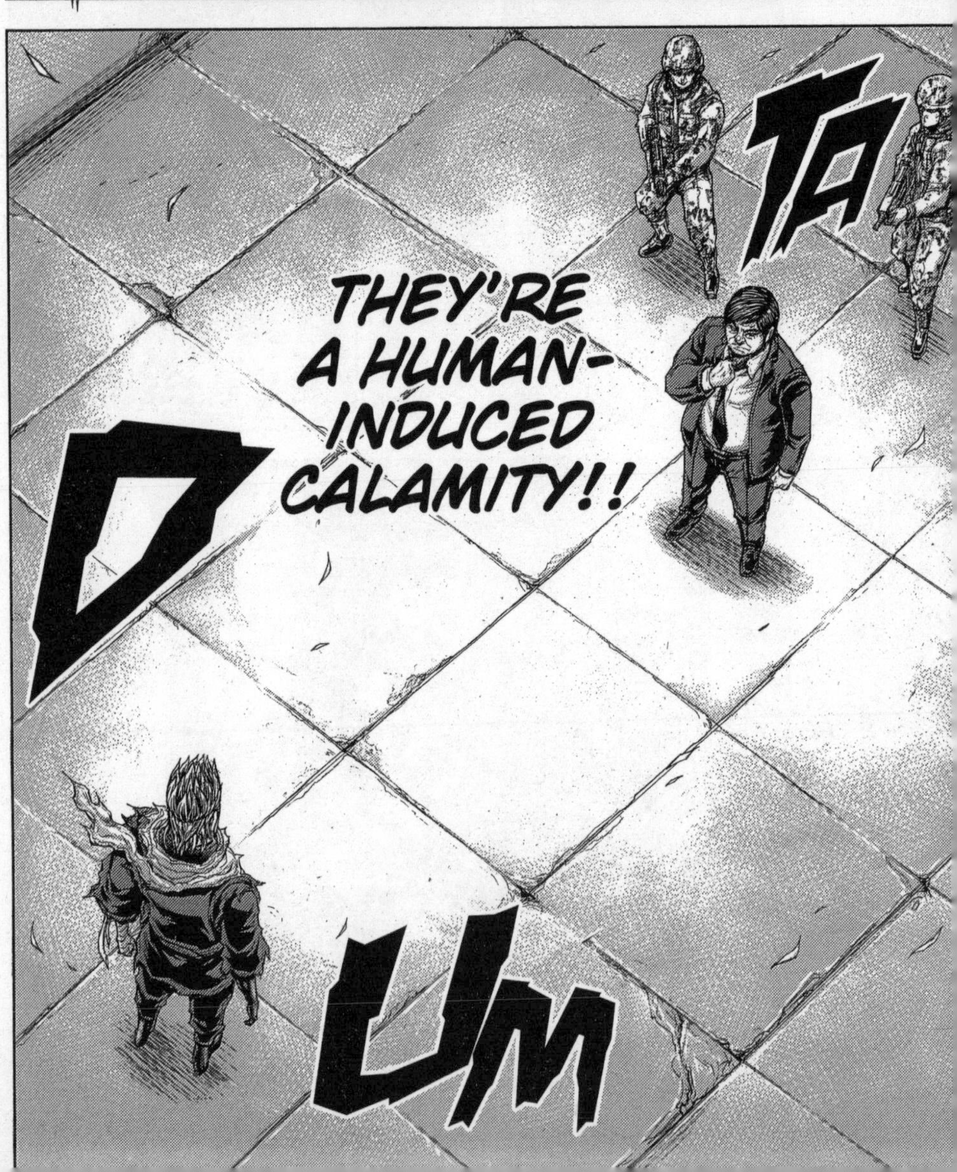
TA
THEY'RE A HUMAN-INDUCED CALAMITY!!
D
UM

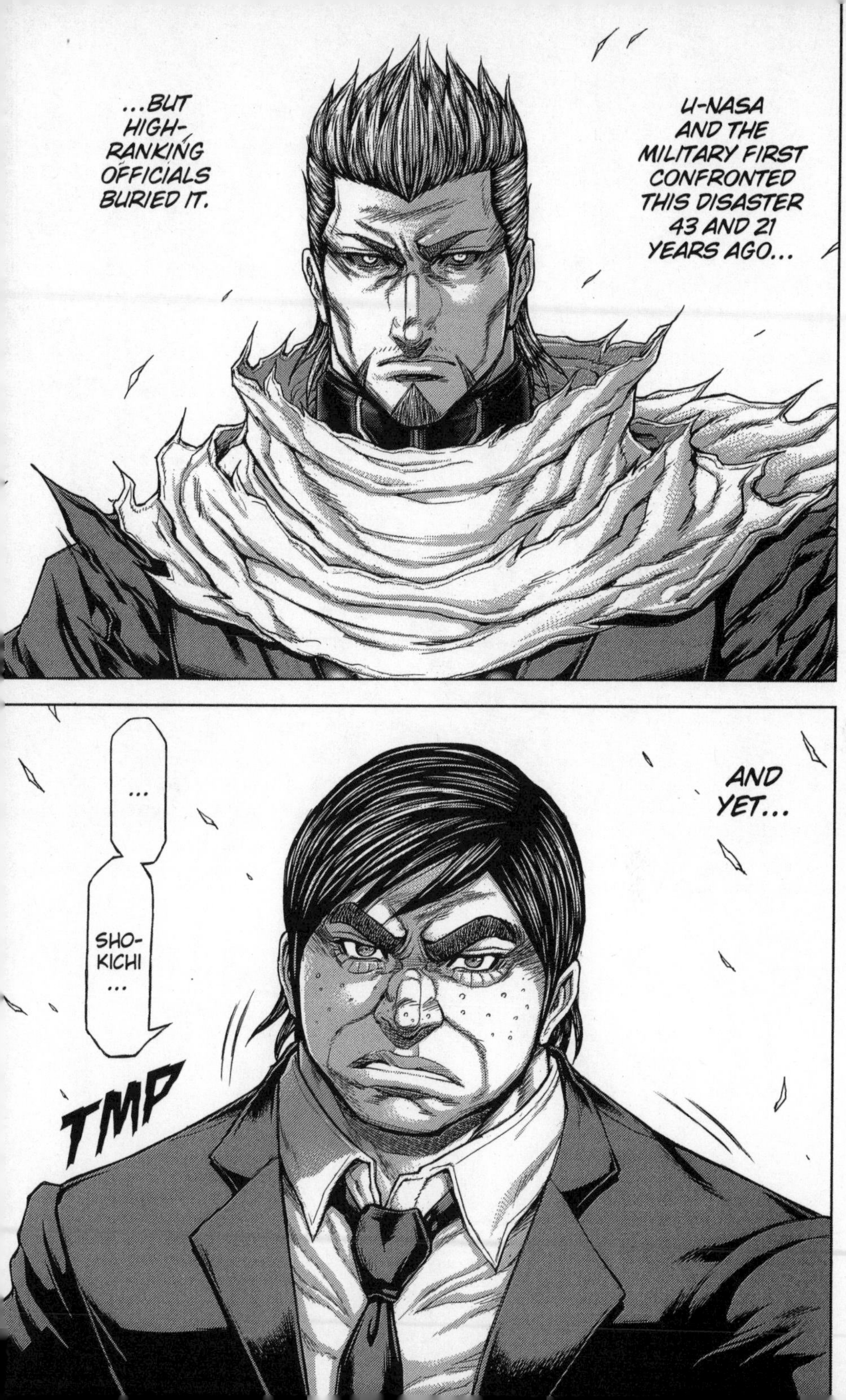
U-NASA AND THE MILITARY FIRST CONFRONTED THIS DISASTER 43 AND 21 YEARS AGO...
...BUT HIGH-RANKING OFFICIALS BURIED IT.
AND YET...
...
SHO-KICHI...
TMP

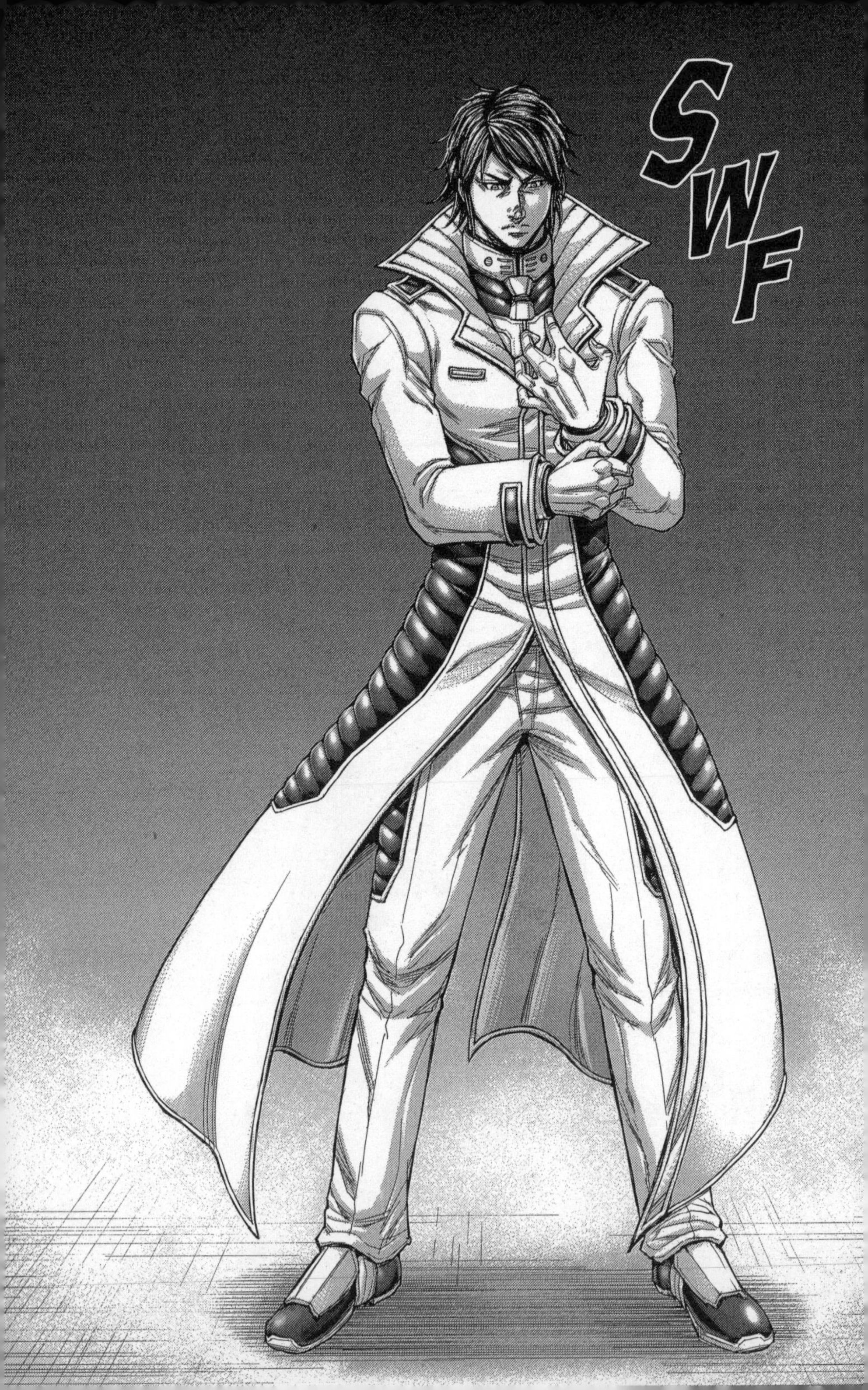
SWF

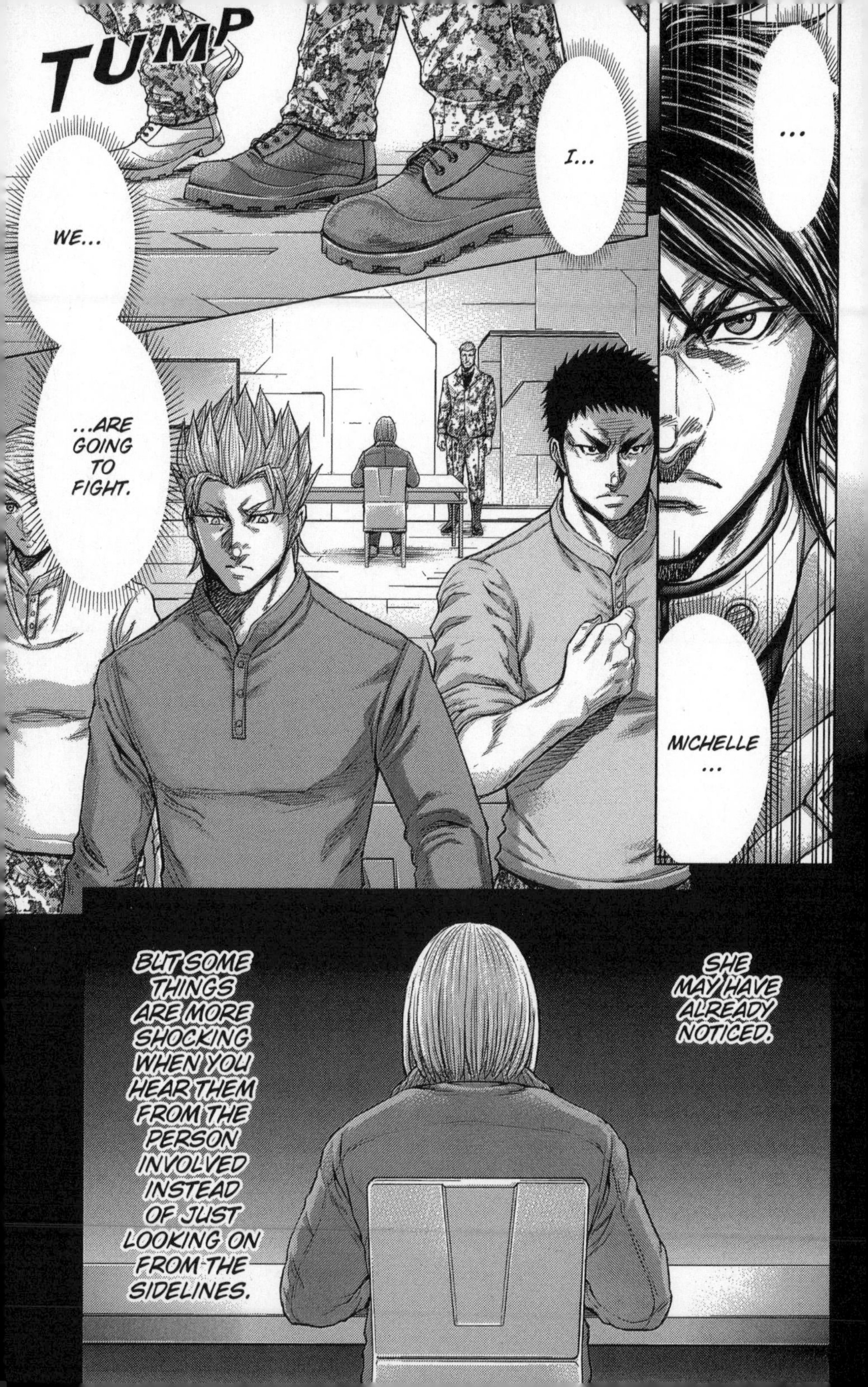
...
MICHELLE ...
TUMP
I...
WE...
...ARE GOING TO FIGHT.
SHE MAY HAVE ALREADY NOTICED.
BUT SOME THINGS ARE MORE SHOCKING WHEN YOU HEAR THEM FROM THE PERSON INVOLVED INSTEAD OF JUST LOOKING ON FROM THE SIDELINES.

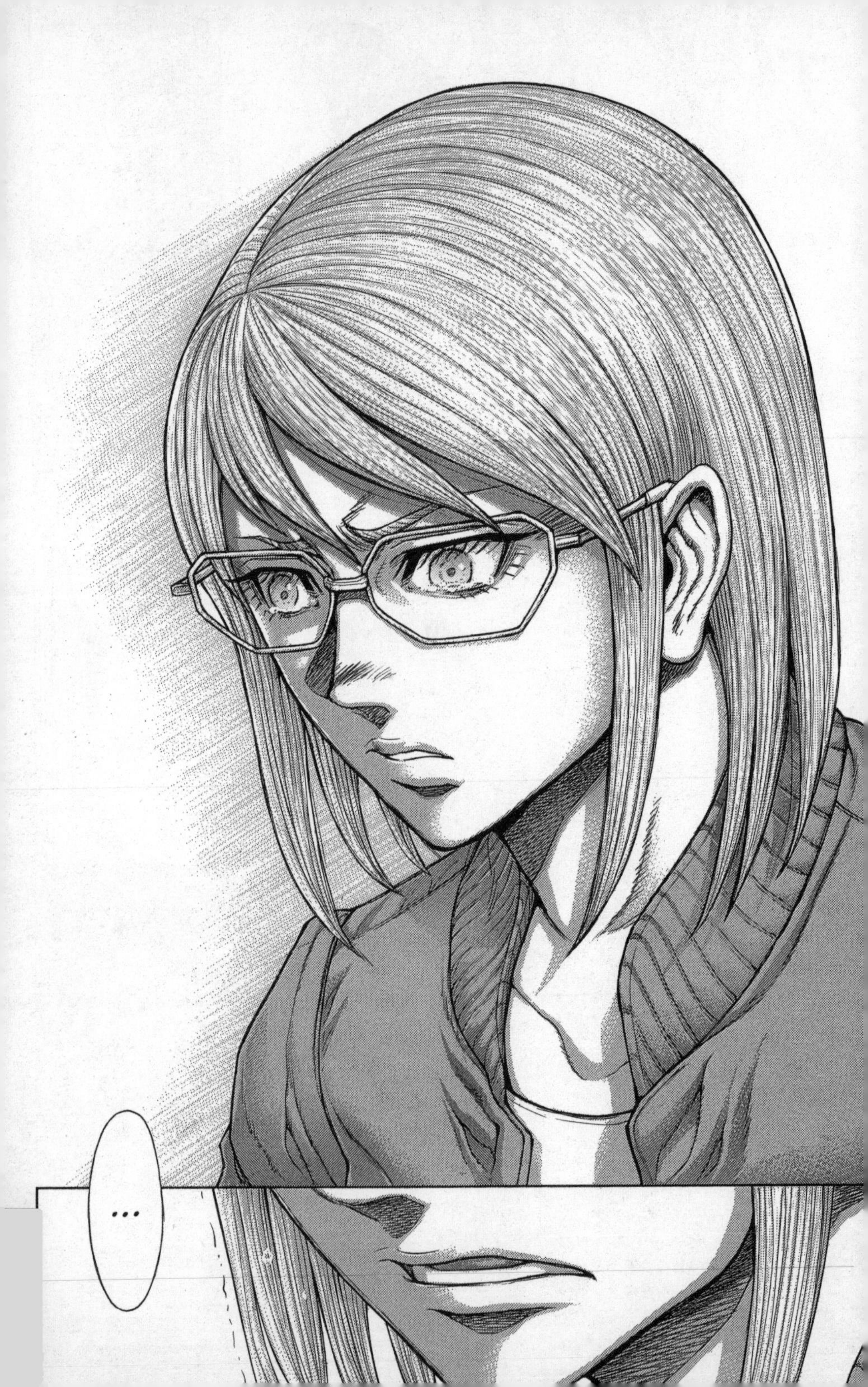
...

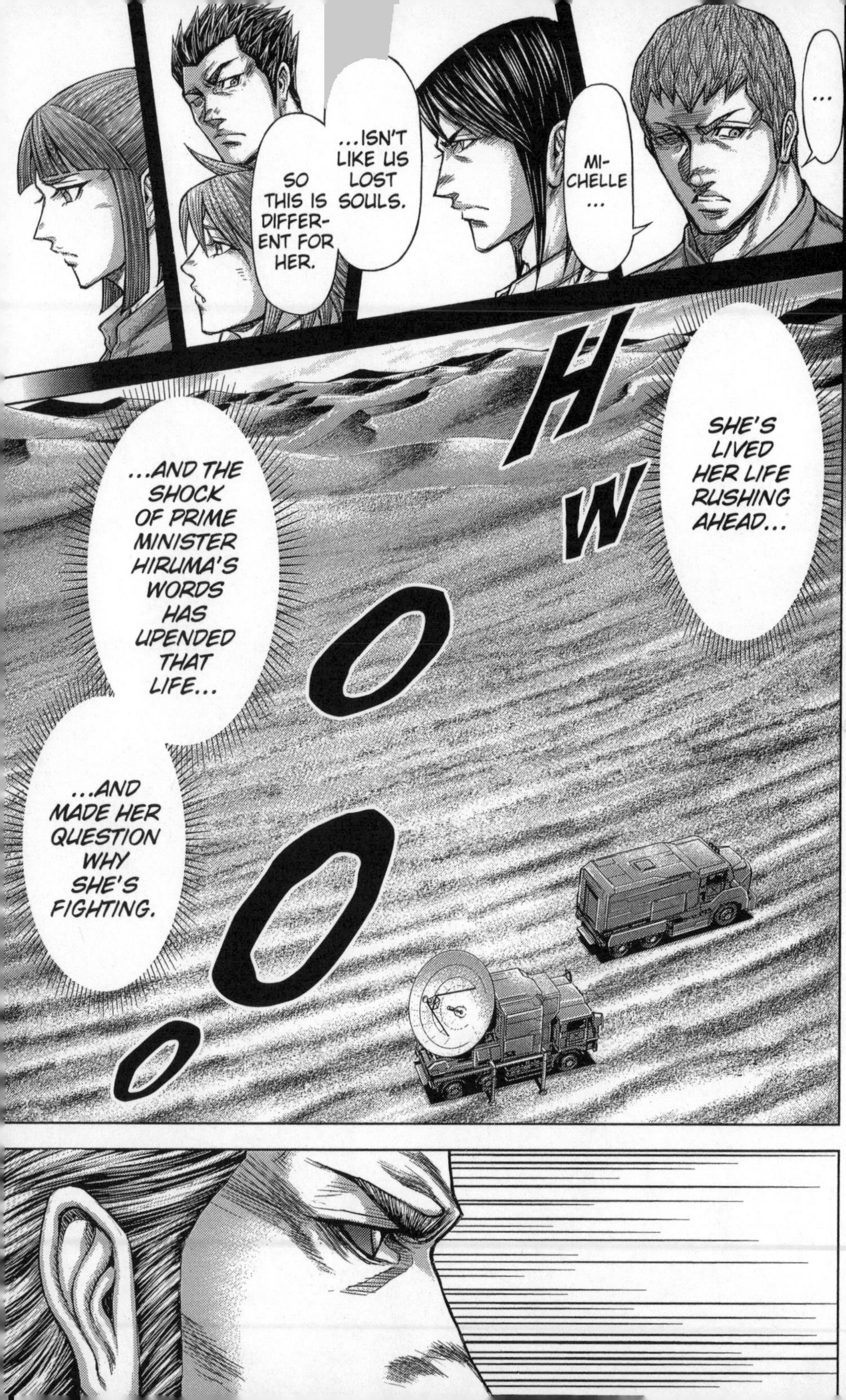
...
MI-CHELLE...
...ISN'T LIKE US LOST SOULS.
SO THIS IS DIFFER-ENT FOR HER.
SHE'S LIVED HER LIFE RUSHING AHEAD...
HWOOOO
...AND THE SHOCK OF PRIME MINISTER HIRUMA'S WORDS HAS UPENDED THAT LIFE...
...AND MADE HER QUESTION WHY SHE'S FIGHTING.

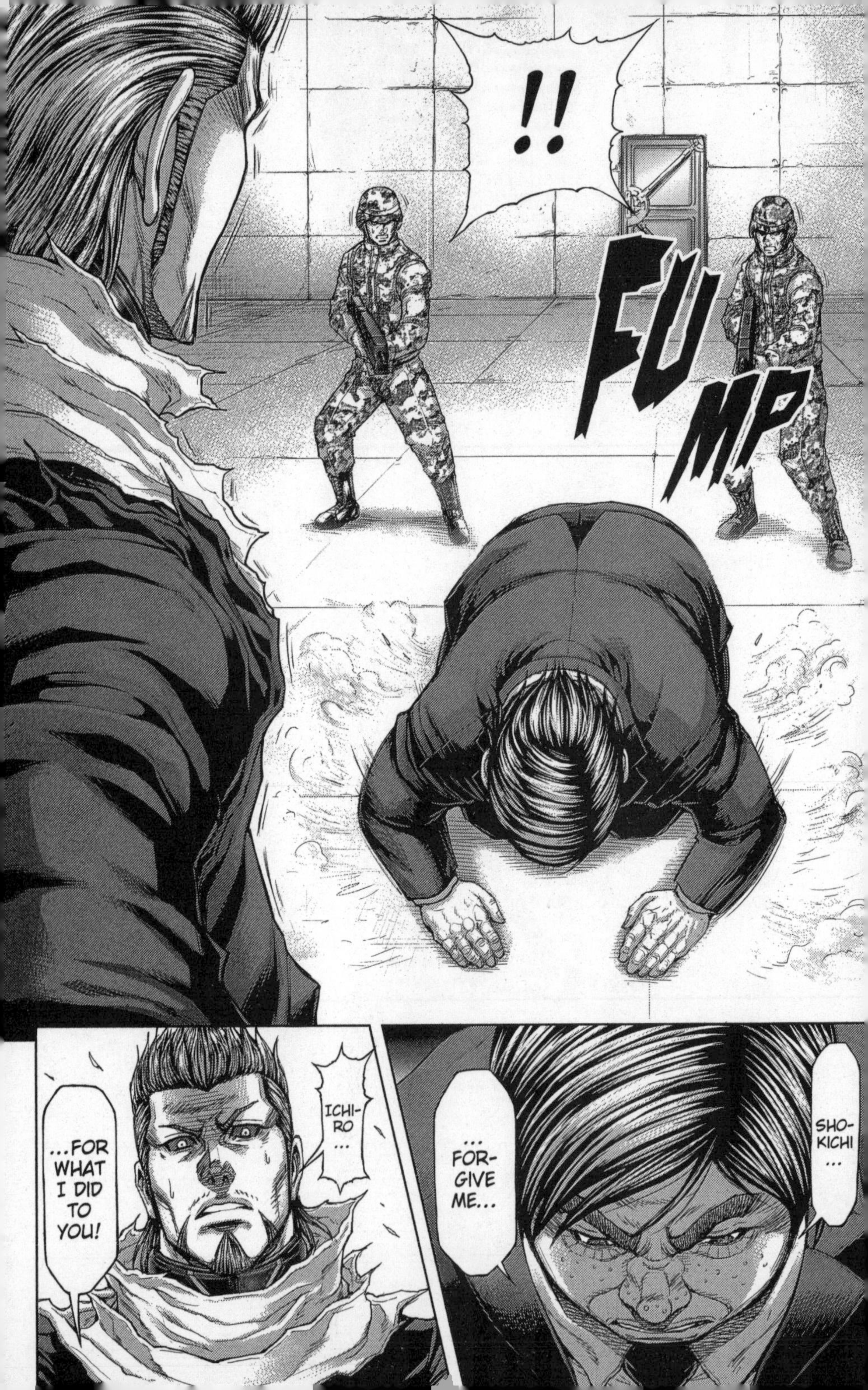
!!
FUMP
SHO-KICHI...
...FOR-GIVE ME...
ICHI-RO...
...FOR WHAT I DID TO YOU!

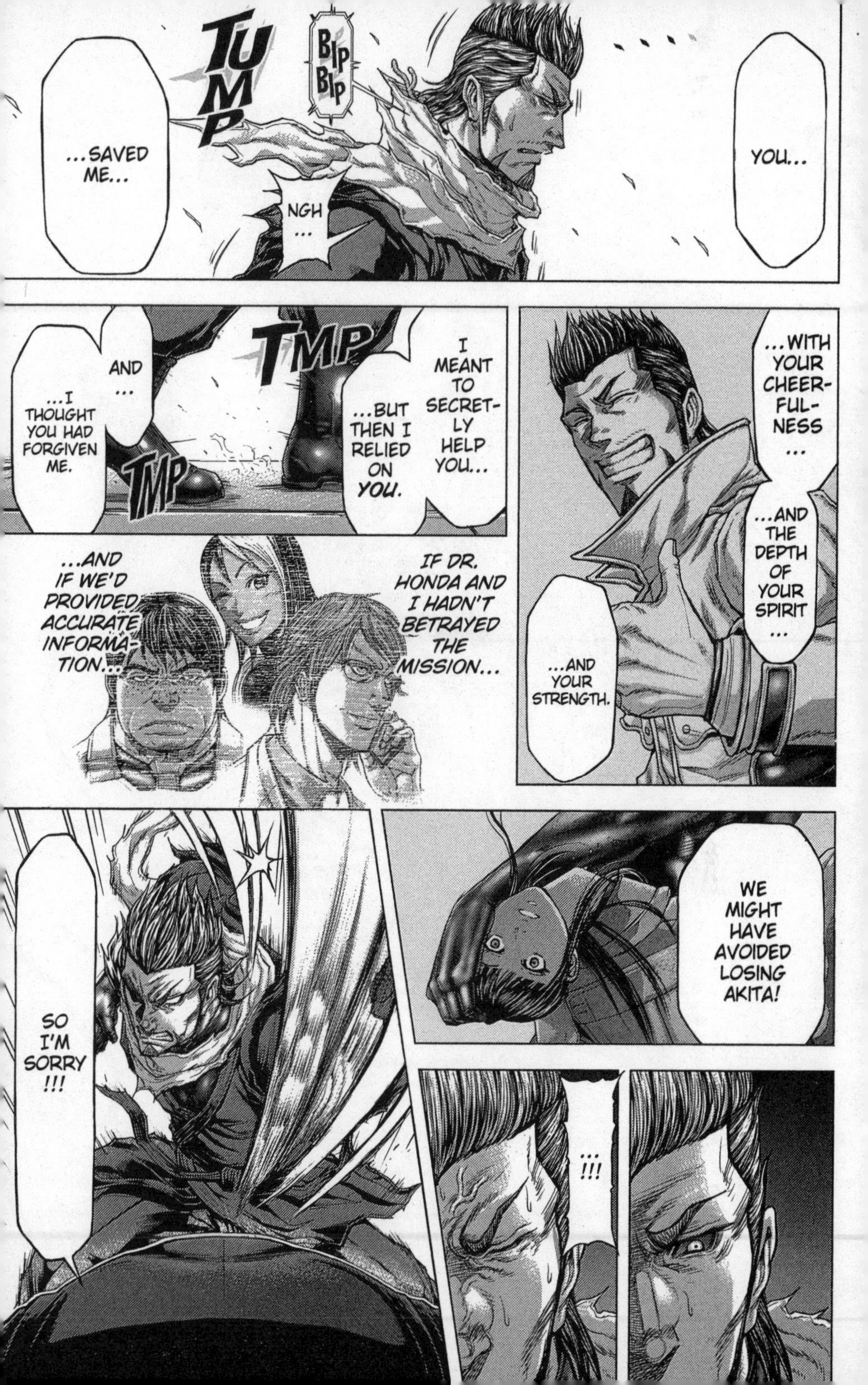
YOU...
. . .
BIP BIP
TUMP
NGH ...
...SAVED ME...
...WITH YOUR CHEERFUL-NESS ...
...AND THE DEPTH OF YOUR SPIRIT ...
...AND YOUR STRENGTH.
I MEANT TO SECRET-LY HELP YOU...
...BUT THEN I RELIED ON *YOU*.
TMP
AND ...
...I THOUGHT YOU HAD FORGIVEN ME.
TMP
IF DR. HONDA AND I HADN'T BETRAYED THE MISSION...
...AND IF WE'D PROVIDED ACCURATE INFORMA-TION...
WE MIGHT HAVE AVOIDED LOSING AKITA!
... !!!
SO I'M SORRY !!!

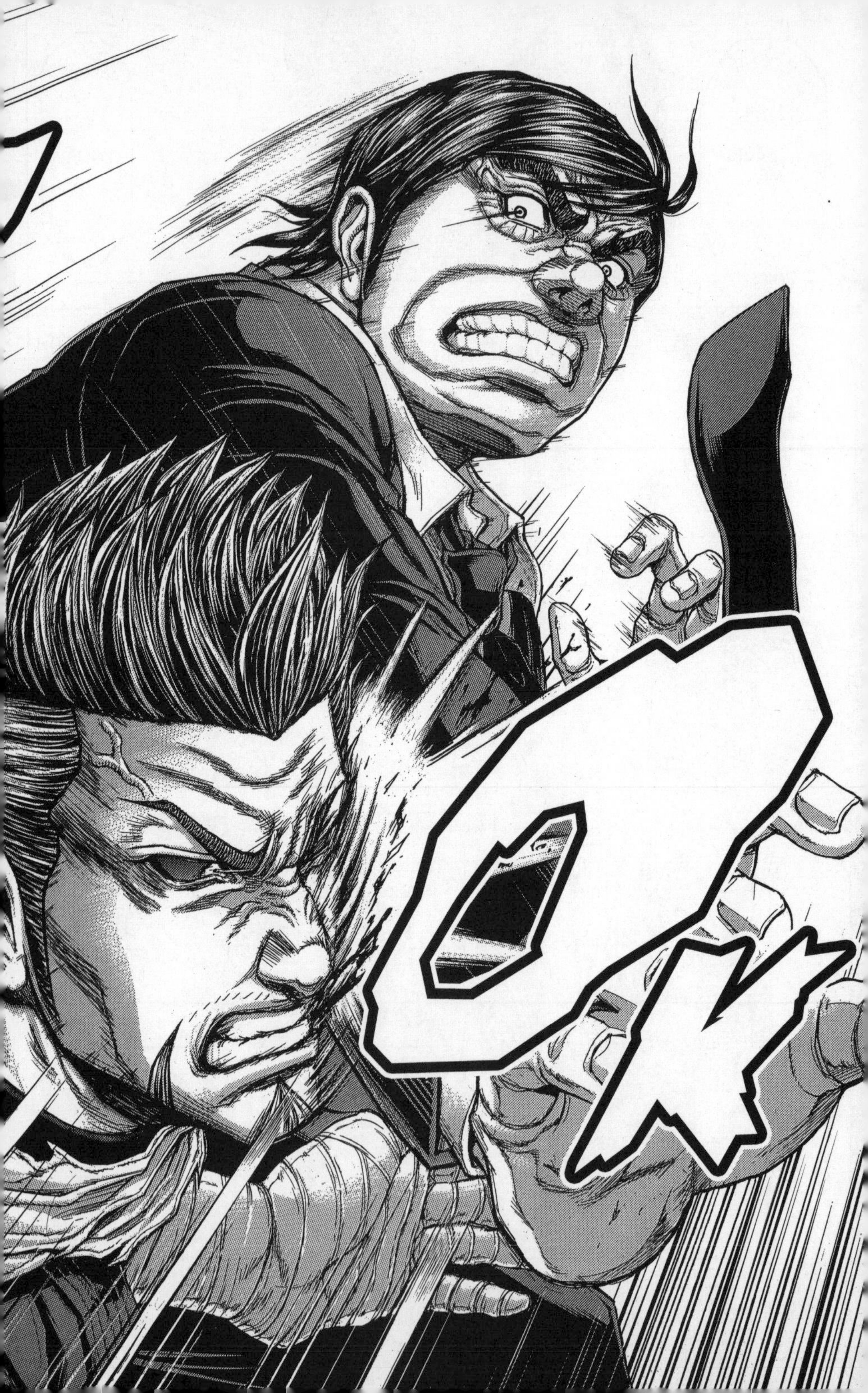

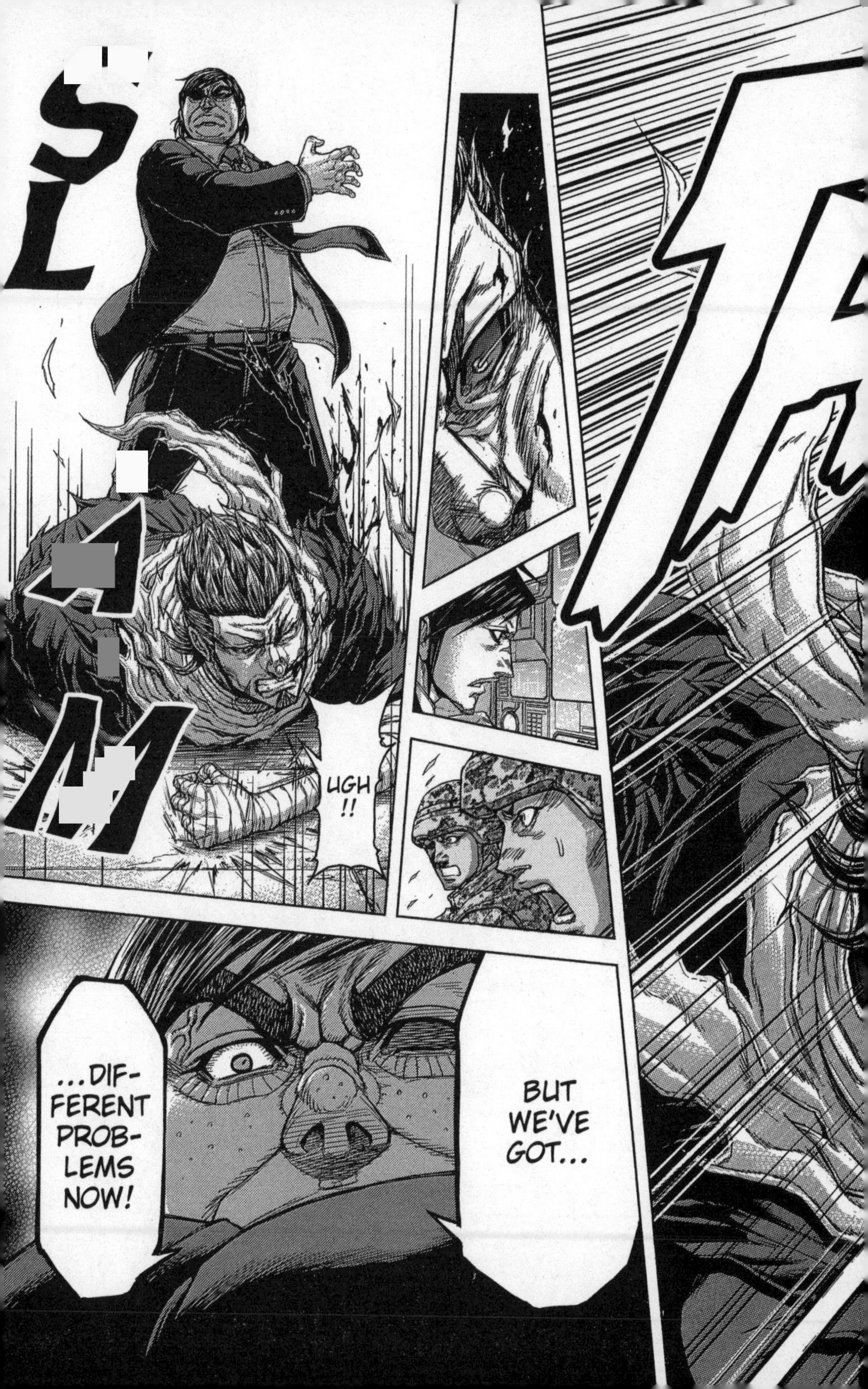
SLAM
UGH!!
BUT WE'VE GOT...
...DIF-FERENT PROB-LEMS NOW!

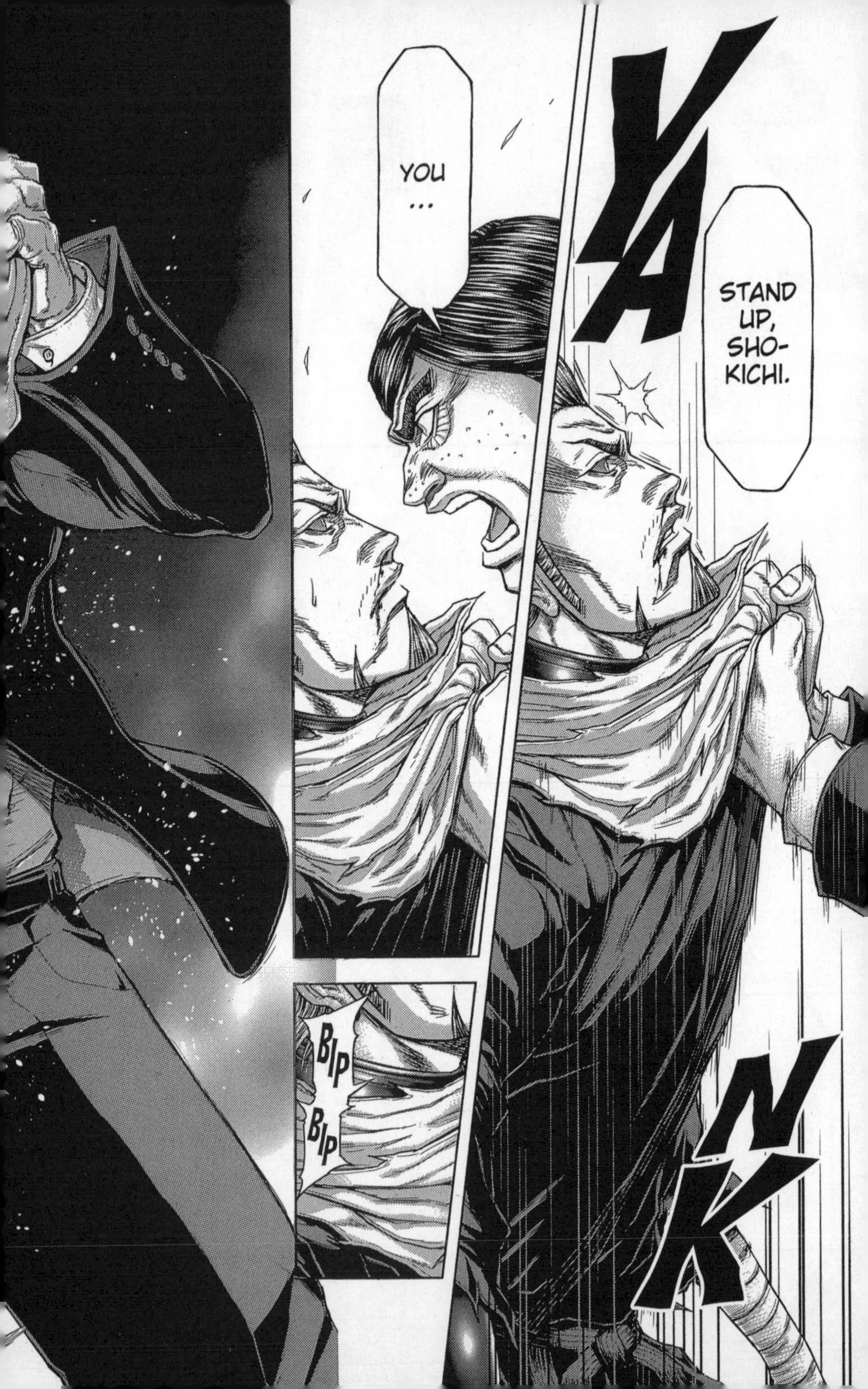
YANK
STAND UP, SHO-KICHI.
YOU ...
BIP
BIP

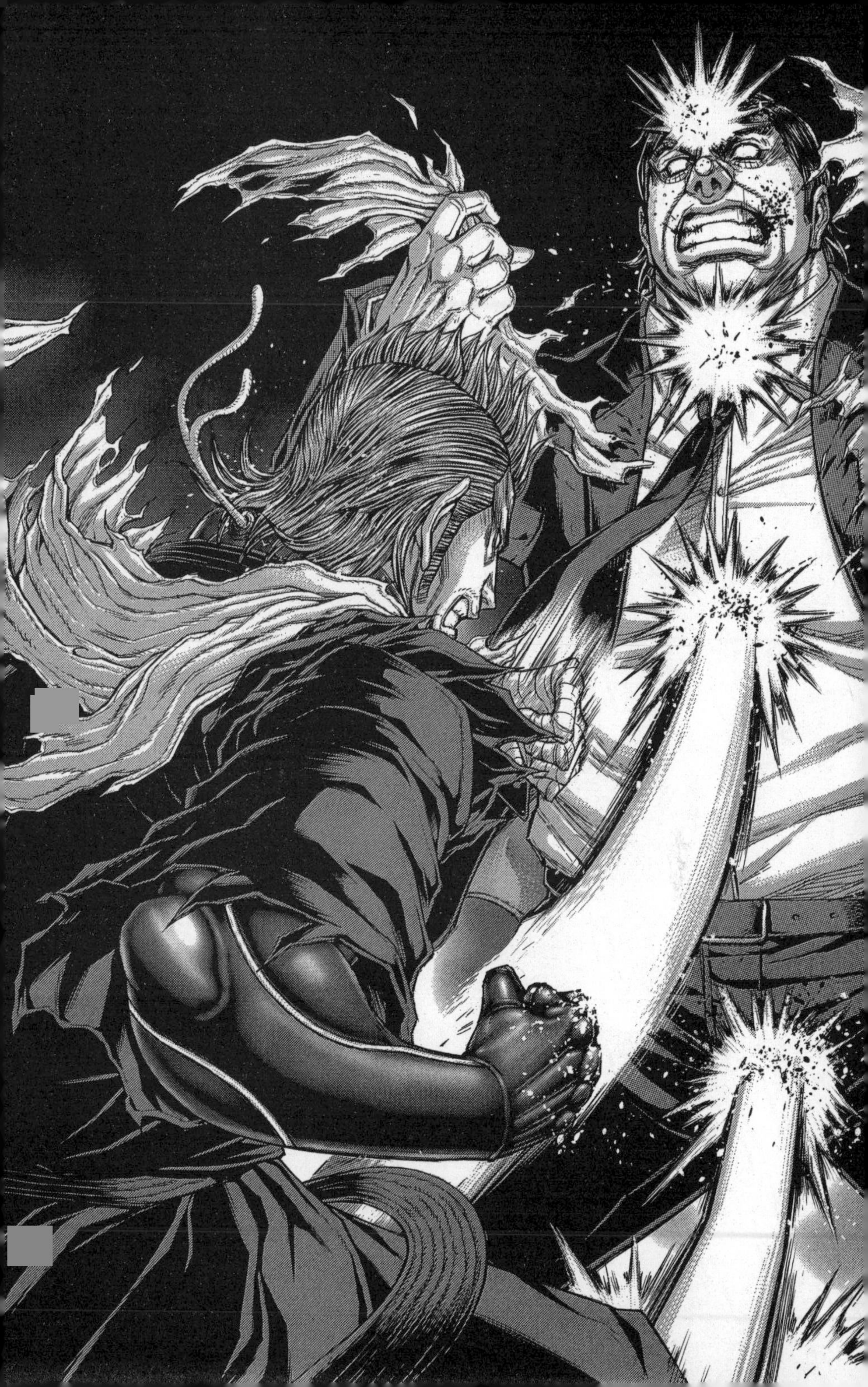

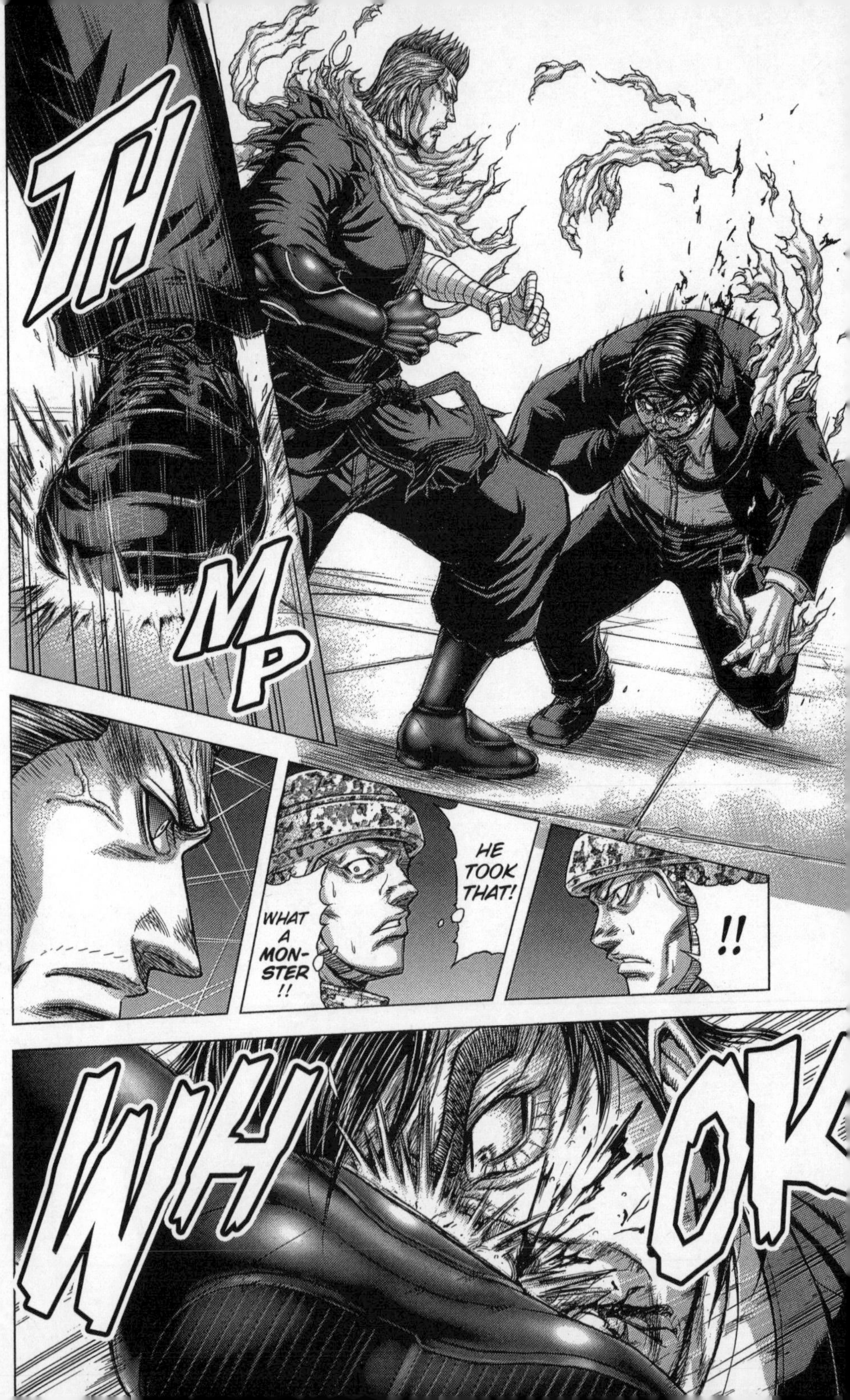
TH
MP
!!
HE TOOK THAT!
WHAT A MON-STER!!
WH
OK

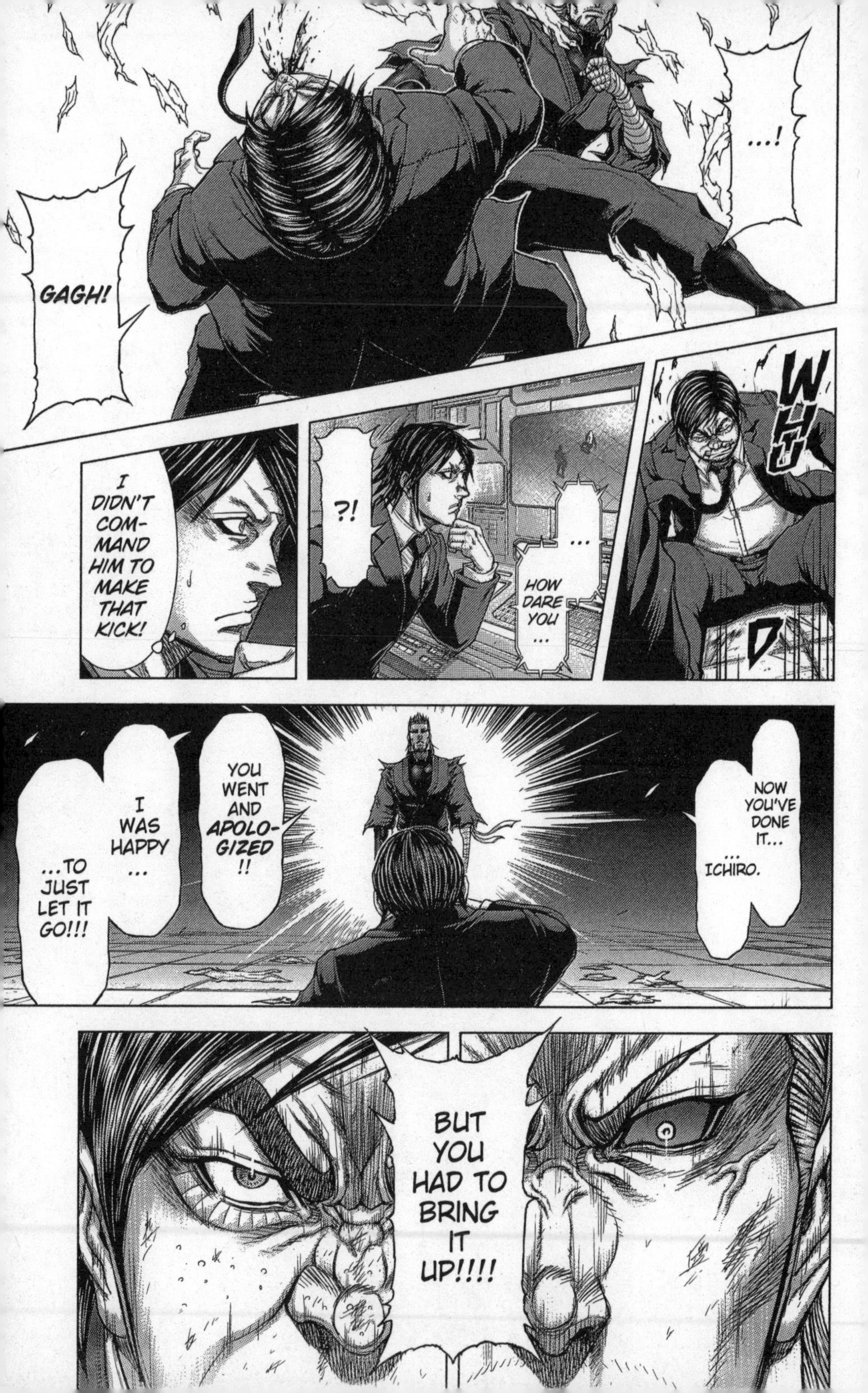
...!
GAGH!
WHUD
...
HOW DARE YOU ...
?!
I DIDN'T COMMAND HIM TO MAKE THAT KICK!
NOW YOU'VE DONE IT... ... ICHIRO.
YOU WENT AND APOLOGIZED!!
I WAS HAPPY ...
...TO JUST LET IT GO!!!
BUT YOU HAD TO BRING IT UP!!!!

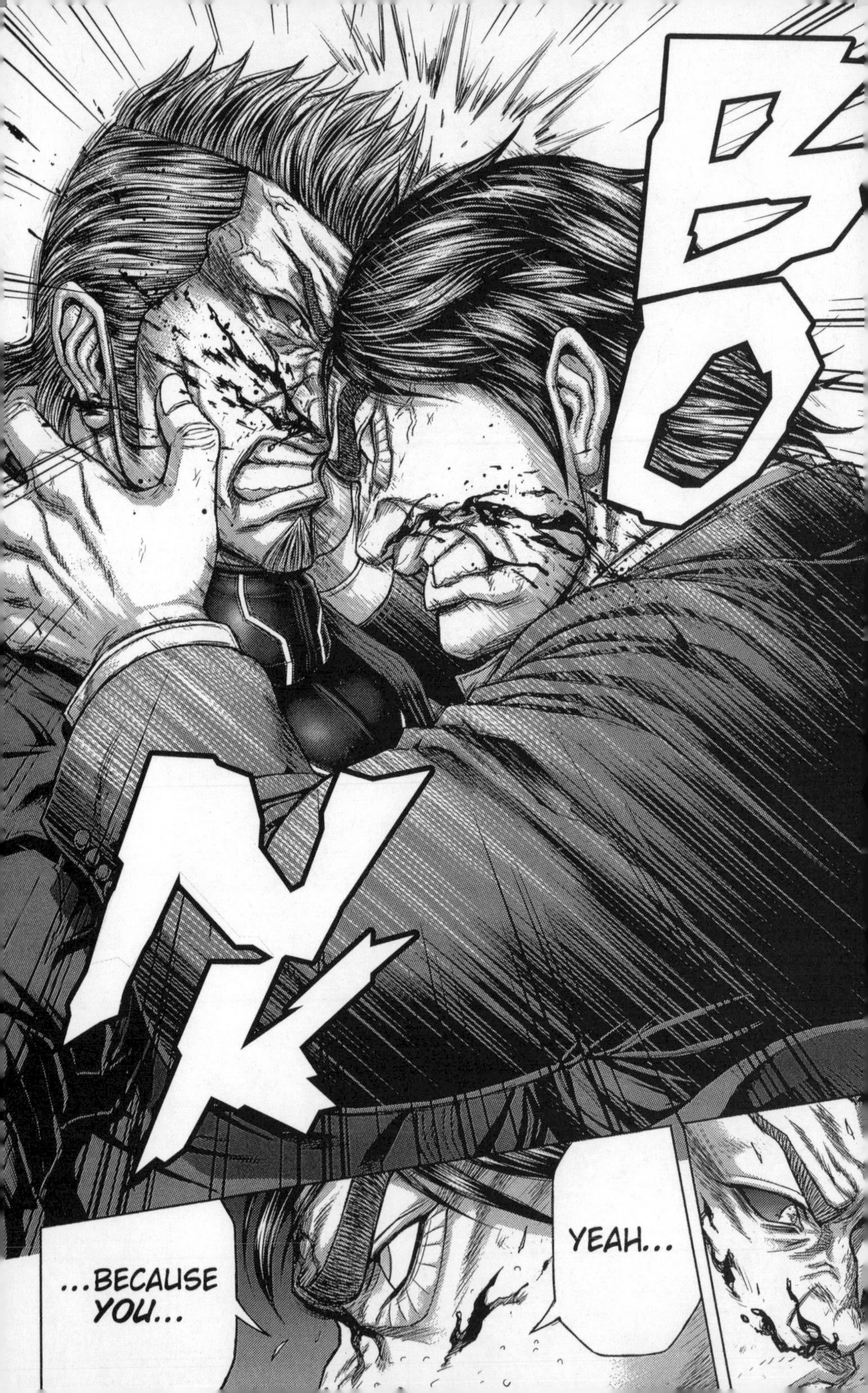
YEAH...
...BECAUSE YOU...

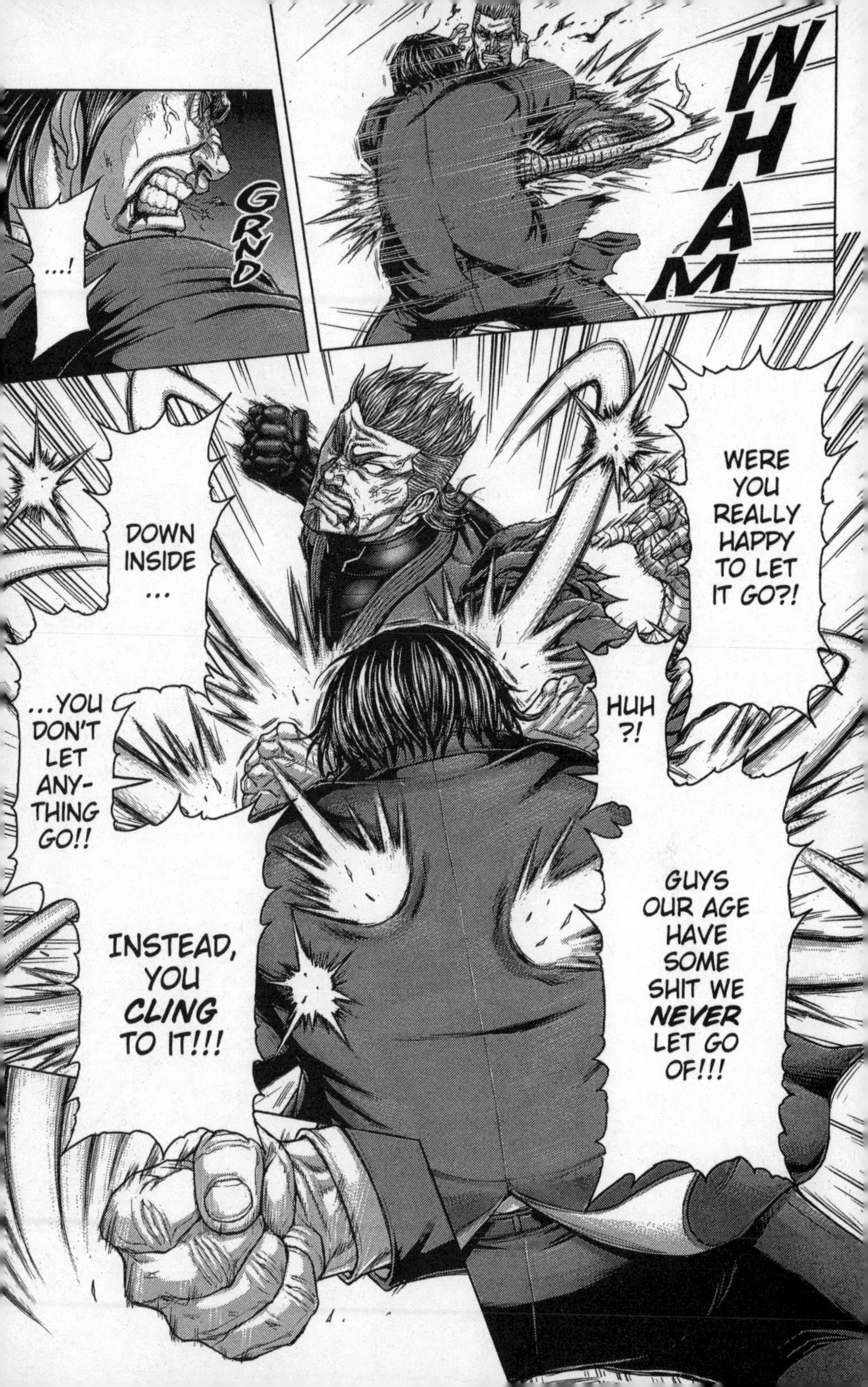
WHAM
GRND
...!
WERE YOU REALLY HAPPY TO LET IT GO?!
DOWN INSIDE ...
HUH?!
...YOU DON'T LET ANYTHING GO!!
GUYS OUR AGE HAVE SOME SHIT WE *NEVER* LET GO OF!!!
INSTEAD, YOU *CLING* TO IT!!!

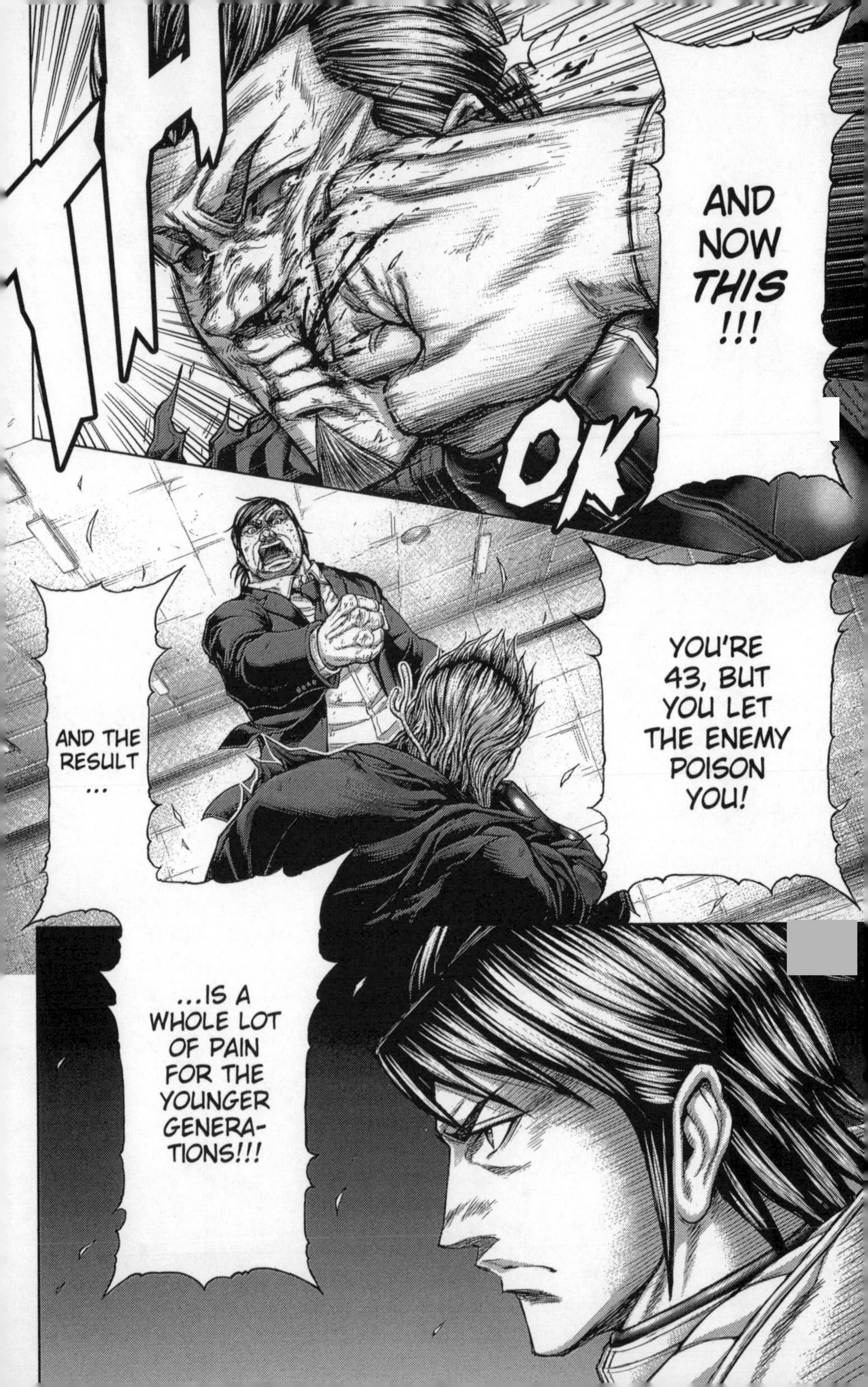
AND NOW THIS !!!
OK
YOU'RE 43, BUT YOU LET THE ENEMY POISON YOU!
AND THE RESULT ...
...IS A WHOLE LOT OF PAIN FOR THE YOUNGER GENERA-TIONS!!!

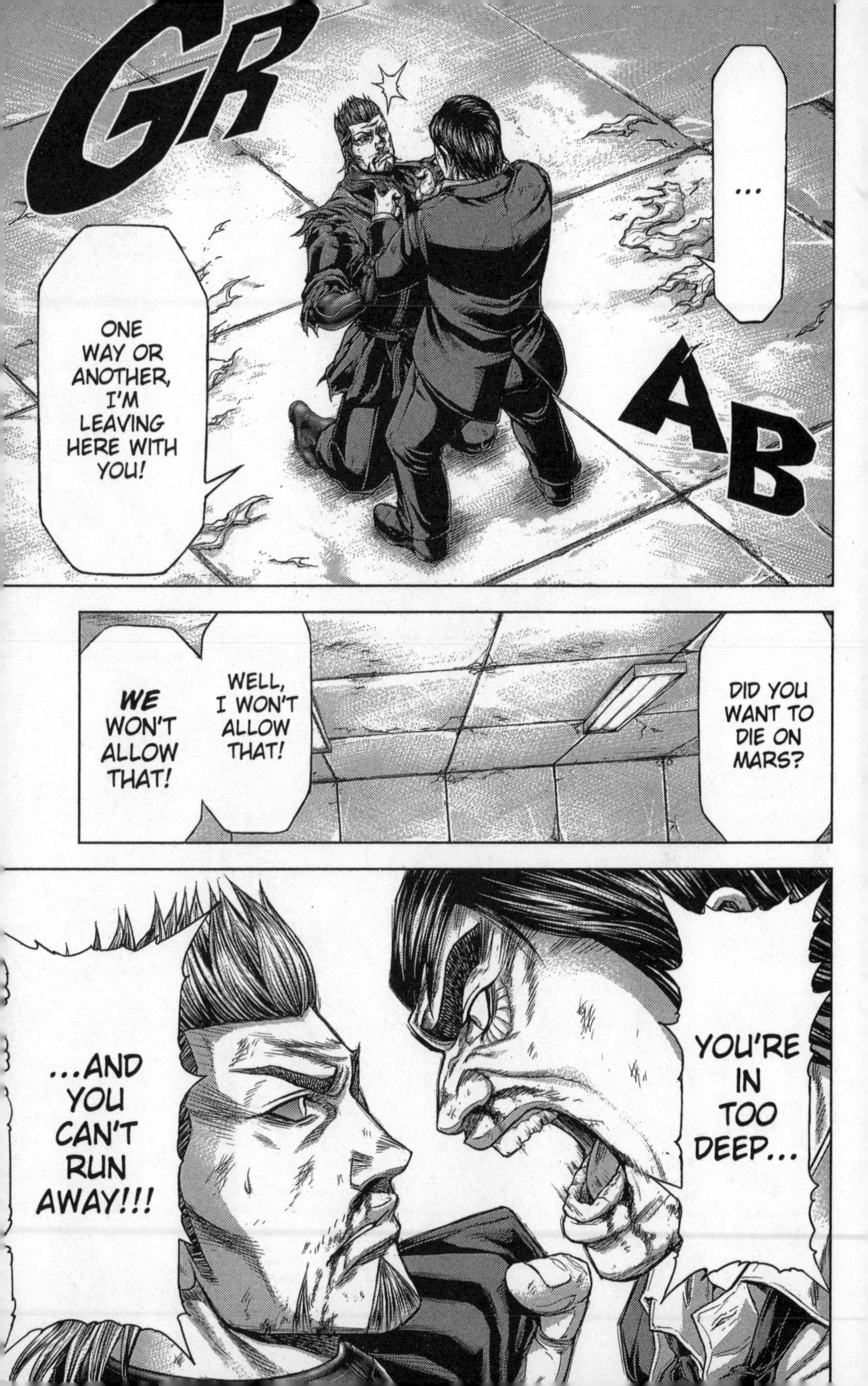
...
GR
AB
ONE WAY OR ANOTHER, I'M LEAVING HERE WITH YOU!
DID YOU WANT TO DIE ON MARS?
WELL, I WON'T ALLOW THAT!
WE WON'T ALLOW THAT!
YOU'RE IN TOO DEEP...
...AND YOU CAN'T RUN AWAY!!!

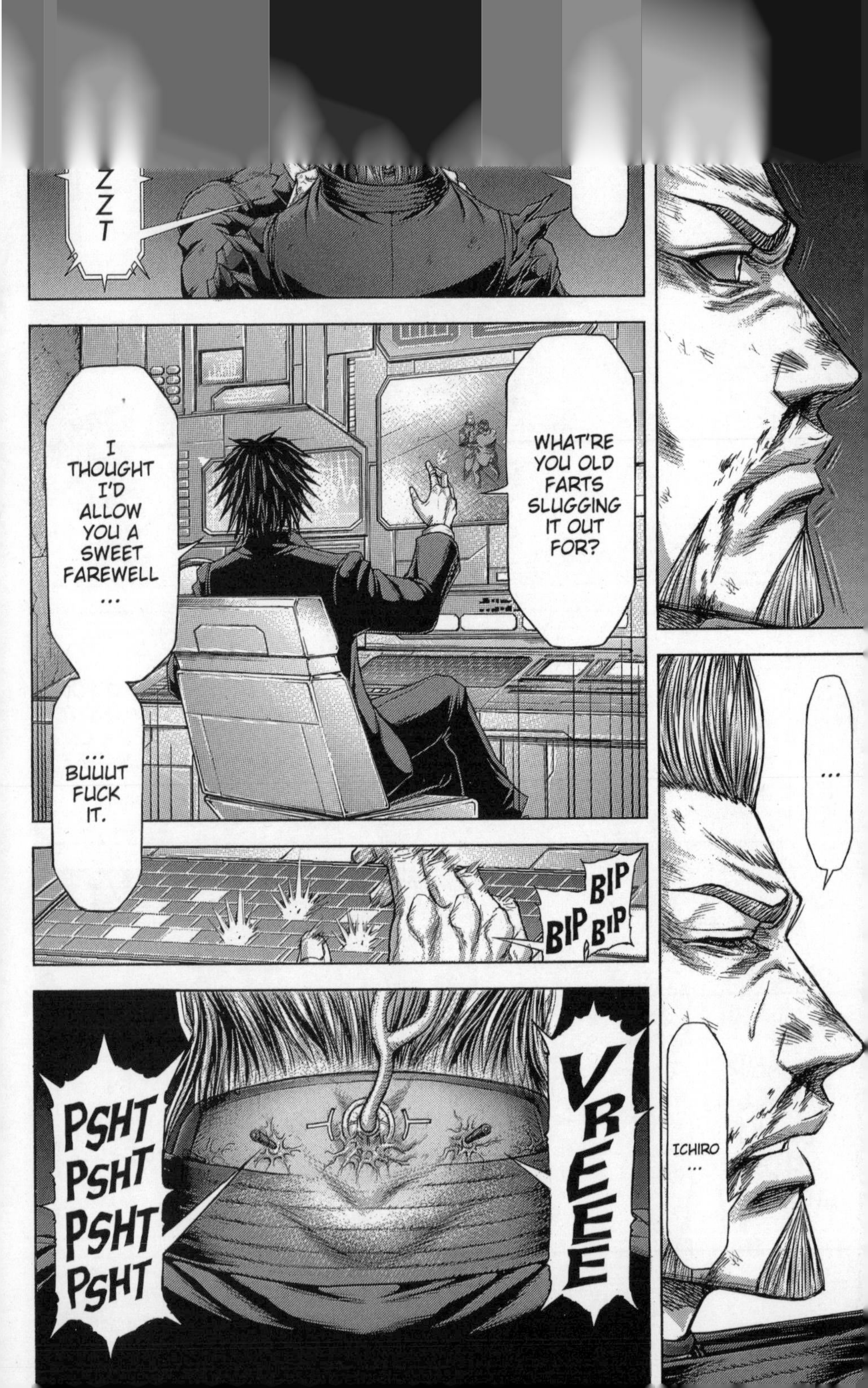
...
ICHIRO ...
ZZZT
WHAT'RE YOU OLD FARTS SLUGGING IT OUT FOR?
I THOUGHT I'D ALLOW YOU A SWEET FAREWELL ...
... BUUUT FUCK IT.
BIP BIP BIP
VREEE
PSHT PSHT PSHT PSHT

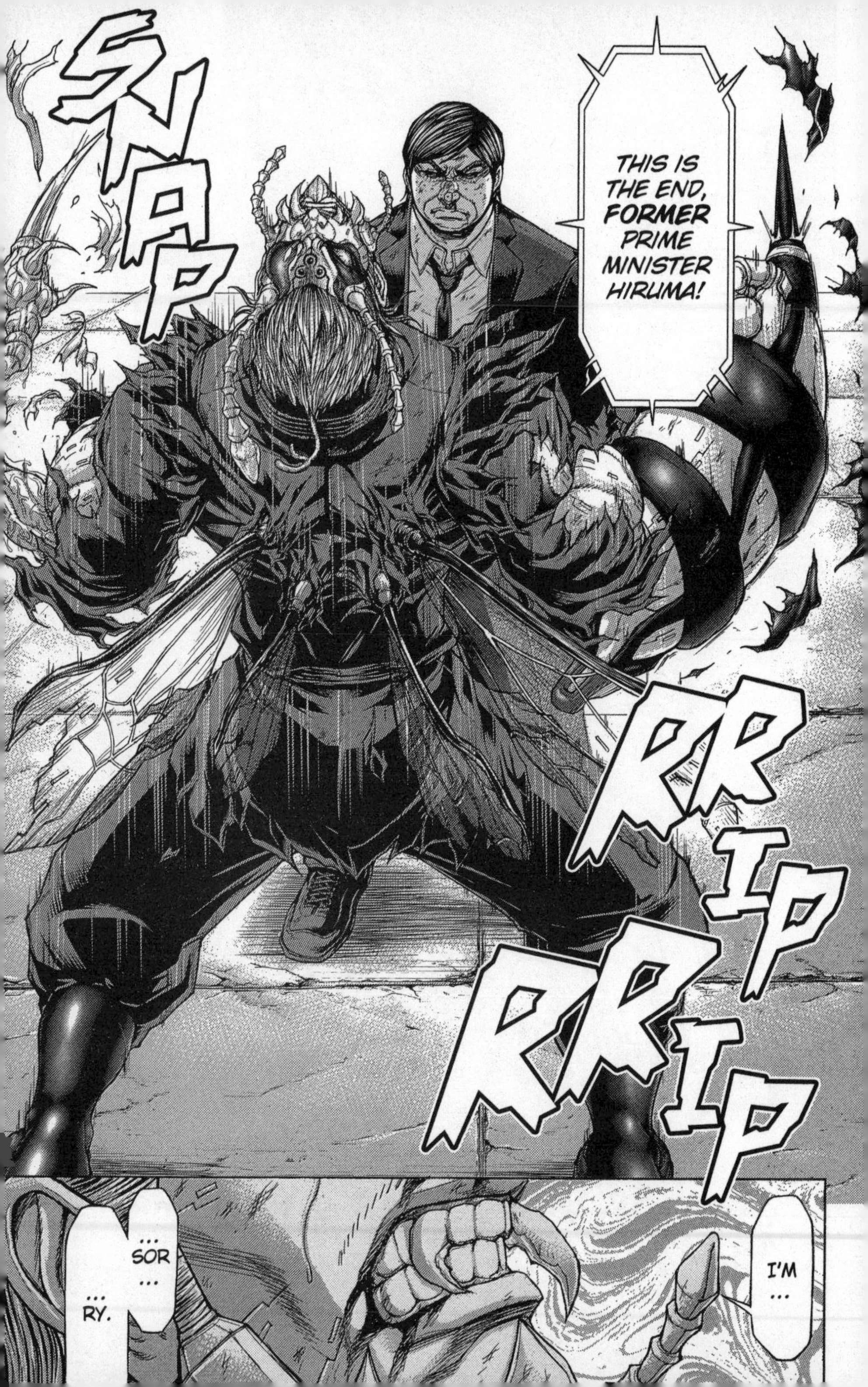
THIS IS THE END, **FORMER** PRIME MINISTER HIRUMA!
SNAP
RRIP RRIP
I'M ...
... SOR ...
... RY.

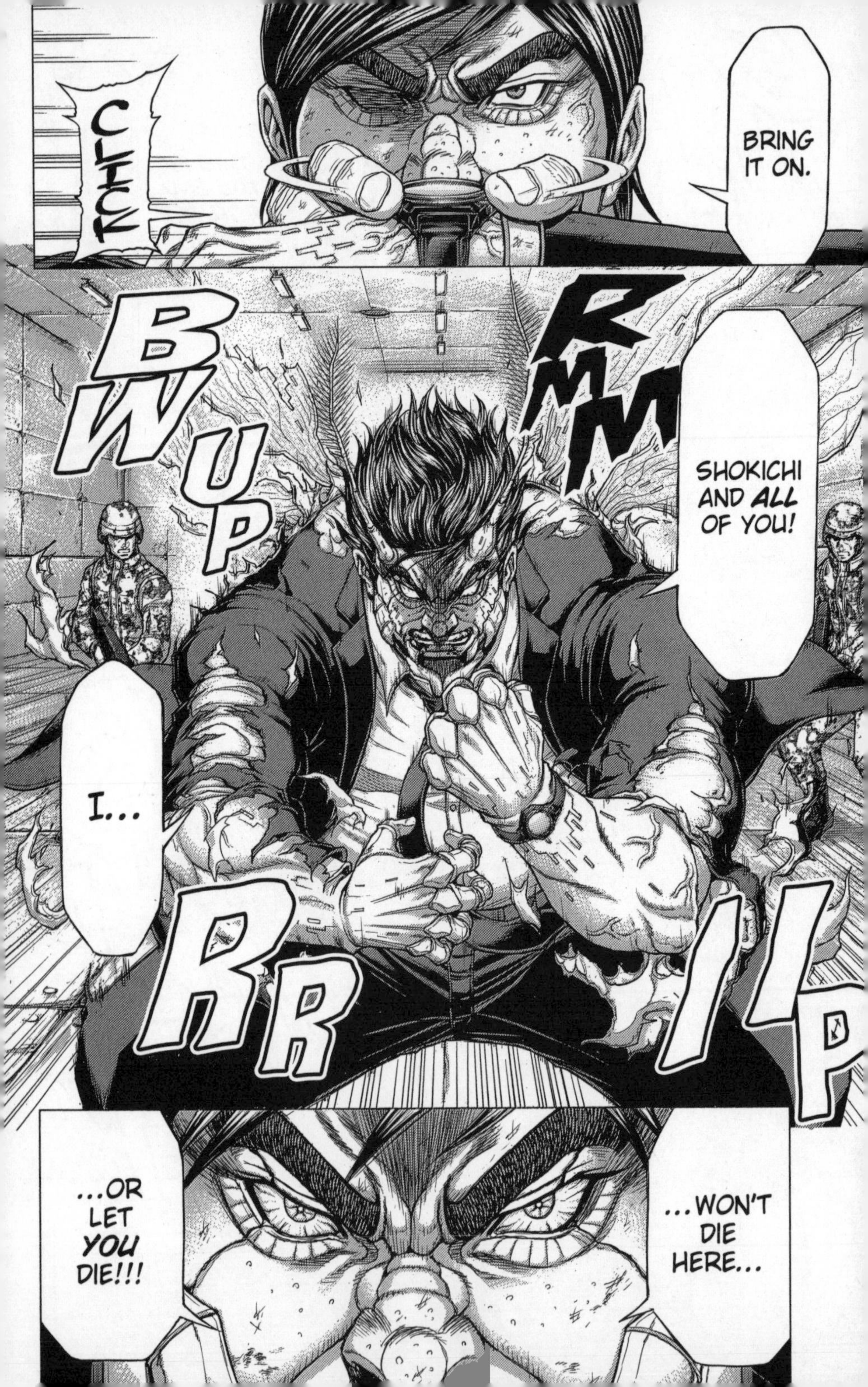
BRING IT ON.
CLICK
RMM
SHOKICHI AND ALL OF YOU!
BWUP
I...
RRIP
...WON'T DIE HERE...
...OR LET YOU DIE!!!

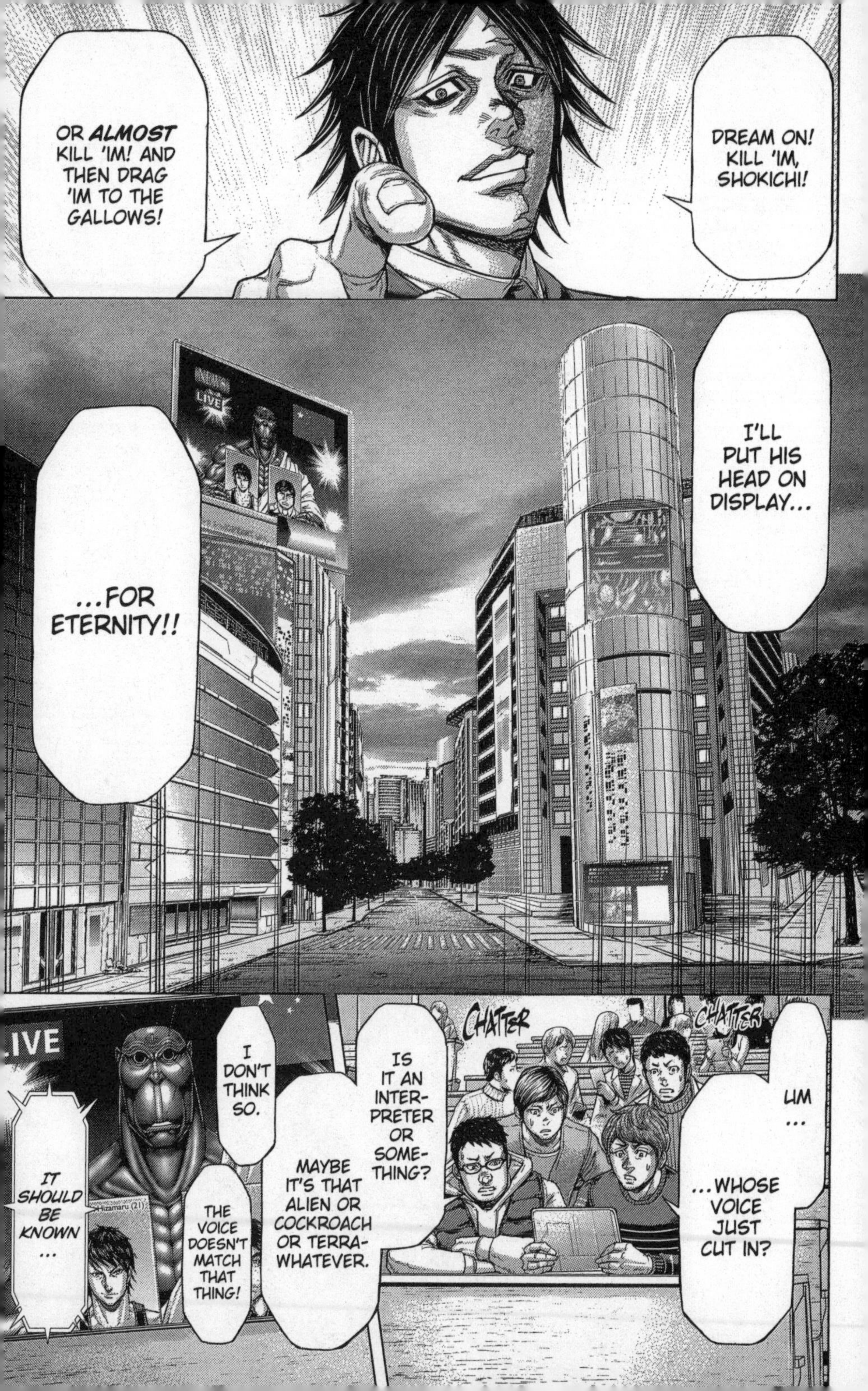
DREAM ON! KILL 'IM, SHOKICHI!
OR ALMOST KILL 'IM! AND THEN DRAG 'IM TO THE GALLOWS!
LIVE
I'LL PUT HIS HEAD ON DISPLAY...
...FOR ETERNITY!!
CHATTER
CHATTER
UM ...
...WHOSE VOICE JUST CUT IN?
IS IT AN INTERPRETER OR SOMETHING?
MAYBE IT'S THAT ALIEN OR COCKROACH OR TERRA-WHATEVER.
I DON'T THINK SO.
THE VOICE DOESN'T MATCH THAT THING!
LIVE
IT SHOULD BE KNOWN ...
Hizamaru (21)

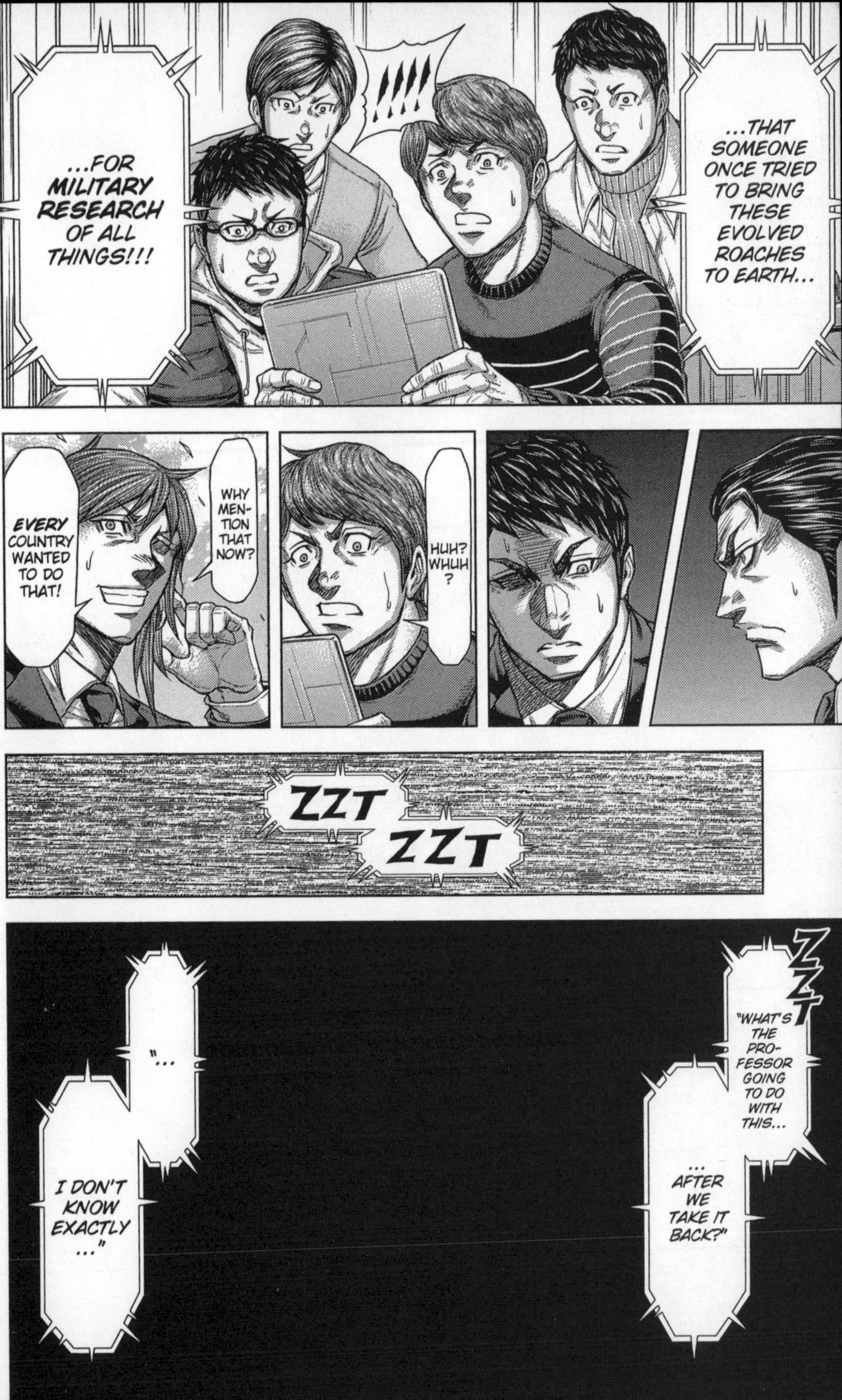
...THAT SOMEONE ONCE TRIED TO BRING THESE EVOLVED ROACHES TO EARTH...
!!!!
...FOR MILITARY RESEARCH OF ALL THINGS!!!
HUH? WHUH?
WHY MEN-TION THAT NOW?
EVERY COUNTRY WANTED TO DO THAT!
ZZT
ZZT
ZZT
"WHAT'S THE PRO-FESSOR GOING TO DO WITH THIS...
... AFTER WE TAKE IT BACK?"
"...
I DON'T KNOW EXACTLY ..."

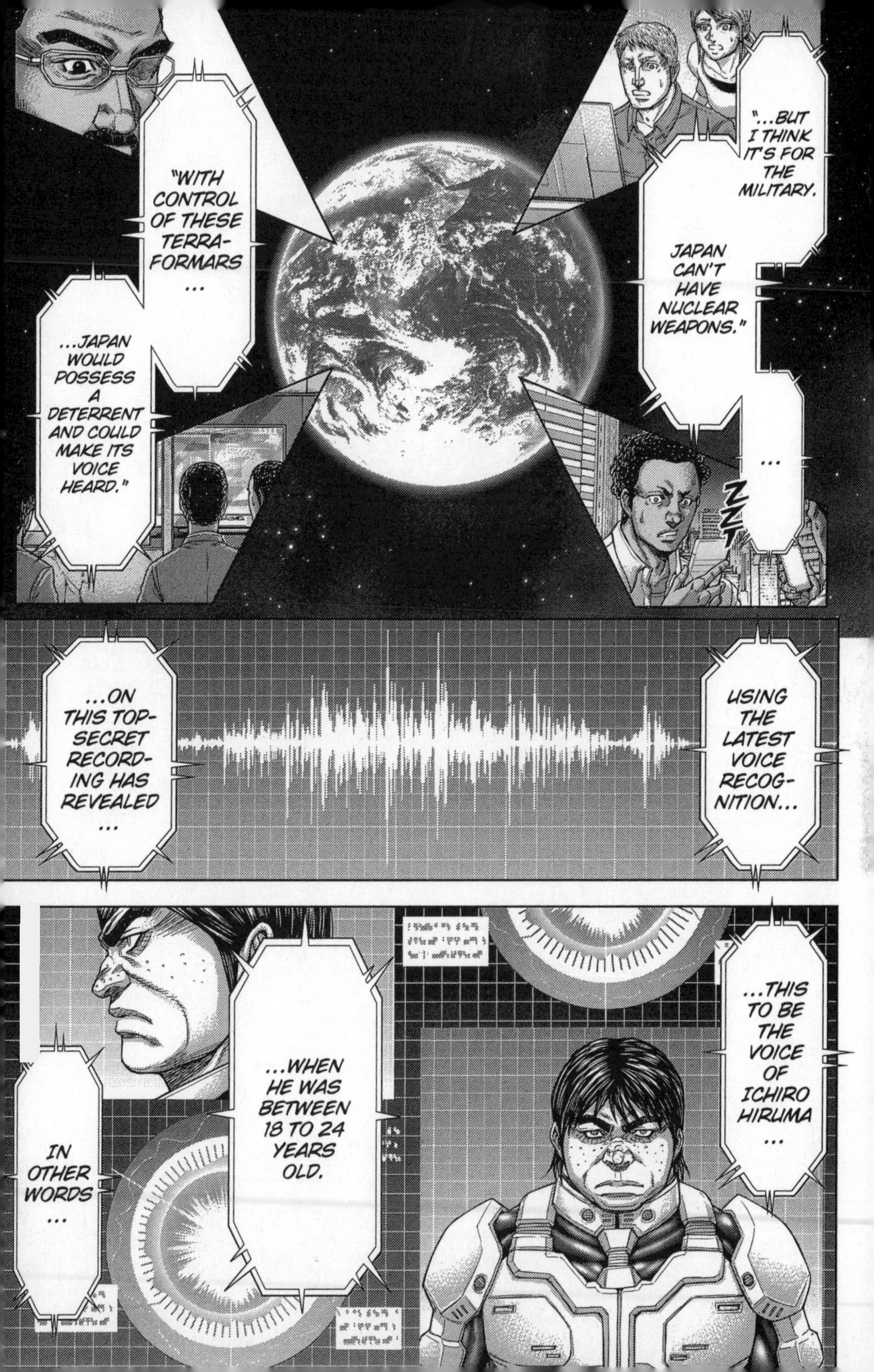
"...BUT I THINK IT'S FOR THE MILITARY.
JAPAN CAN'T HAVE NUCLEAR WEAPONS."
...
ZZT
"WITH CONTROL OF THESE TERRA-FORMARS...
...JAPAN WOULD POSSESS A DETERRENT AND COULD MAKE ITS VOICE HEARD."
USING THE LATEST VOICE RECOG-NITION...
...ON THIS TOP-SECRET RECORD-ING HAS REVEALED...
...THIS TO BE THE VOICE OF ICHIRO HIRUMA...
...WHEN HE WAS BETWEEN 18 TO 24 YEARS OLD.
IN OTHER WORDS...

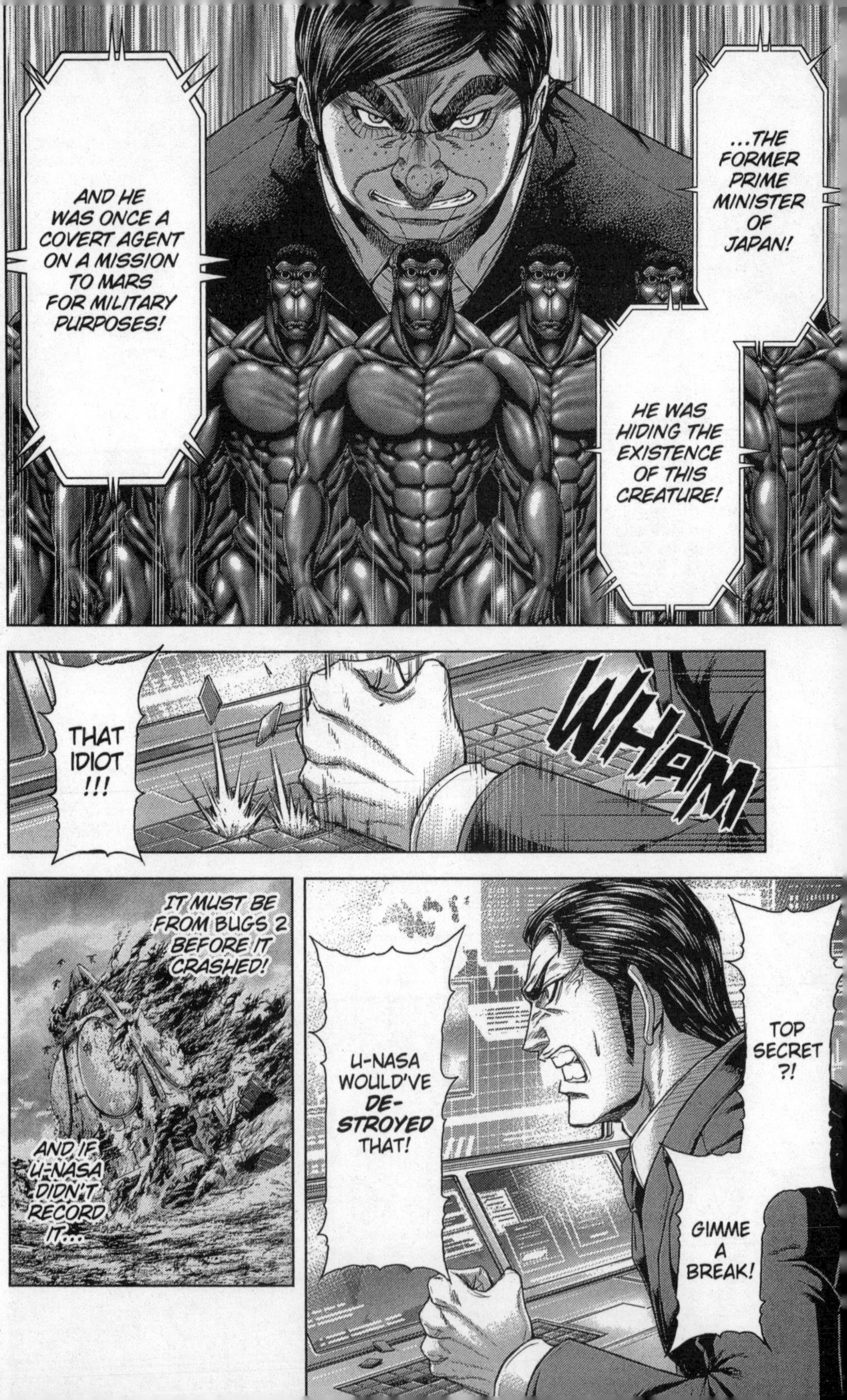
...THE FORMER PRIME MINISTER OF JAPAN!
HE WAS HIDING THE EXISTENCE OF THIS CREATURE!
AND HE WAS ONCE A COVERT AGENT ON A MISSION TO MARS FOR MILITARY PURPOSES!
WHAM
THAT IDIOT!!!
TOP SECRET?!
GIMME A BREAK!
U-NASA WOULD'VE DE-STROYED THAT!
IT MUST BE FROM BUGS 2 BEFORE IT CRASHED!
AND IF U-NASA DIDN'T RECORD IT...

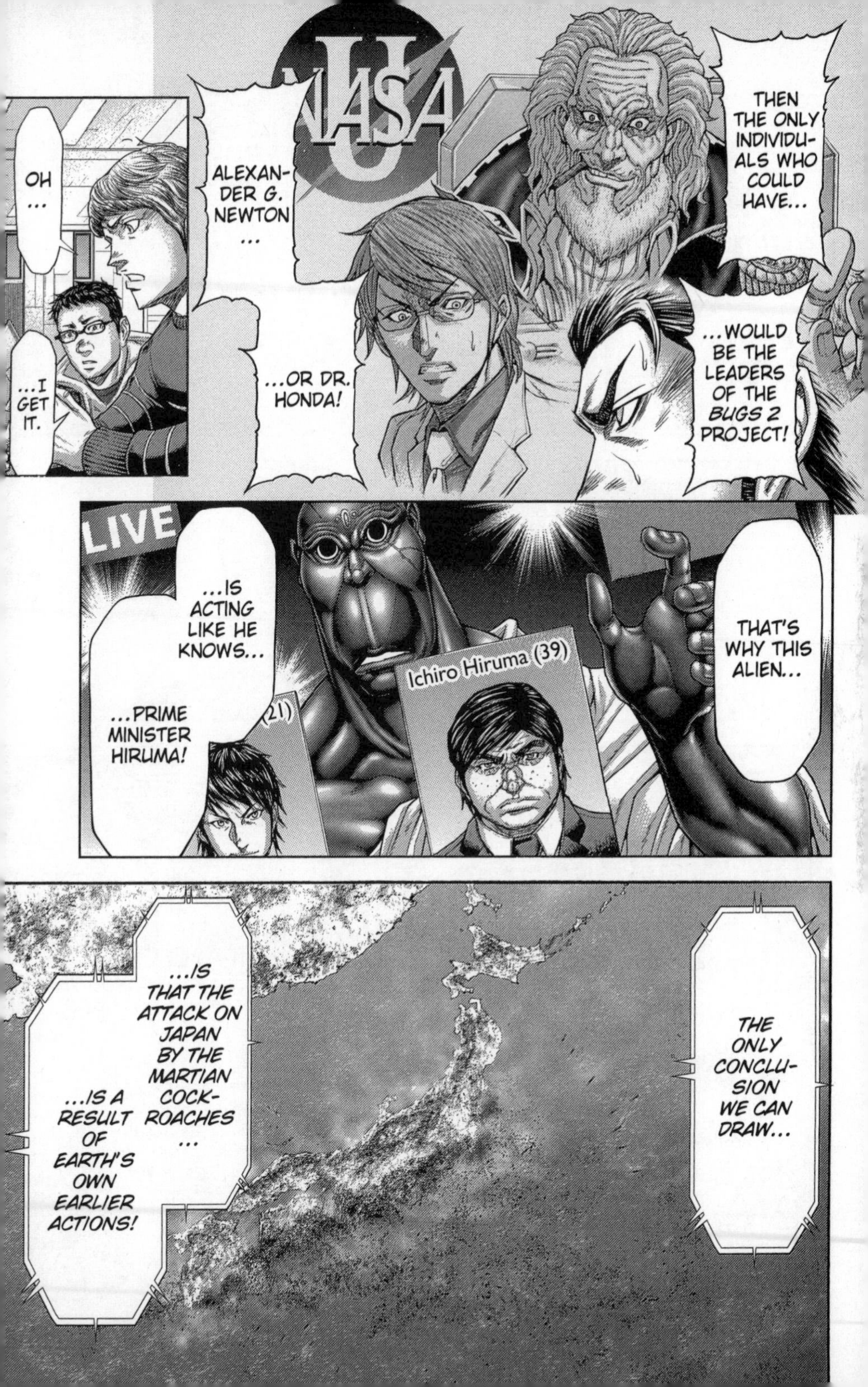
U-NASA
THEN THE ONLY INDIVIDUALS WHO COULD HAVE...
...WOULD BE THE LEADERS OF THE *BUGS 2* PROJECT!
ALEXANDER G. NEWTON...
...OR DR. HONDA!
OH...
...I GET IT.
LIVE
THAT'S WHY THIS ALIEN...
...IS ACTING LIKE HE KNOWS...
...PRIME MINISTER HIRUMA!
Ichiro Hiruma (39)
(21)
THE ONLY CONCLUSION WE CAN DRAW...
...IS THAT THE ATTACK ON JAPAN BY THE MARTIAN COCKROACHES...
...IS A RESULT OF EARTH'S OWN EARLIER ACTIONS!

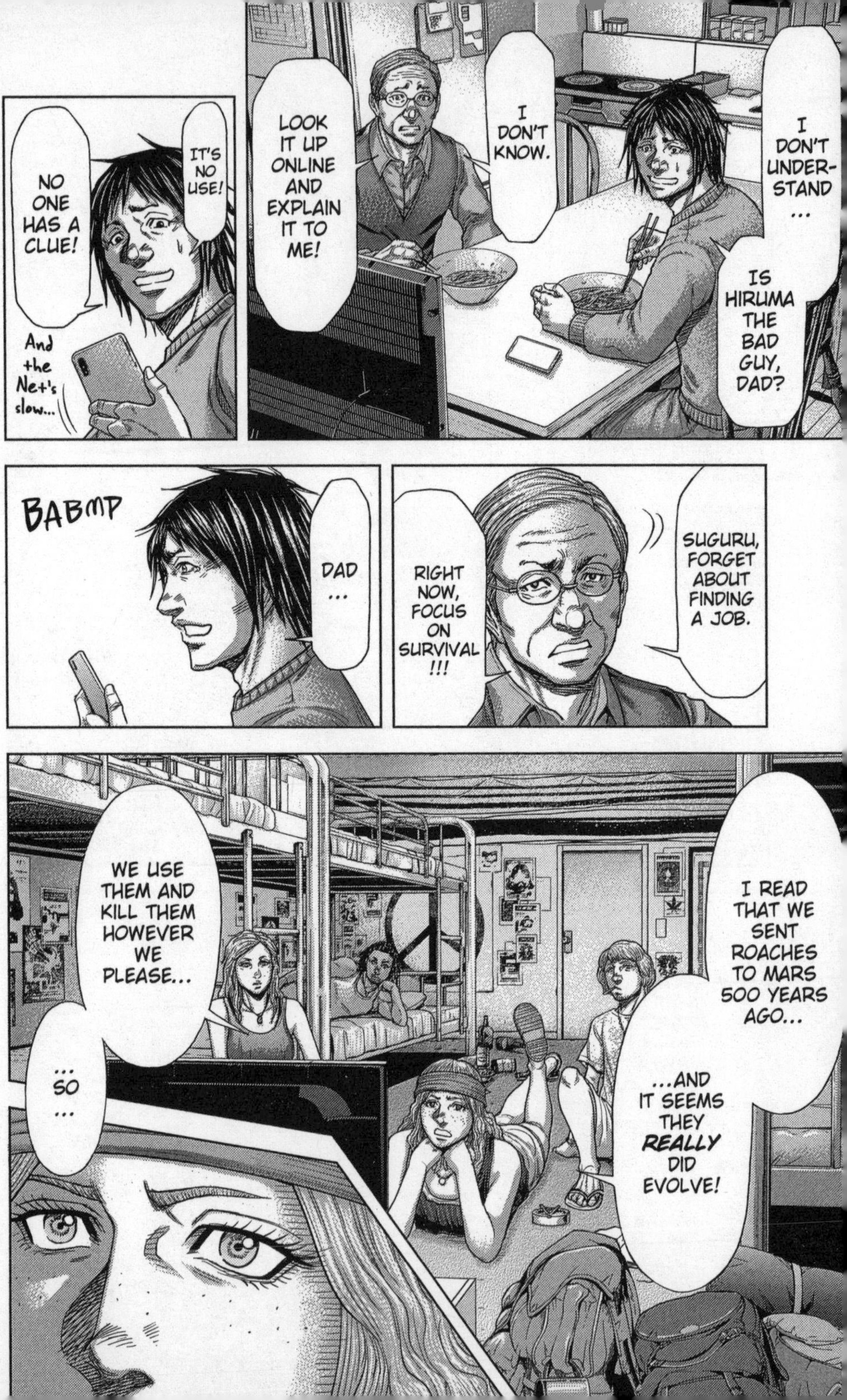
I DON'T UNDERSTAND...
IS HIRUMA THE BAD GUY, DAD?
I DON'T KNOW.
LOOK IT UP ONLINE AND EXPLAIN IT TO ME!
IT'S NO USE!
NO ONE HAS A CLUE!
And the Net's slow...
SUGURU, FORGET ABOUT FINDING A JOB.
RIGHT NOW, FOCUS ON SURVIVAL!!!
DAD...
BABMP
I READ THAT WE SENT ROACHES TO MARS 500 YEARS AGO...
...AND IT SEEMS THEY ***REALLY*** DID EVOLVE!
WE USE THEM AND KILL THEM HOWEVER WE PLEASE...
...SO...

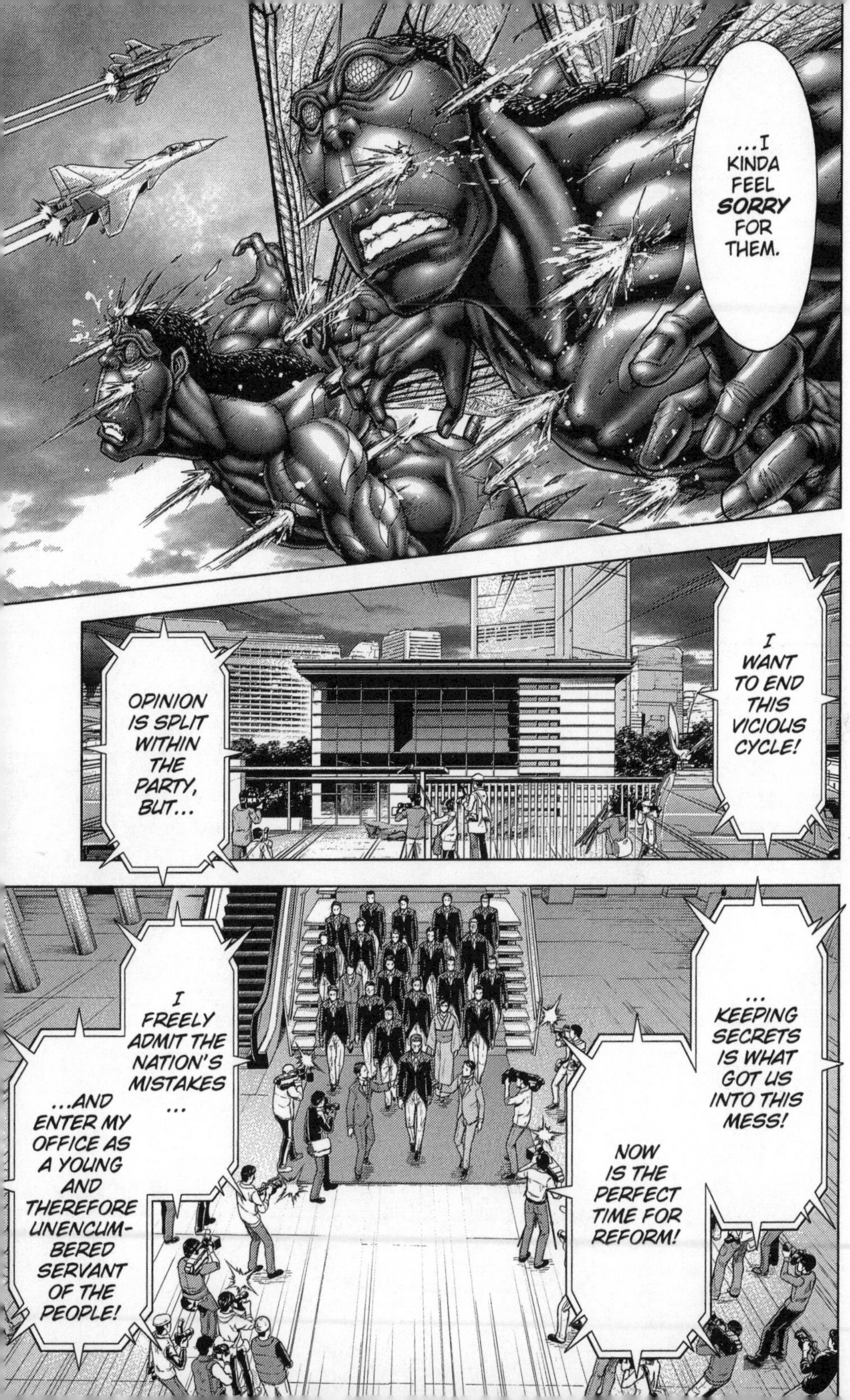
...I KINDA FEEL SORRY FOR THEM.
I WANT TO END THIS VICIOUS CYCLE!
OPINION IS SPLIT WITHIN THE PARTY, BUT...
...KEEPING SECRETS IS WHAT GOT US INTO THIS MESS!
NOW IS THE PERFECT TIME FOR REFORM!
I FREELY ADMIT THE NATION'S MISTAKES...
...AND ENTER MY OFFICE AS A YOUNG AND THEREFORE UNENCUM-BERED SERVANT OF THE PEOPLE!

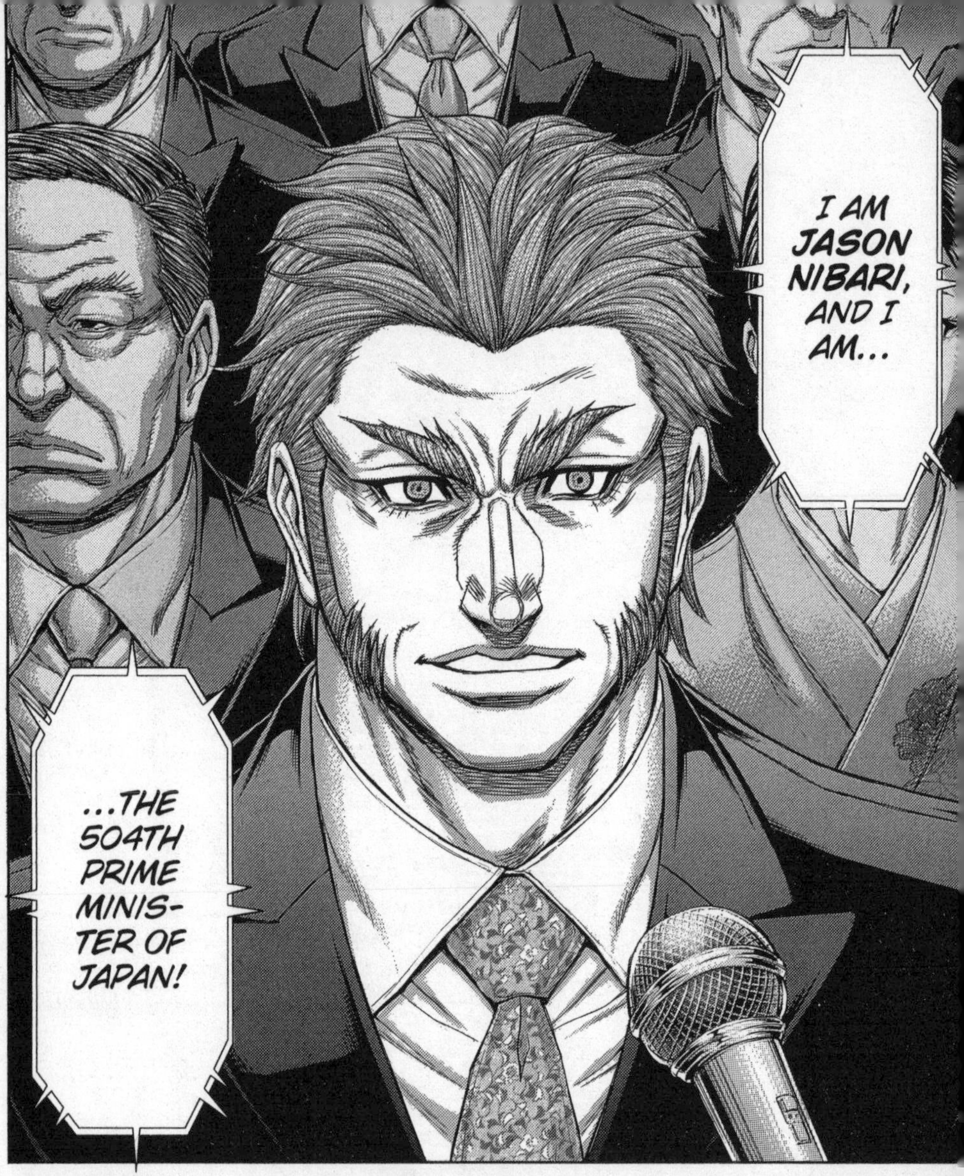
I AM JASON NIBARI, AND I AM...
...THE 504TH PRIME MINIS-TER OF JAPAN!
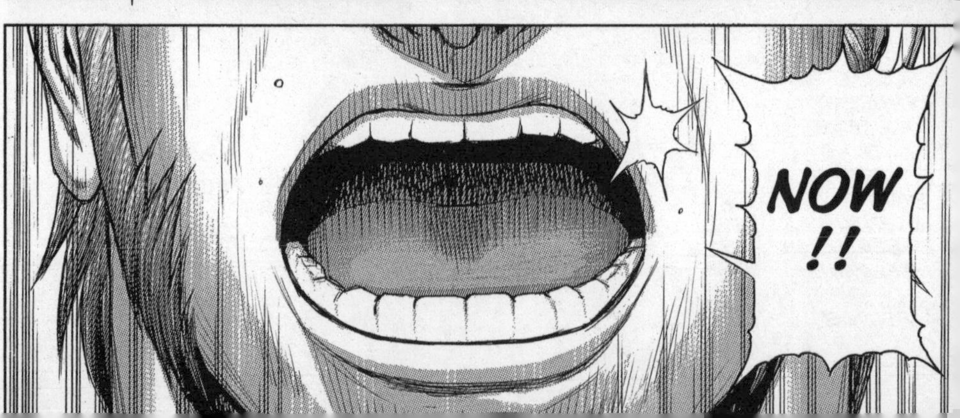
NOW !!

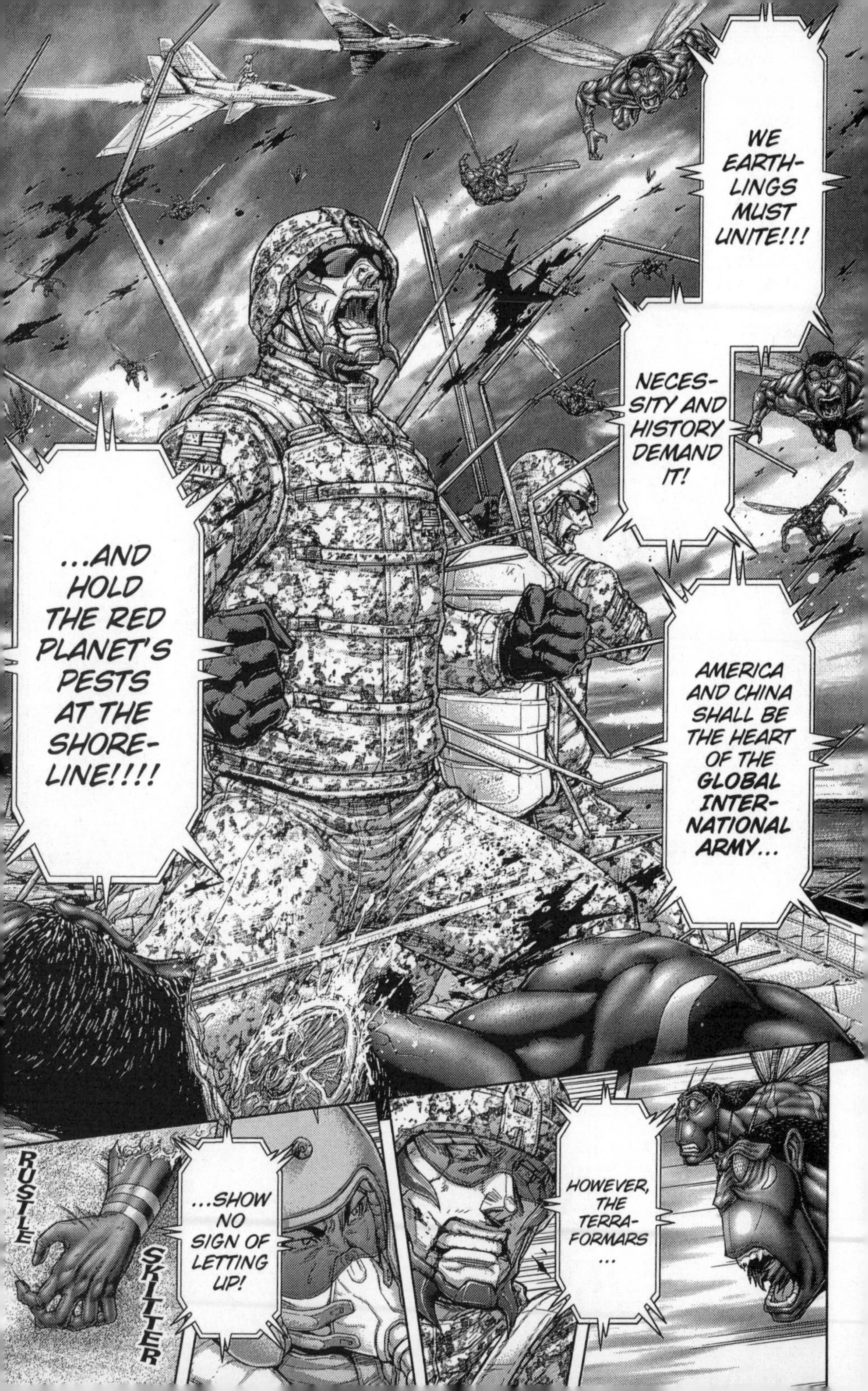
WE EARTHLINGS MUST UNITE!!!
NECESSITY AND HISTORY DEMAND IT!
AMERICA AND CHINA SHALL BE THE HEART OF THE GLOBAL INTERNATIONAL ARMY...
...AND HOLD THE RED PLANET'S PESTS AT THE SHORELINE!!!!
HOWEVER, THE TERRAFORMARS ...
...SHOW NO SIGN OF LETTING UP!
RUSTLE
SKITTER

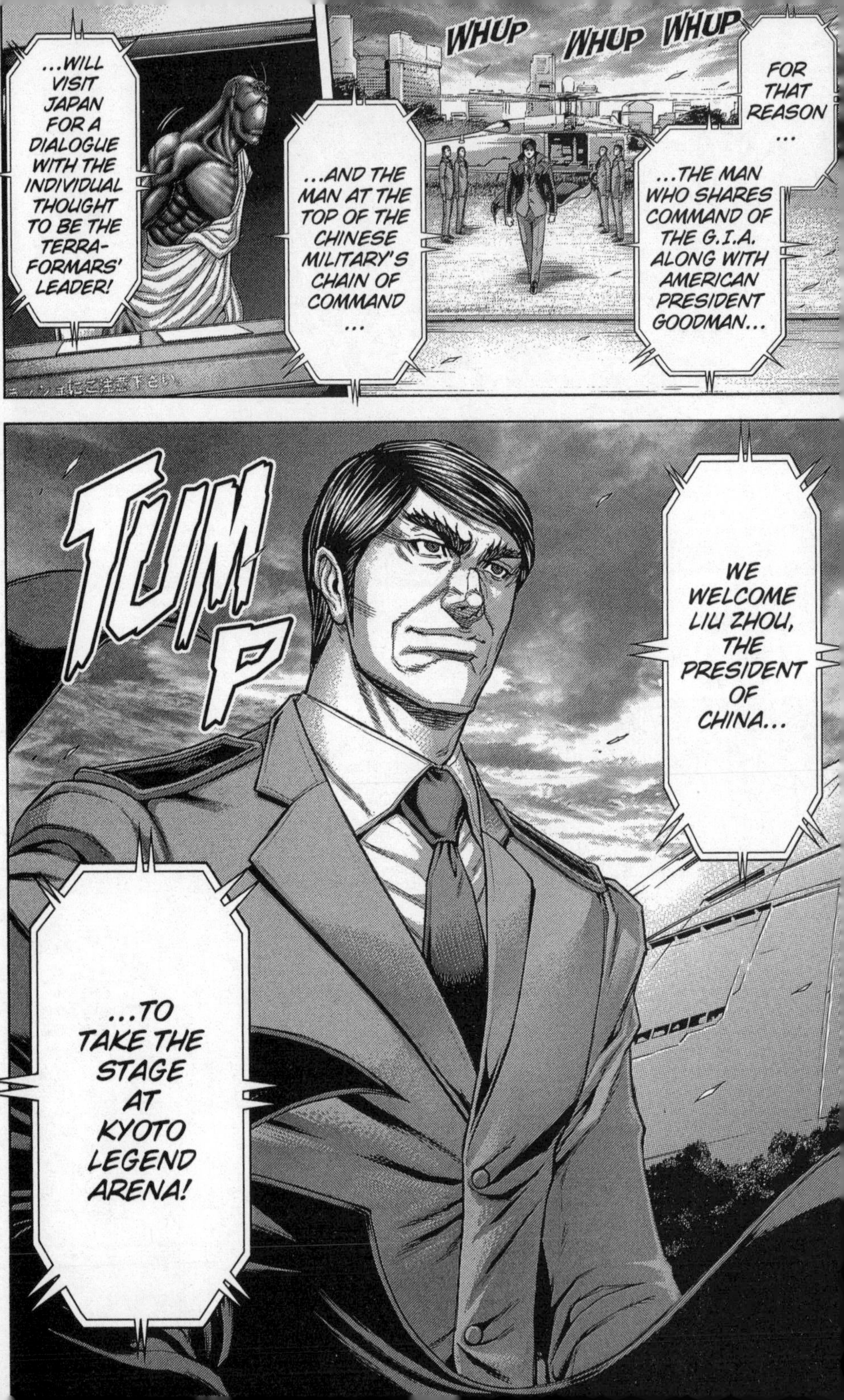
WHUP WHUP WHUP
FOR THAT REASON...
...THE MAN WHO SHARES COMMAND OF THE G.I.A. ALONG WITH AMERICAN PRESIDENT GOODMAN...
...AND THE MAN AT THE TOP OF THE CHINESE MILITARY'S CHAIN OF COMMAND...
...WILL VISIT JAPAN FOR A DIALOGUE WITH THE INDIVIDUAL THOUGHT TO BE THE TERRA-FORMARS' LEADER!
WE WELCOME LIU ZHOU, THE PRESIDENT OF CHINA...
TUMP
...TO TAKE THE STAGE AT KYOTO LEGEND ARENA!

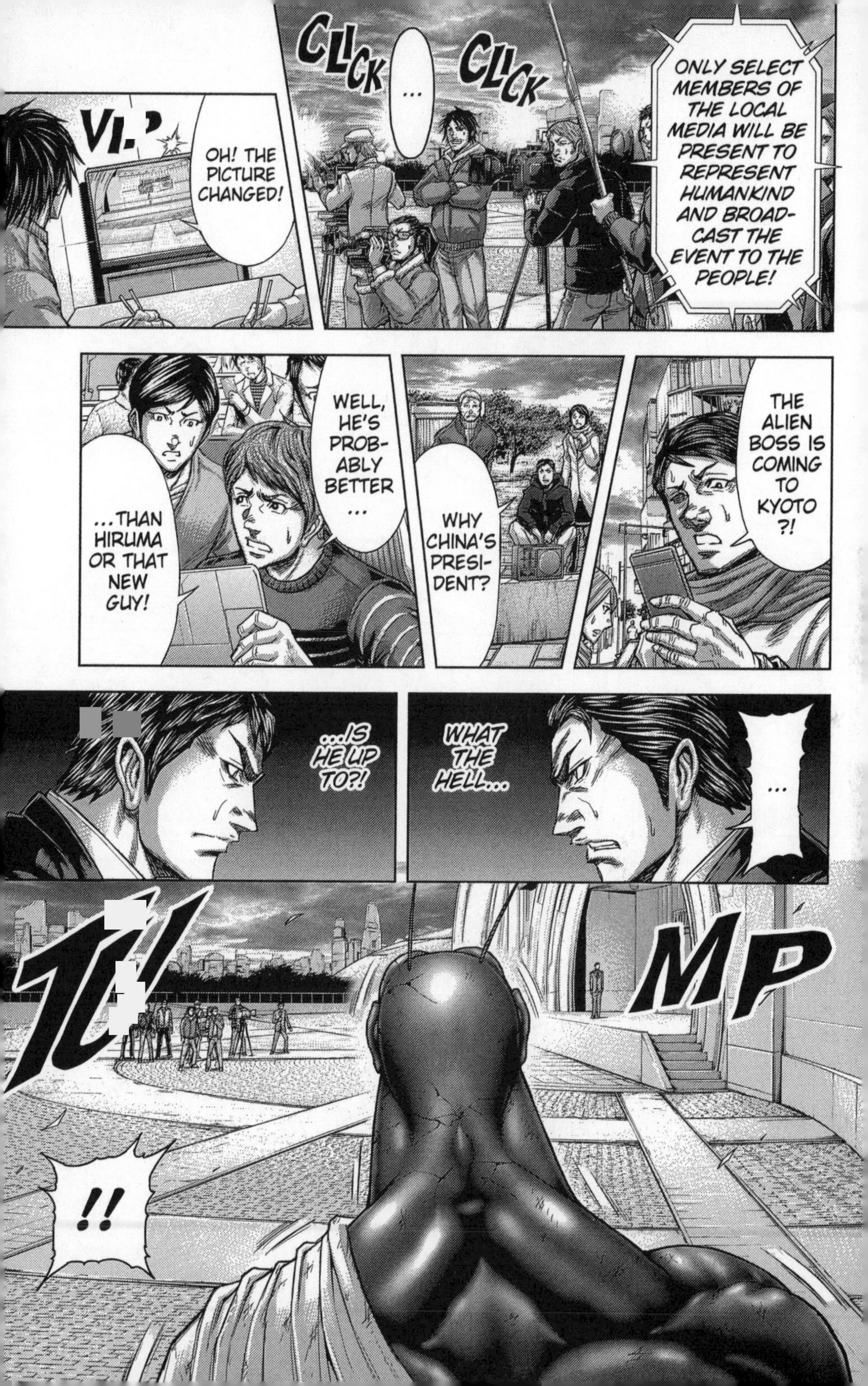
ONLY SELECT MEMBERS OF THE LOCAL MEDIA WILL BE PRESENT TO REPRESENT HUMANKIND AND BROAD-CAST THE EVENT TO THE PEOPLE!
CLICK
...
CLICK
OH! THE PICTURE CHANGED!
THE ALIEN BOSS IS COMING TO KYOTO?!
WHY CHINA'S PRESI-DENT?
WELL, HE'S PROB-ABLY BETTER ...
...THAN HIRUMA OR THAT NEW GUY!
...
WHAT THE HELL...
...IS HE UP TO?!
MP
!!

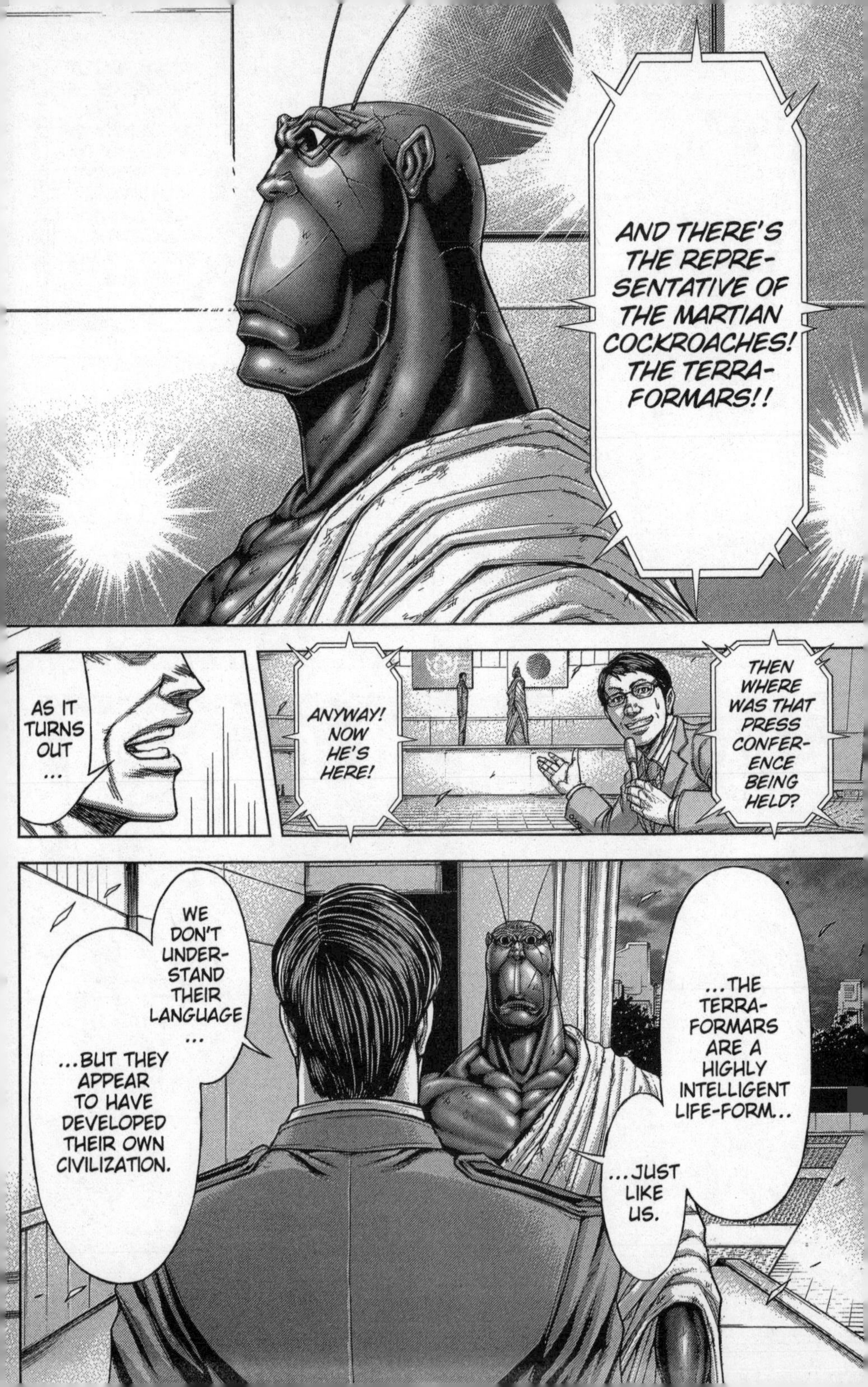
AND THERE'S THE REPRESENTATIVE OF THE MARTIAN COCKROACHES! THE TERRA-FORMARS!!
THEN WHERE WAS THAT PRESS CONFERENCE BEING HELD?
ANYWAY! NOW HE'S HERE!
AS IT TURNS OUT...
...THE TERRA-FORMARS ARE A HIGHLY INTELLIGENT LIFE-FORM...
...JUST LIKE US.
WE DON'T UNDERSTAND THEIR LANGUAGE...
...BUT THEY APPEAR TO HAVE DEVELOPED THEIR OWN CIVILIZATION.

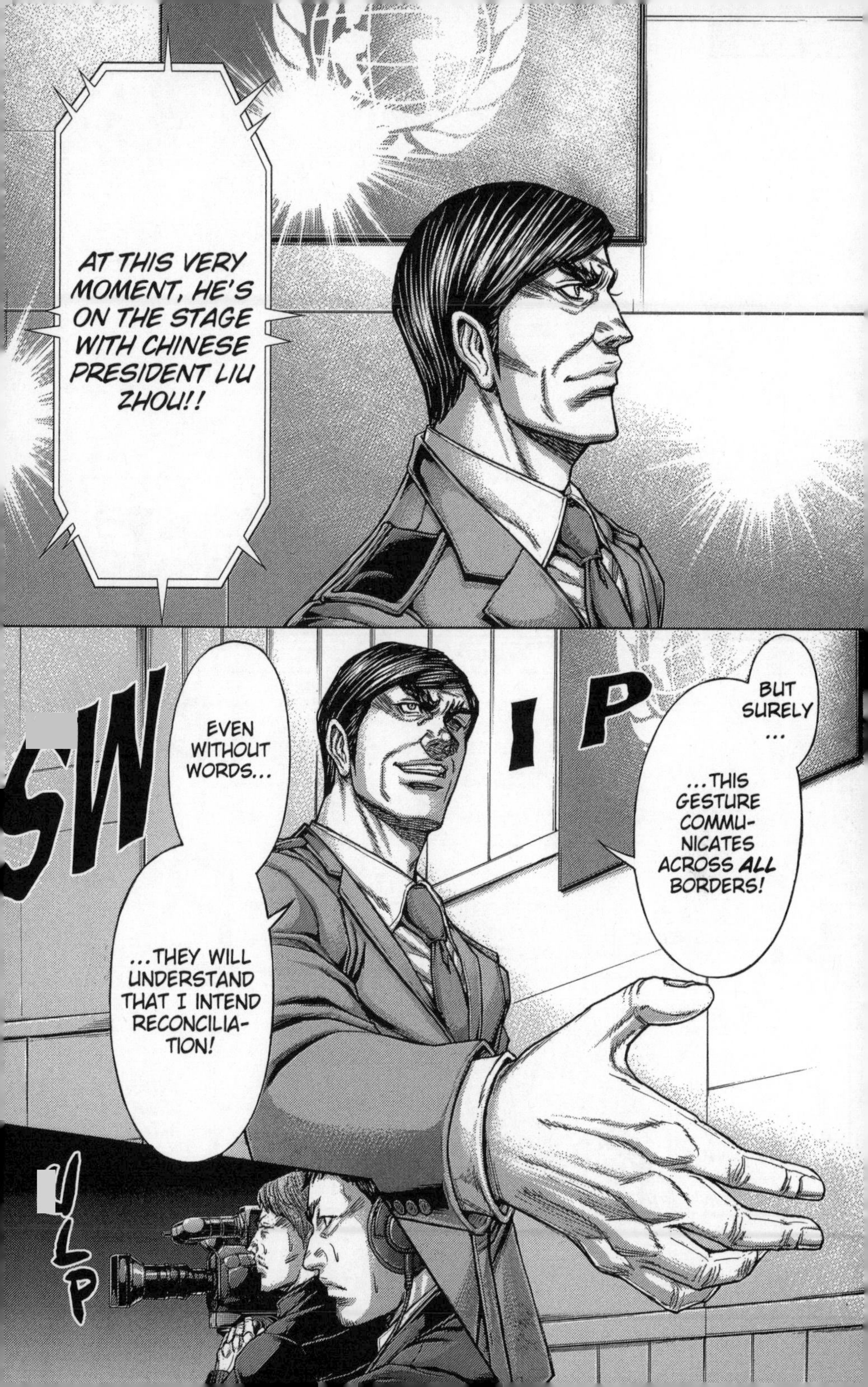
AT THIS VERY MOMENT, HE'S ON THE STAGE WITH CHINESE PRESIDENT LIU ZHOU!!
BUT SURELY...
...THIS GESTURE COMMUNICATES ACROSS **ALL** BORDERS!
SWIP
EVEN WITHOUT WORDS...
...THEY WILL UNDERSTAND THAT I INTEND RECONCILIATION!
ULP

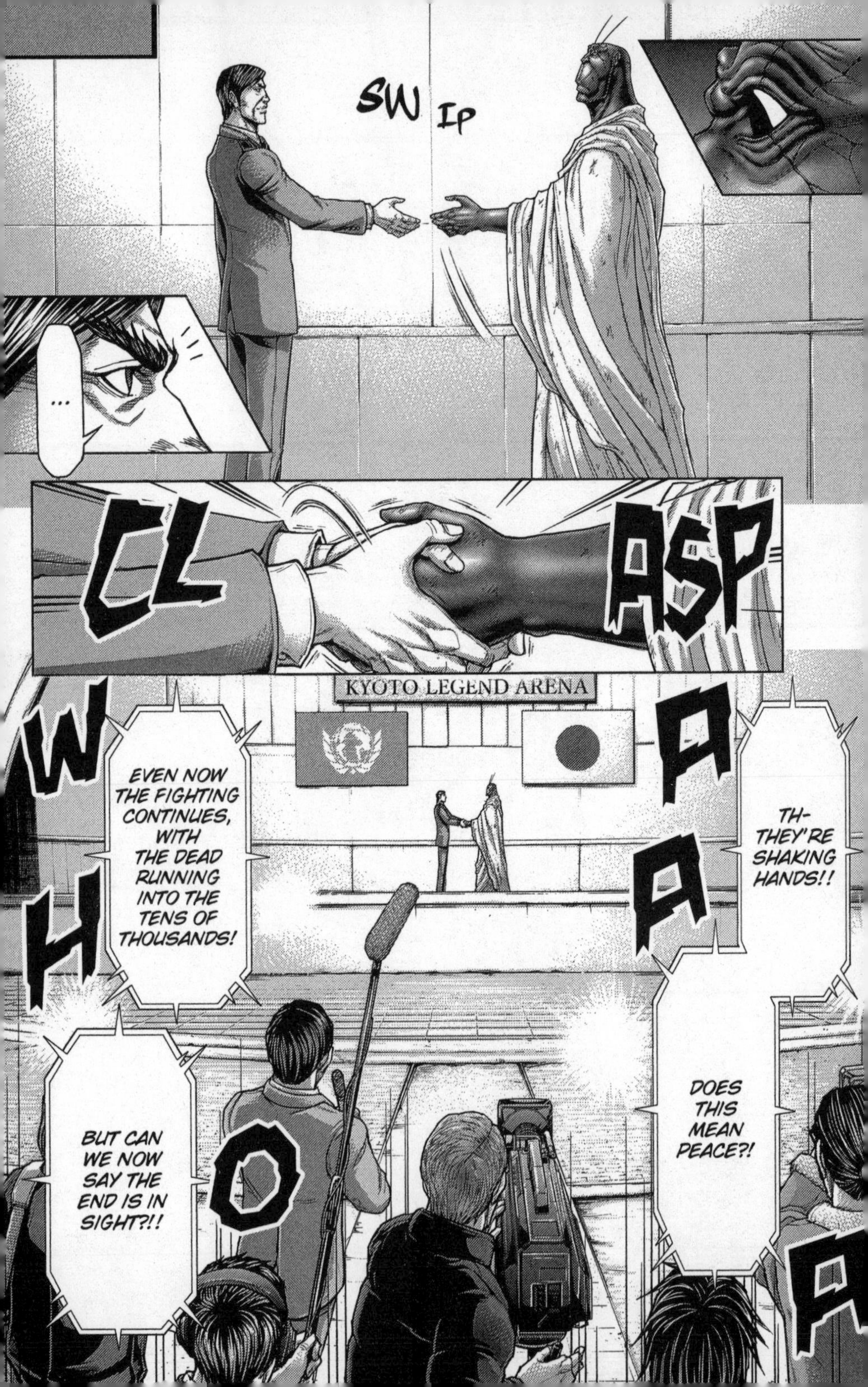
SWIP
...
CLASP
KYOTO LEGEND ARENA
TH- THEY'RE SHAKING HANDS!!
EVEN NOW THE FIGHTING CONTINUES, WITH THE DEAD RUNNING INTO THE TENS OF THOUSANDS!
DOES THIS MEAN PEACE?!
BUT CAN WE NOW SAY THE END IS IN SIGHT?!!
WHOAAAA

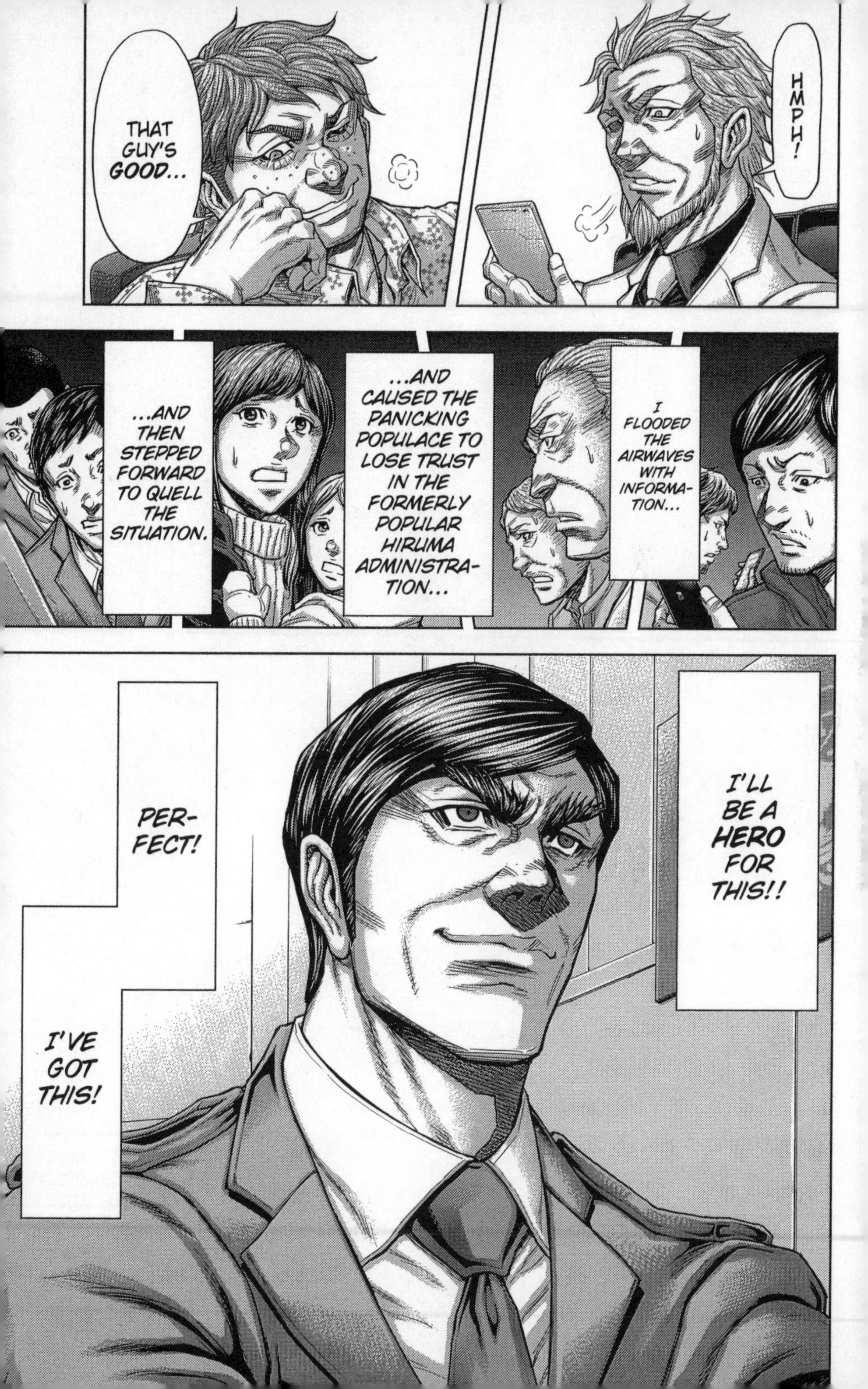
HMPH!
THAT GUY'S GOOD...
I FLOODED THE AIRWAVES WITH INFORMATION...
...AND CAUSED THE PANICKING POPULACE TO LOSE TRUST IN THE FORMERLY POPULAR HIRUMA ADMINISTRATION...
...AND THEN STEPPED FORWARD TO QUELL THE SITUATION.
I'LL BE A HERO FOR THIS!!
PERFECT!
I'VE GOT THIS!

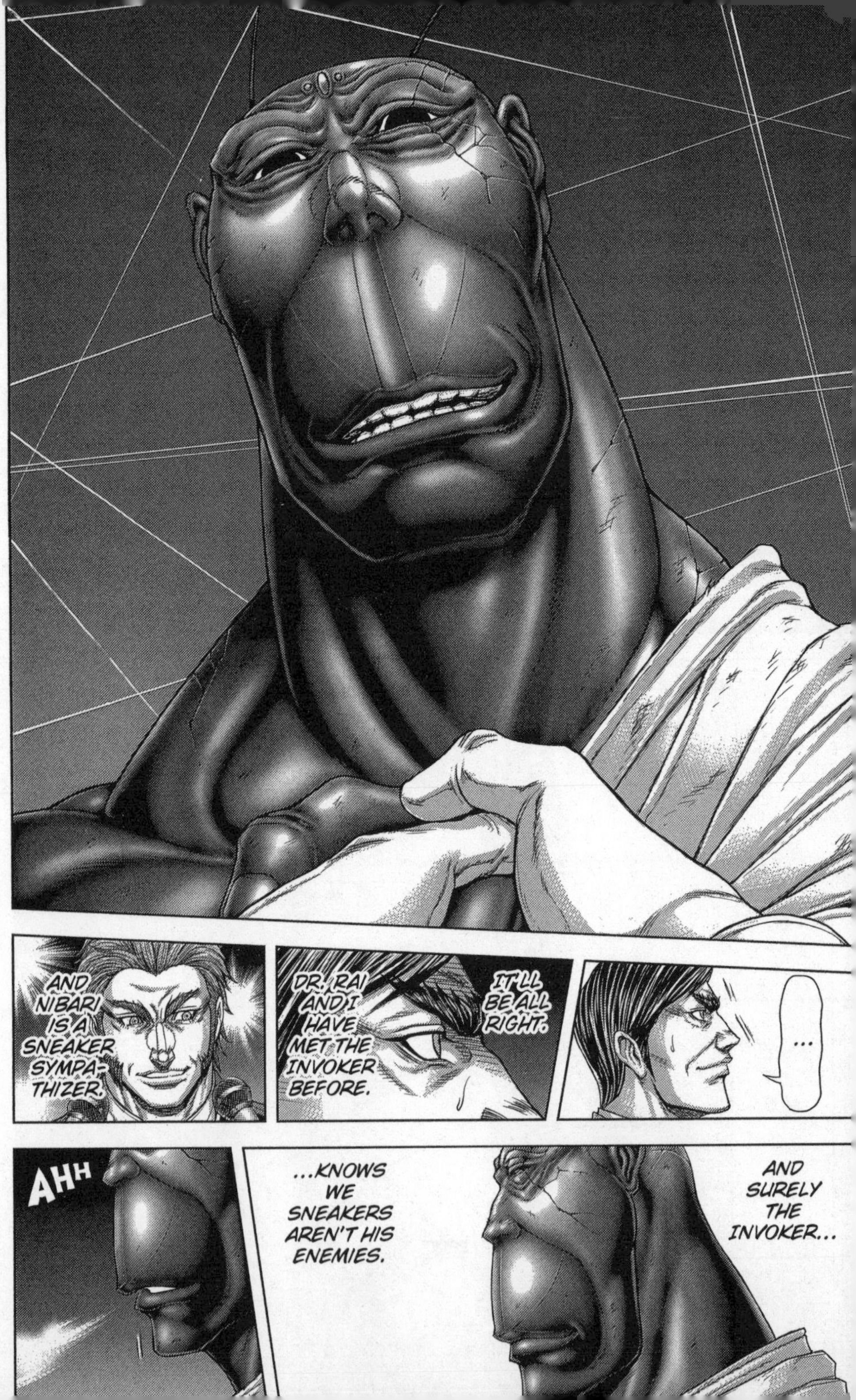
...
IT'LL BE ALL RIGHT.
DR. RAI AND I HAVE MET THE INVOKER BEFORE.
AND NIBARI IS A SNEAKER SYMPATHIZER.
AND SURELY THE INVOKER...
...KNOWS WE SNEAKERS AREN'T HIS ENEMIES.
AHH

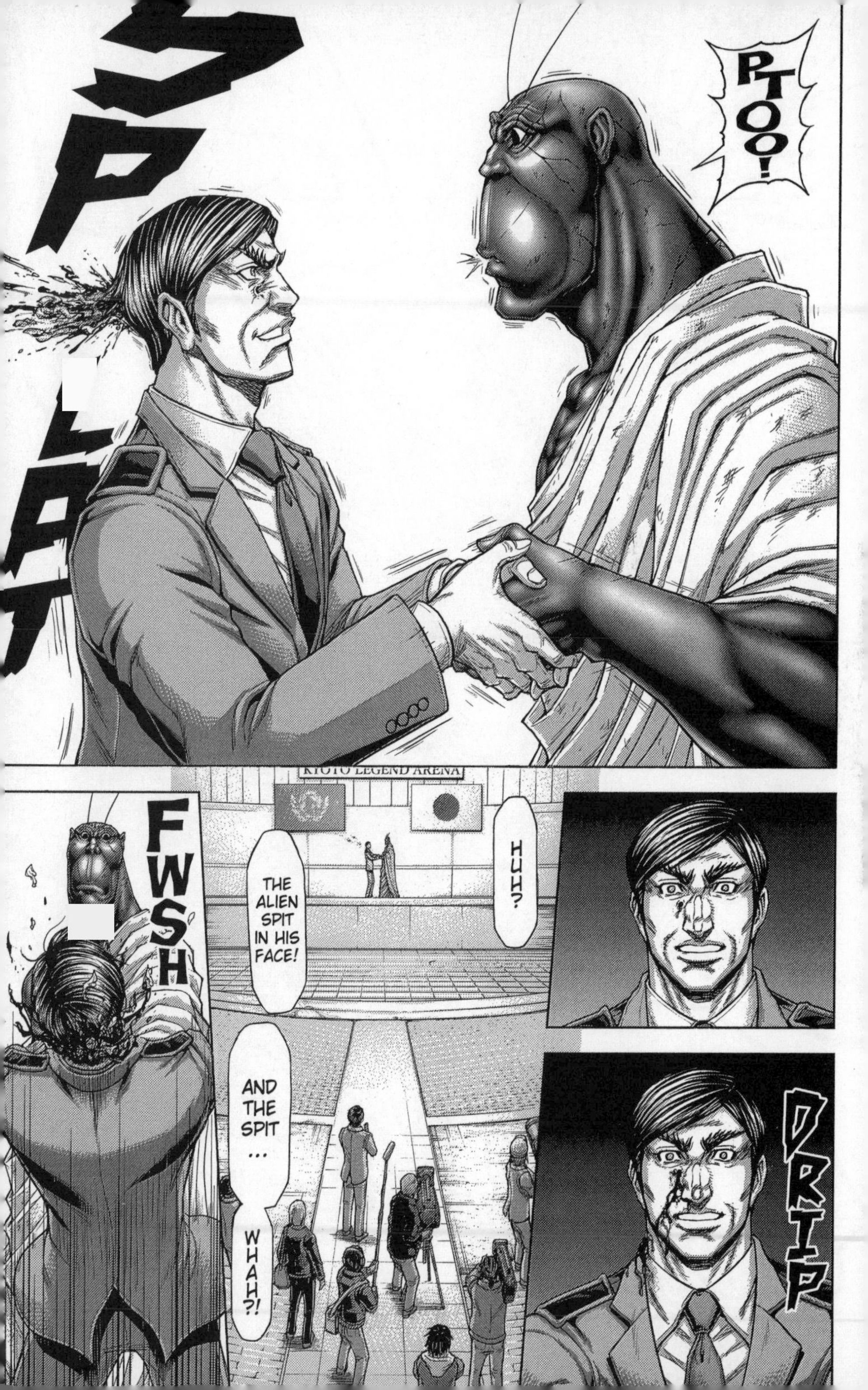
PTOOO!
SPLAT
HUH?
DRIP
KYOTO LEGEND ARENA
THE ALIEN SPIT IN HIS FACE!
AND THE SPIT ...
WHAH?!
FWSH

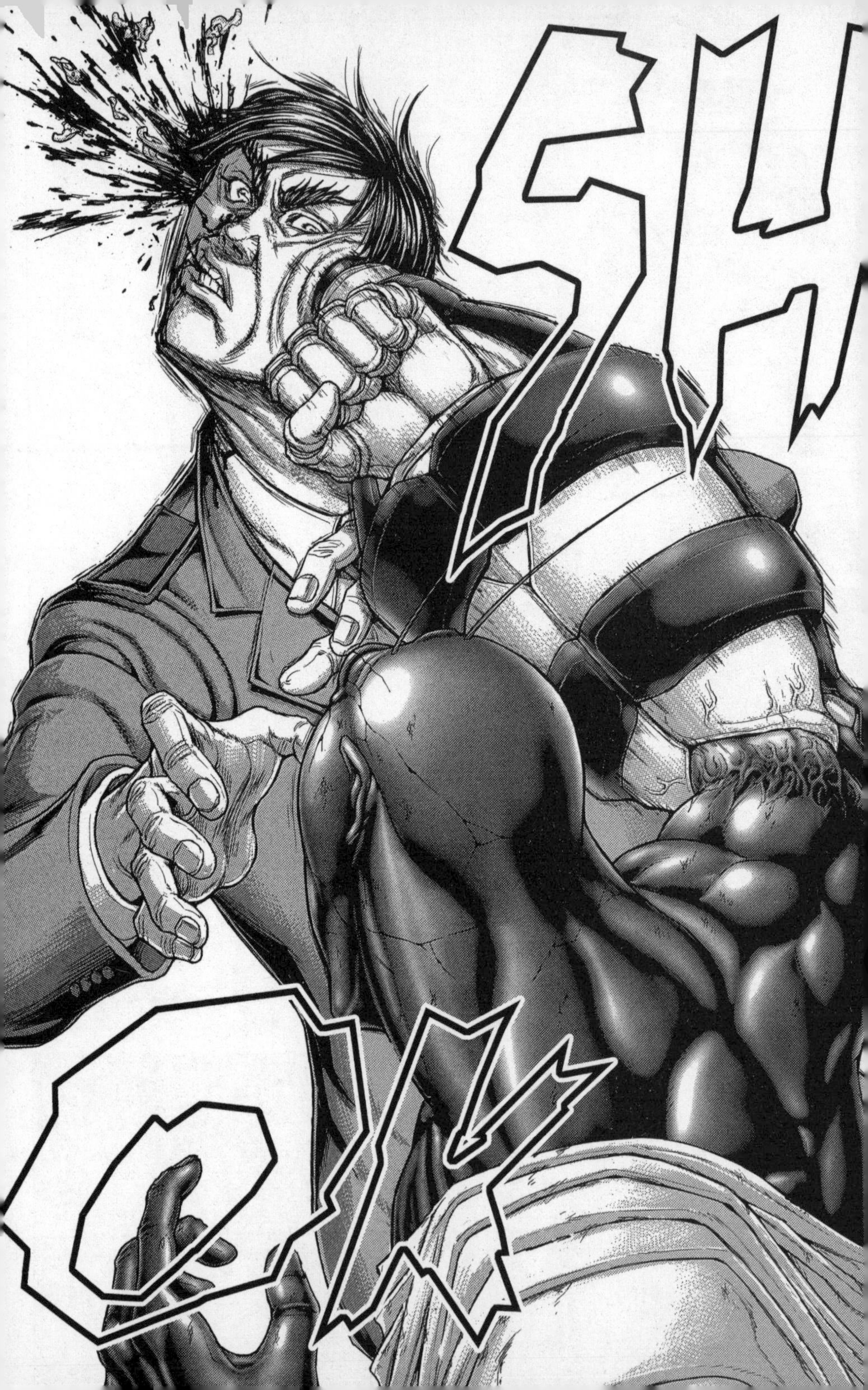
SH

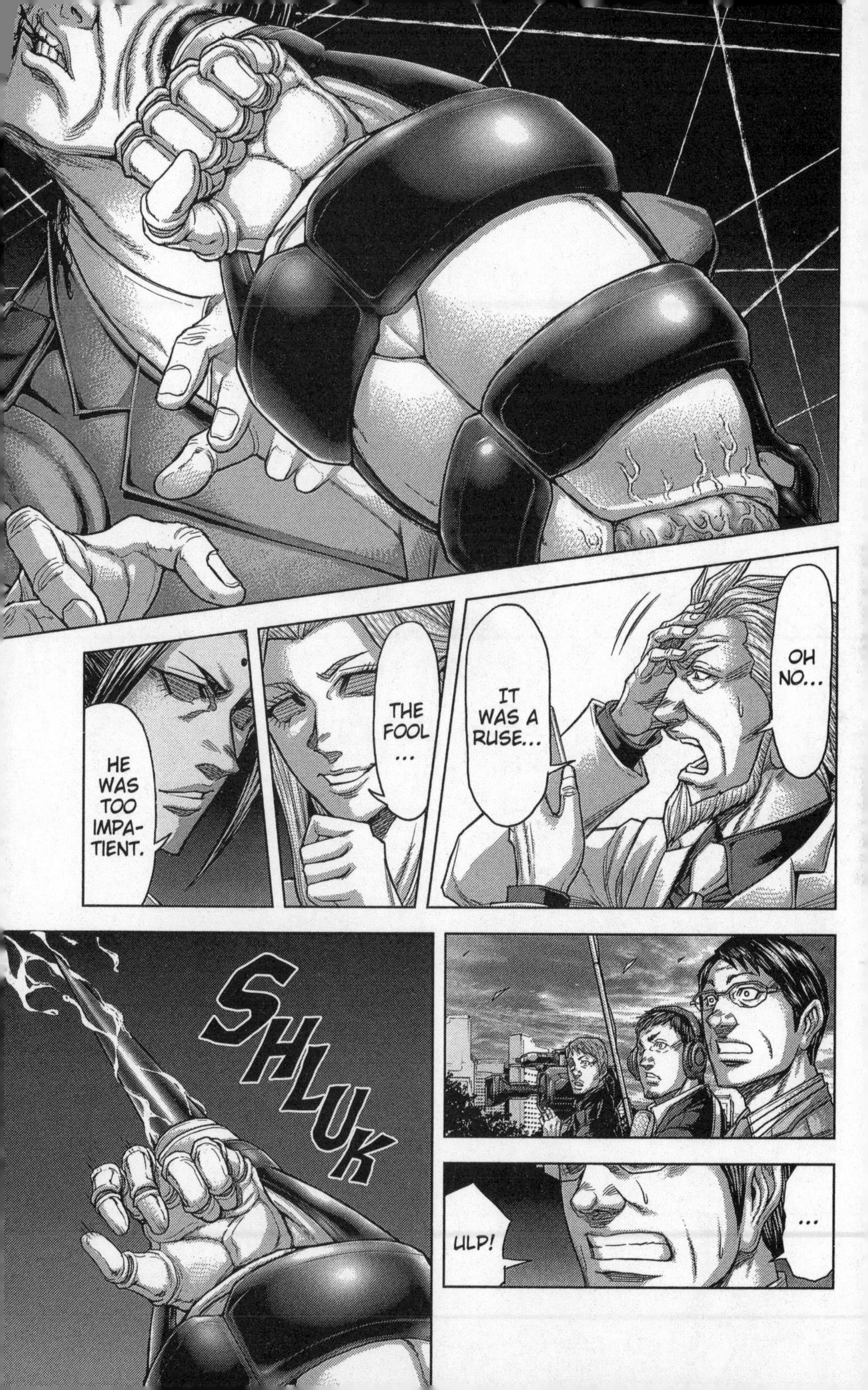
OH NO...
IT WAS A RUSE...
THE FOOL ...
HE WAS TOO IMPATIENT.
...
ULP!
SHLUK

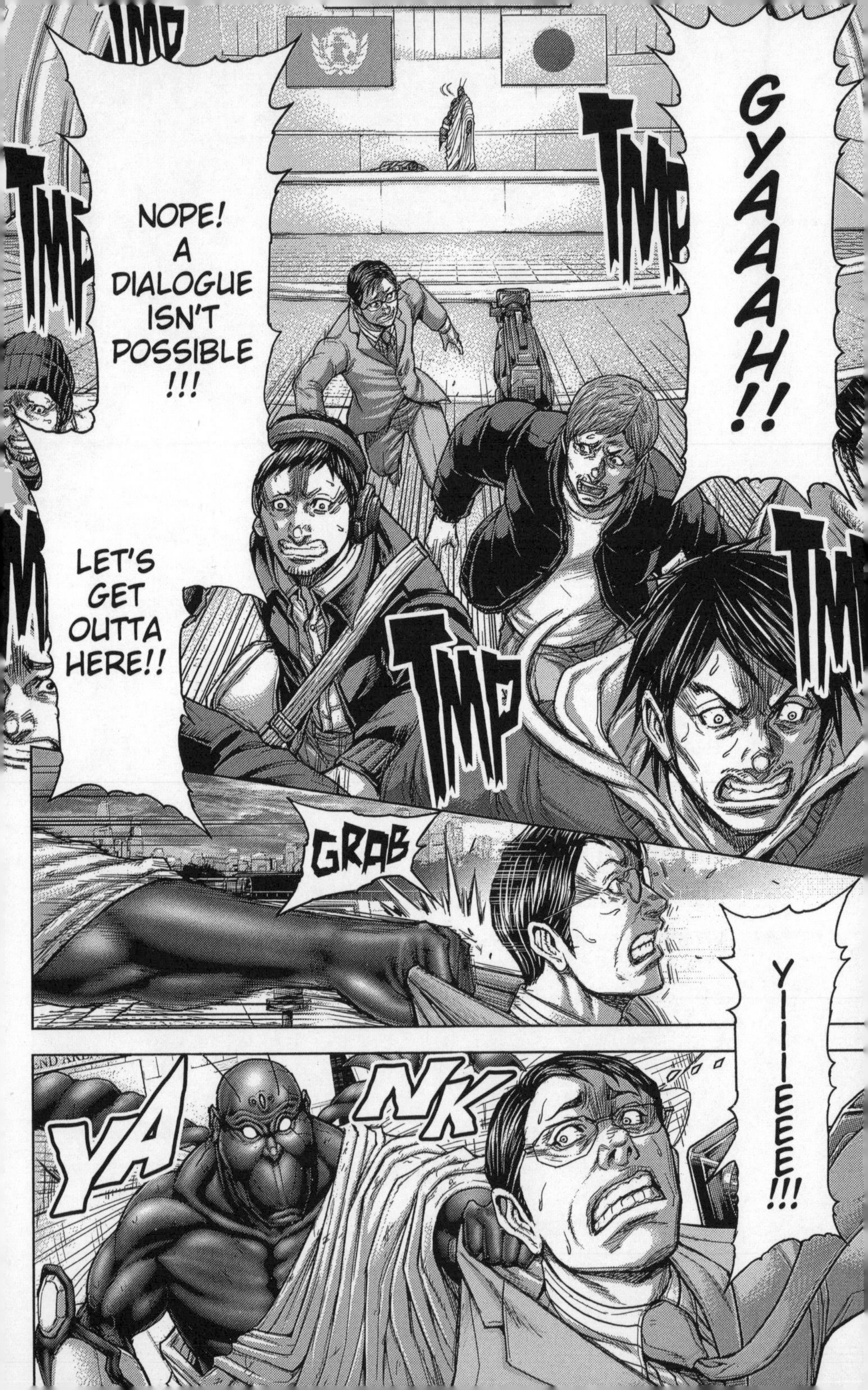
GYAAAAH!!
TMP
TMP
NOPE! A DIALOGUE ISN'T POSSIBLE!!!
LET'S GET OUTTA HERE!!
TMP
TMP
GRAB
YIIIEEEE!!!
YANK

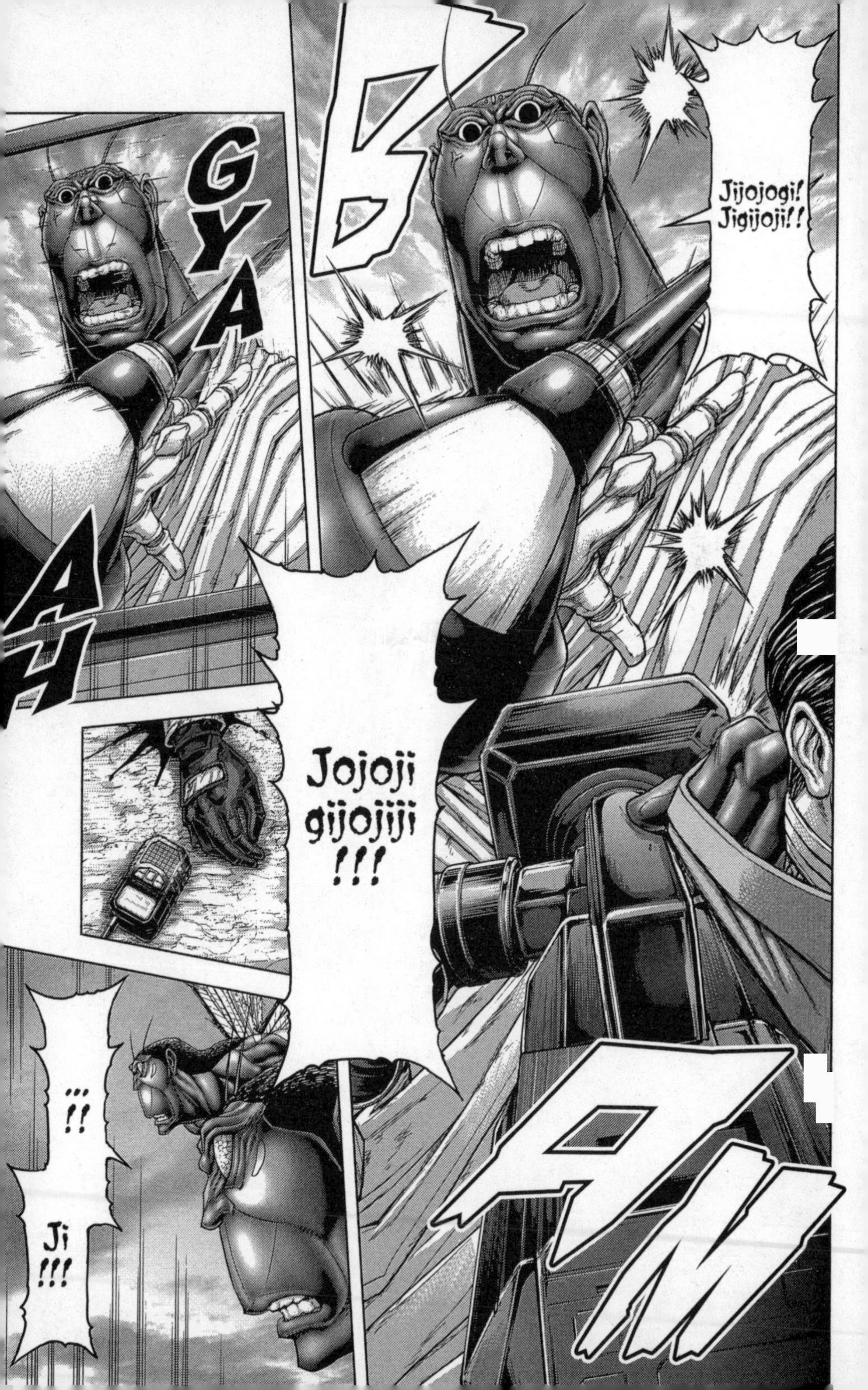
Jijojogi! Jigijoji!!
GYAAH
Jojoji gijojiji!!!
...!!
Ji!!!

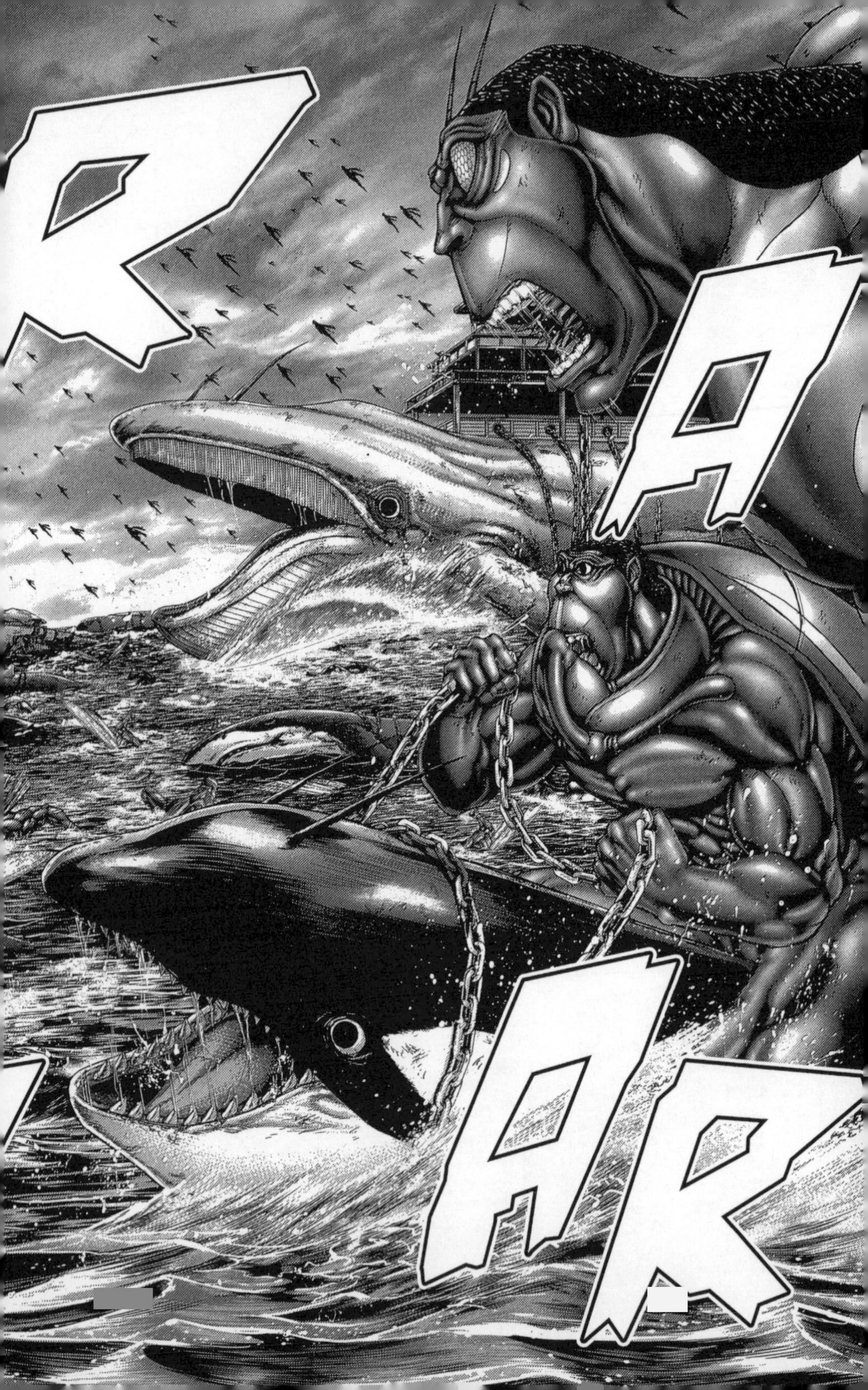
A
R
AR

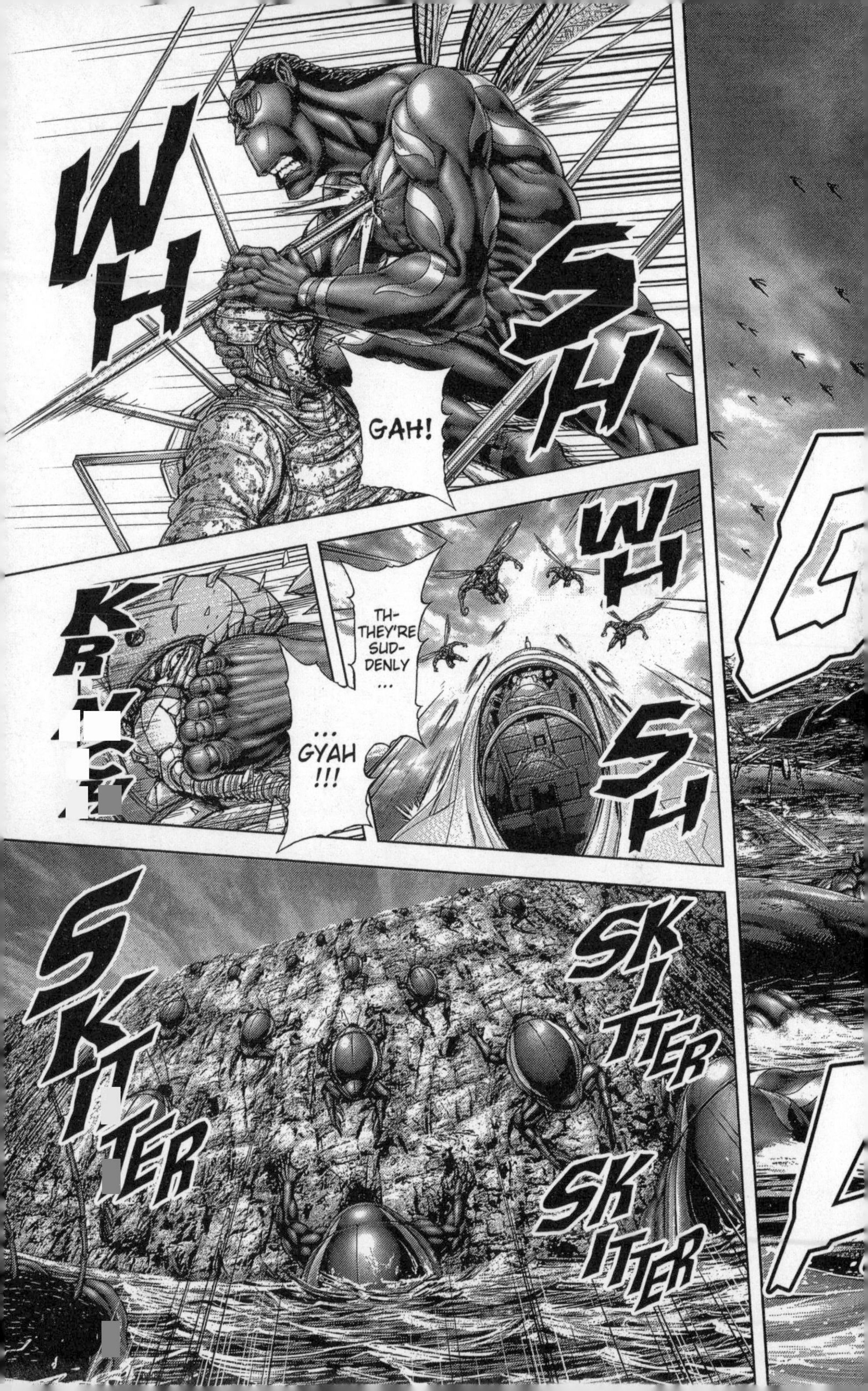
WH
SH
GAH!
WH
SH
TH-THEY'RE SUD-DENLY ...
... GYAH !!!
SKITTER
SKITTER

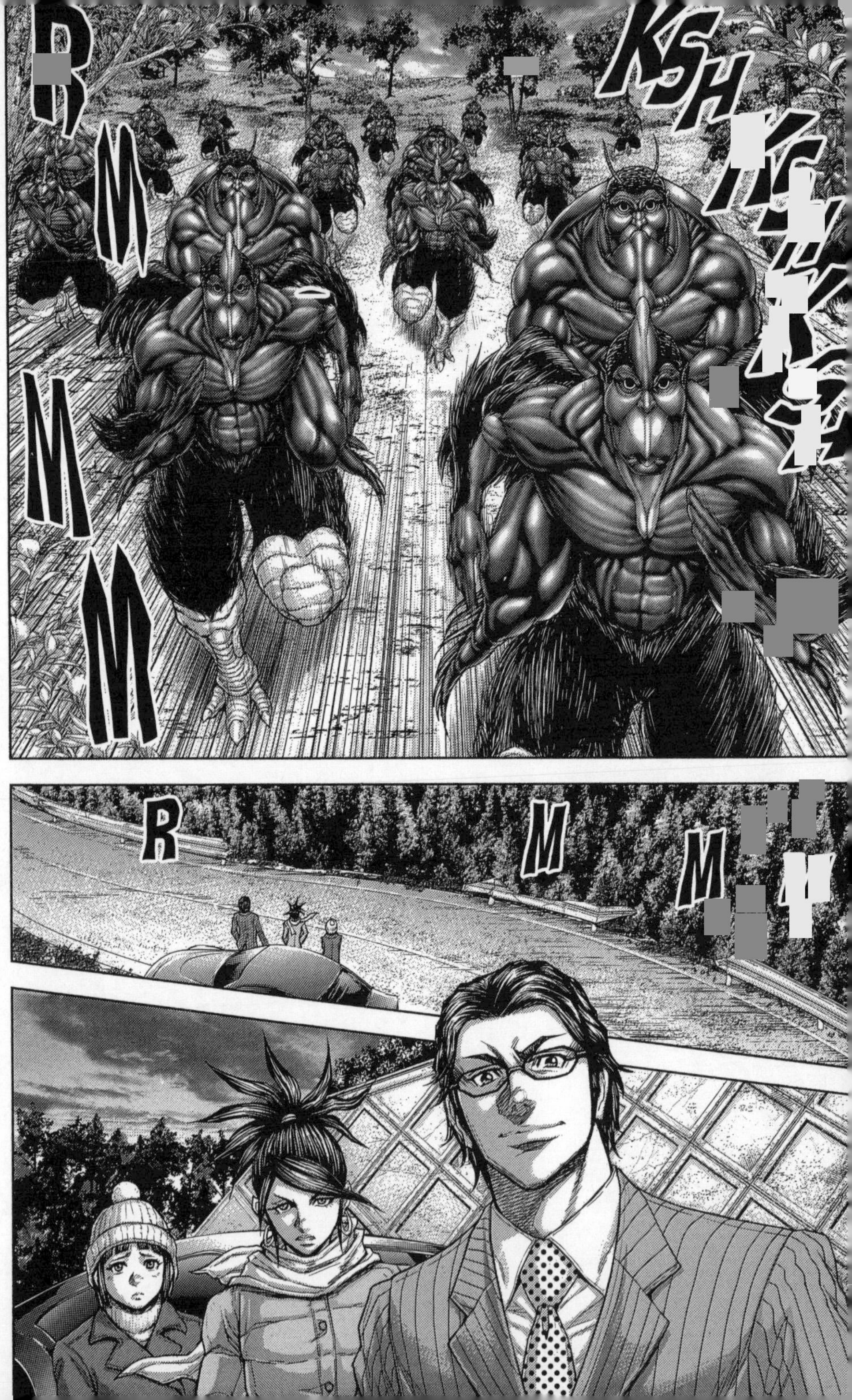
KSH
RMMM
RMM

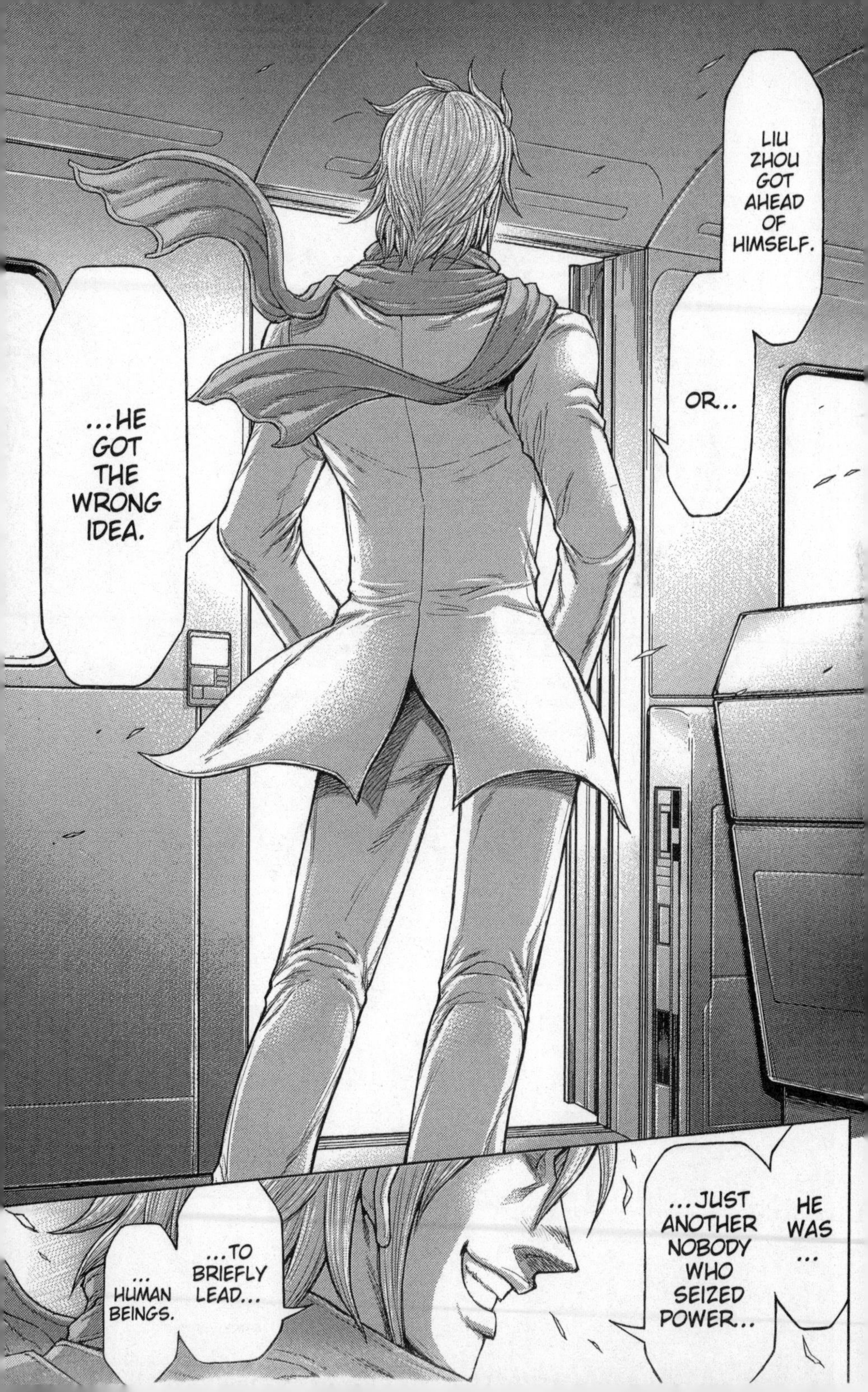
LIU ZHOU GOT AHEAD OF HIMSELF.
OR...
...HE GOT THE WRONG IDEA.
HE WAS...
...JUST ANOTHER NOBODY WHO SEIZED POWER...
...TO BRIEFLY LEAD...
...HUMAN BEINGS.

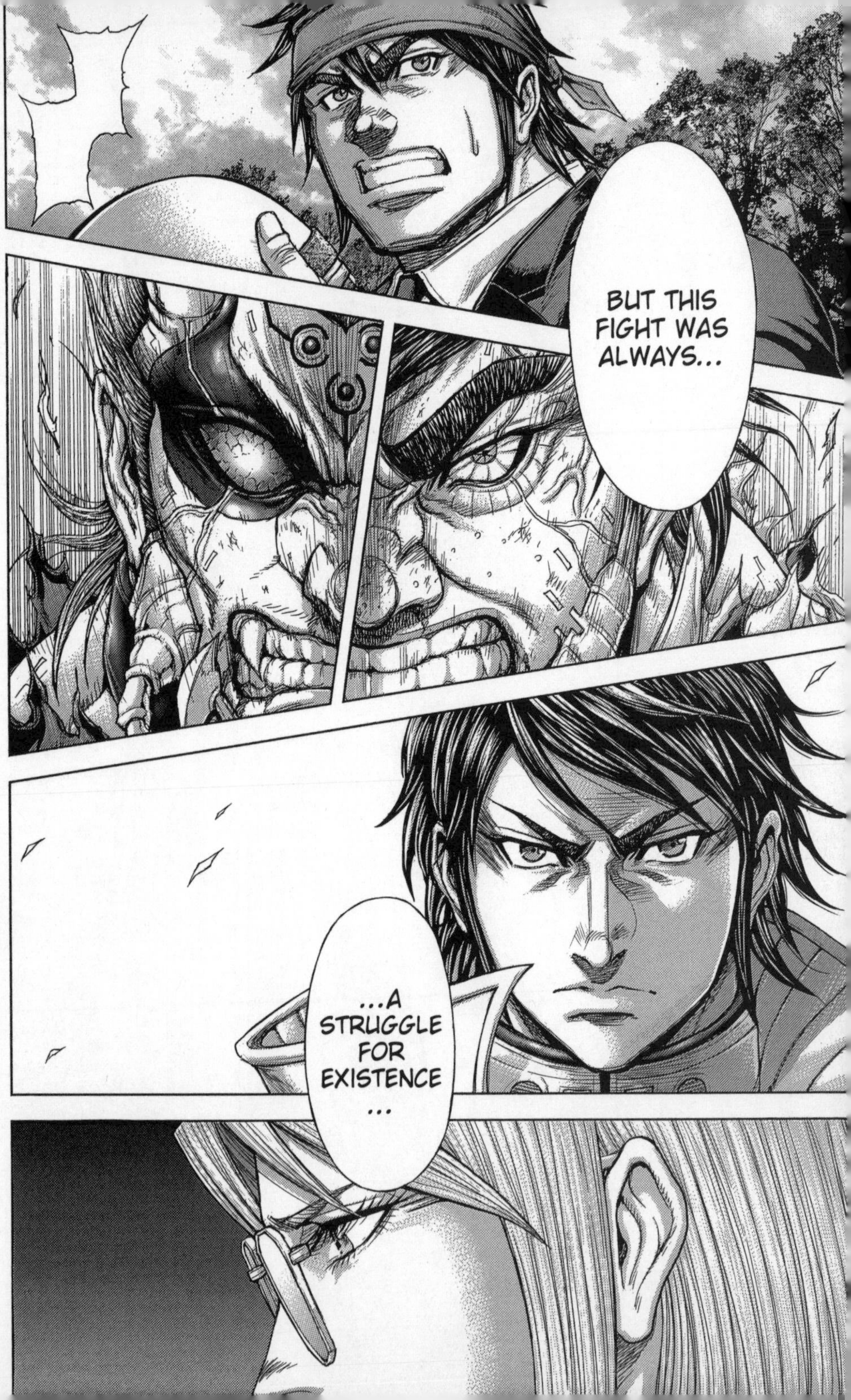
BUT THIS FIGHT WAS ALWAYS...
...A STRUGGLE FOR EXISTENCE ...

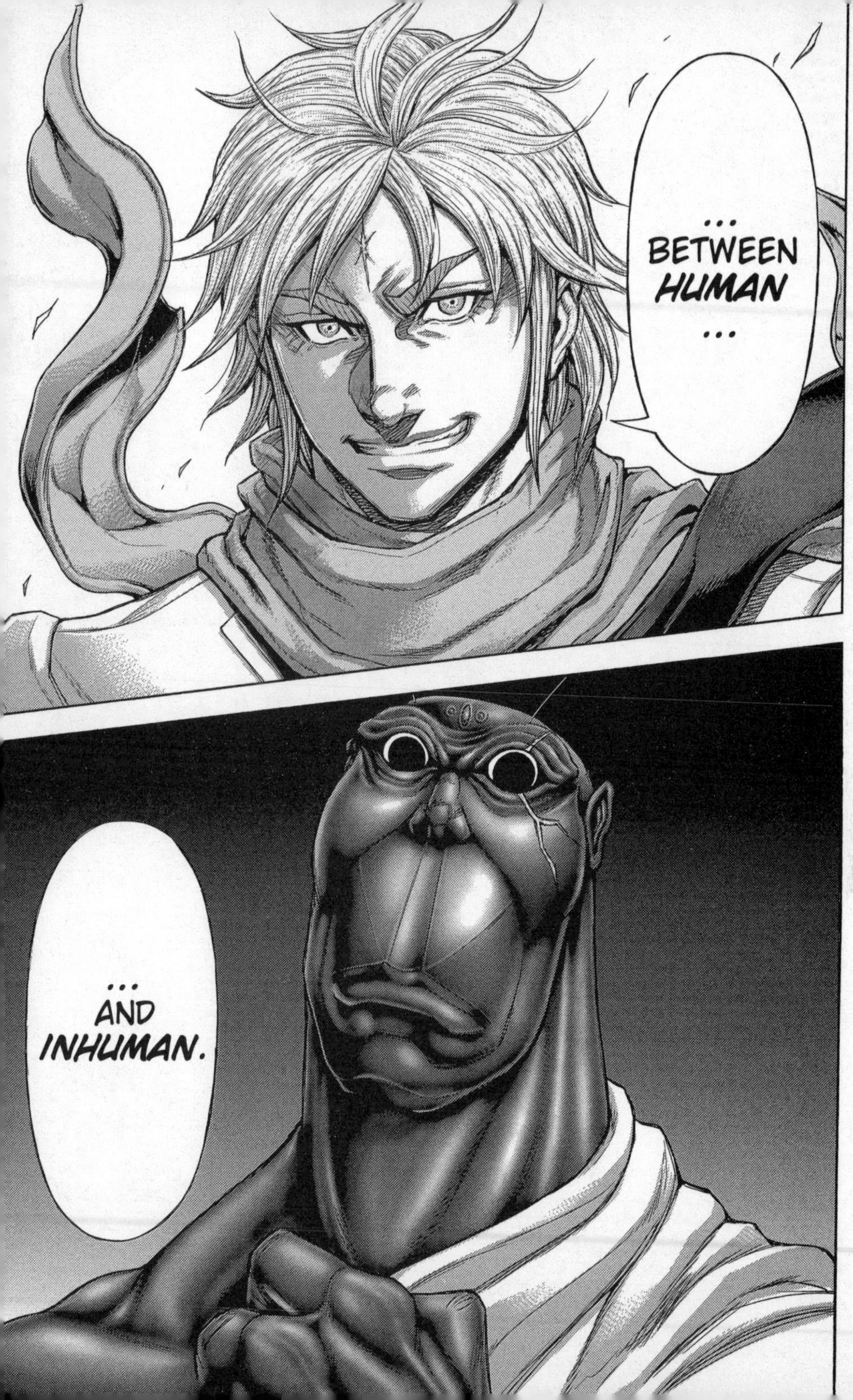
... BETWEEN HUMAN ...
... AND INHUMAN.

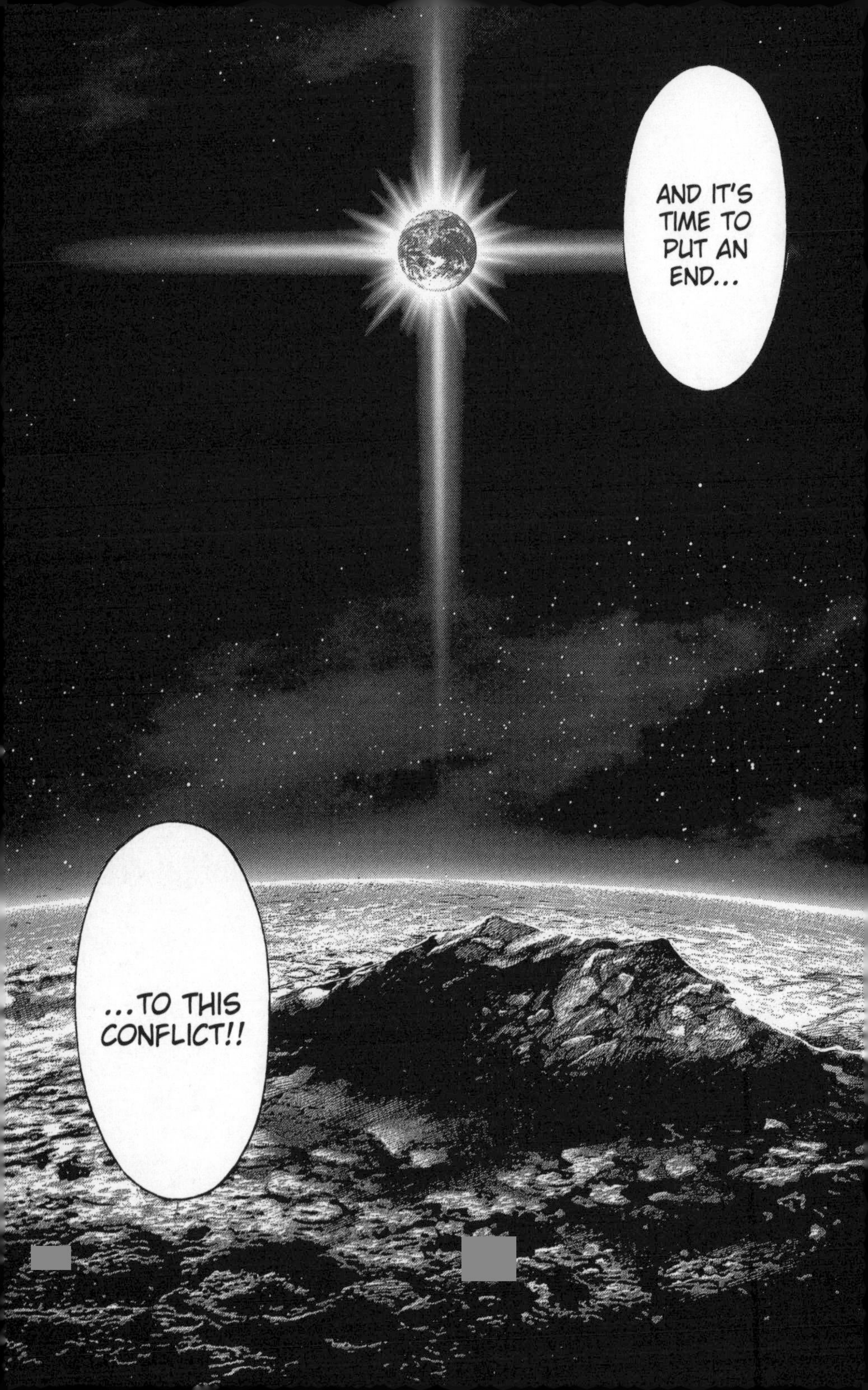
AND IT'S TIME TO PUT AN END...
...TO THIS CONFLICT!!

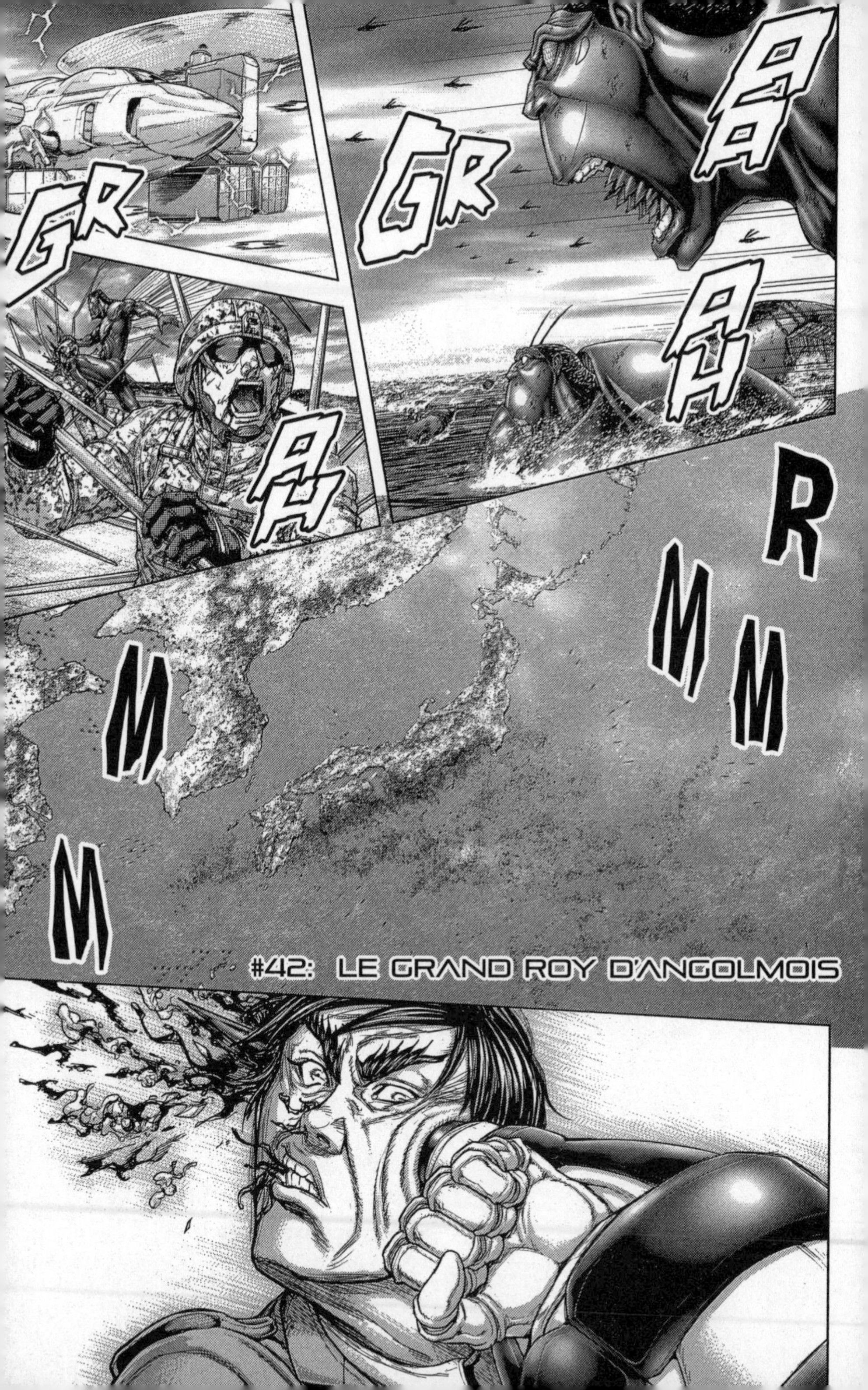
GR
AA
AAH
GR
AAH
RMMMMM
#42: LE GRAND ROY D'ANGOLMOIS

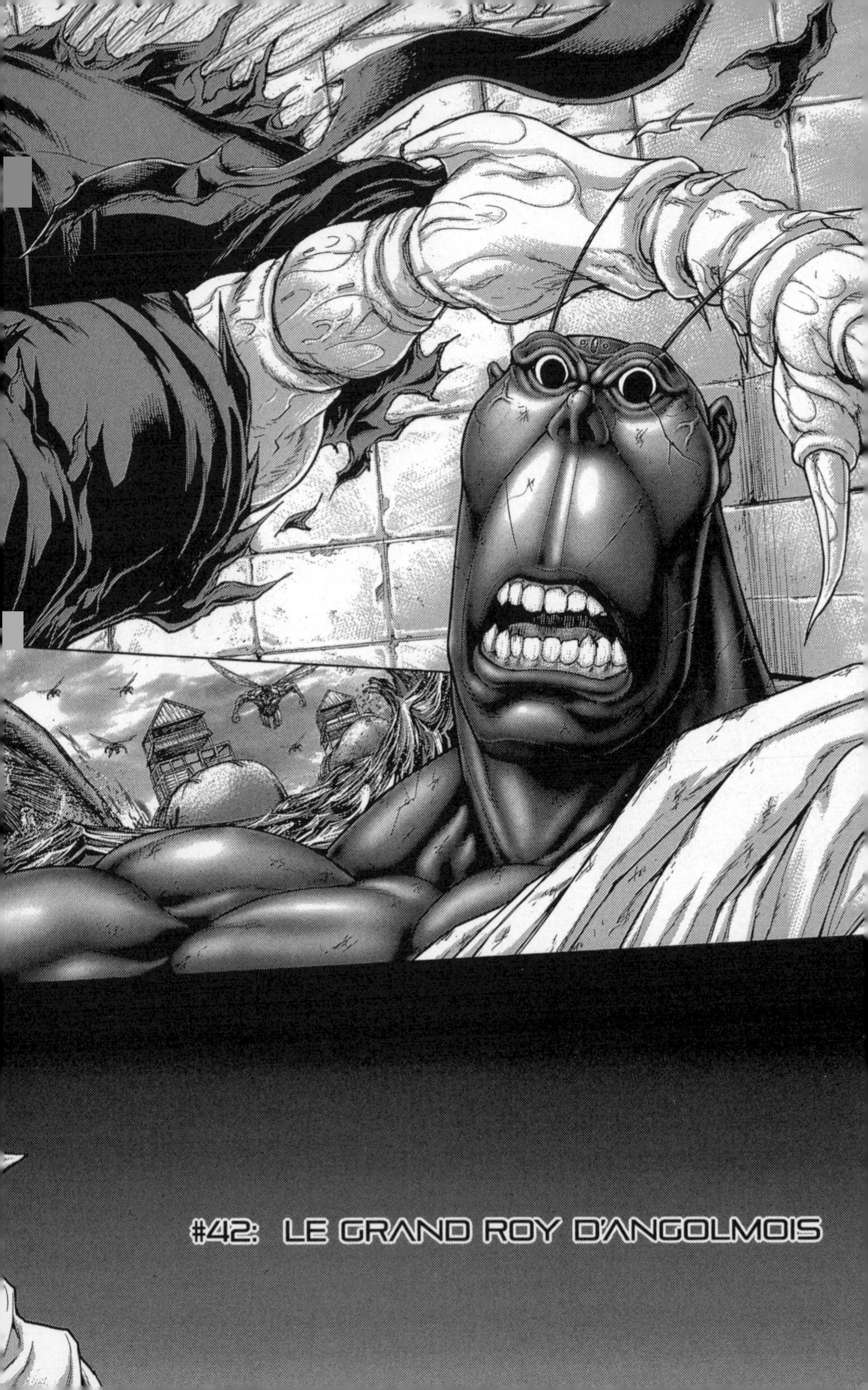
#42: LE GRAND ROY D'ANGOLMOIS

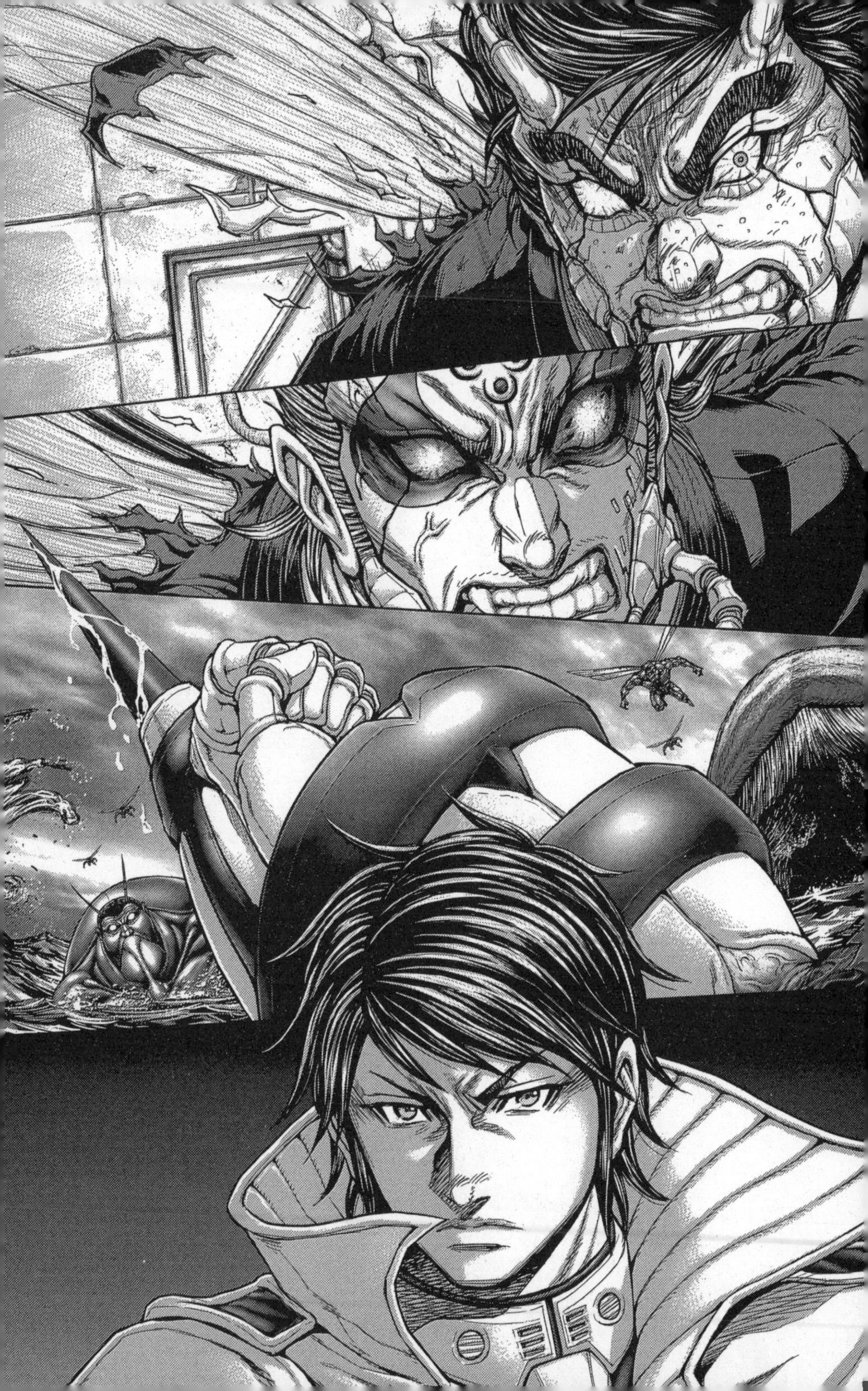

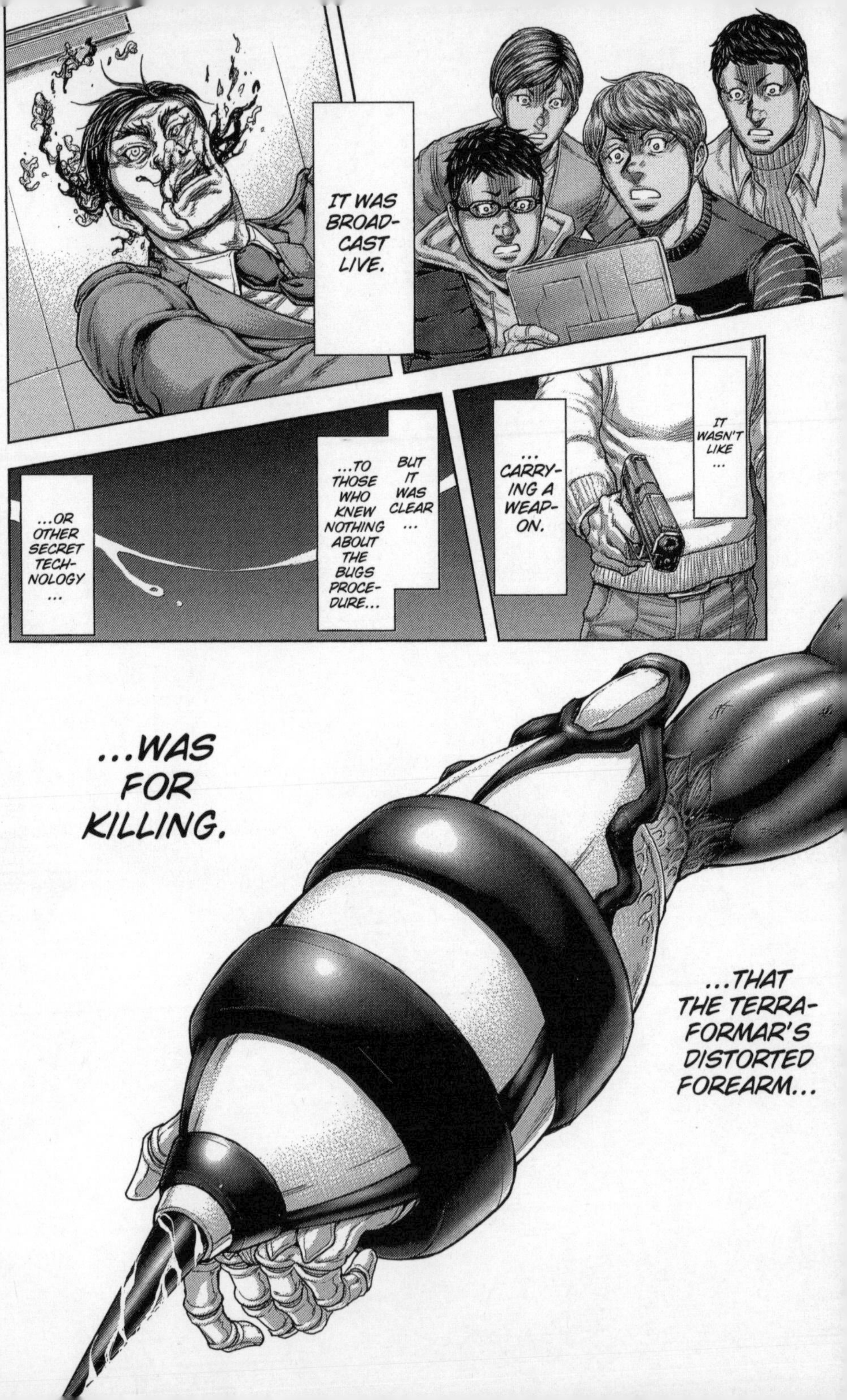
IT WAS BROADCAST LIVE.
IT WASN'T LIKE ...
...CARRYING A WEAPON.
BUT IT WAS CLEAR ...
...TO THOSE WHO KNEW NOTHING ABOUT THE BUGS PROCEDURE...
...OR OTHER SECRET TECHNOLOGY ...
...THAT THE TERRAFORMAR'S DISTORTED FOREARM...
...WAS FOR KILLING.

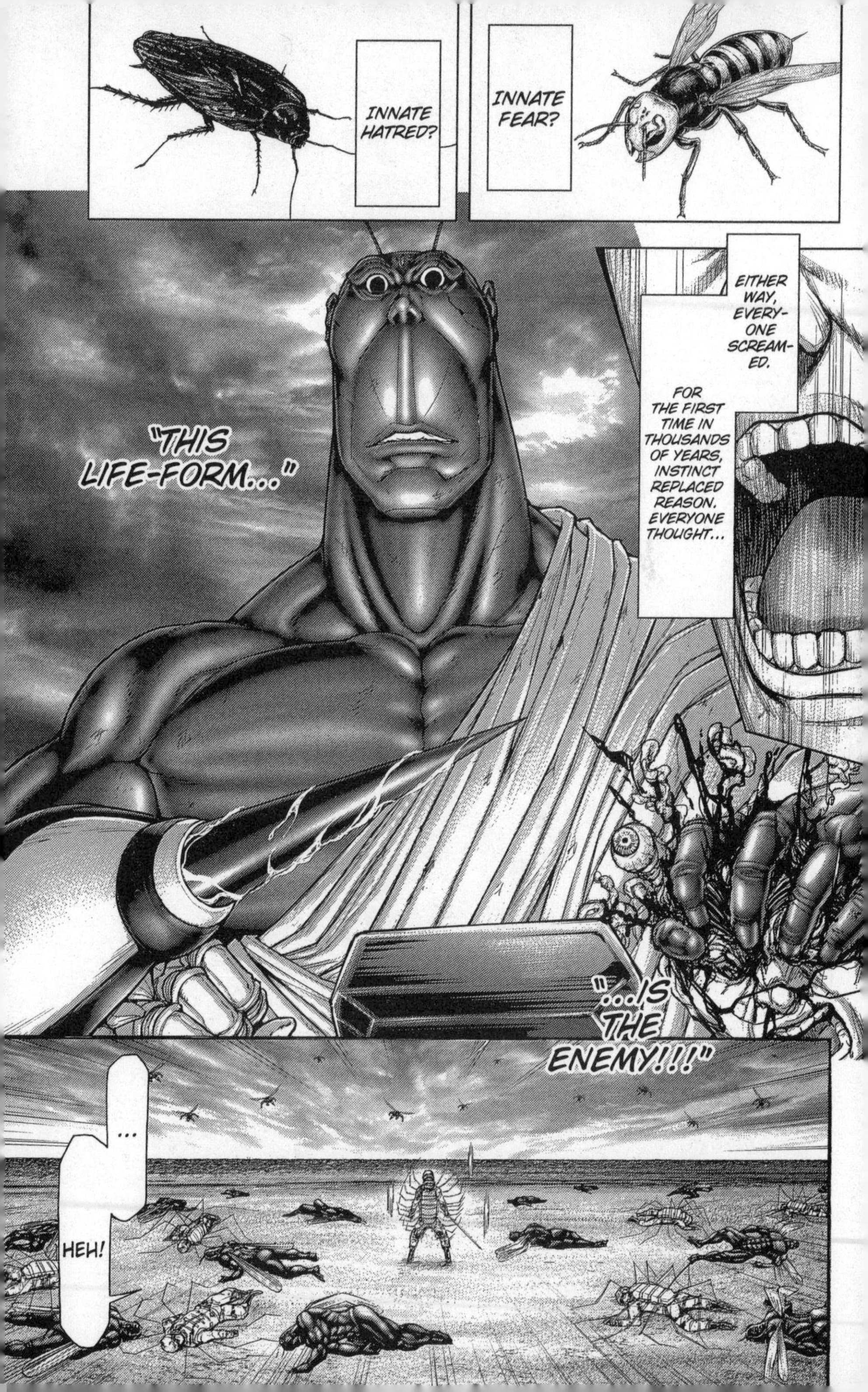

INNATE FEAR?
INNATE HATRED?
EITHER WAY, EVERYONE SCREAMED.
FOR THE FIRST TIME IN THOUSANDS OF YEARS, INSTINCT REPLACED REASON. EVERYONE THOUGHT...
"THIS LIFE-FORM..."
"...IS THE ENEMY!!!"
...
HEH!

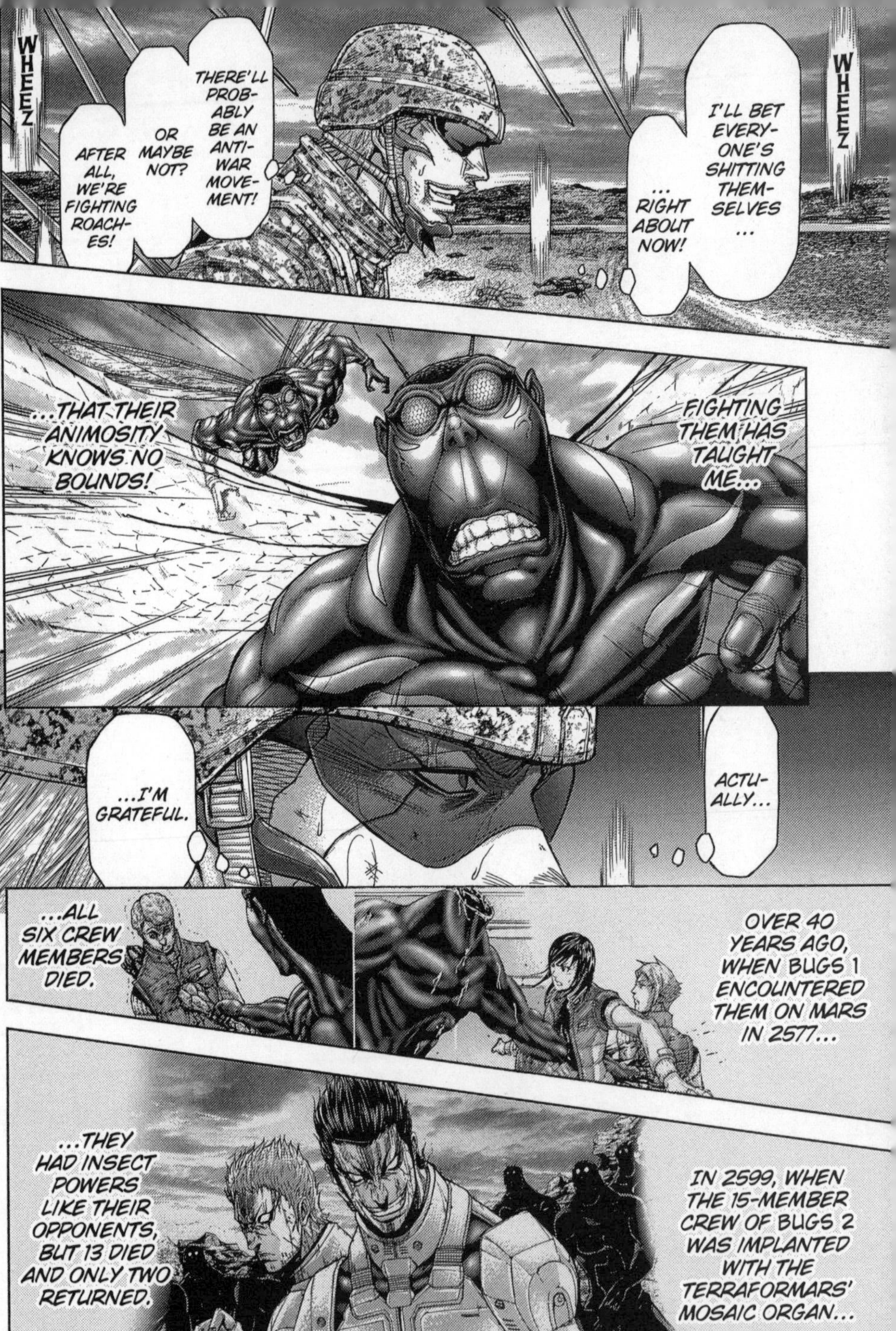
WHEEZ
I'LL BET EVERYONE'S SHITTING THEMSELVES ...
... RIGHT ABOUT NOW!
THERE'LL PROBABLY BE AN ANTI-WAR MOVEMENT!
OR MAYBE NOT?
AFTER ALL, WE'RE FIGHTING ROACHES!
WHEEZ
FIGHTING THEM HAS TAUGHT ME...
...THAT THEIR ANIMOSITY KNOWS NO BOUNDS!
ACTUALLY...
...I'M GRATEFUL.
OVER 40 YEARS AGO, WHEN BUGS 1 ENCOUNTERED THEM ON MARS IN 2577...
...ALL SIX CREW MEMBERS DIED.
IN 2599, WHEN THE 15-MEMBER CREW OF BUGS 2 WAS IMPLANTED WITH THE TERRAFORMARS' MOSAIC ORGAN...
...THEY HAD INSECT POWERS LIKE THEIR OPPONENTS, BUT 13 DIED AND ONLY TWO RETURNED.

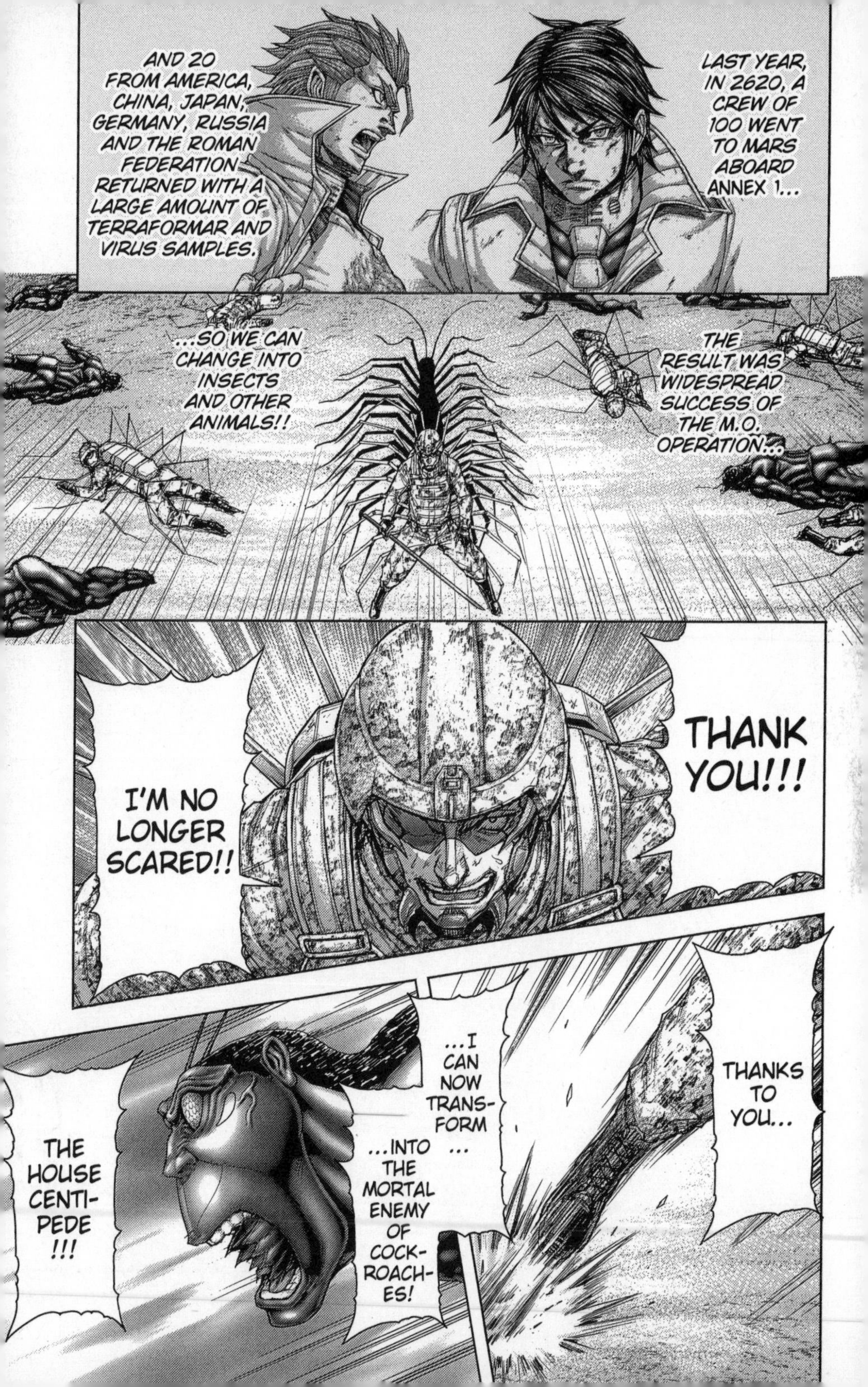
LAST YEAR, IN 2620, A CREW OF 100 WENT TO MARS ABOARD ANNEX 1...
AND 20 FROM AMERICA, CHINA, JAPAN, GERMANY, RUSSIA AND THE ROMAN FEDERATION RETURNED WITH A LARGE AMOUNT OF TERRAFORMAR AND VIRUS SAMPLES.
THE RESULT WAS WIDESPREAD SUCCESS OF THE M.O. OPERATION...
...SO WE CAN CHANGE INTO INSECTS AND OTHER ANIMALS!!
THANK YOU!!!
I'M NO LONGER SCARED!!
THANKS TO YOU...
...I CAN NOW TRANS-FORM ...
...INTO THE MORTAL ENEMY OF COCK-ROACH-ES!
THE HOUSE CENTI-PEDE !!!

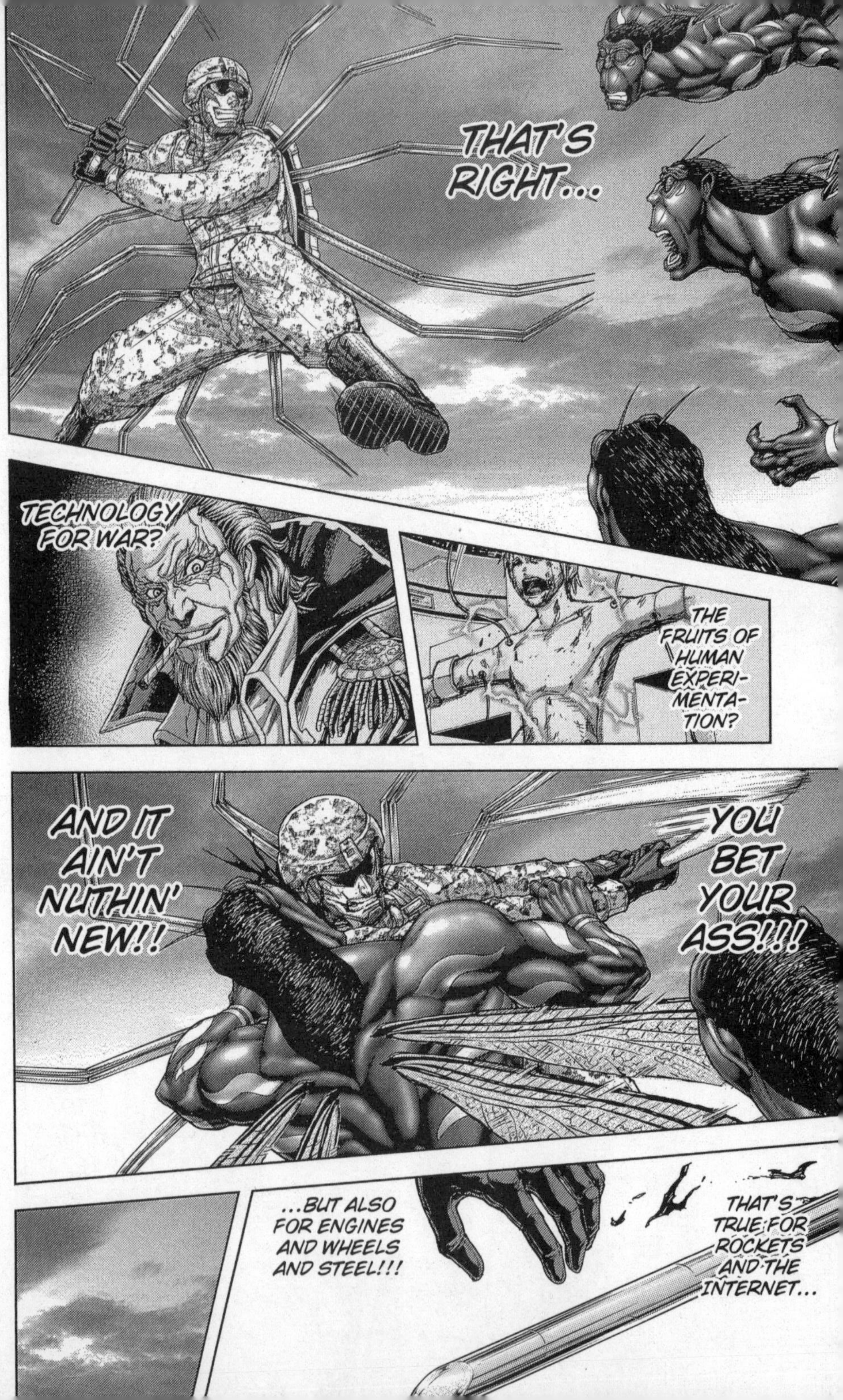

THAT'S RIGHT...
THE FRUITS OF HUMAN EXPERIMENTATION?
TECHNOLOGY FOR WAR?
YOU BET YOUR ASS!!!
AND IT AIN'T NUTHIN' NEW!!
THAT'S TRUE FOR ROCKETS AND THE INTERNET...
...BUT ALSO FOR ENGINES AND WHEELS AND STEEL!!!

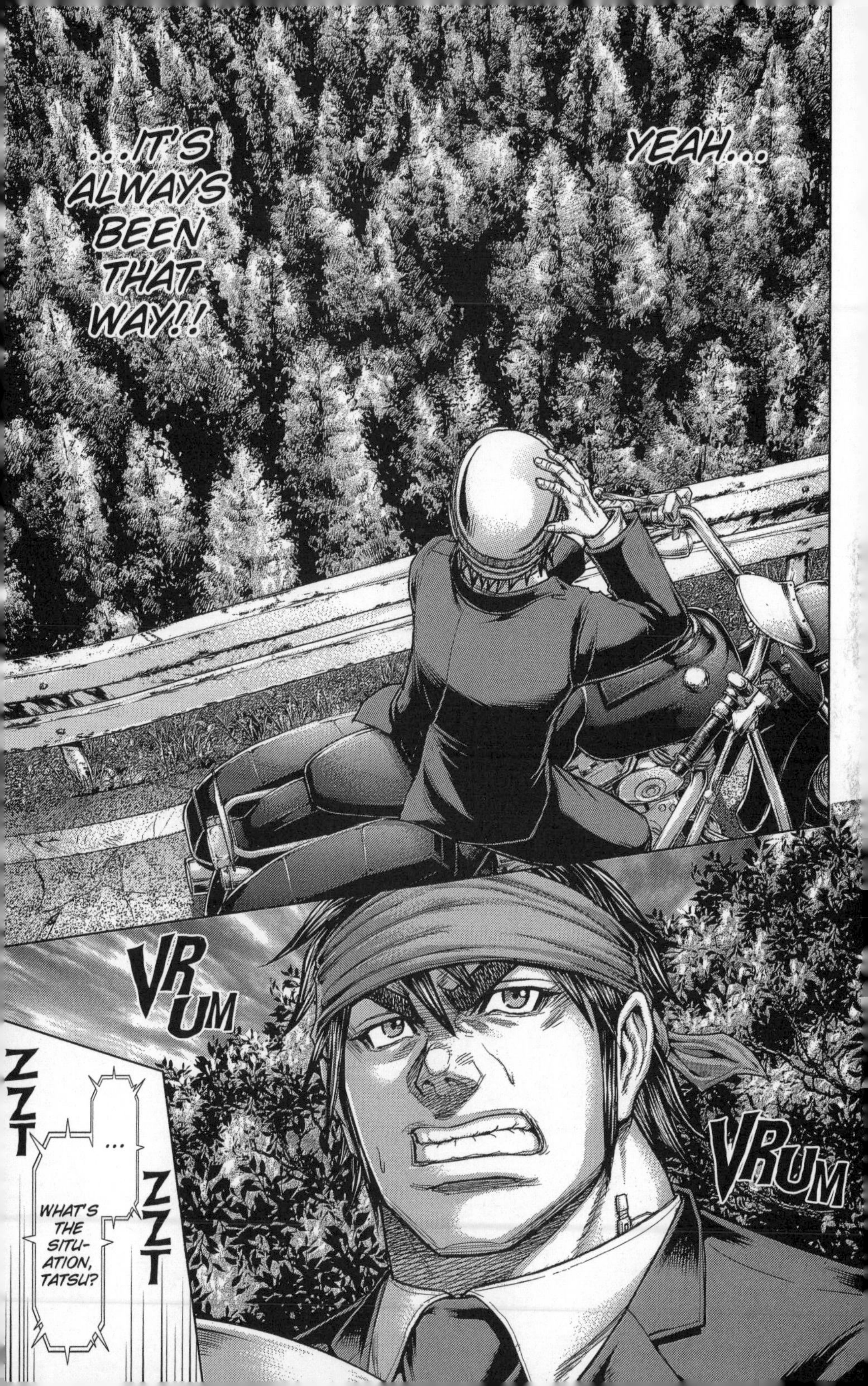
YEAH...
...IT'S ALWAYS BEEN THAT WAY!!
VRUM
VRUM
ZZT
...
ZZT
WHAT'S THE SITU-ATION, TATSU?
ZZT

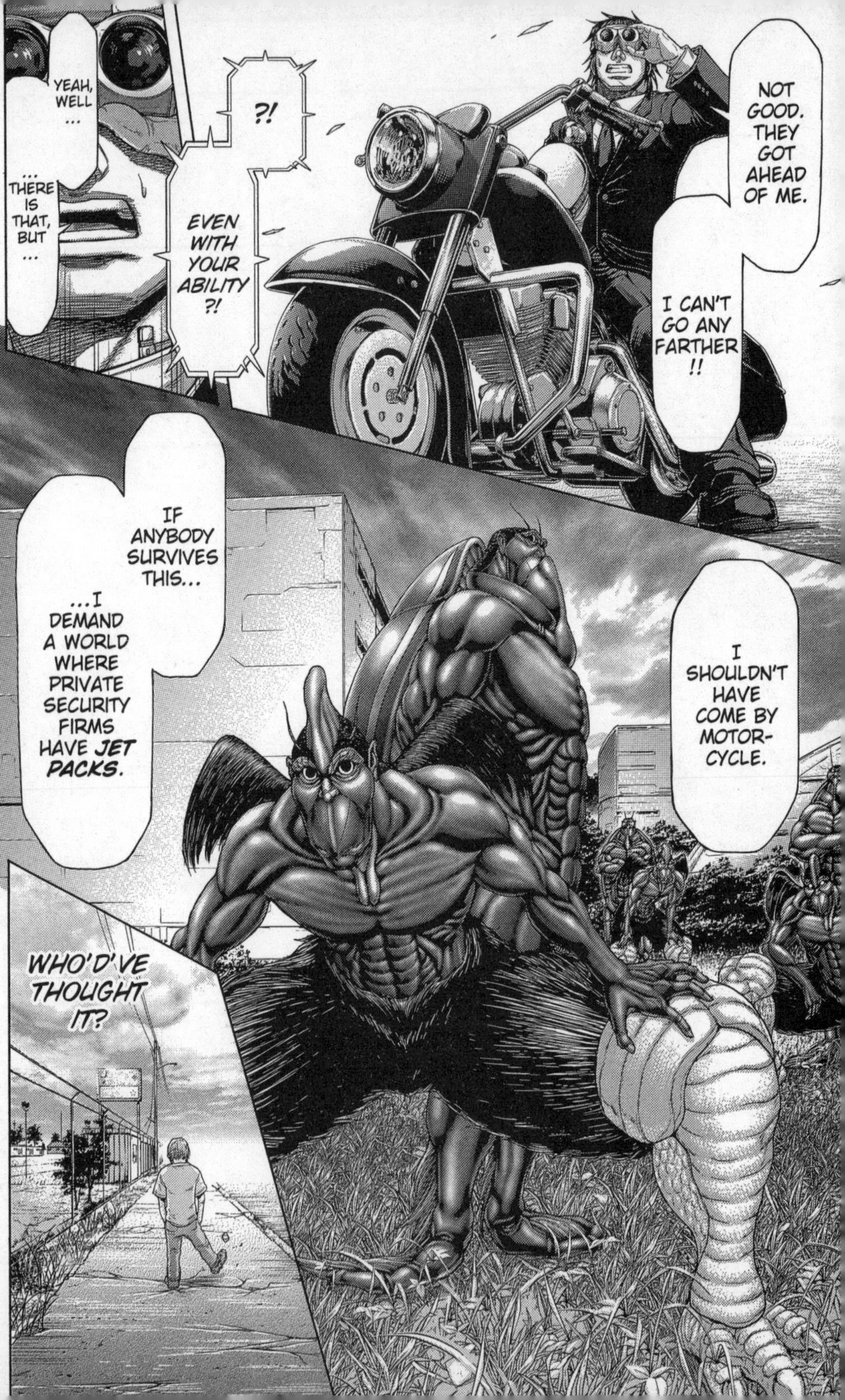
NOT GOOD. THEY GOT AHEAD OF ME.
I CAN'T GO ANY FARTHER!!
?!
EVEN WITH YOUR ABILITY?!
YEAH, WELL...
...THERE IS THAT, BUT...
I SHOULDN'T HAVE COME BY MOTOR-CYCLE.
IF ANYBODY SURVIVES THIS...
...I DEMAND A WORLD WHERE PRIVATE SECURITY FIRMS HAVE *JET PACKS*.
WHO'D'VE THOUGHT IT?

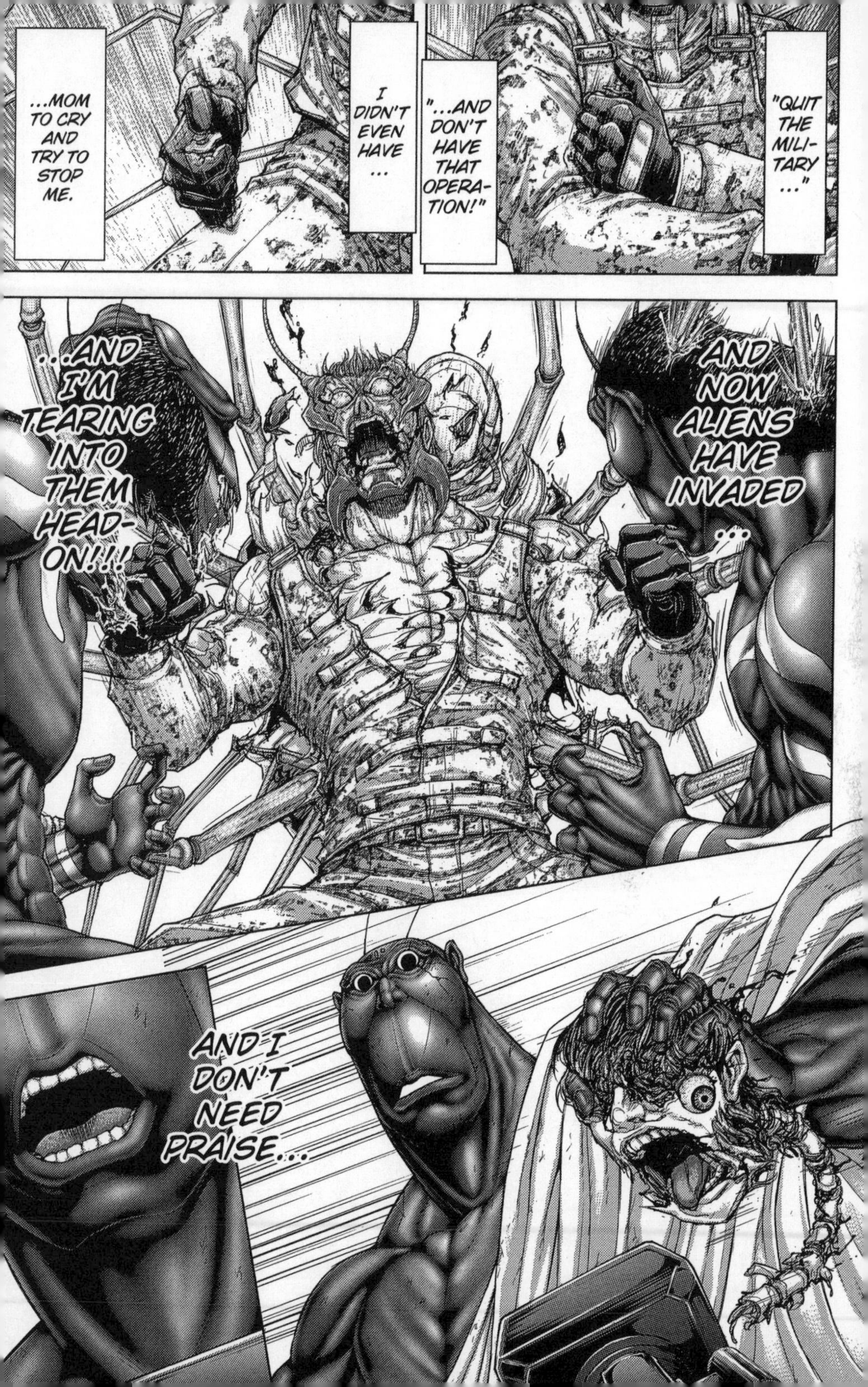
"QUIT THE MILITARY..."
"...AND DON'T HAVE THAT OPERATION!"
I DIDN'T EVEN HAVE...
...MOM TO CRY AND TRY TO STOP ME.
AND NOW ALIENS HAVE INVADED...
...AND I'M TEARING INTO THEM HEAD-ON!!!
AND I DON'T NEED PRAISE...

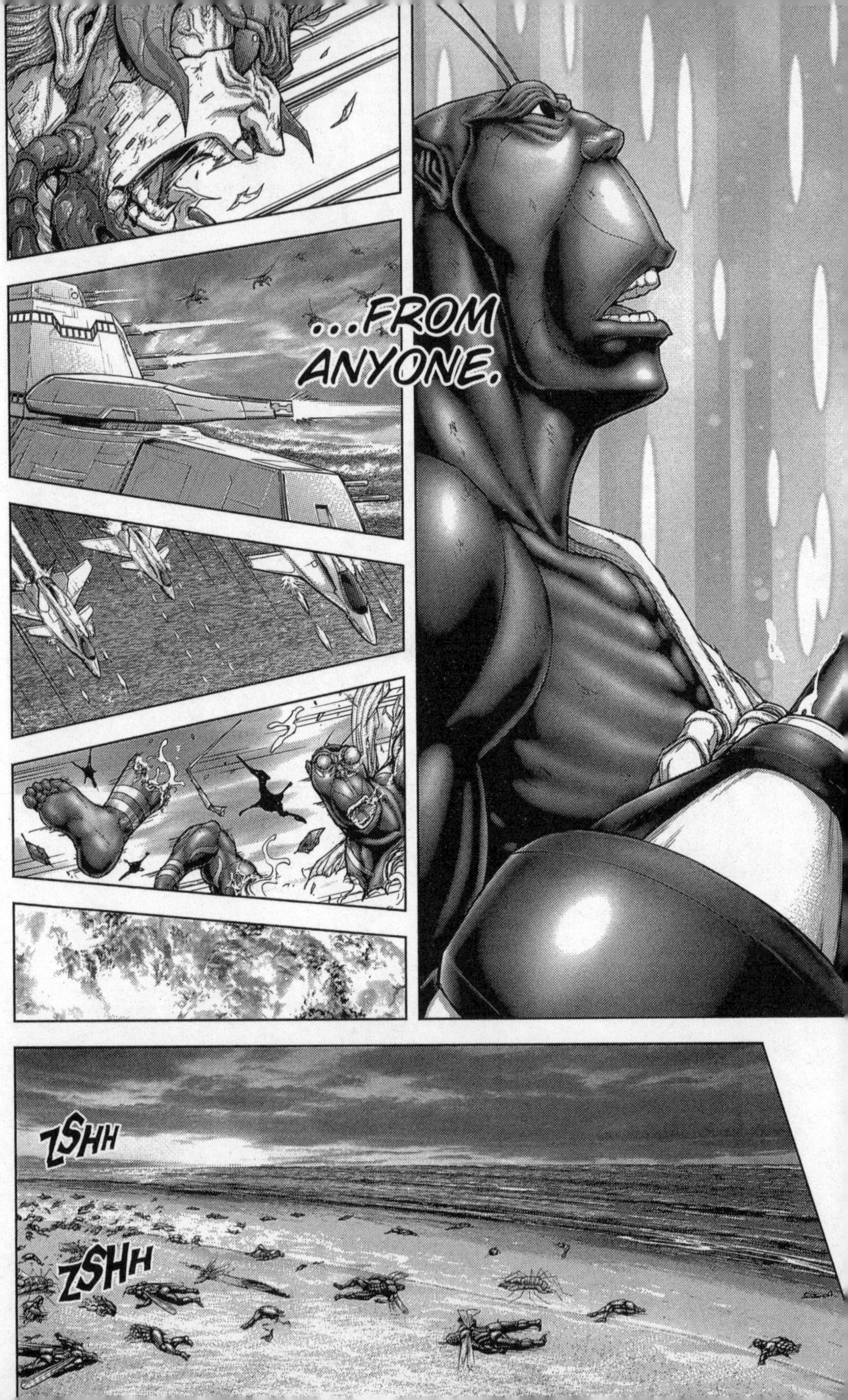
...FROM ANYONE.
ZSHH
ZSHH

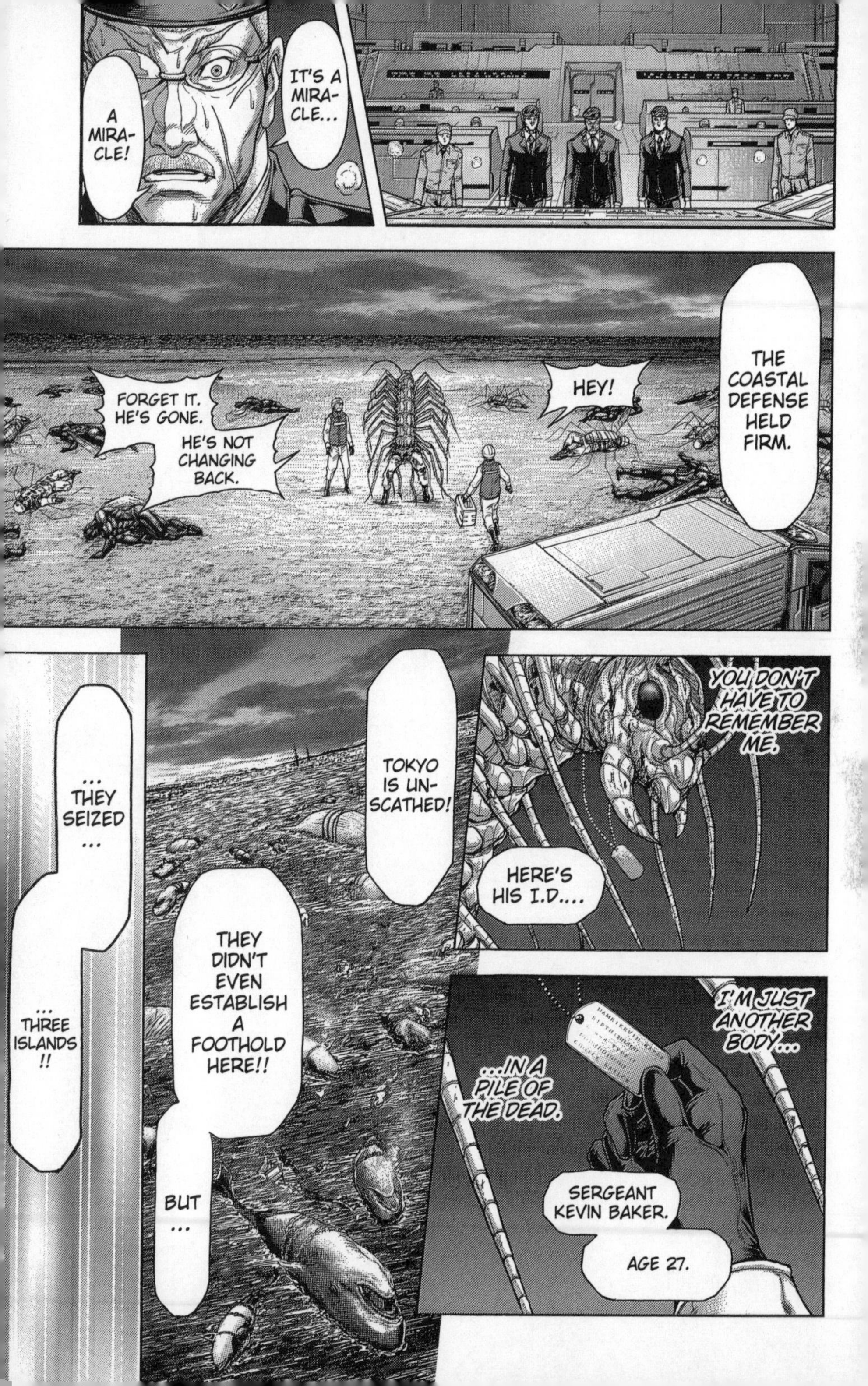
IT'S A MIRA-CLE...
A MIRA-CLE!
THE COASTAL DEFENSE HELD FIRM.
HEY!
FORGET IT. HE'S GONE.
HE'S NOT CHANGING BACK.
YOU DON'T HAVE TO REMEMBER ME.
HERE'S HIS I.D....
I'M JUST ANOTHER BODY...
...IN A PILE OF THE DEAD.
SERGEANT KEVIN BAKER.
AGE 27.
TOKYO IS UN-SCATHED!
THEY DIDN'T EVEN ESTABLISH A FOOTHOLD HERE!!
BUT...
... THEY SEIZED ...
... THREE ISLANDS !!

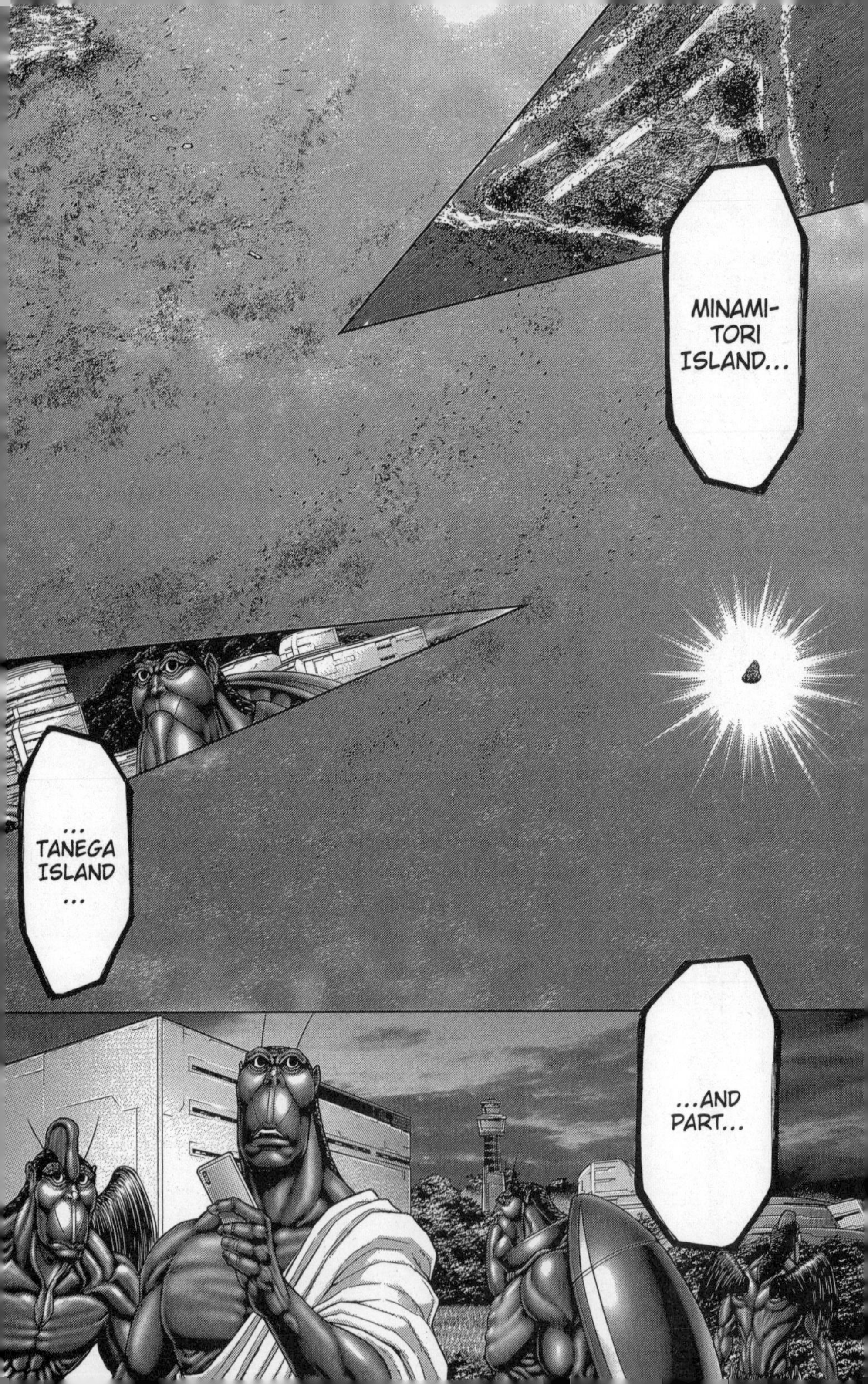
MINAMI-TORI ISLAND...
... TANEGA ISLAND ...
...AND PART...

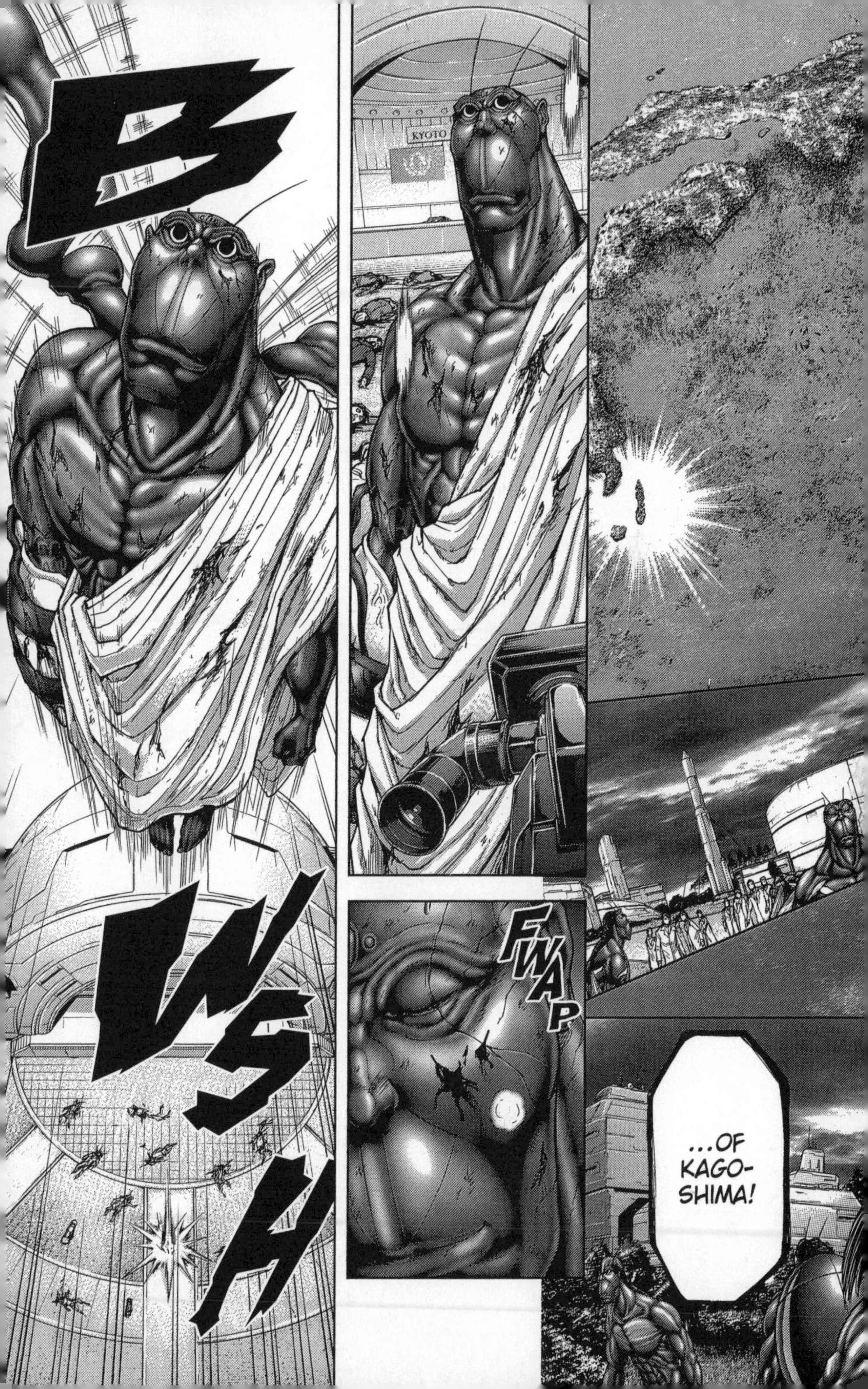
...OF KAGO-SHIMA!
KYOTO
FWAP
WSHH

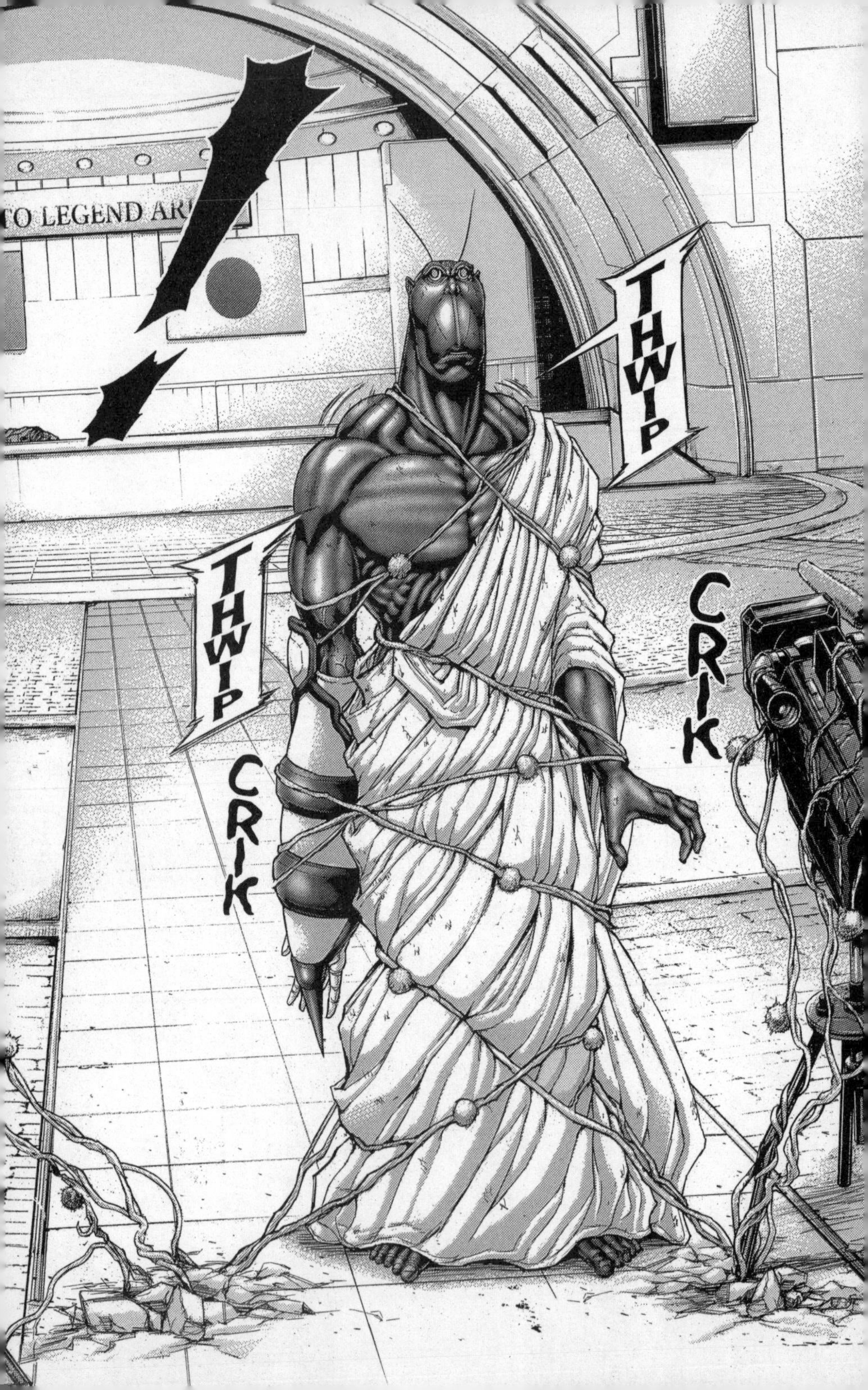
TO LEGEND AR
THWIP
THWIP
CRIK CRIK
CRIK CRIK

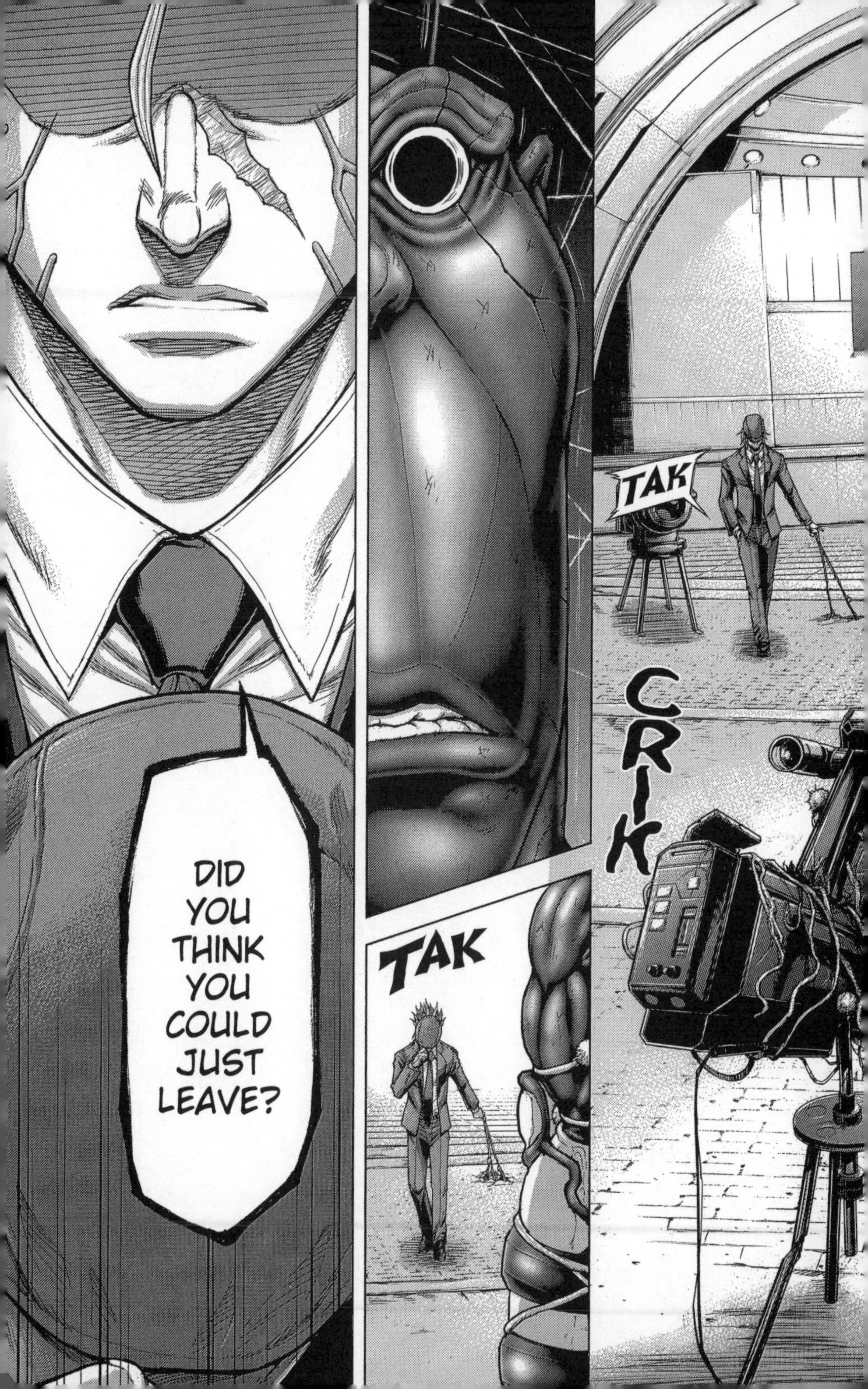
TAK
CRIK
TAK
DID YOU THINK YOU COULD JUST LEAVE?

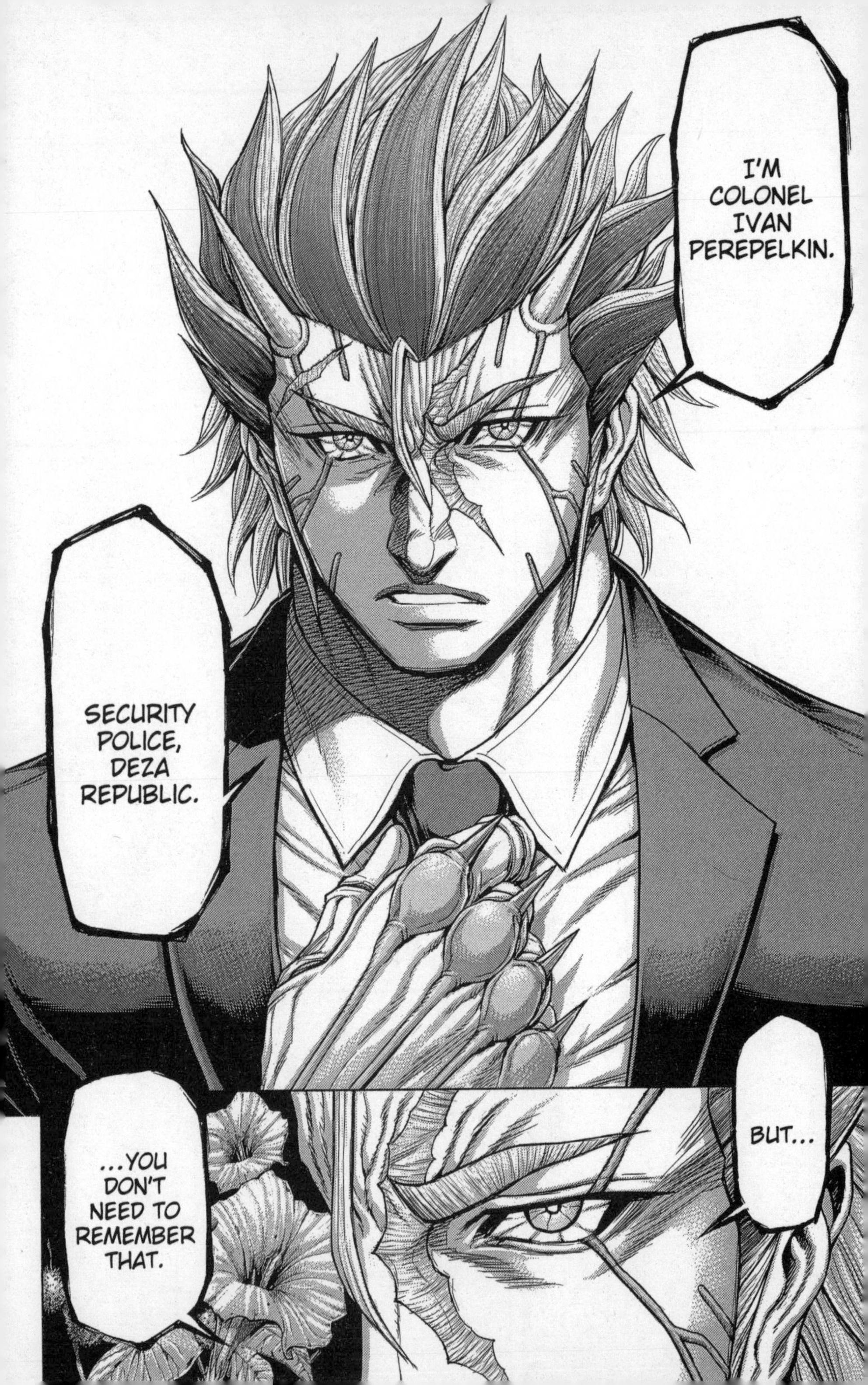
I'M COLONEL IVAN PEREPELKIN.
SECURITY POLICE, DEZA REPUBLIC.
BUT...
...YOU DON'T NEED TO REMEMBER THAT.

Ebi's skill: Ancient Thai massage.
Ikki's recent source of joy:
Pushing his body to the limit. Among other pleasures.

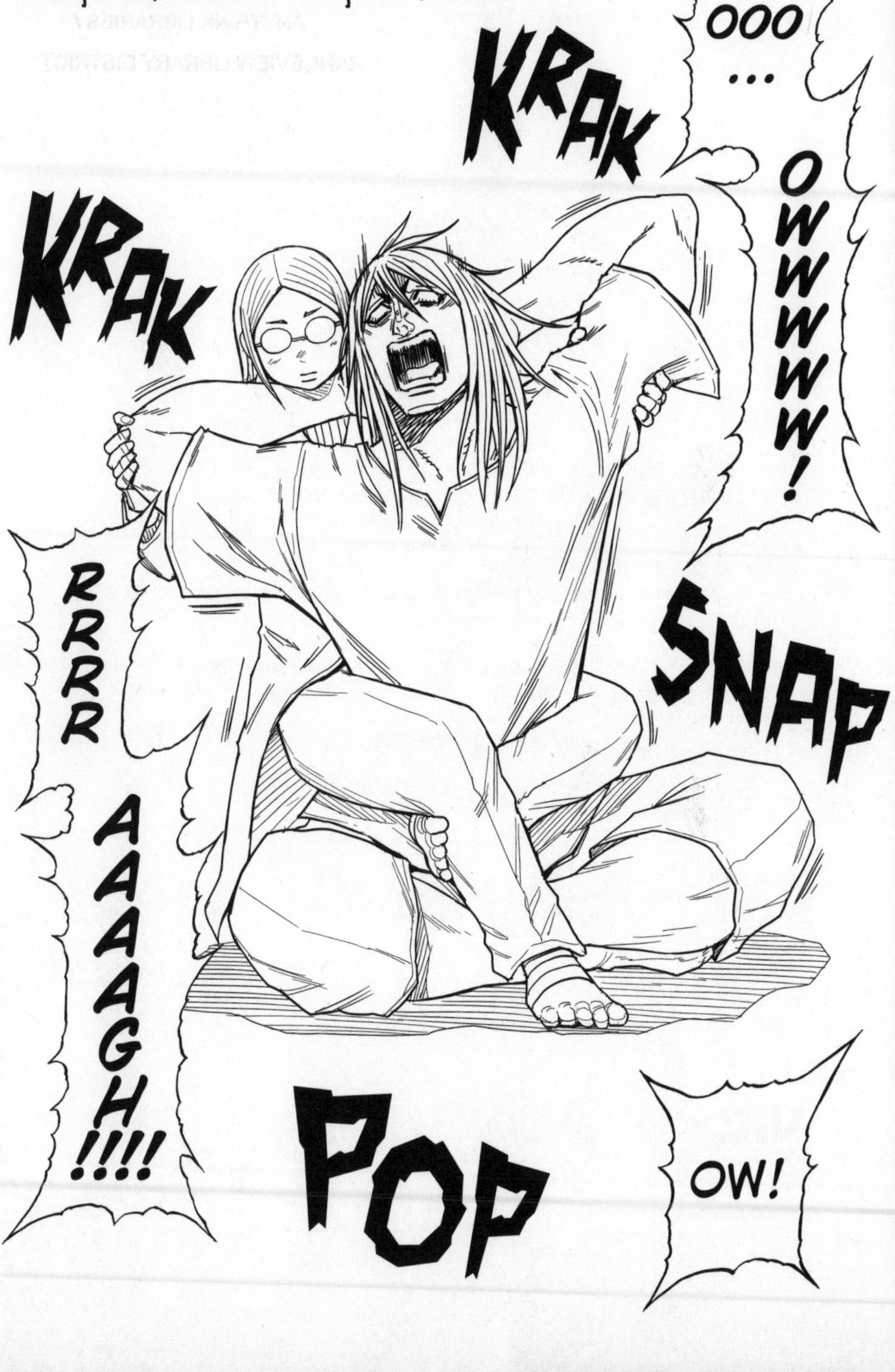
OOO ... OWWWWWW!
KRAK
KRAK
SNAP
RRRR AAAAAGH!!!!
OW!
POP

TERRA FORMARS
Volume 21
VIZ Signature Edition

Story by YU SASUGA
Art by KENICHI TACHIBANA

TERRA FORMARS © 2011 by Ken-ichi Tachibana,Yu Sasuga/SHUEISHA Inc.
All rights reserved.
First published in Japan in 2011 by SHUEISHA Inc., Tokyo.
English translation rights arranged by SHUEISHA Inc.

Translation & English Adaptation/John Werry
Touch-up Art & Lettering/Annaliese Christman
Design/Alice Lewis
Editor/Mike Montesa

Printed in the U.S.A.

Published by VIZ Media, LLC
P.O. Box 77010
San Francisco, CA 94107

10 9 8 7 6 5 4 3 2 1
First printing, July 2019

viz.com

vizsignature.com

TOKYO GHOUL

C O M P L E T E   B O X   S E T

STORY AND ART BY SUI ISHIDA

KEN KANEKI is an ordinary college student until a violent encounter turns him into the first half-human, half-Ghoul hybrid. Trapped between two worlds, he must survive Ghoul turf wars, learn more about Ghoul society and master his new powers.

Box set collects all fourteen volumes of the original *Tokyo Ghoul* series. Includes an exclusive double-sided poster.

COLLECT THE COMPLETE SERIES

VIZ

Hey! You're Reading in the Wrong Direction!

This is the **end** of this graphic novel!

To properly enjoy this VIZ graphic novel, please turn it around and begin reading from **right to left**. Unlike English, Japanese is read right to left, so Japanese comics are read in reverse order from the way English comics are typically read.

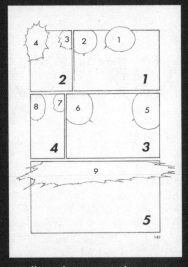

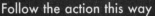

Follow the action this way

This book has been printed in the original Japanese format in order to preserve the orientation of the original artwork. Have fun with it!